Beginner's Guide to SolidWorks 2014 – Level I

Parts, Assemblies, Drawings, PhotoView 360 and Simulation Xpress

Alejandro Reyes, MSME
Certified SolidWorks Professional

Publications

SDC Publications
P.O. Box 1334
Mission, KS 66222
913-262-2664
www.SDCpublications.com
Publisher: Stephen Schroff

ISBN-13: 978-1-58503-841-1
ISBN-10: 1-58503-841-5

Printed and bound in the United States of America.

Acknowledgements

Beginner's Guide to SolidWorks is dedicated to my lovely wife Patricia and my kids Liz, Ale and Hector, all of whom have always been very supportive, patient and comprehensive during the writing of this book. To you, all my love.

Also, I wish to thank the hundreds of students, users, teachers and engineers whose great ideas and words of encouragement have helped me improve this book and make it a great success.

About the Author

Alejandro Reyes holds a BSME from the Instituto Tecnológico de Ciudad Juárez, Mexico in electro-mechanical engineering and a Masters Degree from the University of Texas at El Paso in mechanical design, with strong focus in Materials Science and Finite Element Analysis.

Alejandro spent more than 8 years as a SolidWorks Value Added Reseller. During this time he was a Certified SolidWorks Instructor and Support Technician, CosmosWorks Support Technician, and a Certified SolidWorks Professional, credential that he still maintains. Alejandro has over 20 years of experience using CAD/CAM/FEA software and is currently the President of MechaniCAD Inc.

His professional interests include finding alternatives and improvements to existing products, FEA analysis, and new technologies. On a personal level, he enjoys bicycle riding and spending time with family and friends.

Notes:

Table of Contents

List of commands introduced in each chapter. Note that many commands are used extensively in following chapters after been presented.

PART MODELING

Housing:
New Part
Create Sketch
Confirmation Corner
Sketch Grid
Auto-Rotate view normal to Sketch plane
Sketch Rectangle
Sketch Centerline
Sketch Relations
Smart Dimension
Sketch Status
Extrude Boss/Base
Document Units
View Orientation
Mouse Gestures
Menu Customization
Center Rectangle
Fillet
Magnifying Glass
Extruded Cut
Through All (End condition)
Sketch Fillet
Rename Features
Circle
Instant 3D
Mirror Features
Model Display Styles
Fly-Out FeatureManager
Dimension Tolerance
Hole Wizard
Cosmetic Threads
Sketch Point
Edit Sketch
Rebuild
Circular Pattern
Automatic Relations
Temporary Axes

Sketch Slot
Sketch Numeric Input
Linear Pattern
Edit Material
Mass Properties

Side Cover
Revolved Boss/Base
Trim Entities
Extend Entities
Construction Geometry

Top Cover
Offset Entities
Mirror Entities (Sketch)
Up to Surface (End condition)
Shell
Measure Tool
Select Other
More Fillet options

Offset Shaft
Revolved Cut
Auxiliary Planes
Hide/Show sketch
Convert Entities
Polygon (Sketch)
Flip Side to Cut
Axis (Reference geometry)
Coordinate Systems

Worm Gear
Mid Plane (End Condition)
Chamfer
Dimension to Arc
Direction 2 (End Condition)

Worm Gear Shaft
General Review of previous commands

SWEEP, LOFT, WRAP

Sweep
Thin Feature
Ellipse
Auxiliary Plane at point
Sweep
Up to Next (End condition)
Full Round Fillet
Helix
Variable pitch helix
Open Sketch Cut
Guide Curves

Loft
Offset Plane
Hide/Show Plane
Loft
Start/End Conditions
Model Section View

Wrap
Wrap
Intersection Curve

DETAIL DRAWING

Housing Drawing
Part Configurations
Suppress Feature
Parent Child Relation
Unsuppress
Configure Dimensions
Change Configuration
New Drawing
Make Drawing from Part
View Palette (Drawing)
Projected View
Tangent Edge Display
Section View
Detail View
Model Items
(Import dimensions)

In the next book,
Beginner's Guide to SolidWorks 2014 <u>Level II</u>
you'll learn:

- Multi body part techniques
- Part editing, equations and errors
- Top Down design techniques
- Design sheet metal parts
- How to build and use Libraries
- 3D Sketches
- Design welded structures
- Structural member libraries
- Surface modeling
- Mold design tools
- And more…

Introduction

This book is intended to help new users learn the basic concepts of SolidWorks and good solid modeling techniques in an easy to follow guide. It will be a great starting point for those new to SolidWorks or as a teaching aid in classroom training to become familiar with the software's interface, basic commands and strategies as the user completes a series of models while learning different ways to accomplish a particular task. At the end of this book, the user will have a good understanding of the SolidWorks interface and the most commonly used commands for part modeling, assembly and detailing after completing a series of components and their 2D drawings complete with Bill of Materials. The book is focused on the processes to complete the modeling of a part, instead of the individual commands or operations, which are learned as we progress. We strived hard to cover the commands required in the **Certified SolidWorks Associate** test as listed in the SolidWorks website as of the writing of this book, and added some more.

SolidWorks is easy to use yet powerful CAD software that includes many time saving tools that enable new and experienced users to complete design tasks in a very short time. Most commands covered in this book have advanced options, which may or may not be covered in this book. This book is meant to be a starting point to help new users learn the basic and most frequently used commands, and the Level II book covers more advanced and complex commands including sheet metal, mold making, surfacing, etc.

SolidWorks is a leading 3D mainstream design CAD package with hundreds of thousands of users in the industry going from one man shops to Fortune 500 companies, and has a strong presence in the educational market including high schools, vocational schools and many prestigious universities.

We'd love to hear from you, your experience with this book and any other comments or ideas on how we can make it better for you by sending an email to: alejandro@mechanicad.com.

Prerequisites

This book was written assuming the reader has knowledge of the following topics:

- The reader is familiar with the Windows operating system.
- Knowledge of mechanical design and drafting (detailing).
- Any experience with other CAD systems is a plus.
- Understanding of mechanics of materials – a must to understanding SimulationXpress.

Notes:

The SolidWorks Interface

The very first time we open SolidWorks we are presented with the option to select our default drafting standard and units of measure. Selecting a default doesn't mean we have to use those options; we can change either one at any time as we see fit. Most samples and exercises in the book are presented using the ANSI dimensioning standard and inches for units of measure.

Units and Dimension Standard

Select the initial settings for the default templates:

Units:

IPS (inch, pound, second) ▼

Dimension standard:

ANSI ▼

NOTE: These settings can be changed for individual templates or documents in Tools, Options, Document Properties.

OK   Cancel   Help

The Menu bar is hidden by default. It is automatically displayed when the user moves the pointer over the SolidWorks banner in the upper left corner of the window and is hidden when we move away from it. In order to make the menu bar always visible for ease of clarity in the book, press the pin icon at the end of the menu bar as indicated.

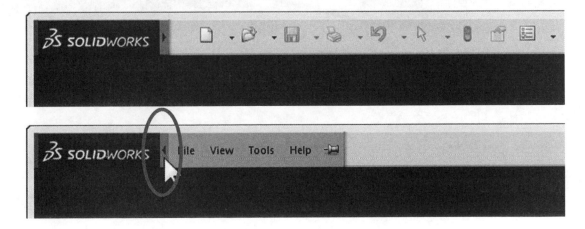

The SolidWorks interface is simple and easy to navigate. The main areas in the interface include toolbars, menus, graphics area, Feature-Manager/PropertyManager and Task Pane. SolidWorks includes an intelligent system of pop up toolbars which is automatically activated when the user selects elements in the FeatureManager or graphics area. SolidWorks has icons and menus similar to those of Microsoft Office applications, and follows Windows rules like drag and drop, copy/paste, etc., typical of any Windows compliant software.

FeatureManager   **Menus and Toolbars**   **View Toolbar**   **Graphics Area**

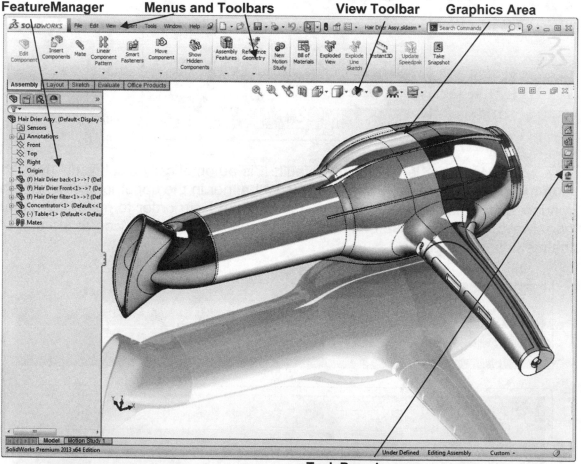

Task Pane Icons

The **graphics area** is the main part of SolidWorks and where most of the action happens; this is where parts, assemblies, and drawings are created, visualized, and modified. SolidWorks lets users Zoom, Pan, Rotate, change view orientations, etc., as well as to change how the models are displayed, either as Shaded, Hidden Lines, Hidden Lines Visible and Wireframe to name a few.

The **FeatureManager** is the graphical browser of features, operations, parts, drawing views and more which can be edited, modified, deleted, etc. and is located on the left side of the screen.

The FeatureManager's space is also shared by the **PropertyManager** and the **ConfigurationManager**. The PropertyManager is where most of the SolidWorks' command options are presented to the user; this is also where a selected entity's properties are displayed and Configurations are created. The PropertyManager is displayed automatically when needed, so the user does not need to worry about it. We'll show the user how to view both Feature and PropertyManagers at the same time later in the book.

In the PropertyManager we are presented with a consistent, common interface for most commands in SolidWorks, including common controls such as check boxes, open and closed option boxes, action buttons, etc.

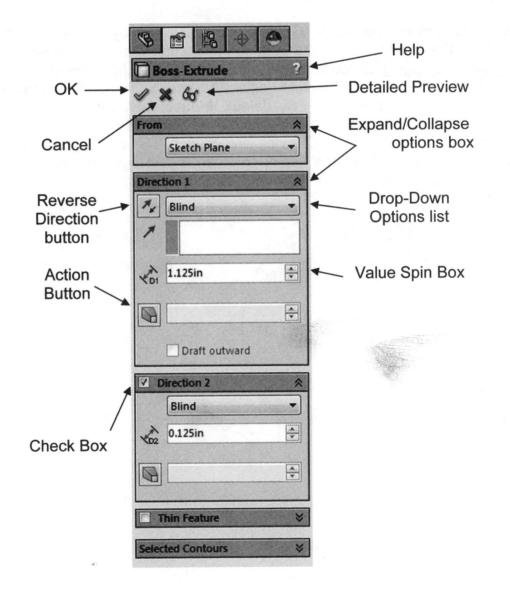

To manipulate the models in the graphics area, a set of tools is available from the menu "**View, Modify**" or the right-mouse-button menu in the graphics screen, to Zoom, Pan, Rotate, etc. Select a view manipulation tool, left click-and-drag the mouse in the graphics area to see its effect.

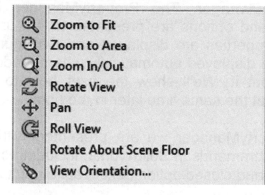

… or using **Mouse Gestures**. Gestures are activated by right-mouse-button-dragging in the graphics area, the gestures shortcuts wheel will appear, and we simply keep dragging to touch the command we want. In order to modify the commands in the wheel we have to select the menu "**Tools, Customize**" and select the Mouse Gestures tab. By default, Mouse Gestures are enabled, but they can be turned off in this tab; we can configure either 4 or 8 gestures for each environment (Part, Assembly, Drawing and Sketch) by selecting the command for each environment from the list of commands and selecting the gesture to assign. In this book we'll use the 8 gesture default settings.

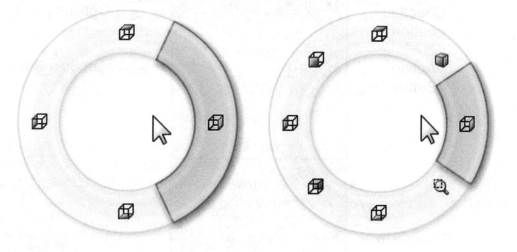

| Customize | | | | | | | ? | ✕ |

| Toolbars | Shortcut Bars | Commands | Menus | Keyboard | **Mouse Gestures** | Customization |

Category: All Commands ▼

☐ Show only commands with mouse gestures assigned

Search for: [＿＿＿＿＿＿＿＿]

☑ Enable mouse gestures
　○ 4 gestures
　◉ 8 gestures

Print List...

Reset to Defaults

Category	Command	Part	Assembly	Drawing	Sketch
File	New..				
File	Open..				
File	Close..				
File	Make Drawing from Part..				
File	Make Assembly from Part..				
File	Save..				
File	Save As..				
File	Save All..				
File	Page Setup..				
File	Print Preview..				
File	Print..				
File	Print3D..				

A few shortcuts to manipulate models: The mouse wheel can be used to zoom in and out in the model (the model is zoomed in at the mouse pointer), and clicking the middle mouse button (the wheel) and dragging the mouse **Rotates** the model in the graphics area. The rotation is automatic about the area of the model where the pointer is located. The **Previous View** (default shortcut "Ctrl+Shift+Z") and **Zoom to fit** (default shortcut "F") are single click commands in the view orientation toolbar.

Use the **Standard Views** icon to view the model from any orthogonal view (Front, Back, Left, Bottom, Top, Right, Isometric, etc.). Another way to rotate the models on the screen is with the arrow keys in the keyboard. Holding down the "Shift" key with the arrow keys rotates the model in 90° increments.

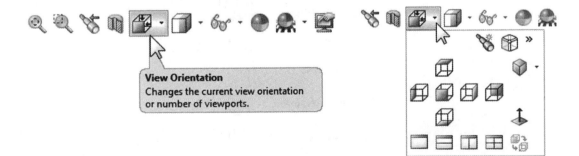

View Orientation
Changes the current view orientation or number of viewports.

Another way to change the view orientation is using the View Selector. We can activate it from the "View Orientation" drop down menu or using the shortcut "Ctrl + Spacebar." After activating the View Selector, every time we click in the "View Orientation" we'll get the View Selector until we turn it off. From here we can select the view we want in the translucent box and the model will be reoriented to that view.

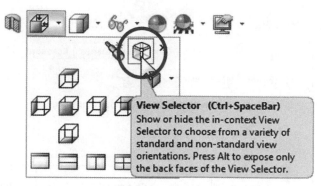

View Selector (Ctrl+SpaceBar)
Show or hide the in-context View Selector to choose from a variety of standard and non-standard view orientations. Press Alt to expose only the back faces of the View Selector.

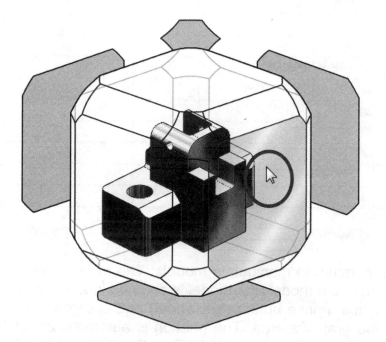

To change the **Display Style** (the way the model looks in the graphics area), the Display Style icon can be selected in the View toolbar; the effects will be immediately visible to the user. Feel free to explore them with your first model to become familiar; sometimes it's convenient to switch to a different view style for visibility or easy selection of internal or hidden entities.

Display Style icon
Shaded with Edges
Shaded
Hidden Lines
Hidden Lines Visible
Wireframe

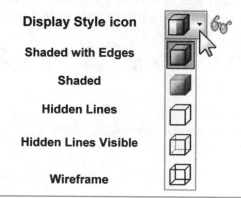

In this book we will make use of the **CommandManager**. The CommandManager is a tool that consolidates many toolbars in a single location, and selecting a toolbar's tab displays commands available, like Features, Sketch, Detailing, Assembly, Sheet Metal, etc. The CommandManager is a smart feature in SolidWorks – depending on the task at hand, different toolbars will be available to the user – and is enabled by default.

To enable or disable the CommandManager, select the menu **"View, Toolbars, CommandManager."** You must have a document open to be able to turn the CommandManager on or off. For clarity, the option "Use Large Buttons with Text" has been enabled; it can be activated by right-mouse-clicking anywhere in

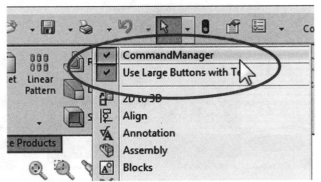

the CommandManager and selecting the option from the pop-up menu.

Models in SolidWorks can be displayed as simple solid colors or with high quality images; depending on the video card (graphics accelerator) used, real time reflections and shadows can be displayed using "RealView" technology. For clarity purposes RealView graphics will be used only from time to time to help the reader more easily understand the concepts presented.

One option the user may wish to change is to display dimensions flat to screen; this way, regardless of the orientation of the part, the dimensions are easier to read. This option can be found in the menu "**Tools, Options**" under the "System Options" tab, in the "Display/Selection" section. The images in this book will use the "**Display dimensions flat to screen**" option toggled on. By default, SolidWorks shows dimensions aligned to a plane, sometimes making it difficult to read dimensions and annotations.

☑ Display dimensions flat to screen
☑ Display notes flat to screen

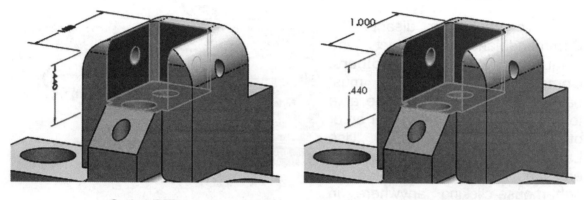

Option OFF   Option ON

The images in your screen *may* be slightly different from this book. The images in the book were made using Windows 7 Professional and SolidWorks' default installation settings. Unless otherwise noted, the only changes made to SolidWorks' default options were adding a white background and in some instances the preview colors were changed to improve clarity in print and/or electronic format.

IMPORTANT NOTE: High resolution images of all the exercises in this book are included in the accompanying disc or can be downloaded from our website for reference.

www.mechanicad.com

With that said, let's design something…

Part Modeling

The design process in SolidWorks generally starts in the part modeling environment, where we create the different parts that make the design of the product or machine. These are later assembled to other parts; at that time the group of parts becomes an Assembly. In SolidWorks, every component of the design will be modeled separately, and each one is a single file with the extension *.sldprt*. SolidWorks is *Feature based software*; this means that the parts are created by incrementally adding features to the model. In the simplest of terms, features are operations that either add or remove material to a part; for example, extrusions, cuts, rounds, etc. There are also features that do not create geometry, but are used as a construction aid, such as auxiliary planes, axes, etc.

This book will cover many different features to create parts, including the most commonly used tools and options. Some features require a **Sketch** or profile to be created first; these are known as Sketched features. A Sketch is a 2D profile created on a plane or flat face that will be later used to generate a 3D feature. It is in the Sketch where most of the design information is added to the model, including dimensions and geometric relations between the different sketch elements and existing geometry. Examples of sketched features include Extrusions, Revolved features, Sweeps and Lofts.

A 2D Sketch can be created only in a Plane or planar (flat) face. By default, every SolidWorks Part and Assembly has three **default planes** (Front, Top and Right) and an Origin. Most parts can be started in any one of these planes. It is not really critical which plane we use to start our designs; however, the plane's initial selection can potentially save us a little time when working in an assembly or when we start detailing the part in the detail drawing for manufacturing.

The initial planning that takes place before we start modeling a part is called the **Design Intent.** The Design Intent basically includes the general plan of how the part is going to be modeled, sort of a "*Step 1, Step 2, etc.*", and how we anticipate (or guess) it may change to accommodate possible future design changes to fit other parts in an assembly or overall design needs. For example, we may choose to create a revolved feature instead of multiple extrusions, or the other way around, based on the particular needs of the task at hand.

SolidWorks is a 3D parametric design software. By *parametric* design, we mean that the models created are driven by parameters. These parameters are dimensions, geometric relations, equations, etc. When a parameter is modified, the 3D model is updated to reflect the changes. Good design practices are evident in how well the Design Intent and model integrity is maintained when parameters are modified. In other words, *the model updates predictably when we change the parameters*.

Notes:

The Housing

Notes:

When we start a new design, we have to decide how we are going to model it. Remember that the parts will be made one feature or operation at a time. It takes a little practice to define the optimum feature sequence for any given part, but this is something that you will master once you learn to think of parts as a sequence of features or operations. To help you understand how to make the *'Housing'* part, we'll show a sequence of features. The order of some of these features can be changed, but always remember that sometimes we have to make some features before others. For example, we cannot round a corner if there are no corners to round! A sequence will be shown at the beginning of each part, and the dimensional details will be given as we progress.

In this lesson we will cover the following tools and features: creating various sketch elements, geometric relations and dimensions, Extrusions, Cuts, Fillets, Mirror Features, Hole Wizard, Linear, and Circular Patterns. For the *'Housing'* part, we'll follow the next sequence of features:

Base Extrusion	Top Extrusion	Fillets	Inside Cut
Front boss	Mirror Front boss	Side boss	Mirror Side boss
Front cut	Side cut	Screw hole	Screw hole pattern
Top tapped holes	Base slot	Slots pattern	Mirror slots pattern

1. -The first thing we need to do, after opening SolidWorks, is to make a **New Part** file. Go to the "New" document icon in the main toolbar and select it.

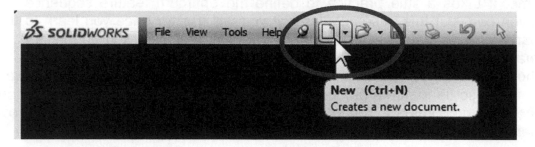

2. - We are now presented with the New Document dialog. (If your screen is different than this, click the "Novice" button in the lower left corner.) Now select the "Part" template, and click OK, this is where we tell SolidWorks that we want to create a Part file. Additional Part templates can be created, with different options and settings, including different units, dimensioning standards, materials, colors, etc. See the Appendix for information on how to make additional **templates** and change the document **units** to inches and/or millimeters. Using the "Advanced" option allows the user to choose from different custom templates when creating new documents instead of using the default templates.

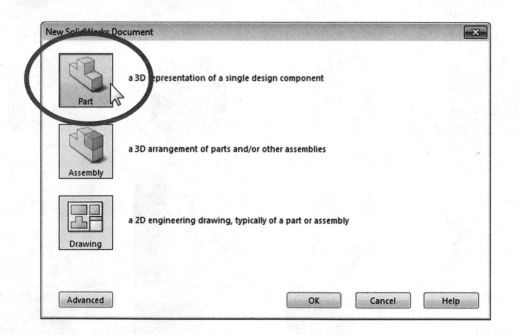

3. - Now that we have made a new Part file, we have to start modeling the part, and the first thing we need to do is to make the extrusion for the base of the *'Housing'.* The first feature is usually one that other features can be added to or one that can be used as a starting point for our model. Select the "**Extruded Boss/Base**" icon from the CommandManager's Features tab (active by default). SolidWorks will automatically start a new **Sketch**, and we will be asked to select the plane in which we want to start working. Since this is the first feature of the part, we will be shown the three standard planes (Front, Top, and Right). Remember the sketch is the 2D environment where we draw the profile before creating an extrusion, in other words, before we make it "3D."

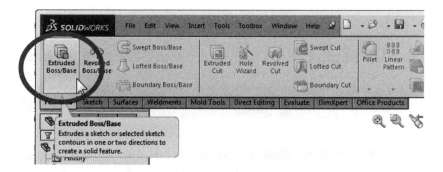

4. - For the *'Housing'* we'll select the *"Top Plane"* to create the first sketch. We want to select the *"Top Plane"* because we are going to start modeling the part at the base of the *'Housing'* and build it up as was shown in the sequence at the beginning of this chapter. Don't get too concerned if you can't figure out which plane to choose first when starting to model a part. At worst, what you thought would be a Front view may not be the front; this is for the most part irrelevant, as the user is able to choose the views at the time of detailing the part in the 2D drawing for manufacturing. Select the *"Top Plane"* from the screen using the left mouse button. Notice the plane is highlighted as we move the mouse to it. The view orientation will be automatically rotated to a Top View.

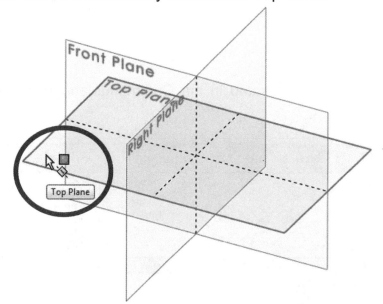

After selecting the *"Top Plane"*, a new **Sketch** is created are now we are working in the sketch environment. This is where we will create the profiles that will be used to make features like Extrusions, Cuts, etc. SolidWorks gives us many indications, most of them graphical, to help us know when we are working in the Sketch environment, like:

a) The **Confirmation Corner** is activated in the upper right corner and displays the Sketch icon in transparent colors.

b) The Status bar at the bottom shows "Editing Sketch" in the lower right corner.

c) In the FeatureManager "Sketch1" is added at the bottom just under "Origin."

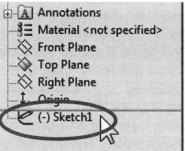

d) The part's Origin is projected in red.

e) The Sketch tab is activated in the CommandManager displaying sketch tools.

f) If the "Display Grid" option is activated, it will be displayed. This can be easily turned on or off *while in the Sketch environment*, by right-mouse-clicking in the graphics area and selecting the "Display Grid" command.

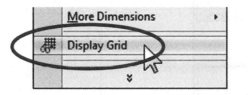

As the reader can see, SolidWorks gives us plenty of clues to help us know when we are working in a sketch.

5. - Notice that when we make the first sketch, SolidWorks rotates the view to match the plane that we selected. In this case, we are looking at the part from *above*. By default, this is done only in the first sketch to help the user get oriented. For subsequent operations we can rotate the view manually using view orientation tools, or turn on the option to always rotate the view to be normal to the sketch plane in the menu "**Tools, Options, System Options, Sketch**" and turn on the option "**Auto-rotate view normal to sketch plane on sketch creation**." Turning this option on will help new users get oriented in 3D. Feel free to turn it ON or OFF as you feel comfortable.

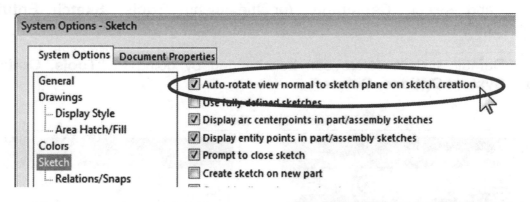

6. - The first thing we need to do in the first sketch is to draw a rectangle and center it about the origin. Select the "**Rectangle**" tool from the "Sketch" tab *or* make a right-mouse-button-click in the graphics area to select it from the pop-up menu, *or* click-and-drag with the right-mouse-button to select it in the Mouse Gestures. Make sure we have the "Corner Rectangle" option selected in the Rectangle's PropertyManager.

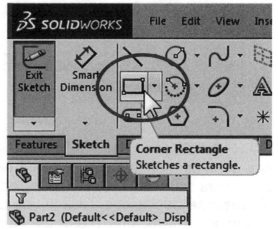

Draw a Rectangle around the origin as shown. To draw it, left-mouse-click-and-drag to the opposite corner. Don't worry too much about the size; we'll dimension it in a later step.

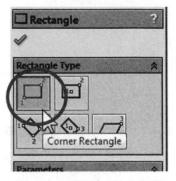 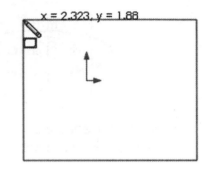

7. - Notice the lines are colored using the selected color defined in the system options after finishing the rectangle. This means the lines are pre-selected immediately after creating them. You can unselect them by hitting the Escape (Esc) key, this will also de-select (turn off) the rectangle tool. Since we only need one rectangle in this sketch, hit the "Esc" key to finish the command. After drawing the rectangle we need to draw a "**Centerline**" from one corner of the rectangle to the opposite corner. The purpose of this line is to help us center the rectangle about the part's origin. (We'll also learn a faster way to do this in the next few steps.) From the Sketch tab select the "**Line**" command's drop down arrow, and select "**Centerline**" (or the menu "**Tools, Sketch Entities, Centerline**").

Default system colors can be changed by going to "**Tools, Options, System Options, Colors.**"

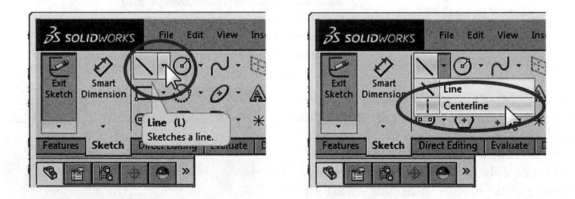

8. - SolidWorks gives the user indications that we will start or finish a line (or any geometric entity) at an existing endpoint using yellow icons; when we locate the cursor near an endpoint, line, edge, origin, etc. it will "snap" to it. With the "**Centerline**" tool active, click in one corner of the rectangle, click in the opposite corner as shown, and press the "Esc" key to finish the centerline. Notice the yellow endpoint feedback icon.

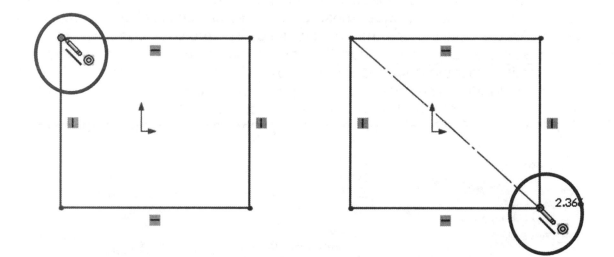

9. - Next we want to make the *midpoint* of the new centerline *coincident* to the part's origin; for this step we will add a "**Midpoint**" geometric relation between the centerline we just drew and the part's origin. Select "Add Relation" from the menu "**Tools, Relations, Add**" or the "**Add Relation**" icon from the "**Display/Delete Relations**" drop-down icon. By adding this relation, the centerline's midpoint will be forced to coincide with the origin; this way the rectangle (and the part) will be centered about the origin. Centering the part about the origin and the model's planes will be useful in future operations.

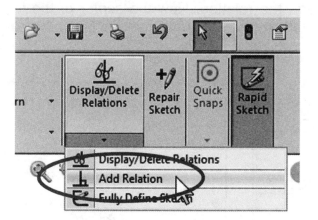

"Add Relation" can also be accessed through the right mouse button menu, or be configured to be available in the **Mouse Gestures** shortcuts.

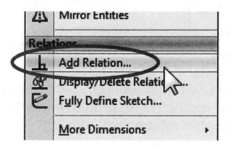

A word about the sketch right mouse button menu: The SolidWorks shortcut menu includes most of the sketch entities and commands available, making the menu very long. To improve workflow, we can customize it to only include the commands we use most frequently. To customize it, select the double down arrow at the bottom of the menu, and select "Customize Menu." The menu will change to show a checkbox next to each menu item; here we can click to turn commands on or off to fit our needs. Feel free to turn them on/off as we progress through the book to better fit your needs.

10. - The "Add Relations" PropertyManager is displayed. The **Property-Manager** is the area where we will make our selections and choice of options for most commands. Select the previously made centerline and the part's origin by clicking on them in the graphics area (notice how they change color and get listed under the "Selected Entities" box.) Click on **"Midpoint"** under the "Add Relations" box to add the relation. Now the *center* of the line is *coincident* with the Origin. Click on OK (the green checkmark) to finish the command.

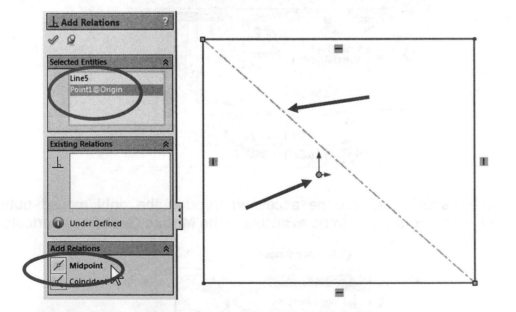

To test the relation we just added, click-and-drag one corner of the rectangle. You will see the rectangle resizing symmetrically *and* centered on the origin because of the geometric relation we added.

11. - What we just did is we *manually* added a **geometric relation**; we also added geometric relations *automatically* when we drew the rectangle and the centerline in the previous step. SolidWorks allows us to view the existing relations between sketch elements graphically by going to the menu "**View, Sketch Relations**," or from the "**Hide/Show Items**" drop down icon in the graphics area. This option is enabled by default.

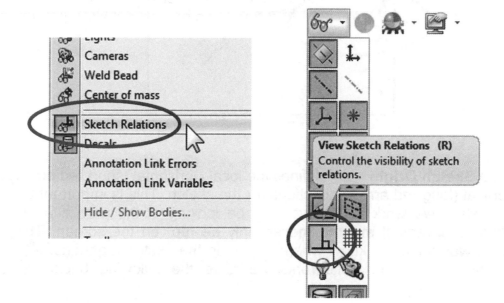

12. - The geometric relations are represented graphically by small icons next to each sketch element. Notice that when we move the mouse pointer over a geometric relation icon, the entity or entities that share the relation are highlighted.

 To delete a geometric relation select the relation icon in the screen and press the "Delete" key, or right-mouse-click on the Geometric Relation icon and select "Delete." (Do not delete any relations at this time!)

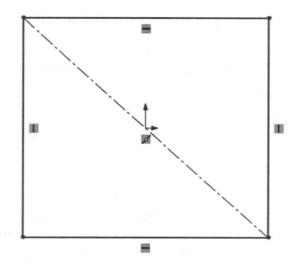

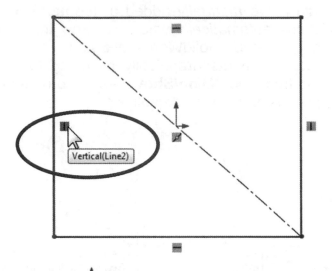

The **Sketch Origin** ⌐► defines the local Horizontal (short red arrow) and local Vertical (long red arrow) directions for the sketch. This is important to know because, when we work in 3D, we may be looking at the part in a different orientation, and vertical may not necessarily be "up" on the screen. This is a convenient way for us to know where "up" is in the sketch regardless of which way we are looking. In SolidWorks we have the following basic types of geometric relations for sketch entities:

	Vertical Parallel to the sketch vertical direction (long red arrow in the origin)
	Horizontal Parallel to the sketch horizontal direction (short red arrow in the sketch origin)
	Coincident is when an endpoint touches another line, endpoint, arc, circle or model edge.
	Midpoint is when a line's endpoint coincides with the middle of another line or a model edge. A Midpoint relation implies it is also Coincident.
	Parallel is when two or more lines or a line and a linear model edge are parallel to each other.
	Perpendicular is when two lines (or a line and a model edge) are 90° from each other. Vertical and horizontal lines are perpendicular. Note that the lines don't have to be connected to each other in order to be perpendicular.

	Concentric is when two arcs or circles share the same center. Concentric can also be between a point or line's endpoint and an arc or circle's center.
	Tangent is when a line and an arc or circle, or two arcs or two circles are tangent to each other.
	Equal is when two or more lines are the same length, or two or more arcs or circles have the same diameter.
	Collinear is when two or more lines lie on the same line. They don't have to be connected.

13. - Once we have added the "Midpoint" geometric relation, the next step is to dimension the rectangle. To avoid visual clutter in the screen we can turn off the geometric relation icons using the menu "**View, Sketch Relations**." Click with the right mouse button in the graphics area and select "**Smart Dimension**" from the pop-up menu or select the "Smart Dimension" icon from the Sketch toolbar. Notice the cursor changes by adding a small dimension icon next to it. This icon will let us know the Smart Dimension tool is selected.

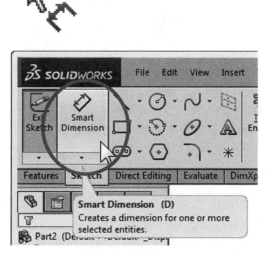

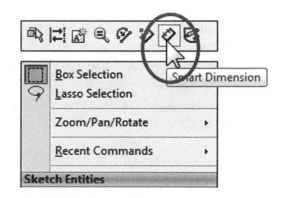

Smart Dimension can also be activated from the Mouse Gestures (default right-mouse-click-and-drag up), or assign a shortcut key using the menu **"Tools, Customize, Keyboard."** Feel free to customize a shortcut that works for you. In the next image we'll add the shortcut key "D" to Smart Dimension.

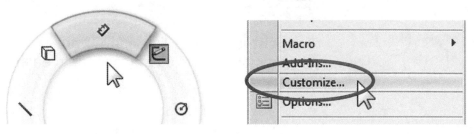

Category	Command	Shortcut(s)	Search Shortcut
Tools	𝔸 Show Curvature..		
Tools	**Dimensions**		
Tools	✏ Smart..	D	
Tools	Horizontal..		
Tools	⍿ Vertical..		
Tools	Ordinate..		
Tools	Horizontal Ordinate..		
Tools	Vertical Ordinate..		
Tools	Angular Running Dimension..		
Tools	Path Length..		

Customize — Toolbars | Shortcut Bars | Commands | Menus | **Keyboard** | Mouse Gestures | Customization
Category: All Commands
Show: All Commands
Search for:
Print List... | Copy List | Reset to Defaults | Remove Shortcut

14. - Adding dimensions in SolidWorks is simple and straight forward. With the Smart Dimension tool active, click to select the right (or left) vertical line and then click next to it to locate the dimension. SolidWorks will show the "Modify" dialog box, where we can enter the 2.625″ dimension. Repeat with the top horizontal line and enter a 6″ dimension. As soon as the dimension value is entered, the geometry updates to reflect the correct size.

If your document is in metric units, you can override the default units by adding "*in*" or ″ at the end of the value in the Modify dialog box. If this is the case, type 2.625in *or* 2.625″ and 6in *or* 6″ to override the document's units to inches.

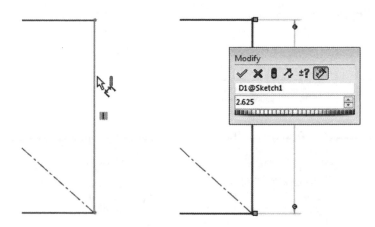

 Another way to pick the units of measure is to move the mouse in the pop-up "Units" menu directly under the value box and select the units of choice.

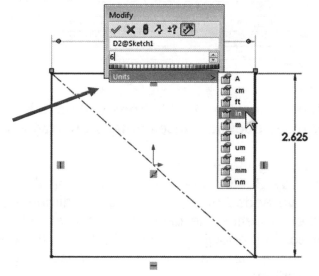

To change a dimension after adding it, double click on it to display the "Modify" box again.

To change the document's units we can either 1) go to the menu "**Tools, Options, Document Properties, Units**", or 2) click in the status bar in the lower right corner to set the units from the quick pick menu, or 3) launch the **"Edit Document Units**…" options page to change units, decimal places, dual dimension units, etc.

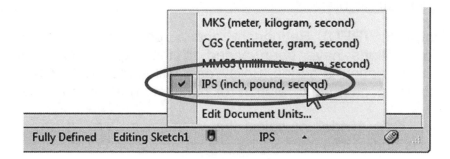

Document Properties - Units

| | System Options | Document Properties | | Search Options |

Drafting Standard
⊞ Annotations
⊞ Dimensions
— Virtual Sharps
⊞ Tables
Detailing
Grid/Snap
Units
Model Display
Material Properties
Image Quality
Sheet Metal
Plane Display
DimXpert
— Size Dimension
— Location Dimension
— Chain Dimension
— Geometric Tolerance
— Chamfer Controls
— Display Options
Configurations

Unit system
○ MKS (meter, kilogram, second)
○ CGS (centimeter, gram, second)
○ MMGS (millimeter, gram, second)
◉ IPS (inch, pound, second)
○ Custom

Type	Unit	Decimals	Fractions	More
Basic Units				
Length	inches	.123		...
Dual Dimension Length	inches	.12		...
Angle	degrees	.123		
		.1234		
Mass/Section Properties		.12345		
		.123456		
Length	inches	.1234567		
Mass	pounds	.12345678		
Per Unit Volume	inches^3			
Motion Units				
Time	second	.12		
Force	pound-force	.12		
Power	watt	.12		
Energy	BTU	.12		

**Most exercises in this book will be in inches
and three decimal places unless otherwise noted.**

After dimensioning the lines, notice the sketch lines changed from Blue to Black. This is the way SolidWorks lets us know that the geometry is *defined*, meaning that we have added enough information (dimensions and/or geometric relations) to completely define the geometry in the sketch. The status bar also shows "Fully Defined" in the lower right corner. This is the preferred state before creating a feature, since there is no information missing and the geometry has been accurately described.

A few more words about a sketch's state. A sketch can be in one of several states; the three main ones are:

- **Under Defined**: (BLUE) Not enough dimensions and/or geometric relations have been provided to completely define the sketch. Sketch geometry is blue and lines/endpoints can be dragged with the left mouse button.

- **Fully Defined**: (BLACK) The Sketch has all the necessary dimensions and/or geometric relations to completely define it. *This is the desired state*. Fully defined geometry is black.

- **Over Defined**: (RED) Redundant and/or conflicting dimensions and/or geometric relations have been added to the sketch. If an over-defining dimension or relation is added, SolidWorks will immediately warn the user. If an over-defining geometric relation (or dimension) is added, delete it or use the menu, **"Edit, Undo"** or select the "Undo" icon . If an over-defining dimension is added, the user will be offered an option to cancel it.

15. - Now that the sketch is fully defined, we will create the first feature of the *'Housing'*; this is when we go from the 2D Sketch to a 3D feature. Select the Features tab in the CommandManager and click in the "**Extrude**" icon, or click in the "**Exit Sketch**" icon in the Sketch toolbar. In the second case, SolidWorks remembers that we wanted to make an Extrusion in the first place, and displays the Extrude command's PropertyManager after exiting the sketch. Notice that the first time we create a feature in a new part, SolidWorks changes the view orientation to an Isometric view and gives us a preview of what the feature will look like when finished.

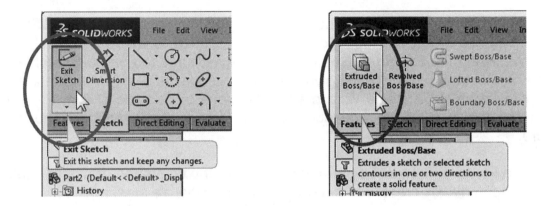

We will make the first extrusion 0.25″ thick. To do this, select the options indicated in the "**Extrude**" command. To finish the extrusion, select the OK button or press the "Enter" key.

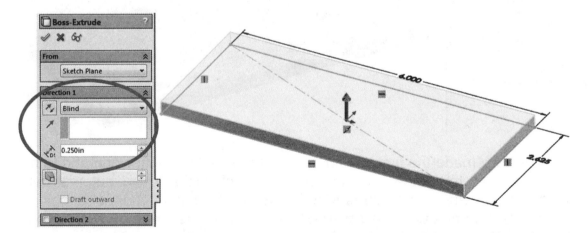

16. - After the first extrusion is completed, notice that "Boss-Extrude1" has been added to the FeatureManager. The confirmation corner is no longer active. The status bar now reads: "Editing Part" to alert us that we are now editing the part and not a sketch.

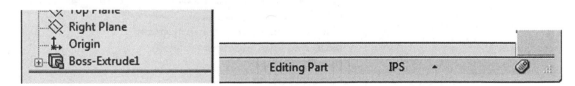

Expanding the "Boss-Extrude1" feature in the FeatureManager by clicking on the "+" on the left side of it, we see that "Sketch1" has been absorbed by the "Boss-Extrude1" feature.

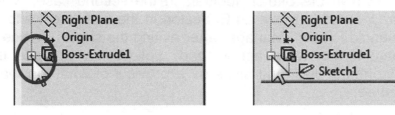

17. - The second feature will be similar to the first one, but with different dimensions. To create the second extrusion, we need to make a new sketch. When we select the **Extruded Boss/Base** in the Features tab or the **Sketch** icon in the Sketch tab, SolidWorks gives us a message in the PropertyManager asking us to select a Plane or a planar (flat) face to add the sketch to. We'll select the top face of the previous extrusion to add the sketch for the next feature.

If a Plane or flat face is pre-selected before the command, the new Sketch is immediately created in that Plane or face without a message.

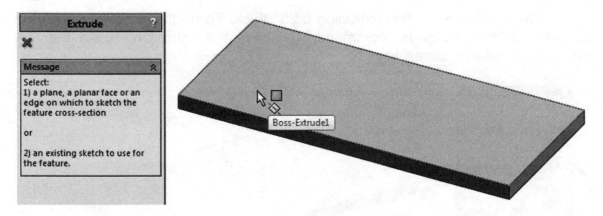

18. - When we made the first sketch, the view was automatically oriented to be normal to the sketch plane. To get subsequent sketches to be automatically oriented normal to the sketch plane and saving us from doing it manually, we can set the option "**Auto-rotate view normal to sketch plane on sketch creation**" found in the menu "**Tools, Options, Sketch**."

30

If you are not looking at the part from the Top view after selecting the top face, or chose *not* to turn on the option, manually change to a **Top View** to see the part from the top using the "**View Orientation**" icon or the default shortcut "**Ctrl+5**", as indicated in the tooltip. Notice that when we place the mouse over a view orientation, we get a pop-up preview of it. In SolidWorks we are free to work in any orientation we like as long as we can see what we are doing. Re-orienting the view helps us get used to 3D in a more familiar way by looking at it in 2D.

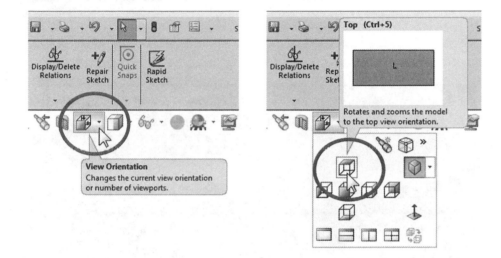

19. - Notice that after starting the second sketch, the Sketch tab in the CommandManager is selected. For the second sketch we'll use the "**Center Rectangle**" command. Click in the Rectangle's tool drop down menu in the Sketch tab, and select "**Center Rectangle**"; if you selected the rectangle as before, you can change the rectangle type to "**Center Rectangle**" from the Rectangle's PropertyManager, too.

To make a Center Rectangle click in the Origin first, then on the top edge of the first extrusion (or the bottom; it really doesn't matter) to finish it. Notice the yellow Coincident icon as the pointer is in the origin and then on the model edge. By doing the rectangle this way we automatically add coincident relations to the

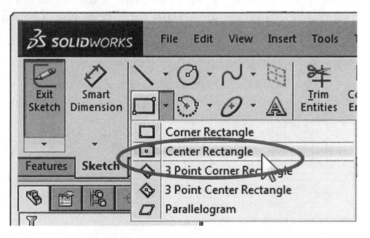

origin and the top edge. The "**Center Rectangle**" command saves us from adding the centerlines and midpoint relations making the rectangle centered about the origin in a single operation.

In the different types of rectangles we can see green numbers; those numbers indicate the number of clicks needed to complete each type of rectangle.

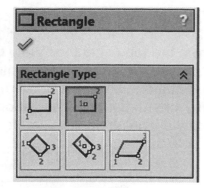

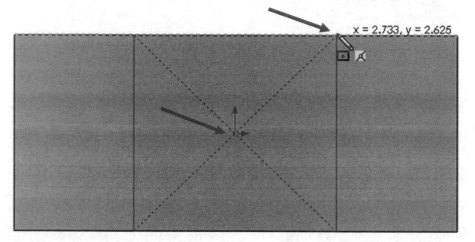

20. - Select the "**Smart Dimension**" tool (toolbar, right mouse menu, Mouse Gesture or keyboard shortcut), and dimension the rectangle 4″ wide by selecting the top (or bottom) line and locating the dimension as shown. Adding this dimension will fully define the sketch since we had automatically added geometric relations when the rectangle was created.

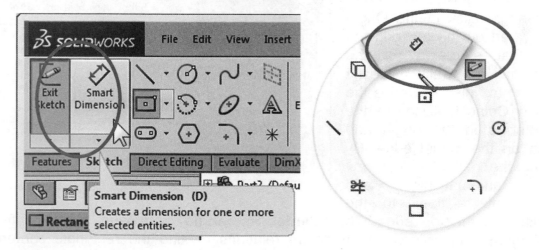

Note: The assigned keyboard shortcut ("D") is displayed in the tooltip.

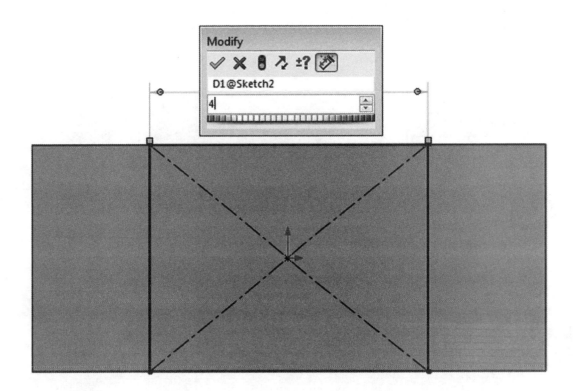

21. - We are now ready to make the second extruded feature. Select the "**Extrude**" command in the Features tab of the CommandManager (or "**Exit Sketch**" if you initially selected "**Extrude**") and make the extrusion 3.5″ high. Also notice the part does not rotate to show an isometric view as it did in the first extrusion, and there is no option to make it do so. Therefore, we have to rotate the view ourselves to see a preview. From the Standard Views icon, select the **Isometric** view ("Ctrl+7" shortcut or Mouse Gesture) to see the preview of the second extrusion. Click OK to complete the command.

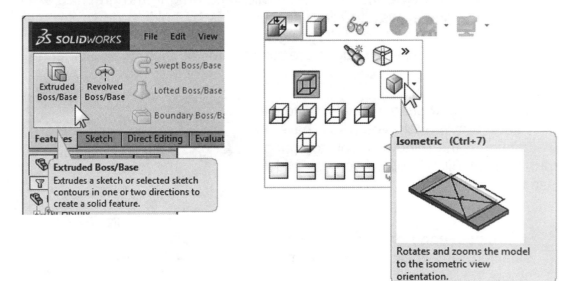

33

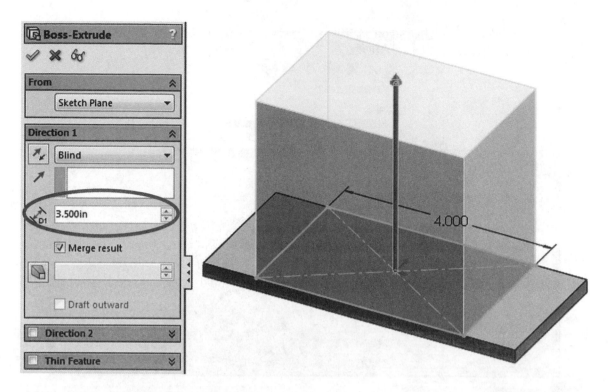

22. - The next step is to round the edges of the two extrusions. To do this, we will select the "**Fillet**" command. The Fillet is what's called an applied feature; we don't need a sketch to create it, and it's applied directly to the solid model. Select the "**Fillet**" icon from the Features Tab of the CommandManager. By default, "**Constant Radius**" type is selected. Change the radius to 0.25"and select the eight vertical corners indicated in the preview. SolidWorks highlights the model edges when we place the cursor on top of them to let us know what we'll be selecting. If an edge to be selected is not visible, rotate the model using the

menu "**View, Modify, Rotate**." Click-and-drag in the graphics area to rotate the part. Another way to rotate the model is by holding down the middle mouse button (scroll wheel), and dragging in the graphics area or using the arrow keys. Click OK when all eight edges are selected to complete the command.

 To use the mouse wheel's button to rotate the model, you *may* have to configure the middle button to change it from the default "Scroll" mode to "Middle Mouse Button."

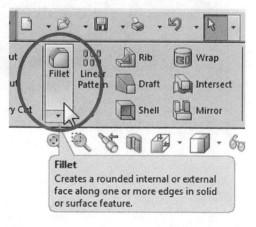

 If a model edge or face is mistakenly selected, simply click on it again to de-select it.

Select the "Full preview" option to see the resulting fillets in the graphics area as we select the edges.

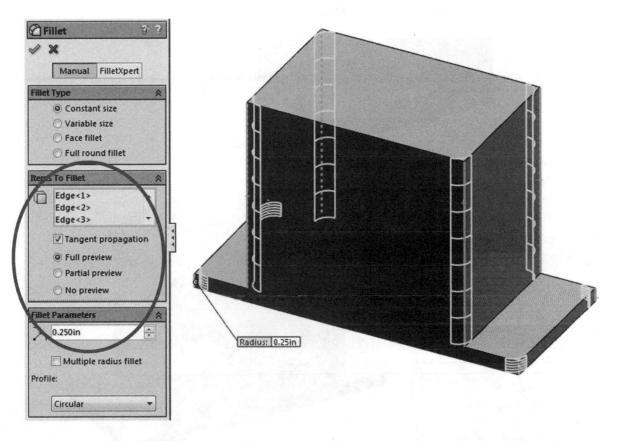

 A handy feature is a "**Magnifying Glass**" to selectively zoom in only one area of the model. To activate it, use the default shortcut "G" in the keyboard. To make multiple selections with it, hold down the "Ctrl" key, otherwise, the Magnifying Glass will turn off after making the first selection or after pressing "G" again. Scrolling with the mouse wheel will zoom inside the Magnifying Glass for more or less magnification.

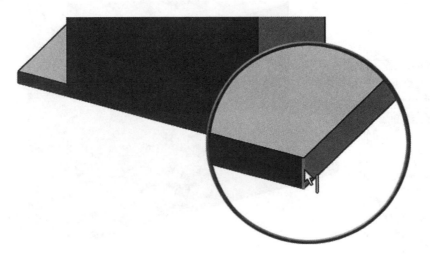

Alternative: Instead of selecting the Fillet command first and then selecting the edges to round, we can select one or more model edges (using the Ctrl key while selecting) and *then* select the Fillet command from the fly-out features toolbar.

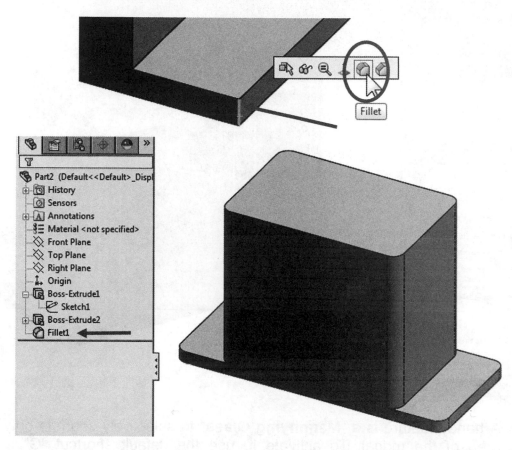

23. - Repeat the **Fillet** command to add a 0.125″ radius fillet at the base of the *'Housing'* but instead of edges we'll select the faces indicated. When we select a face, SolidWorks rounds all the edges connected to it. Click OK to continue.

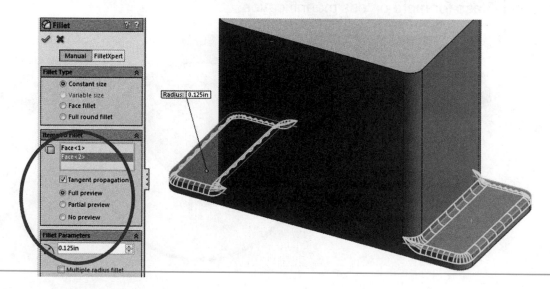

Notice how the new fillets blend with the previous vertical fillets.

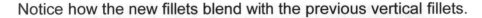

 We can change the appearance of tangent edges (The edges where two tangent faces meet) by selecting the menu, "**View, Display**" and selecting the display option desired: **Visible**, as **Phantom** or **Removed**. Explore the different options to find the one you feel more comfortable with. In this book Phantom lines will be used for clarity, unless otherwise noted.

24. - We will now remove material from the model using the "**Extruded Cut**" command. Switch to a **Top View** using the View Orientation toolbar, Mouse Gesture or shortcut Ctrl+5.

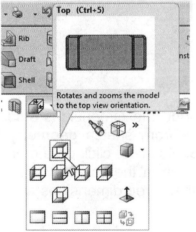

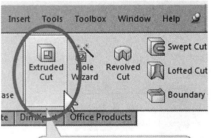

Select the "**Extruded Cut**" command from the Features tab; you will be asked to select a face or planar face just as with the "**Extruded Boss**." Select the top most face to create a new Sketch in it, and using the "**Corner Rectangle**" tool from the now visible Sketch toolbar, draw a rectangle *inside* the top face.

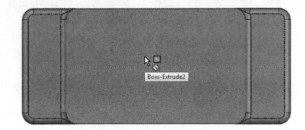

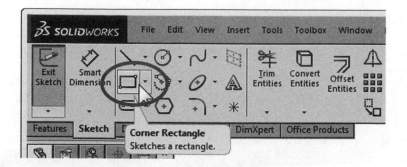

If the option "**Auto-rotate view normal to sketch plane on sketch creation**" is set, the model will automatically rotate to a Top View after selecting the top face.

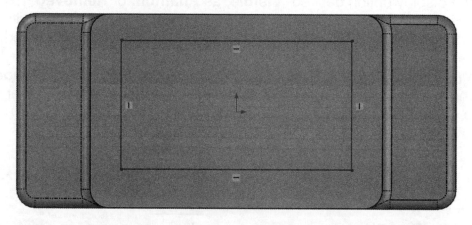

25. - To add the dimensions select the "**Smart Dimension**" tool; we can add dimensions from sketch geometry to model edges simply by selecting them. Select a Sketch line, click on a model edge parallel to it, and finally click to locate the dimension in the screen. When asked, enter a 0.375" dimension. Repeat to add the other three dimensions and also make them 0.375".

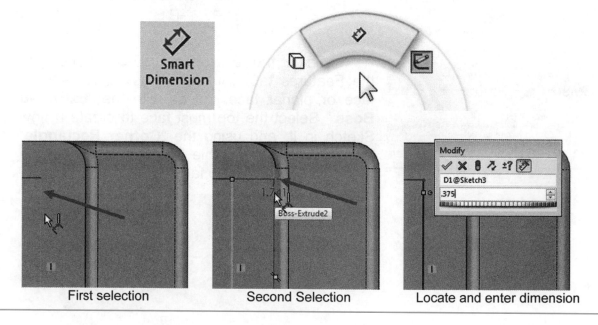

| First selection | Second Selection | Locate and enter dimension |

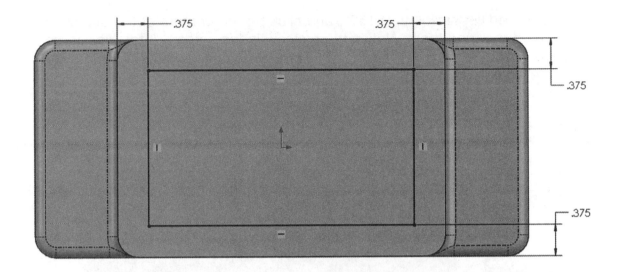

If needed, switch to a "**Hidden Lines Removed**" mode from the **View Style** icon to view the model without shading to facilitate visualization. This change can be done at any time during modeling.

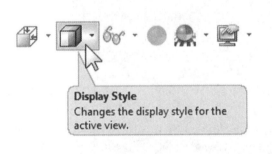

	Display Style menu
	Shaded with Edges
	Shaded
	Hidden Lines Removed
	Hidden Lines Visible
	Wireframe

26. -   In this feature, we will round the corners in the sketch using a **Sketch Fillet**. We can add the fillets to the 3D model as applied features like before, but in this step we chose to show you how to round the corners in the Sketch *before* making the "Extruded Cut" feature. Select the "**Sketch Fillet**" icon from the Sketch toolbar.

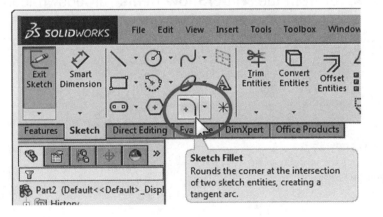

Set the fillet radius to 0.150″, and click on the corners of the sketch lines as indicated to round them. Notice the preview in the screen. After clicking on all 4 corners, click OK to finish the Sketch Fillet command. Adding multiple fillets at the same time results in only one dimension being added; the reason is that SolidWorks adds an equal relation from each fillet to the dimensioned one.

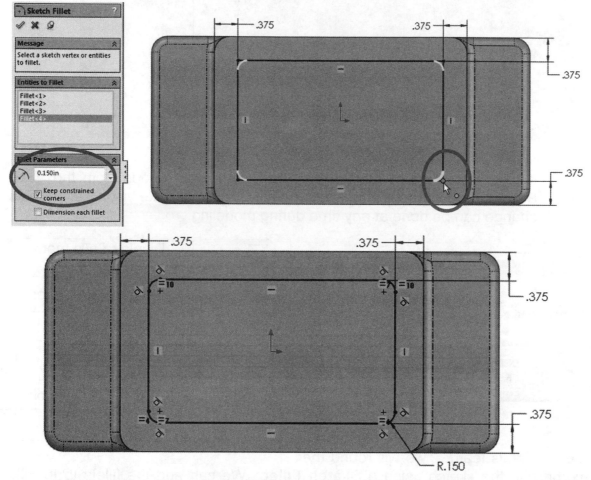

After adding the sketch fillets, we can see the number of geometric relations are starting to clutter the screen. To help clear up the screen, we can turn off geometric relations. Select the menu "**View, Sketch Relations**," or from the "**Hide/Show Items**" dropdown icon, turn off "View Sketch Relations." In this case the keyboard shortcut "R" has been added to the "View Sketch Relations" command.

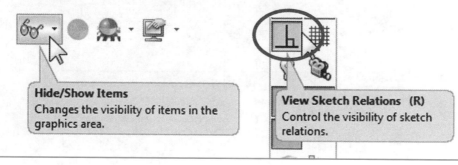

Hide/Show Items
Changes the visibility of items in the graphics area.

View Sketch Relations   (R)
Control the visibility of sketch relations.

27. - Now we select the "**Extruded Cut**" icon from the Features tab in the CommandManager to remove material. Opposite to the Boss Extrude feature that adds material, the Cut feature, as its name implies, removes material from the model.

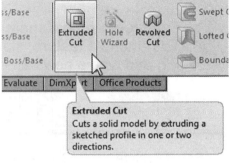

Extruded Cut
Cuts a solid model by extruding a sketched profile in one or two directions.

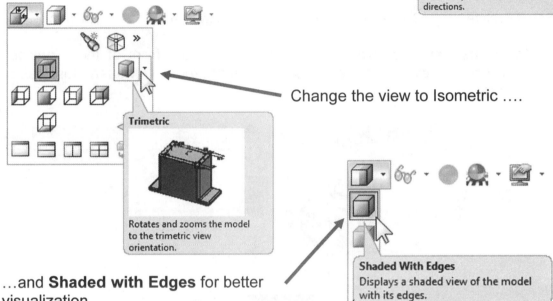

Change the view to Isometric ….

Trimetric

Rotates and zooms the model to the trimetric view orientation.

…and **Shaded with Edges** for better visualization.

Shaded With Edges
Displays a shaded view of the model with its edges.

Make the cut 3.5″ deep and click on OK to finish the cut.

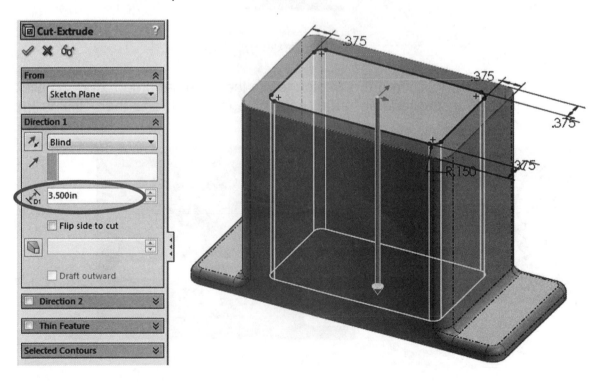

Features can be **Renamed** in the FeatureManager for easier identification. To rename a feature, slowly double-click the feature, or select it and press F2, and type a new name (just like renaming files in Windows Explorer.)

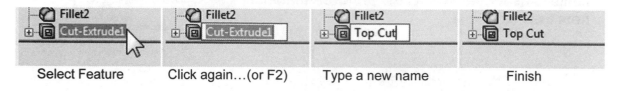

| Select Feature | Click again…(or F2) | Type a new name | Finish |

28. - In the next step we will add a round boss to the front of the *'Housing'*. Switch to a **Front View** using the "View Orientation" toolbar, Mouse Gestures or shortcut Ctrl+1.

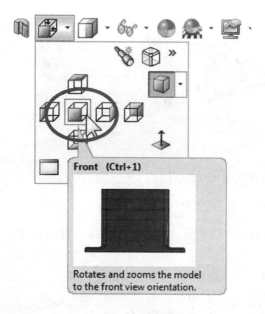

Select the "**Sketch**" icon from the Sketch tab in the CommandManager and click in the front face, or, the reverse order: select the face first, and then click in the "**Sketch**" icon.

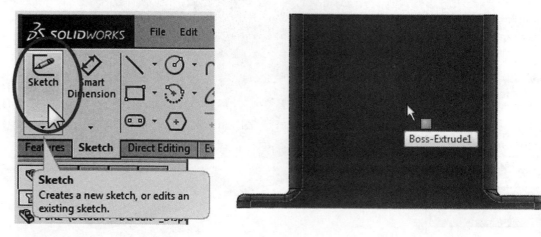

29. - Once we have the sketch created select the "**Circle**" tool from the Sketch tab in the CommandManager or using the Mouse Gestures. Draw a circle approximately as shown; click near the middle of the part to locate the center of the circle, and click again to set its size. (You can also click-and-drag from the center to draw the circle.) Don't worry about the size; we'll dimension it in the next step.

To define the circle's location, select the "**Smart Dimension**" tool. Click on either the center of the circle or its perimeter, and then on the top edge of the *'Housing'*. Finally locate the dimension and enter the value of 1.875". For the Diameter, select the circle and locate the 3.25" diameter dimension as shown.

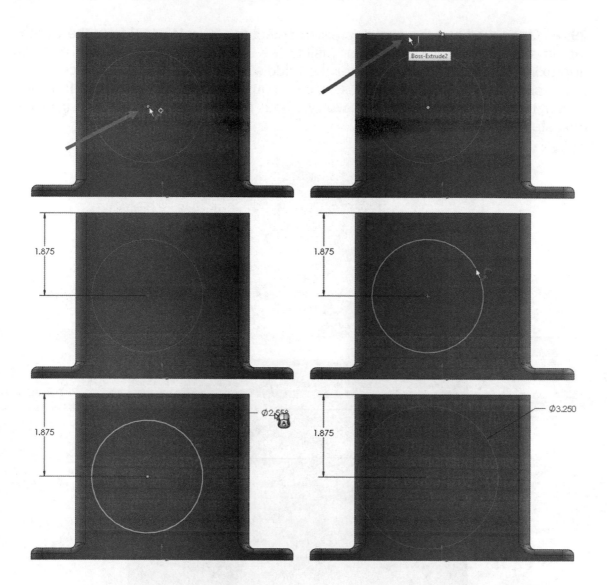

30. - To make the circle horizontally centered in the part, we will manually add a **Vertical Relation** between the center of the circle and the part's origin. SolidWorks allows us to align sketch elements to each other or to existing model geometry (edges, faces, vertices, planes, origin, etc.) From the right mouse button menu, select "**Add Relation**" or use the menu "**Tools, Relations, Add**."

Select the circle's center (not the perimeter!) and the origin. Click on "**Vertical**" to add the relation and make the circle's center vertical to the origin. When done click **OK** to finish. Adding this relation fully defines our sketch. Note the origin's Vertical direction identified by the **long red arrow** (The horizontal is the short red arrow.)

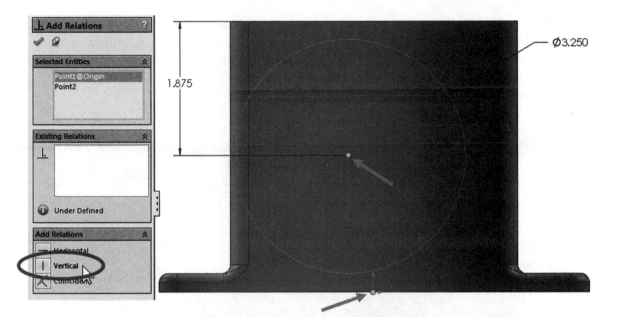

 Alternatively we can add the vertical relation by pre-selecting the origin and the circle's center, and then selecting the "Vertical" relation from the pop-up menu.

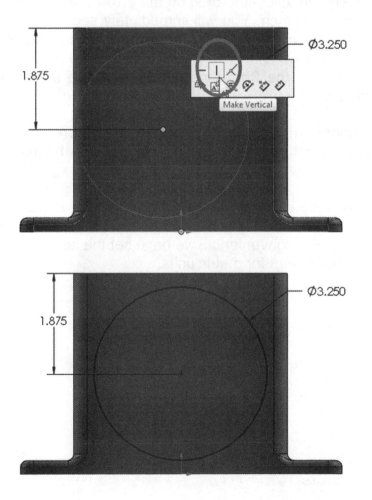

31. - Instead of making an extrusion like we did before, we are going to add material using a different technique. After adding the **Vertical** geometric relation, exit the sketch. We'll use a time saving feature called "**Instant 3D**" to make the extrusion. It should be active by default in the Features tab in the CommandManager; otherwise, click to activate it.

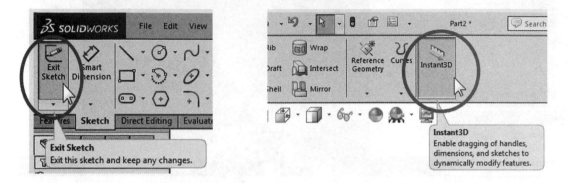

To make the extrusion, switch to an isometric view using the View Orientation toolbar; select the circle of the previously made sketch. Be aware that now we are editing the part, we left the sketch editing environment. Once the sketch circle is selected, click-and-drag on the arrow that appears in it; this is the handle to extrude the sketch. You will immediately see a dynamic ruler that will show the size of the extrusion as you drag it. Make sure to extrude it 0.250″. When you release the handle, a new extrusion will be created. To modify this extrusion, simply select the front face of the extrusion and drag again on the handle to its new size.

 You can control the size of the extrusion with more precision by dragging the handle over the ruler's marks, this way the handle will snap to the markers.

 The smaller step in the ruler is controlled by the default increment in the spin box settings. Go to the menu "**Tools, Options, Spin Box Increments**." For convenience, we have set the length increment to 0.125" for English units and 2.5mm for metric units.

	Length increments	
General		
Drawings	English units:	0.125in
— Display Style		
— Area Hatch/Fill	Metric units:	2.500mm
Colors		
Sketch		
— Relations/Snaps	Angle increments:	1.00°
Display/Selection		
Performance	Time increments:	0.10s
Assemblies		
External References		
Default Templates		
File Locations		
FeatureManager		
Spin Box Increments		

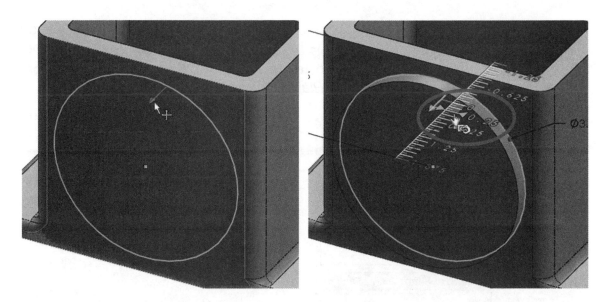

32. - Rename this extrusion as *"Front Boss"* by slowly double-clicking the feature's name in the FeatureManager, or selecting it and then pressing F2.

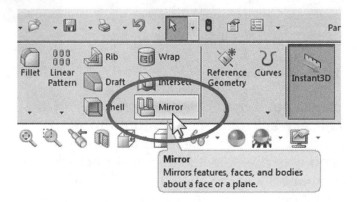

33. - The next step is to create an identical extrusion on the opposite side of the *'Housing'*. To make it we'll use the "**Mirror**" command. It will make an identical 3D copy of the extrusion we just made. Switch to an Isometric view to help us visualize the Mirror's preview and make sure we are getting what we want. Select the "**Mirror**" icon from the Features toolbar in the CommandManager.

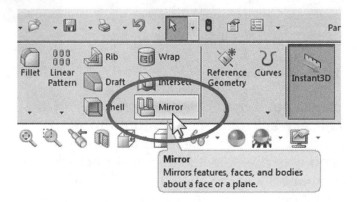

34. - From the Mirror's PropertyManager, we have to make two selections. The first one is the Mirror Face or Plane and the second is the feature(s) we want to make a mirror of. The face or plane that will be used to mirror the feature has to be in the middle between the original feature and the desired mirrored copy. Making the first extrusion centered about the origin caused the *"Front Plane"* to be in the middle of the part, making it the best (and only) option for a Mirror Plane.

To select the "*Front Plane*" (make sure the "**Mirror Face/Plane**" selection box is highlighted, this means it is the active selection box), click on the "**+**" sign next to the part's name to reveal a **fly-out FeatureManager**, from where we can select the "*Front Plane.*"

35. - After selecting the "*Front Plane*" from the fly-out FeatureManager, SolidWorks automatically activates the "**Features to Mirror**" selection box (now highlighted) and is ready for us to select the feature(s) we want to mirror. If the *'Front Boss'* extrusion was pre-selected before we activate the Mirror command, it will be added automatically to the "Features to Mirror" selection box, otherwise we will have to select it either from the FeatureManager or in the graphics area.

 When selecting features from the graphics area be sure to select a face that belongs to the feature. When traversing the FeatureManager, notice how SolidWorks highlights the features in the screen before selecting it.

Notice the preview after making your selections and click OK. Rotate the view to inspect the mirrored feature.

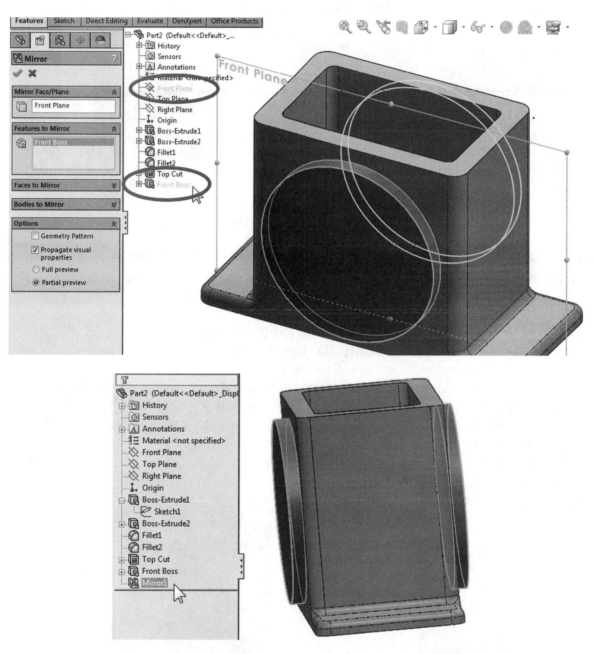

36. - In the next step we'll add the small boss at the right side of the *'Housing'*. Switch to a **Right view** using the View Orientation toolbar (Shortcut Ctrl+4), and select the "**Sketch**" icon from the CommandManager's Sketch tab.

Select the rightmost face to create the Sketch (or select the face and then the Sketch command), draw a circle using the "**Circle**" tool, and add the dimensions shown. Just as we did with the front cylindrical boss, add a **Vertical Relation** between the center of the circle and the part's origin.

From the right mouse button menu or the Sketch toolbar, select "**Add Relation**," select the center of the circle and the origin, and add a "Vertical" relation between them by selecting it in the "Add Relations" box.

Select Sketch plane

Draw & dimension circle

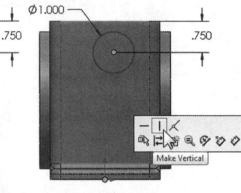
Add vertical relation

When adding relations, if you accidentally select more entities than needed, you can unselect them in the screen, or select them in the selection box and delete them using the "Delete" key.

37. - Now we are ready to extrude the sketch to make the side boss. We'll use the "**Instant 3D**" function as we did in the previous extrusion. Exit the Sketch by selecting "**Exit Sketch**" in the CommandManager's Sketch tab or the Sketch icon in the confirmation corner (*not* the red X), and change to an Isometric view. In the graphics area select the circle of the sketch we just drew, and click-and-drag the arrow along the ruler markers to make the extrusion 0.5″ long. Rename this extrusion '*Side Boss*' in the FeatureManager.

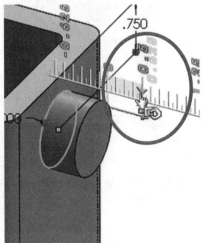

38. - Just like we did with the front circular boss, we'll mirror this extrusion about the *"Right Plane"* (which is also in the middle of the part.) Select the "**Mirror**" command from the Features tab in the CommandManager and, using the fly-out FeatureManager, select the *"Right Plane"* as the "**Mirror Face/Plane**" and the 'Side Boss' extrusion in the "**Features to Mirror**" selection box to complete the Mirror command.

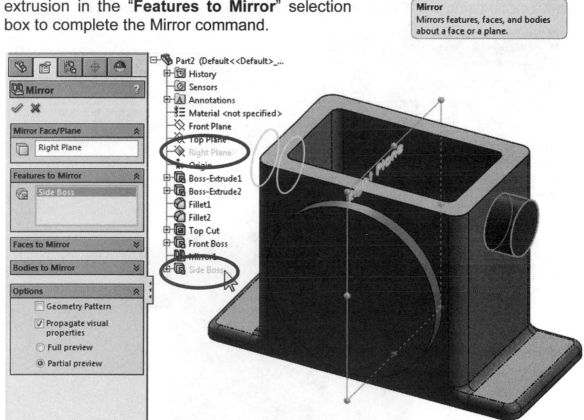

39. - We'll now make the circular cut in the front of the *'Housing'*. Change to a Front view for easier visualization. Select the "**Sketch**" icon from the Sketch tab and click in the round front face of the part (Or select the face first, and then the Sketch icon.)

Draw a circle using the "**Circle**" tool and dimension it 2.250″ in diameter.

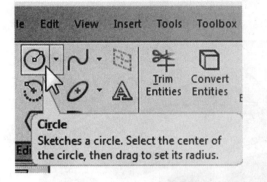

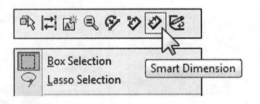

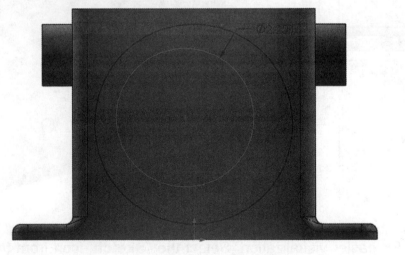

To locate the circle in the center of the circular face, we'll add a "**Concentric Relation**." Select the "**Add Relation**" icon from the right mouse button menu; select the circle we just drew and the edge of the circular face. Click "**Concentric**" to add the relation and center the circle. Click **OK** to finish the command.

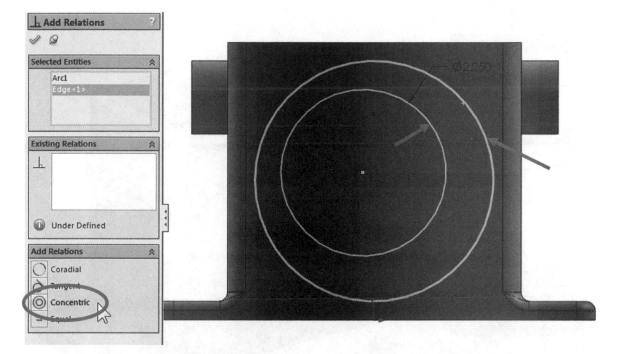

Another way to add a concentric relation is to pre-select the circle and the edge of the "*Front Boss*" (hold down the **Ctrl** key while selecting), and select **Concentric** from the pop-up menu or the PropertyManager. When adding a single geometric relation this is usually a faster way to do it.

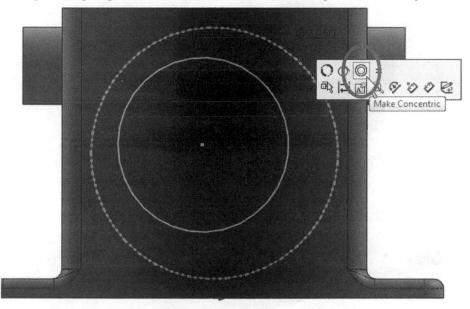

40. - Now that the circle is concentric with the boss, we'll make the cut. Select the "**Extruded Cut**" command from the Features tab and switch to an isometric view for better visualization. From the "**Extruded Cut**" properties select the "**Through All**" option and OK to finish; by using this end condition the cut will go through the entire part regardless of its size. In other words, *if* we change the '*Housing*' to be wider, the cut will still go through it.

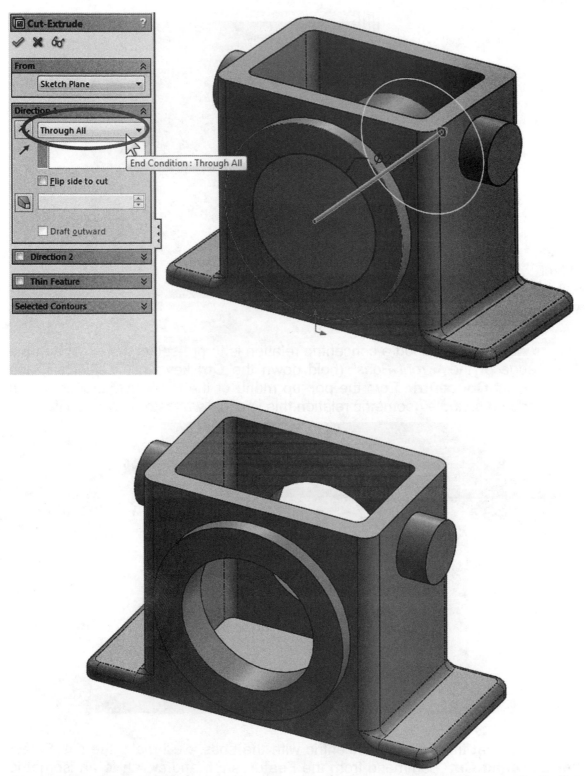

41. - We will now make a hole in the boss added in step 37 for a shaft. Switch to a Right view and create a new sketch on the small circular face of the "*Side Boss*" by selecting the "**Sketch**" icon and then the circular face to locate it.

We know that we want the hole to be concentric with the boss. In order to do this we can draw the circle and add a concentric relation as we did before; however, this is a two step process. Instead, we will do it in one step as follows: Select the "**Circle**" tool icon and *before* drawing the circle, move the cursor and <u>rest it</u> on top of the circular edge as shown, the center of the circular edge is revealed in a fraction of a second. DO NOT CLICK ON THE EDGE. This highlight works only if you have a drawing tool active (Line, Circle, Arc, etc.) This technique can be used to reveal any circular edge's center and reference any other model edges.

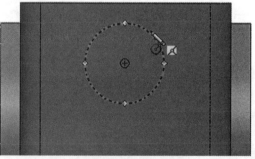

42. - Once the circular edge's center is revealed, click in it to start drawing the circle automatically capturing a concentric relation with the center of the boss. Finish the circle and dimension it 0.575″ in diameter. Now the sketch is fully defined.

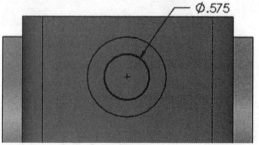

43. - Since this hole will be used for a shaft, we need to add a bilateral **tolerance** to the dimension. Select the 0.575″ dimension in the graphics area, and from the dimension's PropertyManager, under "Tolerance/Precision" select "Bilateral." Now we can add the tolerances. Notice that the dimension changes immediately in the graphics area. This tolerance will be transferred to the *Housing's* detail drawing later on. If needed, tolerances can also be added later in the detail drawing.

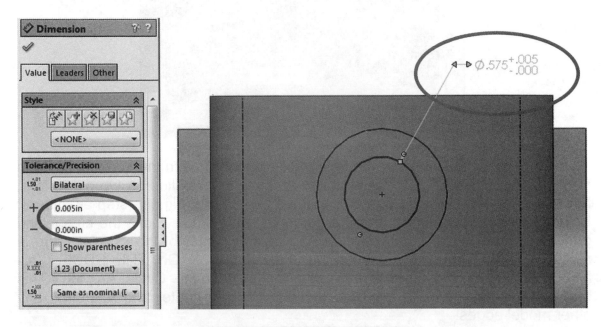

44. - Now we can make a Cut with the **"Through All"** option using the **"Extruded Cut"** command. When finished rename the Feature *"Shaft hole."*

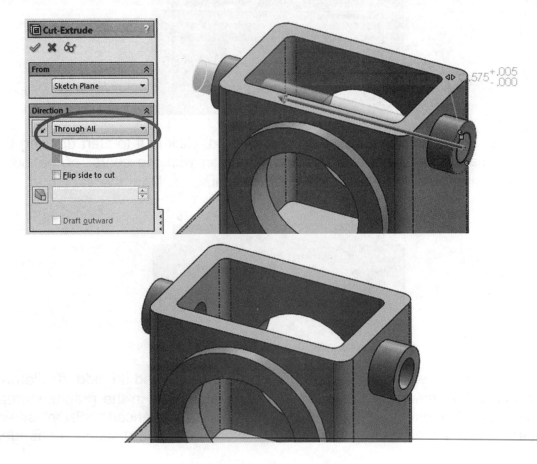

45. - Another way to do this cut is using the "Instant 3D" feature. To use "Instant 3D" to make a cut, click in the "**Exit Sketch**" icon, change to an Isometric view for clarity, and just like we did for the Extrusion, select the sketch circle and click-and-drag the handle *into* the part. You'll see how the part is cut as the arrow is dragged. The only disadvantage to making the cut using this technique is that the "Through All" option is not available, it will be a defined distance only.

46. - For the next feature we'll make a ¼"-20 tapped hole in the front face. SolidWorks provides us with a tool to automate the creation of simple, Countersunk and Counterbore holes, slots, tap and Pipe taps by selecting a fastener size, depth, and location. The "**Hole Wizard**" command is a two-step process: in the first step we define the hole's type and size, and in the second step we define the location of the hole(s). To add the tapped hole, switch to a Front view. The **Hole Wizard** is a special type of feature that uses 2 sketches that are automatically created, so there is no need to add a sketch first; in fact, it works very much like an applied feature.

Change to a Front View for clarity, and select the "**Hole Wizard**" icon from the Features tab in the CommandManager. The first thing we'll do is to define the hole's type and size. Select "**Tap**" for "Hole Type", "ANSI Inch" for Standard, "Tapped Hole" for Screw type and from the drop down selection list pick "¼-20" for size. Change the "End Condition" to "Up to Next", this will make the tapped hole's depth up to the next face where it makes a complete round hole. At the bottom activate the button to add **Cosmetic Threads**.

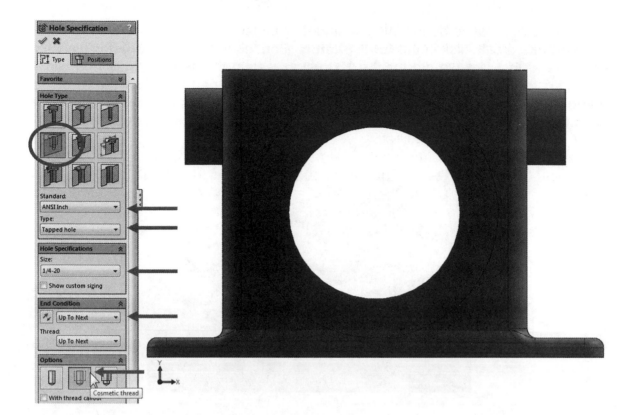

47. - The second step of the "**Hole Wizard**" is to define the hole's location. After selecting the type of hole we want to make, activate the "**Positions**" tab at the top of the properties, SolidWorks will ask to select a flat face to locate the hole(s). Select the round face at the front of the part.

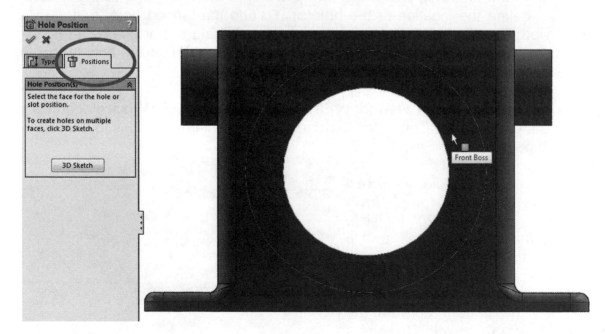

Immediately after selecting the face, SolidWorks will automatically select the "**Sketch Point**" tool and we are ready to define the hole's location. Anywhere we add a sketch point; the Hole Wizard will add a hole. For this exercise we only need to make one, and in order to locate it we'll use regular sketch tools (dimensions and geometric relations; notice that we are working in a Sketch.) We want this hole to be located in the middle of the flat face's width; to locate it, first draw a "**Centerline**" by selecting it from the drop-down menu in the "**Line**" command. Start drawing the centerline at the right quadrant of the outer circular edge, and finish it in the same quadrant of the inner circular edge. The quadrants are activated after selecting the Centerline tool and *touching* (not clicking!) the circular edges. (Notice the reference icons after touching the edges.) Hit the Esc key once to finish the Centerline command.

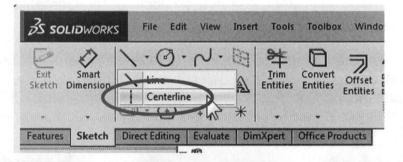

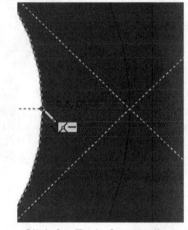
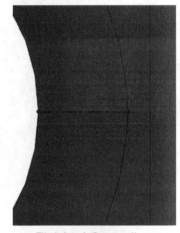

Click for Start of centerline   Click for End of centerline   Finished Centerline

When the centerline is complete, select the "**Sketch Point**" from the Sketch tab in the CommandManager. The idea behind this technique is to make sure the hole is centered in the circular face. To add the sketch point that will define the hole's location, touch the centerline for a split second to reveal its midpoint (like we just did with the circular edges), and click in its center to add the sketch point.

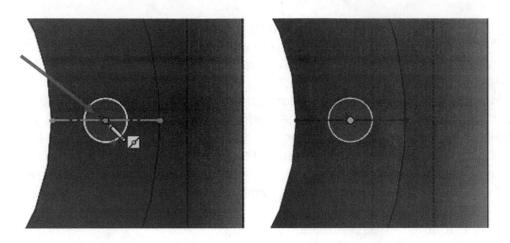

Now the hole will be located in the middle of the Centerline. Click OK to finish the Hole Wizard.

 If the point had been added in a different location, we could add the midpoint relation by Window-Selecting the "**Point**" and the "**Centerline**", and from the pop-up toolbar selecting "**Make Midpoint**." If we had pre-selected the face before selecting the hole wizard command we would have seen this scenario.

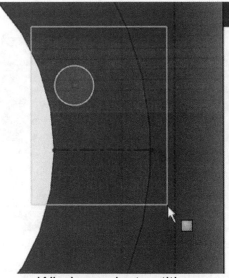
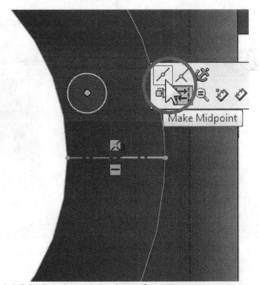

Window select entities   Add Midpoint relation from pop-up menu

 The "Cosmetic Thread" option adds a threaded texture to the holes, instead of an actual thread for looks and performance purposes. To change the "Cosmetic Threads" display right-mouse-click in the "*Annotations*" folder at the top of the FeatureManager, select "Details" and activate the options "Cosmetic Threads" and "Shaded Cosmetic Threads." Remember that there are no real threads in the model. Real helical threads can be made, but it's mostly unnecessary in these cases. Later in the book we'll learn how to model real threads.

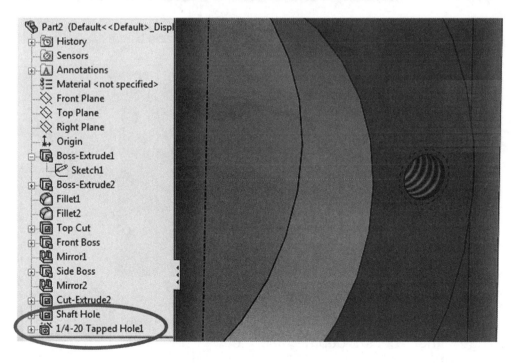

The difference between the two types is:

- *Cosmetic thread* is the annotation that shows up in a 2D drawing to indicate a thread.
- *Shaded cosmetic thread* is a texture added to the holes to give the 3D model the appearance of a thread and it's only for visual effect.

This is the finished ¼"-20 Tapped Hole with cosmetic threads.

48. - After making the Tapped hole, we suddenly realize that the walls of the *'Housing'* need to be thinner, and need to make a change to our design. In order to do this, we find the feature that we want to modify in the FeatureManager (*'Top Cut'* in our case) or in the graphics area, and select it. From the pop-up toolbar, select the **"Edit Sketch"** icon. This will allow us to go back to the original sketch and make changes to it. Notice the selected feature is highlighted in the screen.

There is no real purpose to this dimensional change but to show the reader how to change an existing feature's sketch if needed. While editing a sketch, dimensions, geometry, and geometric relations can be added, edited or removed as needed.

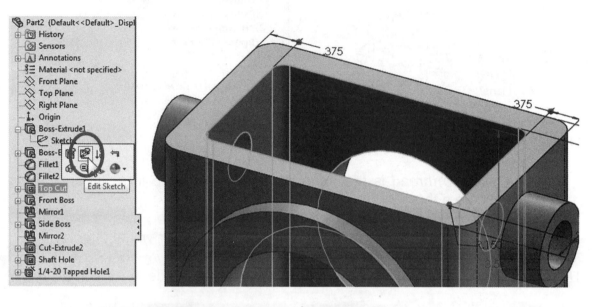

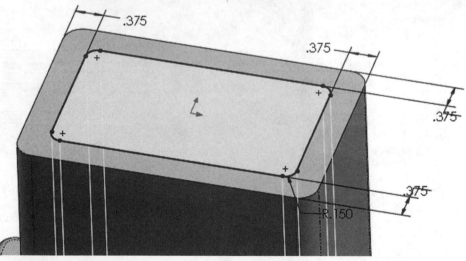

 Selecting the "Edit Feature" icon will show the Cut Extrude command options; this is where we can change the cut's depth and other feature's parameters.

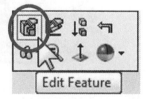

 If we select the feature with a right-mouse-click, we will see the pop-up toolbar along with an options menu. The most commonly used commands are already in the pop-up toolbar

 If the "**Instant 3D**" command is activated, selecting a feature will show its dimensions on the screen (more about that later.)

49. - What we just did was to go back to editing the feature's Sketch, just like when we first created it. Switch to a Top view if needed for visualization. To change a dimension's value double click on it to display the "Modify" dialog box. Change the two dimensions indicated from 0.375″ to 0.25″ as shown.

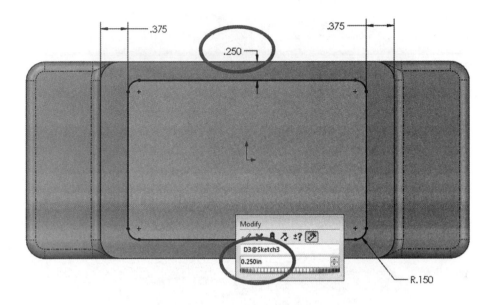

 To arrange the dimensions just click-and-drag to move them around.

50. - After changing the dimensions we cannot select "**Cut Extrude**" because we had already made a cut; what we have to do now is to select "**Exit Sketch**" or "**Rebuild**" the part (Ctrl+B) to update the model with the new dimensions.

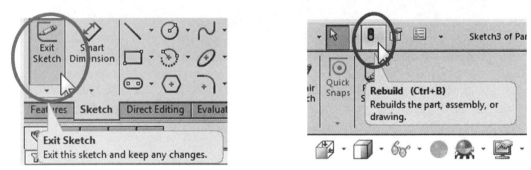

 Another way we can make these changes is using the "**Instant3D**" functionality. The way it works is very simple: instead of having to edit the sketch, we select the feature that we want to modify either in the FeatureManager or the graphics area (in this case one of the inside faces which were made with the Cut Extrude) and click-and-drag the **blue dots** at each of the dimensions that need to be modified until we get the desired value, without having to edit the sketch. Dragging the mouse pointer over the ruler markers will give you values in exact increments. Depending on the speed of your PC and the feature being modified, Instant3D may be slow, as the model is being dynamically updated.

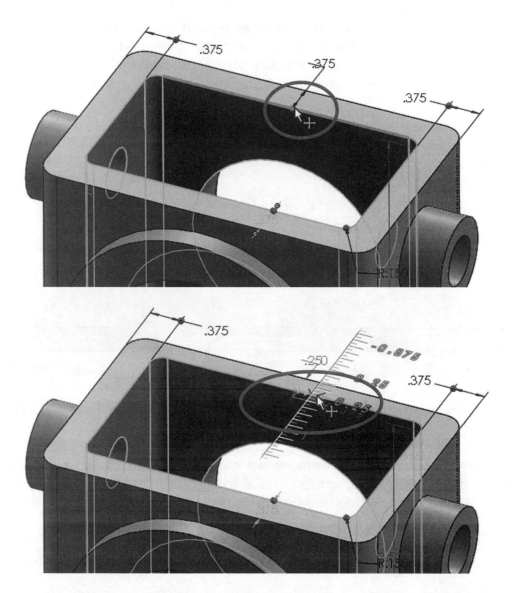

A third option to change the dimensions is to click on the dimension's value and type a new one. If Instant3D is not active, double-click the dimension to change their value; after making the dimension changes we need to rebuild the model.

51. - Now we will add more tapped holes to complete the flange's mounting holes. We'll use the first hole as a "seed" to make copies of it using the "**Circular Pattern**" command. In the Features tab, select the drop-down list below the "**Linear Pattern**" to reveal the drop down menu and select "**Circular Pattern**" or use the menu "**Insert, Pattern/Mirror, Circular Pattern**." Note that commands are grouped by similar functionality.

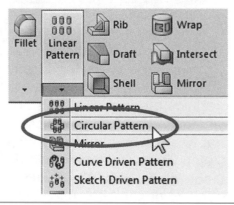

52. - The "**Circular Pattern**" needs a circular edge, a cylindrical surface or an axis as a reference for the direction of the circular pattern. Click inside the Parameters selection box to activate it, and then select the edge indicated for the pattern axis.

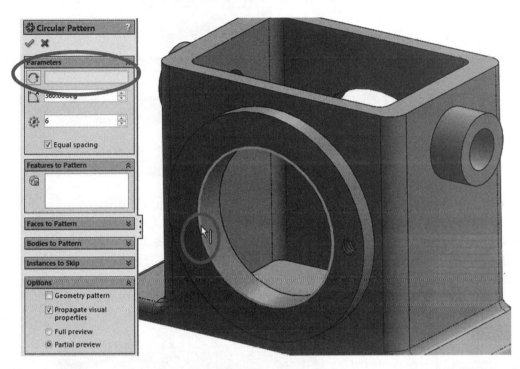

53. - Any circular edge or cylindrical face that shares the same axis can be used for a direction, as shown in the following images.

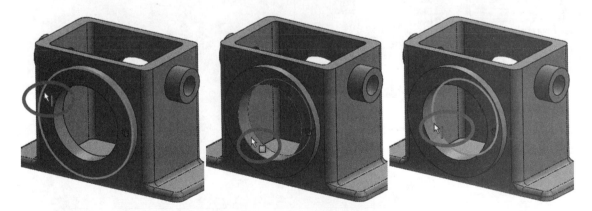

 Another option for Pattern Axis is a temporary axis. Every cylindrical surface has a "Temporary Axis" that runs through its center. To see the temporary axes in a model select the menu "**View, Temporary Axes**" or turn them on in the "**Hide/Show Items**" toolbar.

 Temporary axes (and other auxiliary geometry) can be turned on or off while a command is in progress. In this picture we can see that the shortcut letter "T" was assigned to toggle the temporary axes on and off.

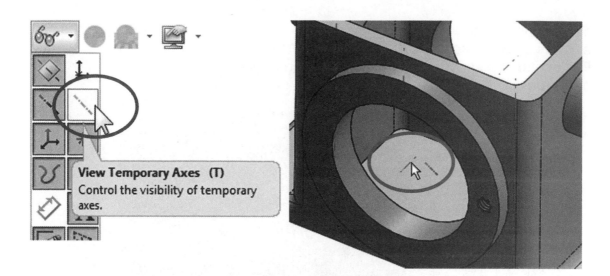

54. - After selecting the Pattern Axis click inside the "**Features to Pattern**" selection box to activate it (Notice it gets highlighted.) Select the "*¼-20 Tapped Hole1*" feature from the fly-out FeatureManager; change the number of copies to six (this value includes the original), and make sure the "Equal spacing" option is selected to equally space the copies in 360 degrees. Notice the preview in the graphics area and click OK to finish the command.

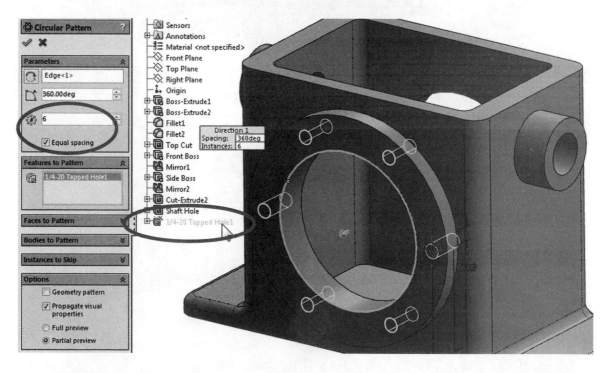

The feature to be patterned can also be selected from the graphics area; in this case <u>a face of the feature</u> needs to be selected. Sometimes a face can be difficult to select because it may be small, like this hole. In this case, we can use the "**Magnifying Glass**" (Shortcut "G") to make selection easier.

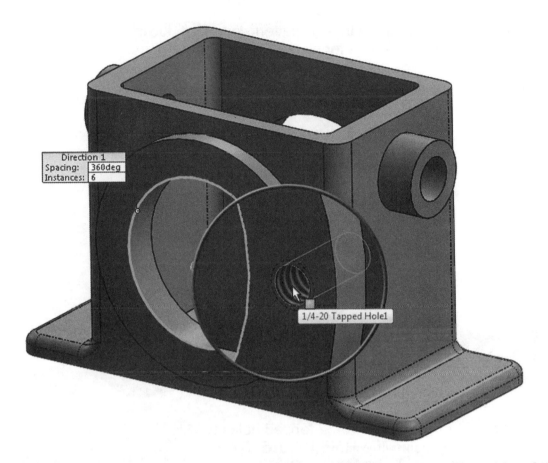

55. - Since we need to have the same six tapped holes in the other side of the *'Housing'*, we will use the "**Mirror**" command to copy the Circular Pattern about the *"Front Plane."* Make this mirror about the *"Front Plane"* and mirror the *"CircPattern1"* feature created in the previous step. Click OK to finish.

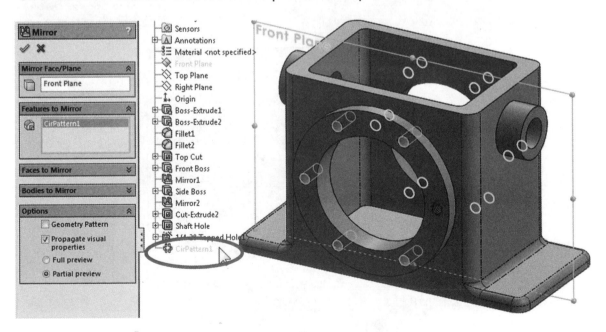

After mirroring the circular pattern our part looks like this (Cosmetic Threads have been turned off for clarity):

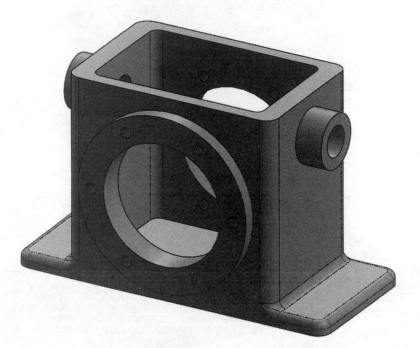

56. - We will now add four #6-32 tapped holes to the topmost face using the **Hole Wizard**. Switch to a Top view (Ctrl+5 or Mouse Gestures) for visibility and select the "**Hole Wizard**" icon.

57. - In the Hole Wizard's PropertyManager, select the "**Tap**" Hole Specification icon, and select the options shown for a #6-32 Tapped Hole. The "Blind" condition tells SolidWorks to make the hole an exact depth.

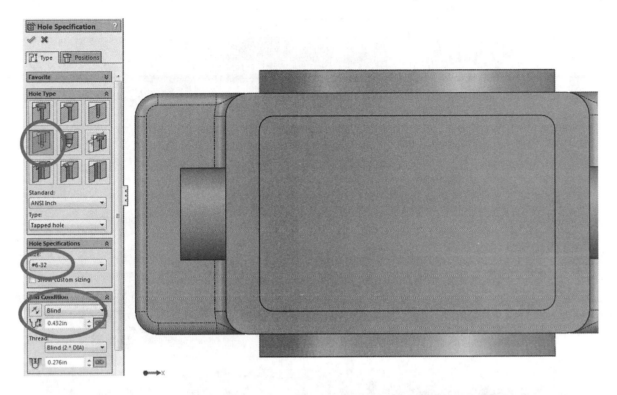

58. - Click in the "Positions" tab to define the hole locations. Select the top face to add the tapped holes, and notice that immediately after we select the face the "**Sketch Point**" tool is automatically selected, we are editing a sketch and the Sketch toolbar is activated.

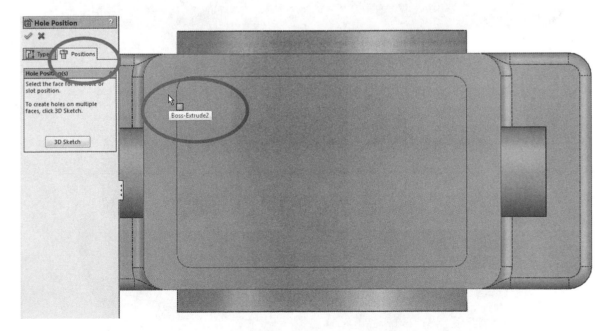

59. - With the "**Point**" tool active, *touch* each of the round corner edges to reveal their centers, and then click in their centers to add a point in each one; this way we'll make the points concentric to each corner fillet's center. Click OK to finish the Hole Wizard.

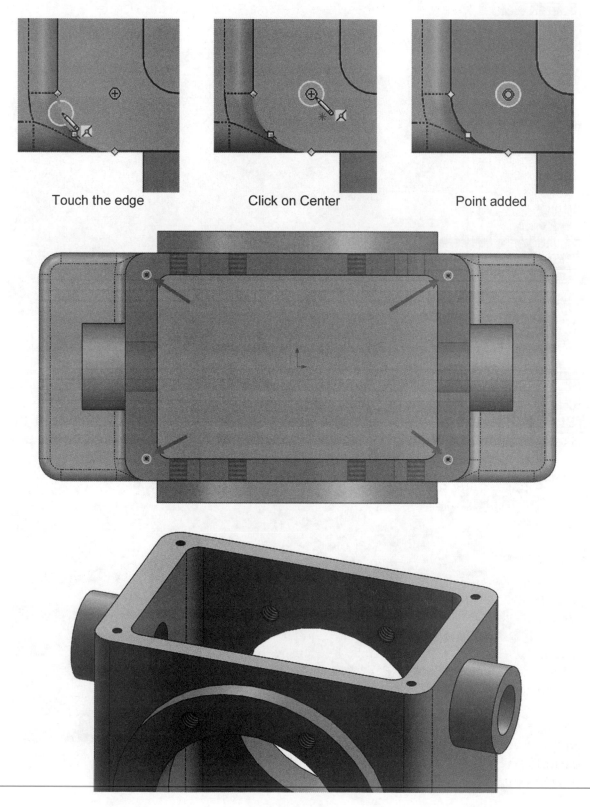

Touch the edge   Click on Center   Point added

60. - We are now ready to make the slots at the base of the *'Housing'*. For this task it will be easier to switch to a Top view. To add a new sketch, we can select the "**Sketch**" command and click on the selected face as before, but in this case we'll learn how to use the pop-up toolbar. Select the face, and from the pop-up toolbar, select "**Sketch**." Notice there are two similar looking icons, the one on top is "**Edit Sketch**" and is used to modify the sketch of the feature we selected, the one below is "**Sketch**" to create a new sketch on the selected flat face.

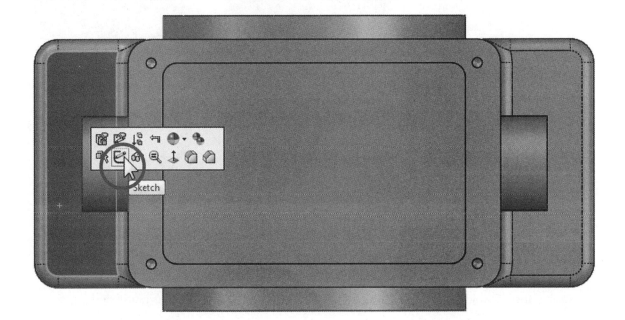

 If "**Edit Sketch**" is selected instead of "**Sketch**," simply click on the red "X" in the confirmation corner in the upper right corner of the graphics area to cancel any changes made to the sketch and go back to editing the model.

To make the slot, we'll use the "**Straight Slot**" command from the Sketch tab in the CommandManager. This tool will create a slot by first drawing the centerline and then defining the width of the slot. Select the "**Straight Slot**" icon and activate the "Add Dimensions" option, it will automatically add dimensions when we finish. First click to locate the center of one arc, click to locate the second, and click a third time to define the width. When finished, double click the dimensions to change them and make the slot 0.375″ long and 0.250″ wide.

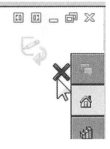

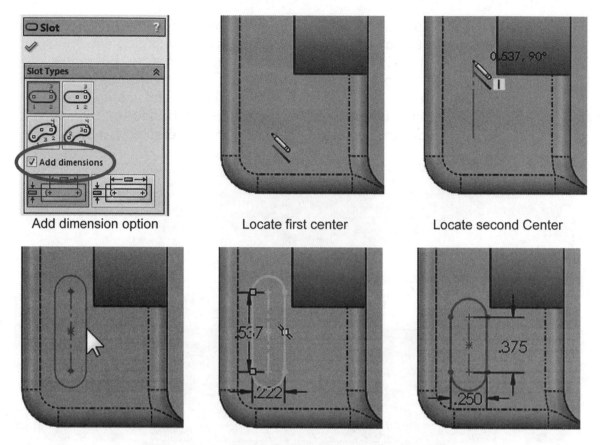

Add dimension option	Locate first center	Locate second Center

Define the slot width	Automatic dimensions added	Corrected dimensions

 The "**Slot**" command has more options, including arc slots and overall slot length dimension.

 To enable auto dimension while adding other sketch elements, select the menu "**Tools, Options, System Options, Sketch**" and activate:

☑ Enable on screen numeric input on entity creation

Another way to activate the option is by right-mouse-click and turn on "**Sketch Numeric Input**." This option will allow you to type the dimensions (entity size) as you sketch. To automatically add the dimensions select a sketch tool (line, arc, circle, etc.) right-mouse-click and turn on the option "**Add Dimension**."

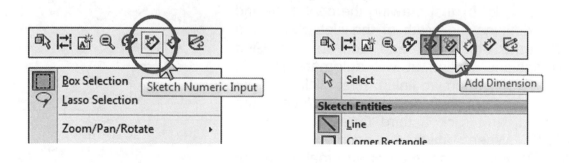

After the slot's size is defined, locate the slot by adding two 0.5″ dimensions to the lower and left edges of the base as shown. Finish the slot by making an "**Extruded Cut**" using the "Through All" option. Rename this feature "*Slot*."

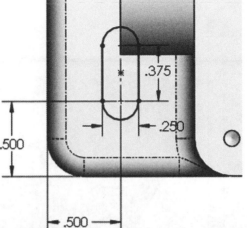

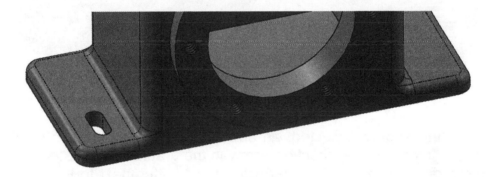

 Slots can also be made using the Hole Wizard

61. - We will now create a "**Linear Pattern**" of the slot. A linear pattern allows us to make copies of one or more features along one or two directions (usually along model edges.) Select the "**Linear Pattern**" command from the Features tab in the CommandManager or the menu "**Insert, Pattern/Mirror, Linear Pattern**."

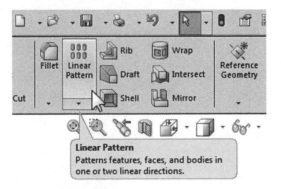

 Using the Mirror command keeps the design intent better, but we chose to show the user how to use the Linear Pattern command instead.

62. -In the Linear Pattern's Property-Manager, the "Direction 1" selection box is active; select the edge indicated for the direction of the copies. The copies will follow this direction. Any linear edge can be used as long as it is in the desired direction of the pattern.

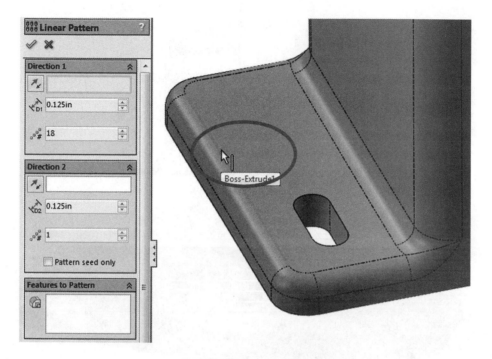

Once the edge is selected, an arrow indicates the direction in which the copies will be made. If the Direction Arrow in the graphics area is pointing in the wrong direction click in the "**Reverse Direction**" button next to the "Direction 1" selection box.

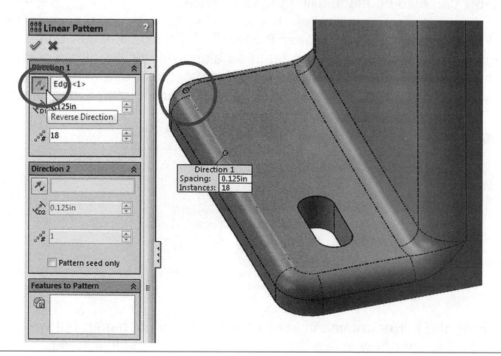

63. - Now click inside the "Features to Pattern" selection box to activate it and select the slot feature either from the fly-out FeatureManager or the graphics area. Change the spacing between the copies to 1.25″ and total copies to 2. This value includes the original just like in the Circular Pattern. Click OK to finish the command.

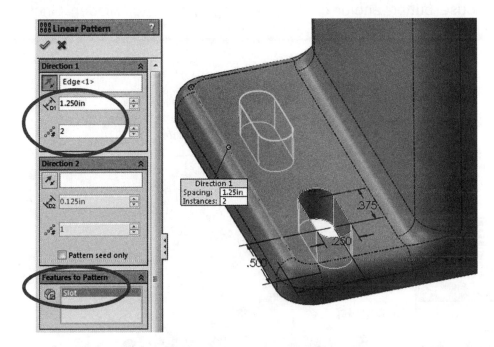

64. - We need the slots on both sides, so we'll copy the previous linear pattern to the other side of the *'Housing'* using the "**Mirror**" command about the "*Right Plane*." Click on the "**Mirror**" icon in the Features tab of the CommandManager; select the "*Right Plane*" as the mirror plane and the "*LPattern1*" in the "Features to Mirror" selection box to copy the slots.

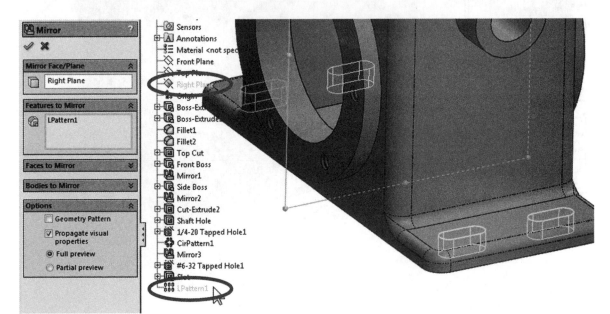

Selecting the Linear Pattern feature for the mirror also includes the pattern's seed feature, the "*Slot*."

65. - Using the "**Fillet**" command from the Features tab, add a 0.125″ radius **fillet** to the edges indicated as a finishing touch. Rotate the model using the **middle mouse button** and/or change the display style to "Hidden Lines Visible" **mode to make selection easier.** Click OK to finish.

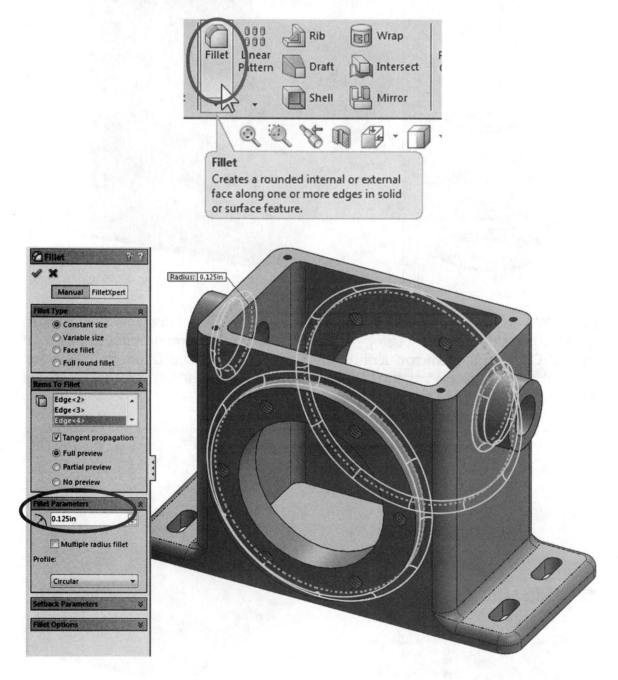

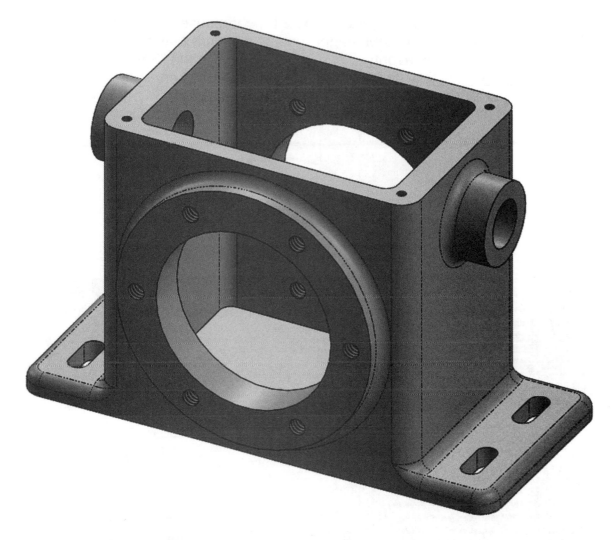

66. - Now that the model is finished, we can easily determine its physical properties, such as **Weight, Volume, Center of Mass and Moments of Inertia**. SolidWorks includes a built in materials library with many different metals and alloys, plastics, woods, composite materials and others like air, glass and water.

The library includes mechanical and thermal properties such as:

- Mass density
- Elastic and Shear modulus
- Tensile, Compressive and Yield strengths
- Poisson's ratio
- Thermal expansion coefficient
- Thermal conductivity
- Specific heat

 These properties are used by SolidWorks to determine a part's **weight**, or determine if a component will fail under a given set of loading **conditions** using SimulationXpress (the built in structural analysis software.)

To assign a material to a component, right-mouse-click in the **"Material"** icon at the top of the FeatureManager, and select "Edit Material" or pick one of the materials listed. The favorites list can be changed in the "Favorites" tab in the Materials library. For this part select "Cast Alloy Steel" from the "Steel" library. Click on "Apply" to accept the material and Close the library.

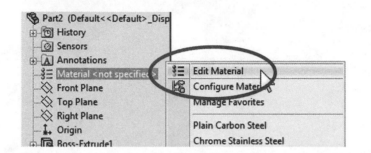

Now the FeatureManager reads "*Cast Alloy Steel*" instead of "*Material.*" Select **"Mass Properties"** from the Evaluate tab in the CommandManager. We'll see the Density (provided by the material selection), Mass (Calculated from the volume and density), Volume, Surface Area and Center of Mass coordinates relative to the origin (also indicated by a magenta triad in the graphics area), Principal Axes of inertia and Moments of inertia about the Center of Mass and the part's origin all listed in a new window, where we can copy the text for later use in reports.

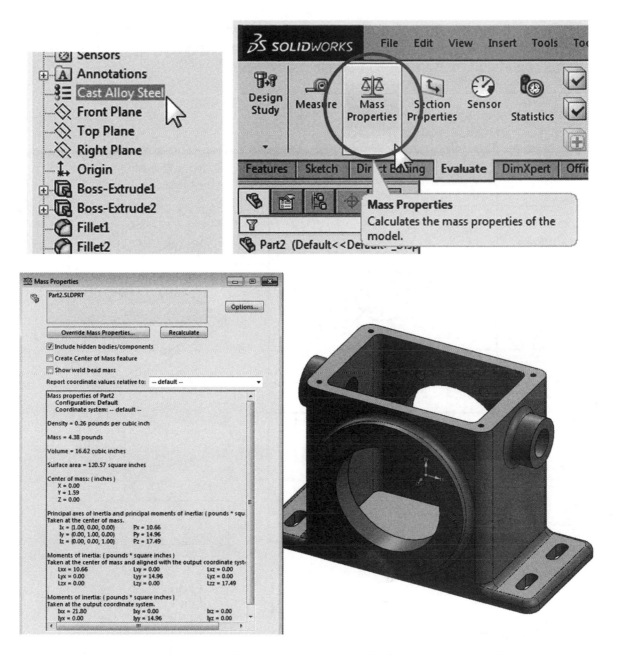

Mass properties are referenced to the origin by default, but they can also be referenced to a user defined coordinate system by selecting one from the "Output coordinate system" drop down list. In the "Options" button we can change the units we want the results to be displayed with, by default mass properties are displayed using the document's units.

Save the finished part as *'Housing'* and close the file.

79

Exercises: Build the following parts using the knowledge acquired in this lesson. Try to use the most efficient method to complete each model. High resolution images are included in the accompanying disc.

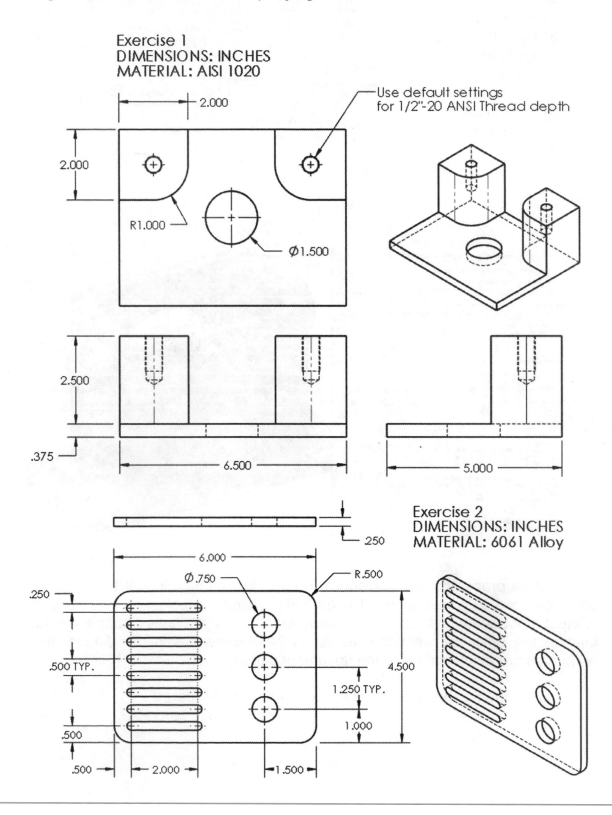

Exercise 1
DIMENSIONS: INCHES
MATERIAL: AISI 1020

2.000

Use default settings for 1/2"-20 ANSI Thread depth

2.000

R1.000

Ø1.500

2.500

.375

6.500

5.000

.250

Exercise 2
DIMENSIONS: INCHES
MATERIAL: 6061 Alloy

6.000

Ø.750

R.500

.250

.500 TYP.

4.500

1.250 TYP.

1.000

.500

.500

2.000

1.500

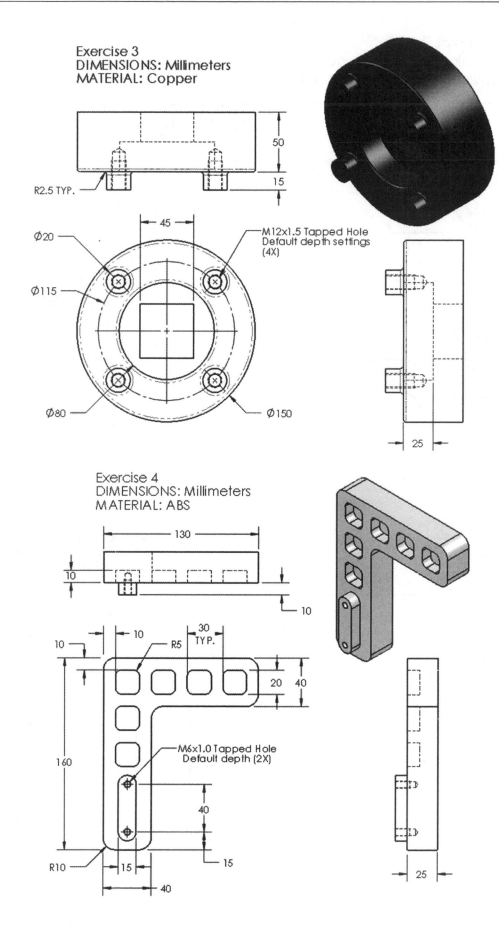

Exercise 3
DIMENSIONS: Millimeters
MATERIAL: Copper

50

15

R2.5 TYP.

45

Ø20

M12x1.5 Tapped Hole
Default depth settings
(4X)

Ø115

Ø80

Ø150

25

Exercise 4
DIMENSIONS: Millimeters
MATERIAL: ABS

130

10

10

10

R5

30
TYP.

10

20   40

M6x1.0 Tapped Hole
Default depth (2X)

160

40

R10   15   15

40

25

81

Engine Project Parts:
Make the following components to build the engine. Save the parts using the name provided. High resolution images at www.mechanicad.com

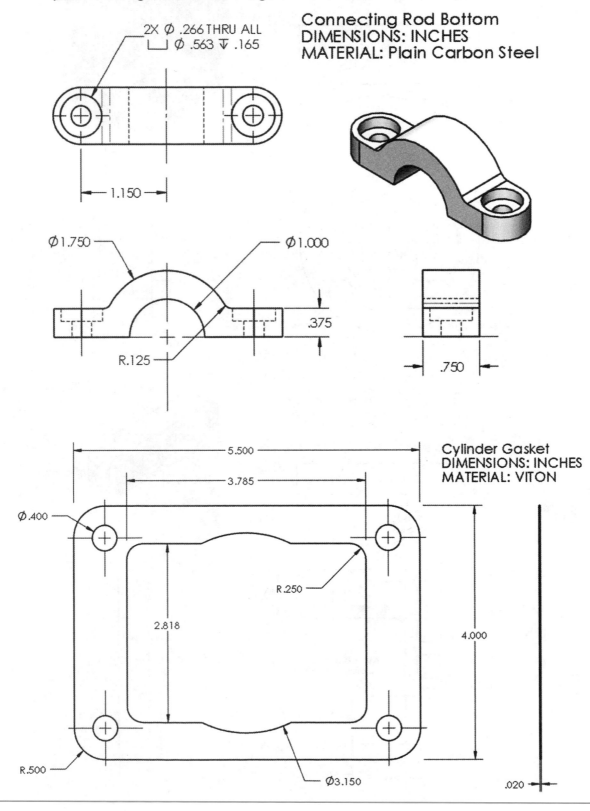

2X Ø .266 THRU ALL
⌴ Ø .563 ▼ .165

Connecting Rod Bottom
DIMENSIONS: INCHES
MATERIAL: Plain Carbon Steel

1.150

Ø1.750   Ø1.000

.375

R.125

.750

5.500
3.785

Cylinder Gasket
DIMENSIONS: INCHES
MATERIAL: VITON

Ø.400

R.250

2.818

4.000

R.500

Ø3.150

.020

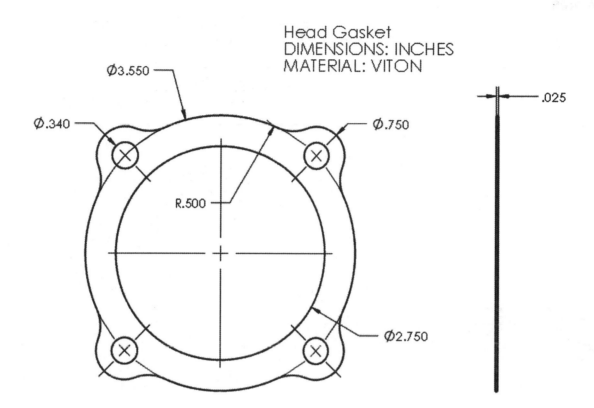

Head Gasket
DIMENSIONS: INCHES
MATERIAL: VITON

Notes:

The Side Cover

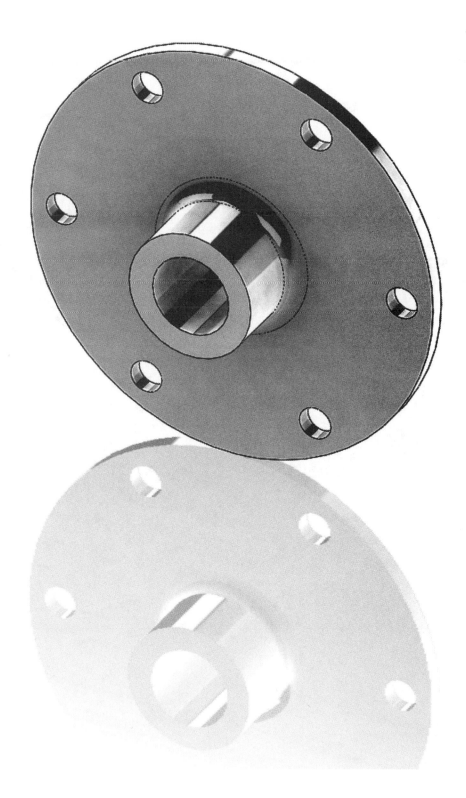

Notes:

In making the *'Side Cover'* part we will learn the following features and commands: Revolved Feature, Sketch Trim, and Extend and construction geometry. We will also review some of the commands previously learned in the *'Housing'* part. The sequence of features we'll follow for the *'Side Cover'* is:

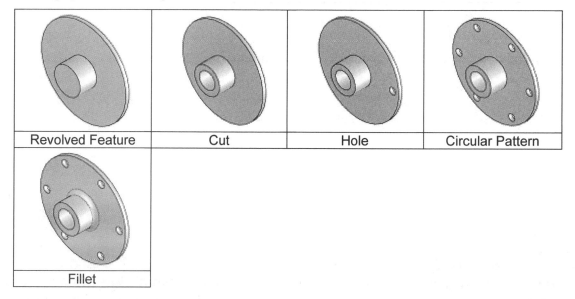

Revolved Feature	Cut	Hole	Circular Pattern

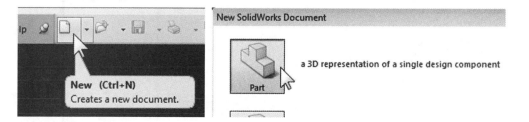

Fillet

67. -   Let's make a new part. Select the "**Part**" template and click OK. Be sure to change the units to Inches and three decimal places.

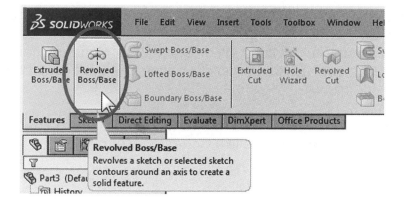

The first feature we'll create is a **Revolved Feature**. As its name implies, it is created by revolving a sketch about an axis. Select the "**Revolved Boss/Base**" icon from the Features tab in the CommandManager. When asked to select a plane for the sketch, select the "*Right Plane*" (no particular reason to choose this plane except to have a good looking isometric view ☺.)

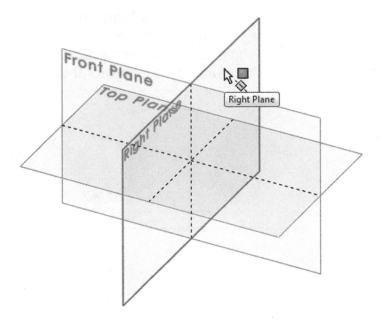

68. - Select the "**Rectangle**" command from the Sketch toolbar and draw the following sketch using two rectangles, starting at the origin and to the left (there will be two lines overlapping in the middle.) Don't be too concerned with their size; we'll add the correct dimensions later.

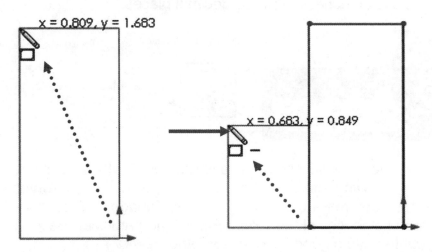

69. - It is a good practice to have single, non-intersecting profiles in the sketch, and no more than 2 lines sharing an endpoint. It is possible to use a sketch with intersecting lines using a function called "**Contours.**" Contours can be a powerful tool when properly used. This command is covered in the Level II book.

In general it is a good idea to work with single contour sketches and advance to other techniques like Contours later on.

To clean up the sketch, we will use the "**Trim**" command from the Sketch toolbar, from the lower left corner in the Mouse Gestures or the menu "**Tools, Sketch Tools, Trim**."

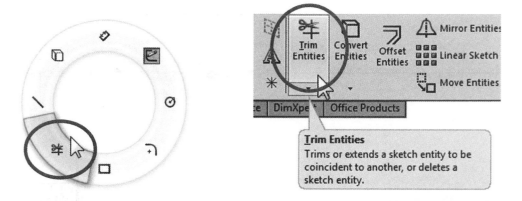

70. - The Trim tool allows us to cut sketch entities using other geometric elements as a trim boundary. After selecting the "**Trim Entities**" icon, select the "Power Trim" option from the PropertyManager. The Power Trim allows us to click-and-drag *across* the entities that we want to trim. Click-and-drag the cursor crossing the two lines indicated next. Notice the lines are trimmed as you cross them.

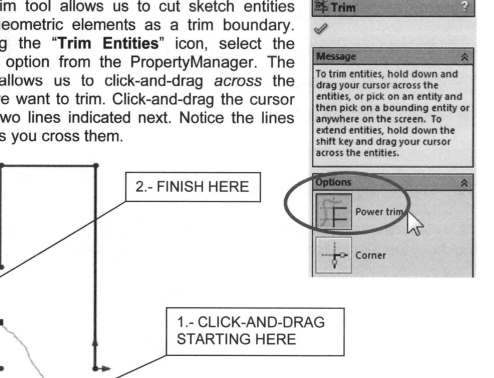

71. - The next step is to extend the short line to close the sketch and have a single closed profile. Select the "**Extend Entities**" icon from the drop down menu under "**Trim Entities**" or if the "Trim Entities" command is enabled, from the right-mouse-button menu. Click on the short line indicated; a preview will show you how the line will be extended. If the extension does not cross a line, you will not get a preview.

Extend Entities can also be accessed with the right mouse button menu when using the **Trim Entities** command.

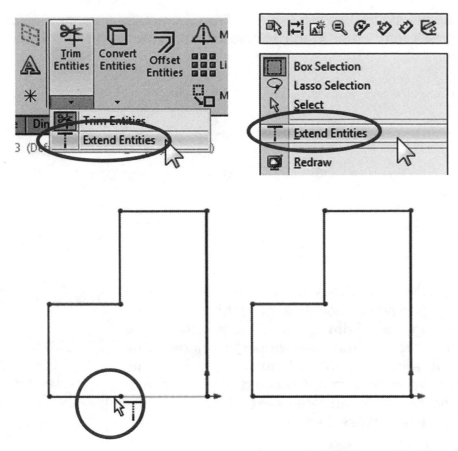

Another way to extend the line is to click-and-drag its endpoint onto other entities without selecting any tool.

72. -   Add the following dimensions to the sketch using the "**Smart Dimension**" tool from the Sketch tab in the CommandManager, or the Mouse Gestures.

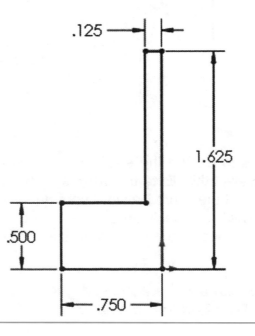

73. - Now that the Sketch is fully defined we'll make the **Revolved Boss/Base**. Select "**Exit Sketch**" or the **Revolved Boss/Base** icon from the Features tab.

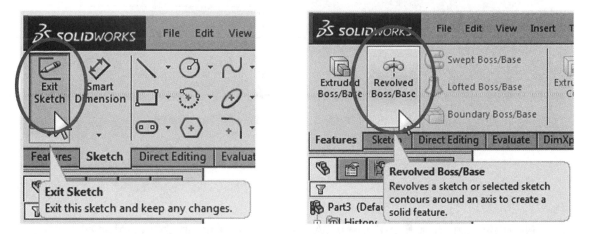

74. - The **Revolve** Property-Manager is presented and waits for us to select a line or centerline to make the revolved feature about it; if the sketch has a single centerline, it is automatically selected as a default axis of rotation. Select the line that we extended as the axis of rotation to make the revolved base.

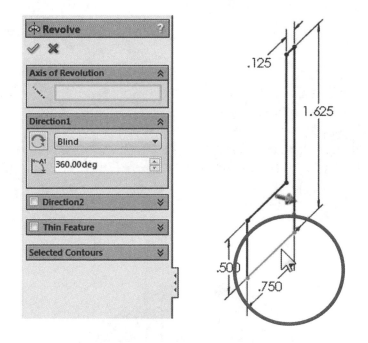

75. - After selecting the line, notice the preview in the graphics area. The default setting for a revolved feature is 360°. Click OK to complete the revolved feature and rename it "*Flange Base*."

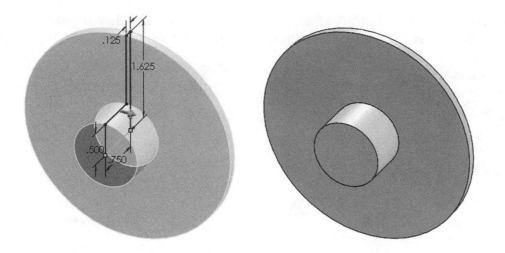

76. -   Now switch to a Front view. We'll make a hole in the center of the cover for a shaft. Create a new sketch in the front most face of the cover (Small round face), or, select the small face and click in the "**Sketch**" icon from the pop-up toolbar. Draw a circle starting at the origin and dimension as indicated. Make a cut using the "**Extruded Cut**" command using the "Through All" option.

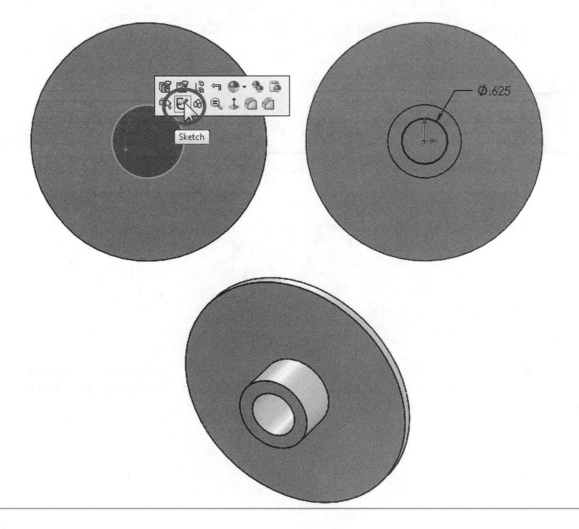

77. - The next step will be to make the first hole for the screws to pass through. We'll make one hole, and then use a Circular Pattern to make the rest as we did in the *'Housing'*, but in this case we'll use the **"Cut Extrude"** feature and not the **"Hole Wizard"** to show a different approach. To make this hole select the large circular face and create a new sketch. Draw a centerline from the origin toward the right, and at the end of the centerline draw a circle. Dimension as shown and make a cut using the "Through All" option as in the previous step.

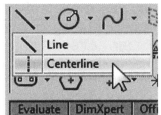

 The centerline is used as reference geometry to locate the center of the circle. Optionally we can add a Horizontal relation between the circle's center and the origin to fully define it.

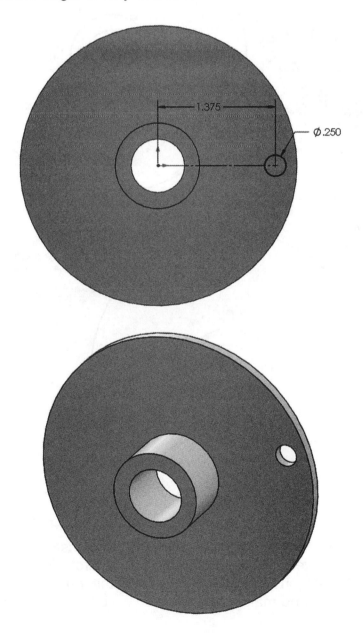

93

78. - A different way to do this sketch is to draw a circle and then convert it to construction geometry, this way you can dimension the circle's diameter. To convert any sketch element to construction geometry, simply select it in the graphics area and activate the "For construction" check box in the element's PropertyManager or click the "**Construction Geometry**" icon from the pop-up toolbar. After changing it the circle is displayed as construction geometry. Change to "Hidden Lines Removed" if necessary for clarity as we did in this step.

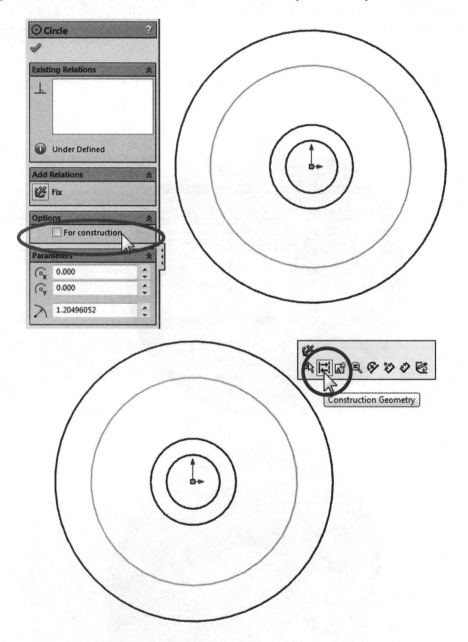

Now that the location circle is defined as construction geometry (also known as *reference geometry*), draw the second circle for the hole making its center coincident with one of the quadrants of the reference circle as shown. Dimension the sketch and make the cut.

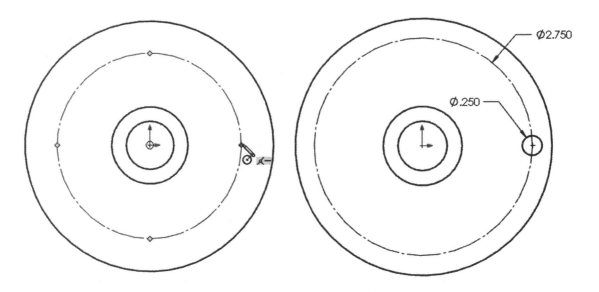

 An advantage of making the sketch using this approach is that you can add a diameter dimension to the circle locating the holes.

79. – To complete the rest of the holes, we'll make a circular pattern. Select the "**Circular Pattern**" icon from the Features tab in the CommandManager and select any circular edge for the pattern direction.

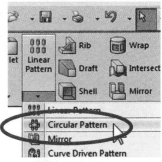

Now click inside the "Features to Pattern" selection box, and if not already selected, select the last cut operation from the fly-out FeatureManager or in the graphics area, using the "Magnifying Glass" (Shortcut "G") may help. Change the number of copies to 6; remember this count includes the original. Click OK to complete.

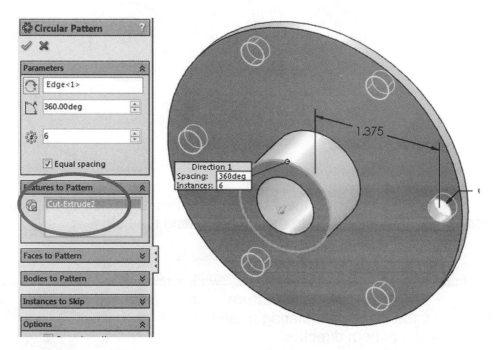

80. - Now select the Fillet command and round the edge as shown with a 0.125″ fillet radius.

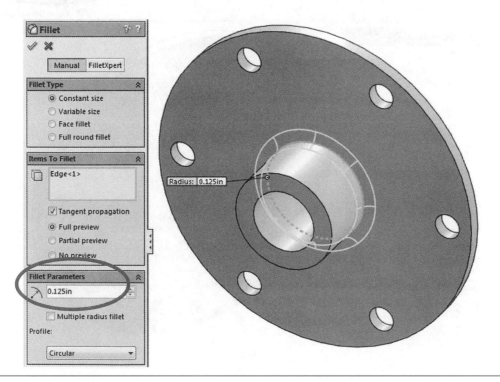

81. – Edit the material for the part, and assign AISI-1020 steel. If it is not in the materials favorite list, select it from the library.

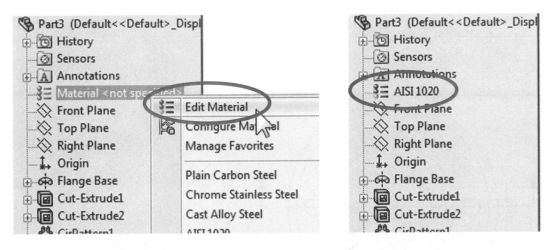

Save the finished component as *'Side Cover'* and close the file.

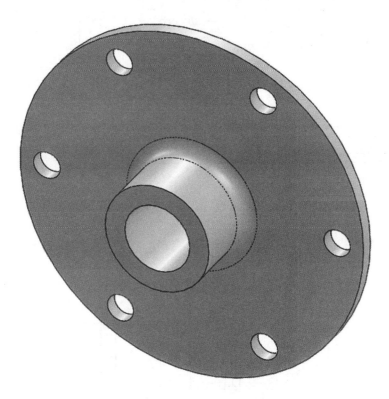

Exercises: Build the following parts using the knowledge acquired so far. Try to use the most efficient method to complete each model.

Exercise 5
DIMENSIONS: INCHES
MATERIAL:

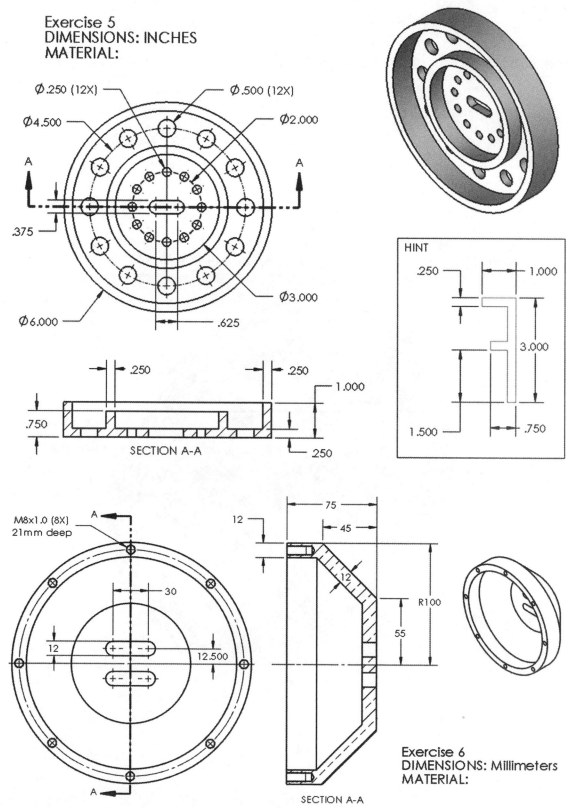

HINT

Exercise 6
DIMENSIONS: Millimeters
MATERIAL:

Engine Project Parts: Make the following components to build the engine. Save the parts using the name provided. High resolution images are included in the accompanying disc.

The '*Oil Seal*' is made using a single feature.

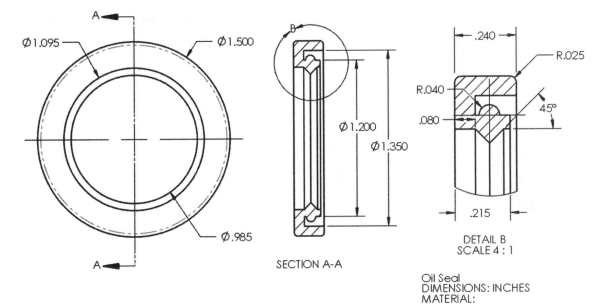

SECTION A-A

DETAIL B
SCALE 4 : 1

Oil Seal
DIMENSIONS: INCHES
MATERIAL:

Notes:

The Top Cover

Notes:

For the *'Top Cover'* part we will follow the next sequence of features. In this part we will learn a new feature called Shell, new options for Fillet, new end conditions for features (Boss, Cut, Revolve, etc.) and we'll practice some of the previously learned features and options.

Base Extrude	Top Extrude	Corner cuts	Corner Fillet
Shell	Bottom Extrude	Top Fillet	Shell Fillet
Holes			

82. - We'll start by making a new document selecting the **Part** template from the "**New Document**" command, and just like we did with the *'Housing'*, we'll create a new sketch. Select the "**Extruded Boss**" command and then select the *"Top Plane."*

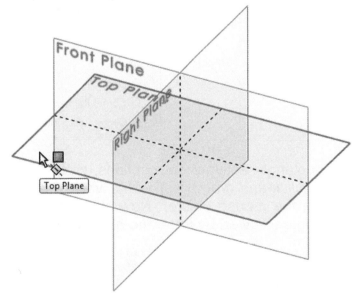

Draw a rectangle using the "**Center Rectangle**" command; first click in the origin to locate the center and then outside to complete the rectangle. Add the dimensions shown with the "**Smart Dimension**" tool and round the corners with the "**Sketch Fillet**" command using a 0.25"radius.

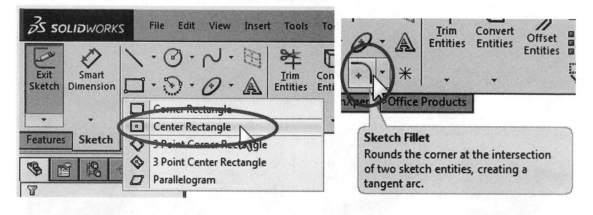

A slightly different way of making this sketch (or any sketch) is by using the "**Sketch Numeric Input**." What this option does is to allow us to define geometry's exact size as we sketch, making it the correct size from the start. This option can be turned on in the menu "**Tools, Options, Sketch, Enable on screen numeric input on entity creation**", or the right mouse button menu. If using this option, it may be a good idea to also activate the "**Add Dimension**" option (this option is only available if a sketch tool is active.) The differences are:

Sketch Numeric Input allows the user to enter the exact size of geometry.
Add Dimension will add the dimensions to the geometry created.
Add Dimension is only available when *Sketch Numeric Input* is activated and a sketch drawing tool is selected, as seen in the following images.

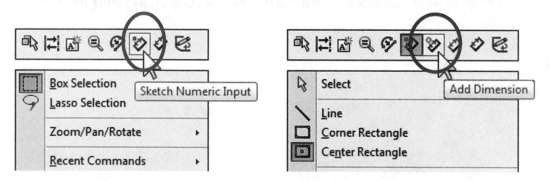

To make the rectangle activate both options, click to select the center of the rectangle (*do not click-and-drag.*) Notice the value boxes are immediately displayed as we move the mouse pointer. Now start typing the dimensions for each side of the rectangle followed by Enter, no need to click again.

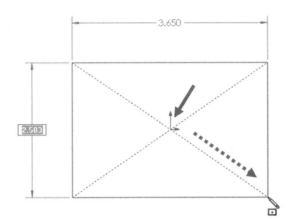

Click on center and move the mouse

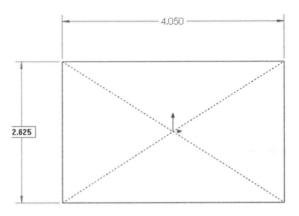

Type vertical dimension, press Enter

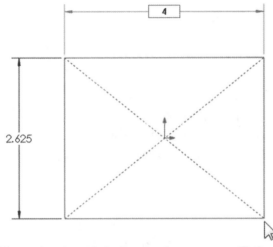

Type horizontal dimension, press Enter

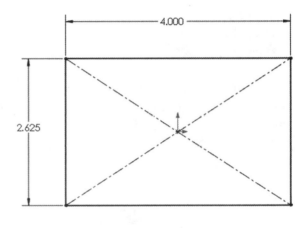

Finished rectangle with dimensions

Using the "Sketch Fillet" command round the corners 0.25".

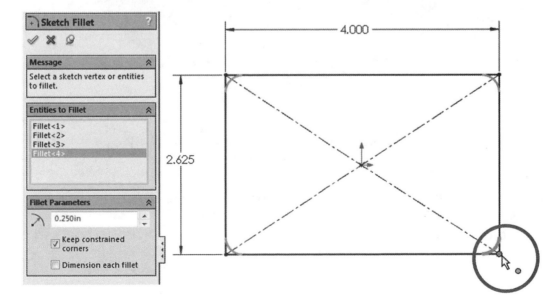

83. - To make the first extrusion, click on **"Exit Sketch"** or **"Extruded Boss/Base"** and set the distance to 0.25″. Rename the extrusion *'Base'*.

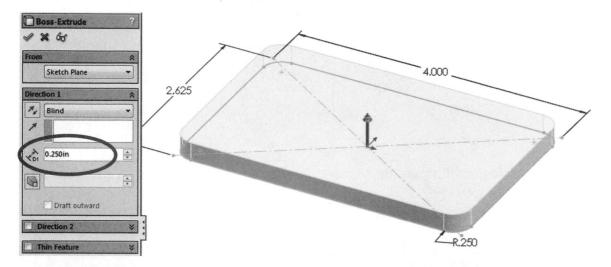

84. - For the second feature, we'll make an extrusion of similar shape to the first one, but smaller. For this feature we will use the **"Offset Entities"** function, this way the sketch will be created automatically by offsetting the edges of the previous feature face's edge. Click in the top face of the model and select the **"Sketch"** command from the pop-up toolbar to create a new sketch.

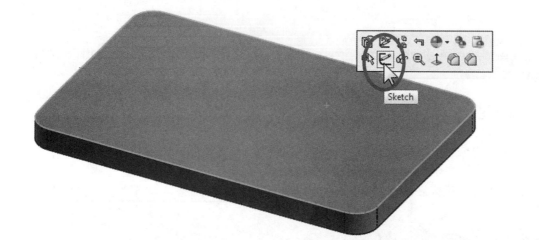

85. - After creating the sketch, notice the top face of the first feature is selected (in highlighted color); while it is selected activate the **"Offset Entities"** icon in the Sketch tab of the CommandManager. You will immediately see a preview of the offset of the selected face edges.

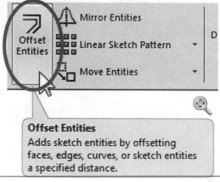

86. - Change the offset value to 0.375″ and then click in the "Reverse" checkbox to make the offset inside, not outside. Notice that when we change the direction the preview updates accordingly. Click OK when done.

87. - The Sketch is now Fully Defined (all geometry is black) because the sketch geometry is related to the edges of the face and only the offset dimension is added.

 Notice the offset command is powerful enough to eliminate the rounds in the corners if needed.

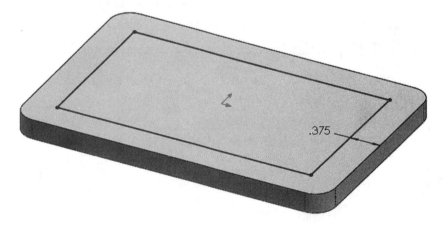

88. - To make the second feature select "**Extruded Boss**" from the Features toolbar in the CommandManager and extrude it 0.25″. Rename the feature *"Top Boss."*

89. - For the next feature, we'll make round cuts in the corners of the top extrusion to allow space for a screw head, washer, and tools. Switch to a Top view and create a sketch in the topmost face. Make a circle as shown making sure the center is coincident to the corner. Feel free to use the Sketch Numeric Input in this sketch. Add two centerlines starting in the origin, one vertical, and one horizontal; they'll be used in the next step. The model view was changed to Hidden Lines Removed mode for clarity.

 The sketch grid can be turned on or off for better visualization if needed, from the right mouse button menu.

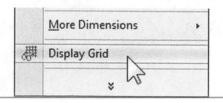

The "Sketch Numeric Input" option can be left on or turned off as the reader sees fit. It will be turned off in the following exercises to make explanation easier.

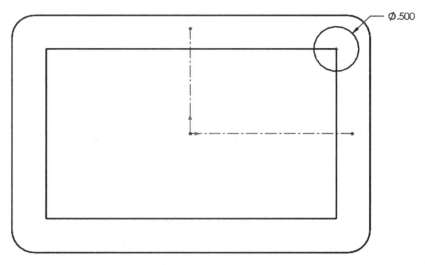

Ø.500

90. - We will now use the "**Mirror Entities**" from the Sketch tab in the CommandManager. This tool will help us make an exact copy of any sketch entity, in this case the circle, about any line, edge, or for our example, the vertical centerline; then we'll copy both circles about the horizontal centerline to make a total of four equal circles. Select the "**Mirror Entities**" icon.

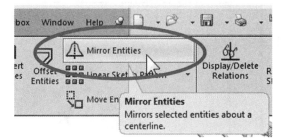

91. - In the "Entities to Mirror" selection box select the circle. Then click inside the "Mirror About" selection box to activate it (it will be highlighted) and select the vertical centerline. Click OK to complete the first sketch mirror.

 In certain commands after making a selection, the mouse pointer will change to indicate us that pressing the Right Mouse Button will activate either the next selection box or finish the command, helping us reduce mouse travel and work more efficiently. If we ignore the Right Mouse Button nothing happens and it will be dismissed.

Next   Finish/OK

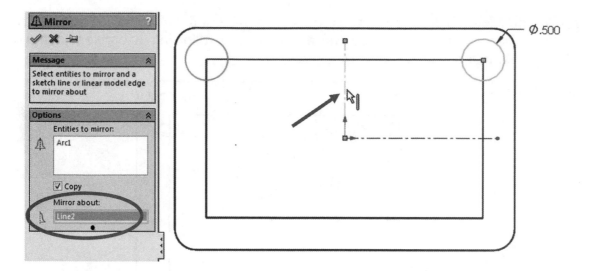

92. - Now repeat the "**Mirror Entities**" command selecting both circles in the "Entities to Mirror" selection box, and using the Horizontal centerline in the "Mirror About" selection box. Click OK to finish the Mirror. Since the new circles are mirror copies of the original, and the original was fully defined, the sketch is therefore fully defined. The new circles are added a "Symmetric" relation about the centerline.

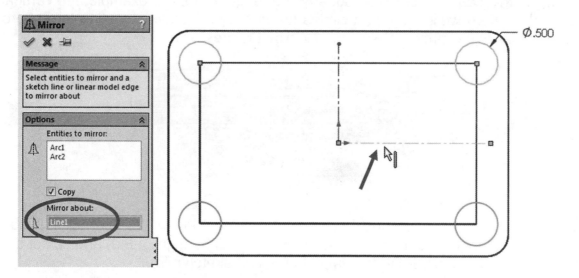

93. - We are now ready to make the cut. In this step we'll cut all four corners at the same time. SolidWorks allows us to have multiple closed contours in a sketch for one operation as long as they don't intersect or touch each other in one point. To add intelligence to our model (Design intent) we'll use an end condition for the cut called **Up to Surface**; with this end condition we can define the stopping face for the cut instead of giving it a depth. Select the "**Extruded Cut**" icon and select "Up To Surface" from the "Direction 1" options drop down selection box. A new selection box is displayed and activated; this is where we'll select the face where we want the cut to stop. Select the face indicated as the end condition and click OK to finish the feature.

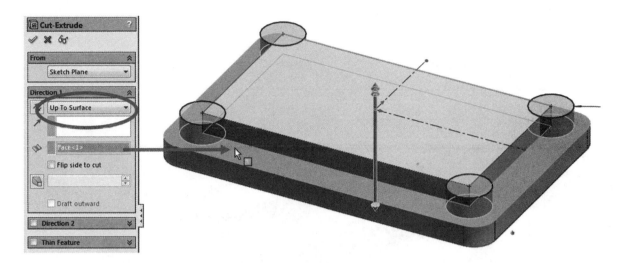

 The reason for selecting a face as an end condition is that if the height of the "Top Boss" changes, the cut will still go up to the intended depth. This is how design intent is maintained and intelligence added to our model.

Our part should now look like this:

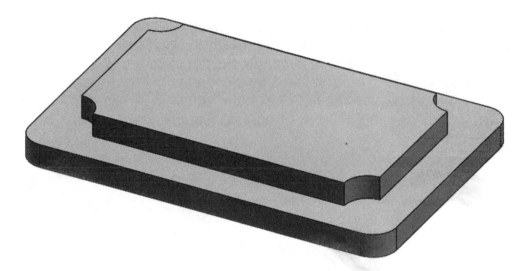

94. - Using the "**Fillet**" command add a 0.25"radius fillet to the edges indicated in the corner cuts. There are eight (8) edges to be rounded. To make selection easier, SolidWorks has a built in tool to help us select multiple edges. After selecting the first edge, a pop-up toolbar gives the user options to select different groups of edges. By moving the mouse over the different selection options highlights the edges that would be selected. For this example select the "Connected to end loop" option is exactly the edges we are interested in. In subsequent exercises the user will be able to explore other selection options.

After clicking in the icon to select the rest of the edges, the mouse changes to give us the OK/Finish in the right mouse button.

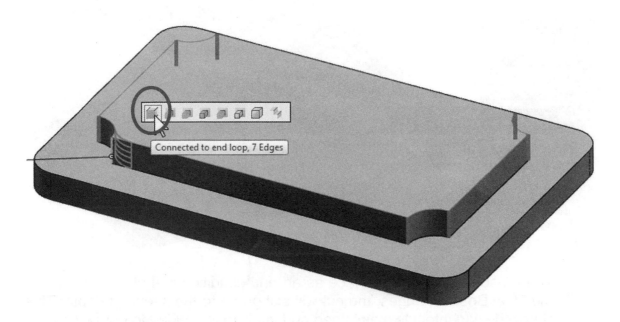

Connected to end loop, 7 Edges

 If selecting small edges is difficult, try using the "**Magnifying Glass**" to make selection easier (default shortcut "G.")

95. - Since this is going to be a cast part, we want to remove some material from the inside, and make its walls a constant thickness (common practice for castings and injection molded plastic parts.) In this case the "**Shell**" command is the best tool for the job. The Shell creates a constant thickness part by removing one or more faces from the model. Select the "**Shell**" icon from the Features tab in the CommandManager. This is an applied feature, which means it does not require a sketch.

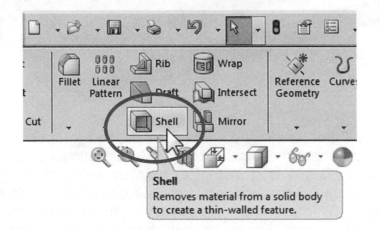

Shell
Removes material from a solid body to create a thin-walled feature.

96. - In the Shell's PropertyManager under "Parameters" set the wall thickness to 0.125″, rotate the part and select the bottom face; this is the face that will be removed making the remaining faces in the part 0.125″ thick. Click OK to finish the command. Since we only have one shell feature in this part, there is no reason to rename it.

If no faces are selected the "**Shell**" command creates a hollow part.

97. - With the finished shell operation the part looks like this, with every face in the part 0.125″ thick.

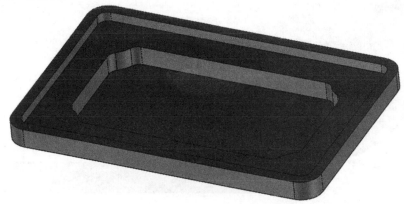

How can we tell if the walls are really 0.125″ thick? Using the "**Measure**" tool. It is located under the Evaluate tab in the CommandManager. This tool is like a digital measuring tape, where we can select faces, edges, vertices, axes, planes, coordinate systems, or sketch entities to measure to and from.

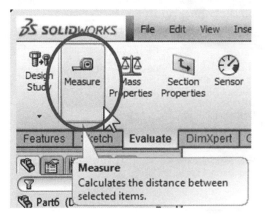

Activate the "**Measure**" tool and select the indicated face and edge; for better visibility expand the Measure box clicking in the double arrow icon. Notice the result in the Measure window as well as the tag (Dist .125in) in the graphics area giving the distance in all three X, Y and Z axes, as well as the normal distance between the selected entities. The dX, dY, and dZ dimensions are measured distances between the points we selected. In this case we are interested in the dZ or the Normal Distance values, which are the same.

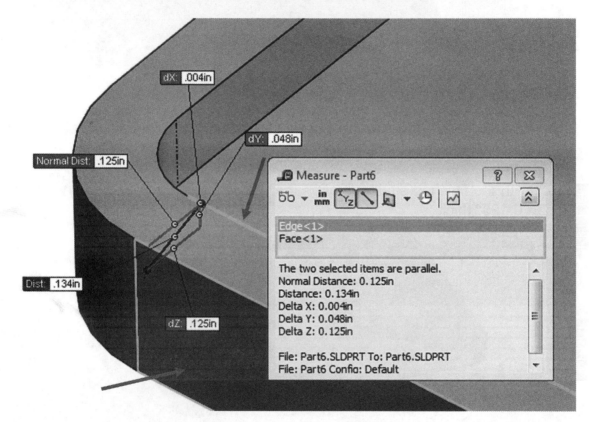

 To measure a different set of entities, click on an empty area of the graphics window, or make a right-mouse-click inside the selection box, and select "**Clear Selections**." This option works with every selection box.

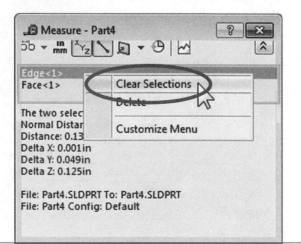

98. - To select a hidden face without having to rotate the component, make a right-mouse-click close to the face that we want to select, and use the "**Select Other**" command from the pop-up menu.

When we use the "Select Other" command, SolidWorks automatically hides the face we made a right-mouse-click on. Now we can see the faces behind it. When we touch them they are highlighted, and this way we know which face we are selecting. We also get a list of faces behind the one removed where we can select the one we need. If we still cannot see the face we need right-mouse-click in other visible faces and hide them as needed. When we see the face we want left-mouse-click to select it. Every hidden face will be made visible again after making a selection.

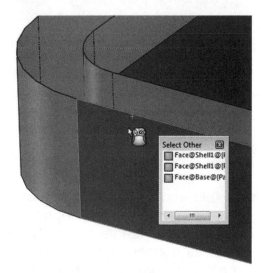

Right mouse button to hide face   Left mouse button to select hidden face

Select the hidden face indicated above, and then select the inner shell face. Feel free to make different measurements between Edge-Face, Edge-Vertex, Edge-Edge, Face-Vertex, and Vertex-Vertex to see the results.

When we select a face first we are immediately presented with the area and perimeter of the selected face. Selecting a second face gives the distance between them plus the total area of both faces.

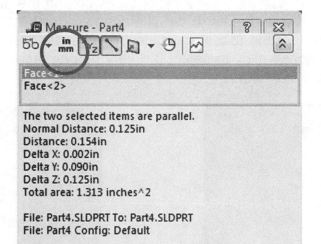

 In the "**Measure**" tool options, we can change the units of measure and precision if needed.

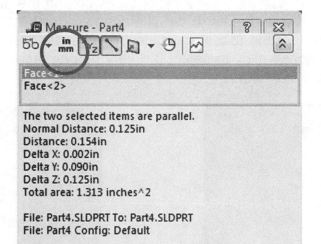

99. - The Shell operation left the outside corners thin and now we have to add material to reinforce them by adding an extrusion and have enough support for screws in the corners. Switch to a Bottom view (Ctrl+6) and create a sketch on the bottommost face as indicated and draw four circles concentric to the corner fillets. Do not worry about the size of the circles; we'll take care of that in the next step. Remember to touch the round edges to reveal their centers, and then draw the circle starting in the center to capture the concentric relation automatically.

100. - In order to maintain the design intent we are going to make the circles the same size as the corner fillets using an Equal geometric relation. Select the "**Add Relation**" icon from the Sketch Tab in the CommandManager or from the right mouse button pop-up menu. Select all four circles and under "Add Relations," select **Equal** to make all circles the same size.

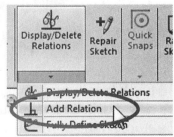

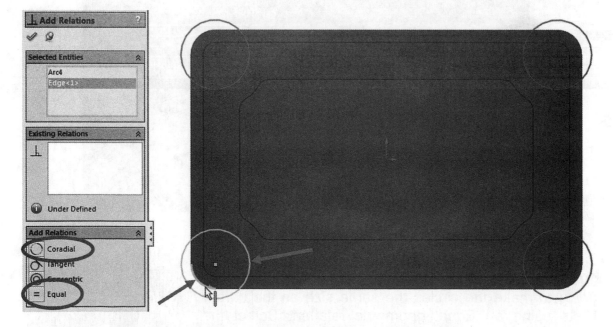

Now that all circles are the same size, select one and make it either "Coradial" (same size and concentric) or "Equal" to a rounded corner to fully define the sketch.

101. - We will now make the extrusion using the "**Up to Surface**" end condition as we did in the last cut. Select the "**Extrude Boss/Base**" command from the Features tab, and use the option "**Up to Surface**." Select the face indicated as the end condition and click OK. By doing the extrusion this way we can be sure that our design will update as expected if any of the previous features changes.

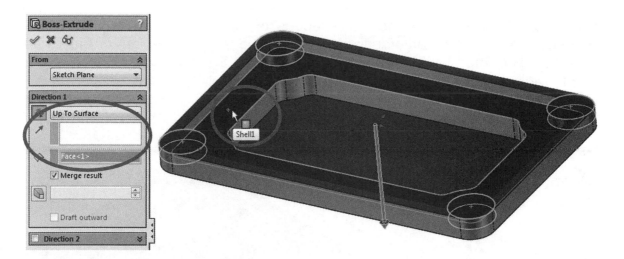

Our part should now look like this:

102. - Add a 0.031″ radius fillet using the "**Fillet**" command from the Features tab. Select the two faces on top of the cover as indicated. Notice all the edges on the top side of the part are rounded with only two selections, maintaining our design intent and making our job easier at the same time.

103. - To add fillets to all the inside edges of the part we will use a slightly different approach. Instead of individually selecting the inside edges or faces, we will only select the "Shell1" feature from the fly-out FeatureManager, and add a 0.031″ radius. Adding the fillet using this technique will round every edge of the "Shell1" feature, making it much faster and convenient, not to mention that it maintains the design intent better.

Selecting a feature to fillet as in this example can only be done using the fly-out FeatureManager or pre-selecting it in the FeatureManager before selecting the "**Fillet**" command.

Now every edge inside the part is rounded in one operation with only one selection.

104. - We are now ready to make four clearance holes for the #6-32 screws on the top. We'll use the "**Hole Wizard**" feature from the Features tab. Switch to a Top view for visibility and select the "**Hole Wizard**" icon.

105. - In the first step of the "**Hole Wizard**", select the "Hole" specification icon. From the "Type" drop down list select "**Screw Clearances.**" From the "Size" selection list pick "# 6" and from "End Condition" select "Through All." This will create a hole big enough for a #6 size screw to pass freely through it.

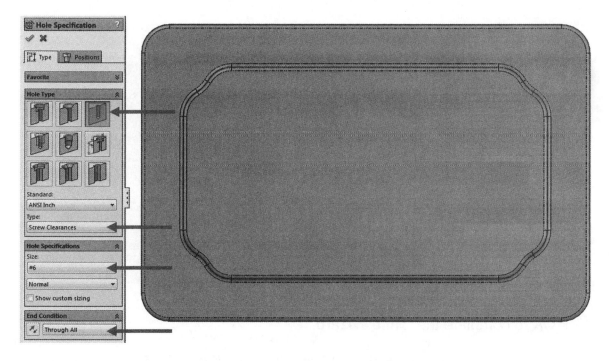

106. - For the second step, click in the "Positions" tab and select the face indicated to add the hole's location sketch. After selecting the face, the **"Point"** tool is automatically selected and we are ready to add four points for the holes' centers. Touch the round corner edges to reveal their centers as we did in the *'Housing'* part, and click in one

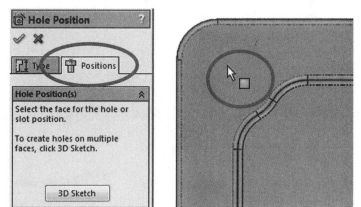

center to locate the hole. Repeat in the remaining corners to add all four holes.

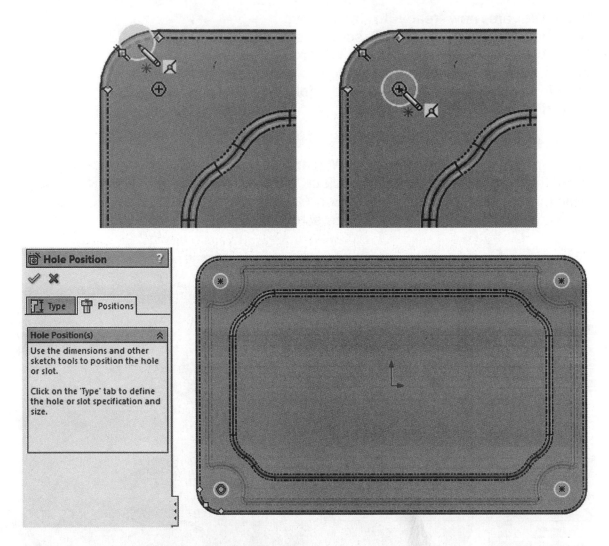

Click OK to complete the "**Hole Wizard**."

107. - Change the part's material to "Cast Alloy Steel" as a final step. Save the part as *'Top Cover'* and close the file.

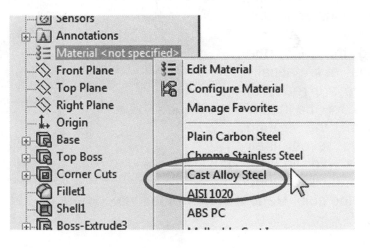

The finished part should look like this.

Exercises: Build the following parts using the knowledge acquired in this lesson. Try to use the most efficient method to complete the model.

Exercise 7
DIMENSIONS: INCHES
MATERIAL: AISI 1020

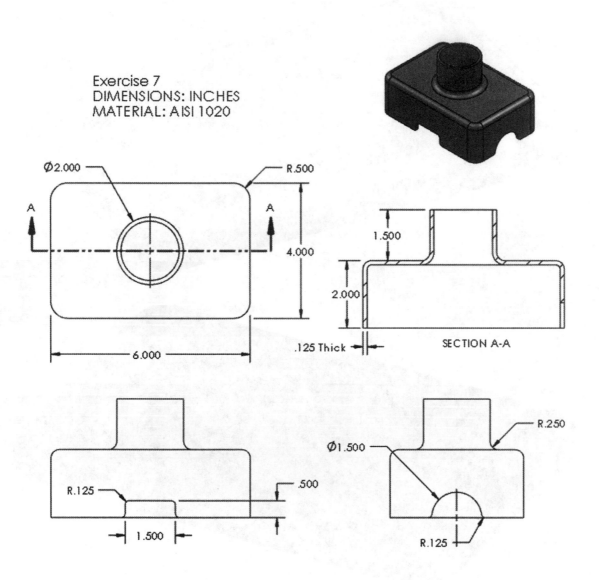

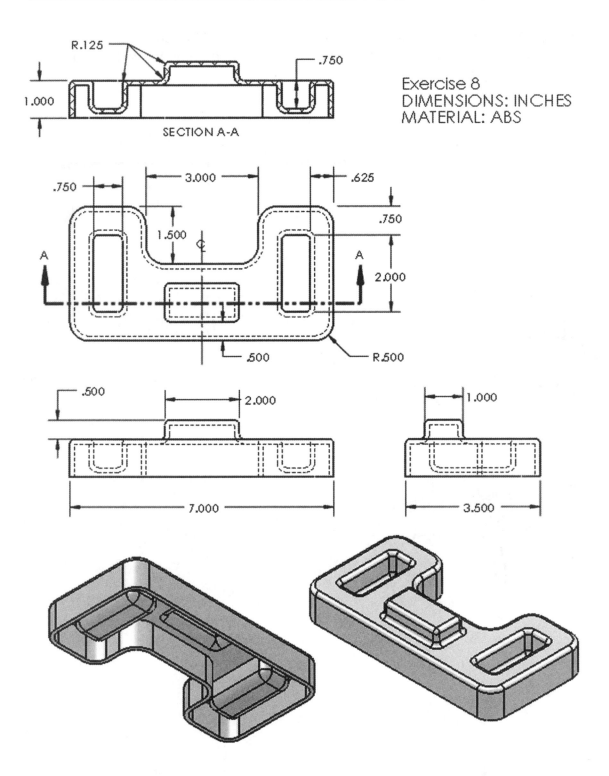

R.125

.750

1.000

SECTION A-A

Exercise 8
DIMENSIONS: INCHES
MATERIAL: ABS

.750

3.000

.625

.750

1.500

⊄

A

A

2.000

.500

R.500

.500

2.000

7.000

1.000

3.500

Engine Project Parts: Make the following components to build the engine. Save the parts using the name provided. High resolution images are included in the accompanying disc.

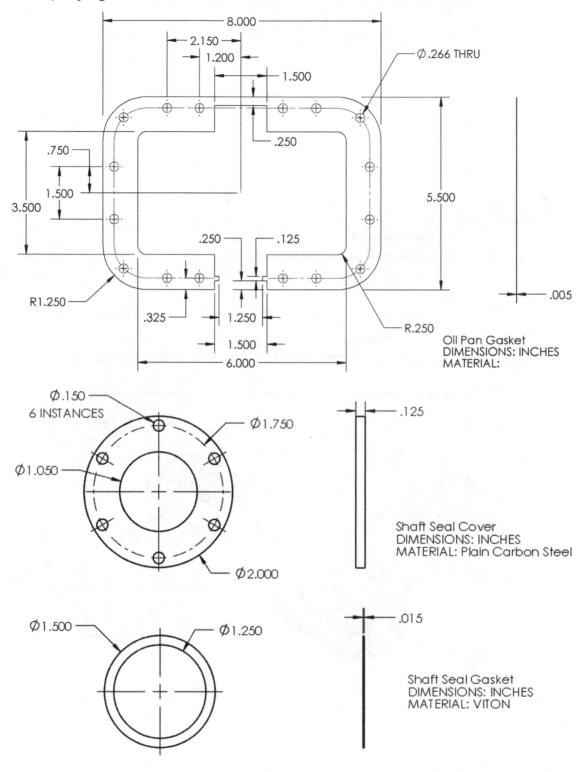

8.000

2.150

1.200

1.500

Ø.266 THRU

.250

.750

1.500

3.500

5.500

.250 .125

R1.250

.325 1.250

1.500

6.000

R.250

.005

Oil Pan Gasket
DIMENSIONS: INCHES
MATERIAL:

Ø.150
6 INSTANCES

Ø1.750

Ø1.050

Ø2.000

.125

Shaft Seal Cover
DIMENSIONS: INCHES
MATERIAL: Plain Carbon Steel

Ø1.500

Ø1.250

.015

Shaft Seal Gasket
DIMENSIONS: INCHES
MATERIAL: VITON

The Offset Shaft

Notes:

For the *'Offset Shaft'* we'll follow the next sequence of operations. In this part we only need a few features. We'll learn how to make polygons in the sketch, a new option for the **"Cut Extrude"** feature, auxiliary planes and a Revolved cut.

Boss Extrude	Cut Revolve	Offset Plane
Second Cut	Hex cut	

108. - Start by making a new document selecting the Part template. For the first feature in this part create a sketch in the *"Right Plane."* A different way to create a sketch to how we've been doing it so far is to select the *"Right Plane"* in the FeatureManager, and from the pop-up toolbar select "**Sketch.**"

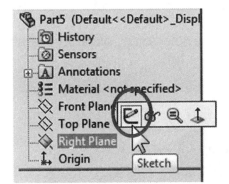

The view will be oriented to the Right view automatically. Draw a circle starting at the origin and dimension it 0.600″ using the "**Smart Dimension**" tool. Since this shaft will need to meet certain tolerances for assembly, we will give a tolerance to the diameter.

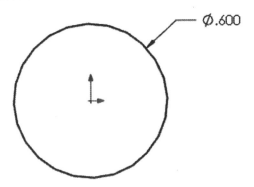

109. - To add (or change) the tolerance of the shaft's diameter, select the dimension in the graphics area. Notice the dimension's properties are displayed in the PropertyManager. This is where we can change the tolerance type. For this shaft select "Bilateral" from the **"Tolerance/Precision"** options box and add +0.000"/-0.005".

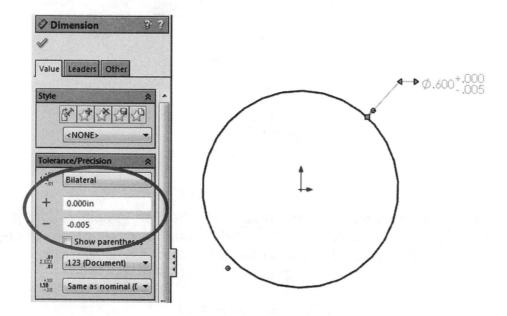

110. - When finished with the tolerance, extrude the shaft 6.5" using **"Extruded Boss/Base"** from the Features tab.

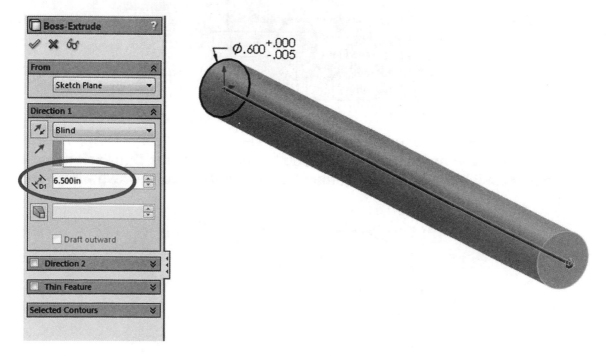

111. - For the second feature we'll make a "**Revolved Cut**." As its name implies, we'll remove material from the part similar to a turning (Lathe) operation. Switch to a Front view and select the "*Front Plane*" from the FeatureManager. From the pop-up menu select the "**Sketch**" icon as before to create a new sketch on it. Draw the following sketch and be sure to add the centerline. This is the profile that will be used as a "cutting tool." The centerline will be automatically selected as the axis of revolution for the cut.

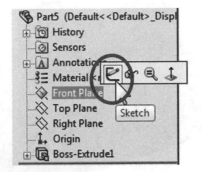

 The reason for selecting the "*Front Plane*" for this sketch is because there are no flat model faces to create the sketch in this orientation.

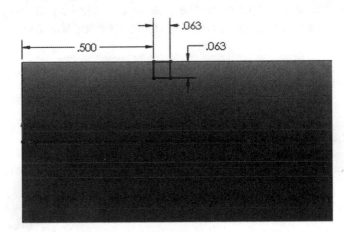

112. - Now that we are finished with the sketch, select the "**Revolved Cut**" icon from the Features toolbar.

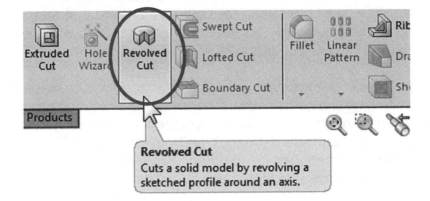

Revolved Cut
Cuts a solid model by revolving a sketched profile around an axis.

113. - Since we only have one centerline in the sketch, SolidWorks automatically selects it as the axis to make the revolved cut about it. By default a revolved cut is 360 degrees. Rotate the view to see the preview. Feel free to use the value spin box to change the number of degrees to cut, this will illustrate the effect of a revolve cut very clearly. Click OK to complete the feature and rename it *'Groove'*.

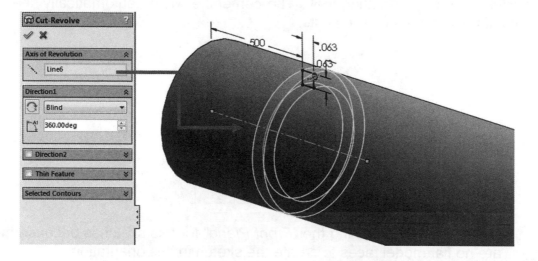

 If there is more than one centerline in the sketch or none at all, we will be asked to select a line or model edge to use for the axis of revolution.

Our part now looks like this.

114. - For the next feature, we need to make a cut exactly like the one we just did, but in the right side of the shaft. We could have done it at the same time with the previously made Revolved Cut feature, but we'll show a different way to make it and learn additional functionality at the same time.

For this feature, we'll create an auxiliary plane for a new sketch. Auxiliary Planes help us to locate a sketch where we don't have any flat faces or planes to use. To create an auxiliary plane, select "**Reference Geometry, Plane**" from the Features tab in the CommandManager or from the menu "**Insert, Reference Geometry, Plane**." Planes can be defined using many different options using model vertices, edges, faces, sketch geometry, existing planes, and/or axes.

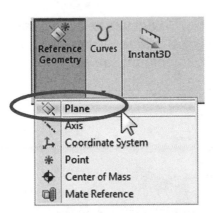

As we start selecting references to define a new plane, the possible ways to define it are dynamically shown in the PropertyManager, along with a preview of the plane in the graphics area. Some plane definitions require 1, 2, or 3 references depending on each case, but SolidWorks helps us by letting us know when the necessary options have been selected with a **"Fully Defined"** message at the top of the PropertyManager.

 Notice that references are color coded in the PropertyManager and matched in the graphics area to easily identify them.

Here are some of the most common ways to define an auxiliary plane:

Through Lines/Points– Select 3 non-collinear vertices, or one straight edge and one non-collinear vertex. Two or three references needed.

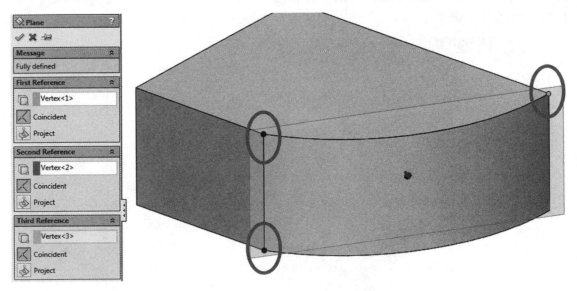

Parallel Plane at Point – Select an existing Plane or a flat face and a point. Note that when we select a Plane or flat face we get additional options like Parallel, Perpendicular, Coincident, at angle or distance. Two references are needed.

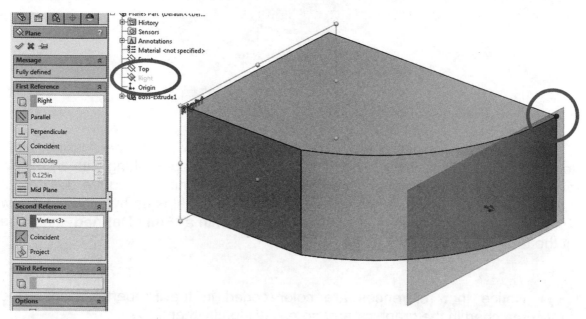

At an angle – Select a Plane or flat face and an Edge and enter the angle. The Plane's direction can be reversed using the "Flip" checkbox. In this case the face in the back was selected and the Edge indicated. The Edge acts as a "hinge" to the new plane. Change the angle using the value spin box to see the effect. The "Flip" checkbox will change the direction of the plane. Two references needed.

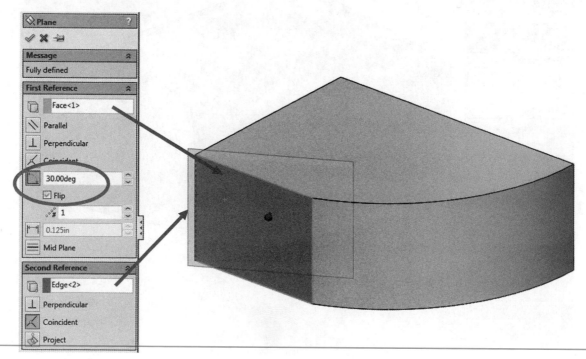

Offset Distance – Select a Plane or flat face, and define the distance from it to create the new Plane. "Flip" can be used to change the side on which the new plane is created. In this case the face in the back was selected and the new plane created to the right. We can optionally create multiple parallel planes changing the number of planes to create (default is 1.) One reference needed.

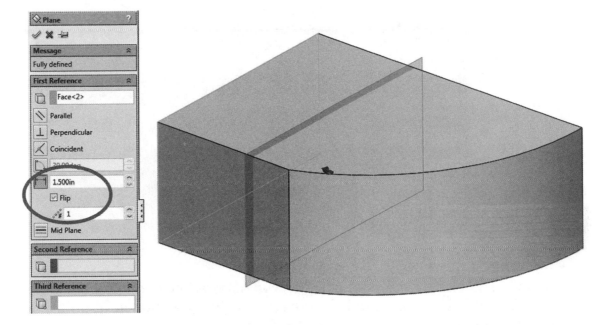

Normal to Curve – The plane is created by selecting an edge and a vertex of the edge. The plane created is perpendicular to the curve at the vertex. In this case we selected the edge and the vertex indicated. Two references needed.

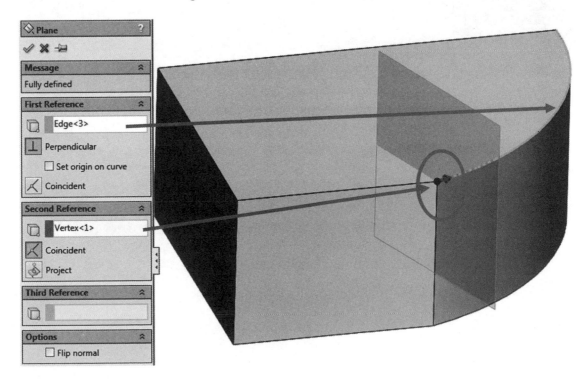

On Surface – The plane is created selecting a surface (any surface) and a vertex (or sketch point/endpoint) on the surface. In this case the face is curved and the resulting plane is tangent to the face at the selected vertex. Two references are needed.

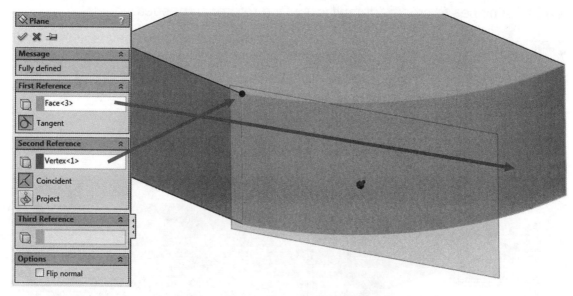

Mid Plane – The plane is created between two selected planes or faces. If the planes and/or faces are not parallel the new plane will be created at an angle half the angle between the reference planes/faces.

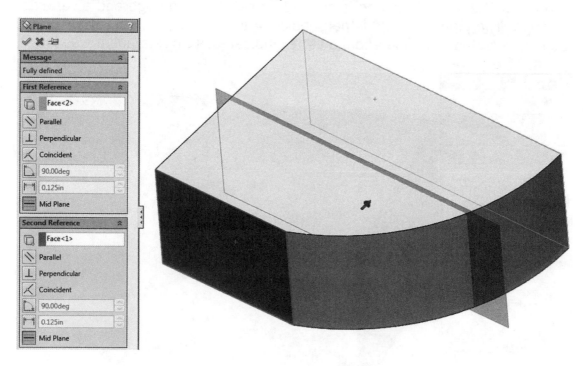

When creating auxiliary planes, we can use as references existing Planes, Faces, Vertices, sketch elements, Axes and Temporary Axes, the Origin, etc. To make sketch elements visible, expand a feature in the FeatureManager, select the sketch that we want to make visible, and from the pop-up toolbar select the **Show/Hide** icon. If the sketch is hidden, it will be made visible and vice versa.

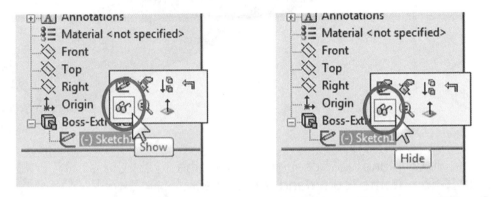

115. - Back to our part, we'll make an Auxiliary Plane parallel to a face of the groove. Select "**Auxiliary Geometry, Plane**" from the Features tab. We'll make an auxiliary plane a set distance from the right face of the groove. Using the "**Select Other**" function (right mouse button menu or pop-up icon), select the indicated face below (hidden in this view.)

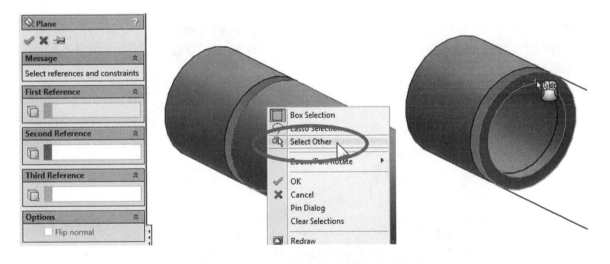

 Notice the mouse pointer changes, letting us know that the left button is to select a face, and the right button to hide a face.

116. - Set the distance to 5″ and select the "Flip" checkbox if necessary. Notice the preview. After creating the plane, rename it to *"Offset Plane."*

If the new plane is not visible, use the "**Hide/Show Items**" command."*Front Plane*," "*Top Plane*" and "*Right Plane*" are hidden by default; you can hide and show any plane the same way we did with the sketch. Note we added the keyboard shortcut "P" to hide/show the planes.

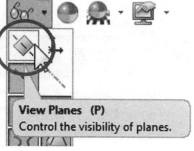

117. - Switch to an Isometric view (for visibility) and select the *"Offset Plane"* in the graphics area; from the pop-up toolbar click on "**Sketch**" to create a new sketch on it.

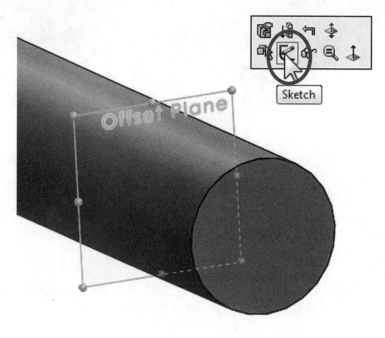

The "**Convert Entities**" command is used to project existing geometric entities onto a sketch, such as model edges or other sketch entities and convert them to new sketch entities at the same time. Click on "**Convert Entities**" from the Sketch tab in the CommandManager; select the two edges indicated from the "*Groove*" feature and click OK to finish.

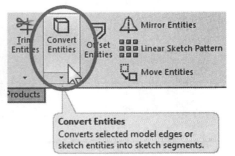

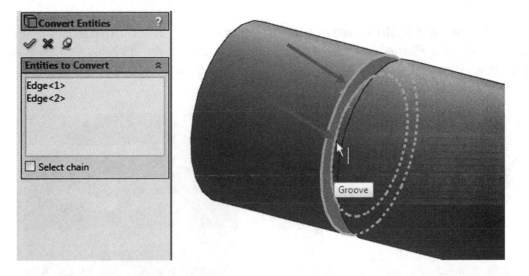

The two edges are projected onto the sketch plane and are automatically fully defined since they are a projected copy of the edges they came from adding an "On Edge" geometric relation; if the original geometry changes, so will the converted entities. Make an "**Extruded Cut**" feature 0.063″ deep, going to the right. Rename the feature *"Offset Groove."*

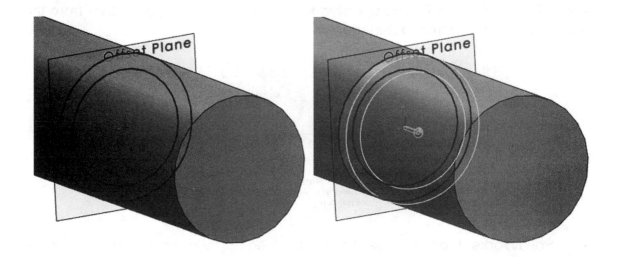

118. - For the last feature, we'll add a hexagonal cut at the right end of the shaft. Hide the "*Offset Plane*" (or turn off all planes) for easier visibility and switch to a Right view. Insert a sketch in the rightmost face of the shaft as indicated.

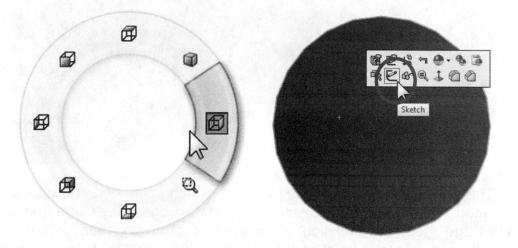

119. - We can make a polygon using lines, dimensions and geometric relations, but we really want to make it easy, so we'll use the "**Polygon**" tool. Go to the menu, "**Tools, Sketch Entities, Polygon**" or select the "**Polygon**" tool from the Sketch tab in the CommandManager.

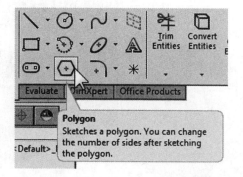

SolidWorks toolbars can be customized to add or remove icons as needed. Right-mouse-click on any toolbar, select "**Customize**" and from the "Commands" tab drag the commands needed to and from toolbars.

120. - After we select the **"Polygon"** tool, we are presented with the options in the PropertyManager. This tool helps us to create a polygon by making it either inscribed or circumscribed to a circle. For this exercise we'll select the "Circumscribed circle" with 6 sides in the "Parameters" options. Don't worry too much about the rest of the options, as we'll fully define the hexagon using two additional geometric relations.

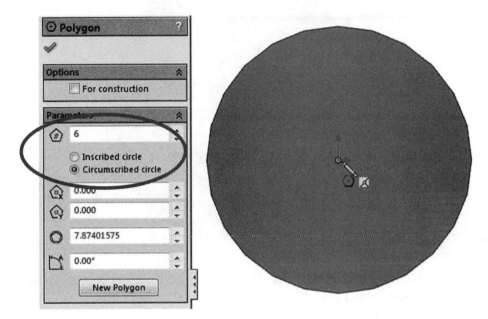

121. - Since the polygon is defined by a circle (Inscribed or circumscribed), it is drawn like a circle. Start at the center of the shaft as shown and notice that we immediately get a preview of the hexagon, its radius and angle of rotation.

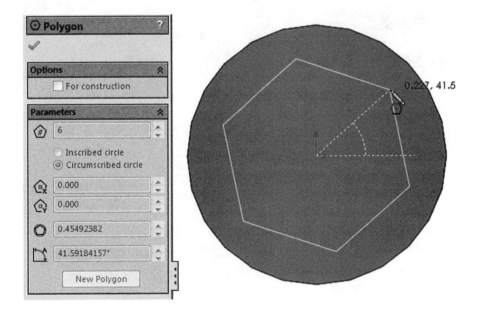

122. - Draw the circle a little smaller (or larger) than the shaft, the idea is to make the construction circle the same size as the shaft using a geometric relation. Hit "Esc" or OK to finish the polygon tool when done.

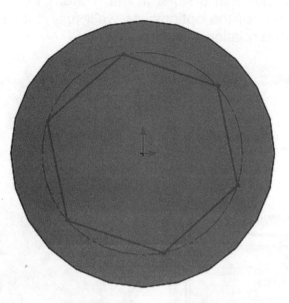

123. - Now select the "**Add Relation**" tool from the Sketch tab and select the polygon's construction circle and the edge of the shaft; add an "Equal" geometric relation to make them the same size.

 Remember that the "**Add Relation**" tool can also be found in the right mouse button menu.

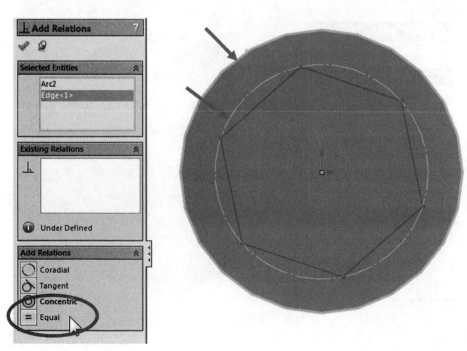

124. - Now select one of the hexagon's lines and add a "**Horizontal**" relation to fully define the sketch.

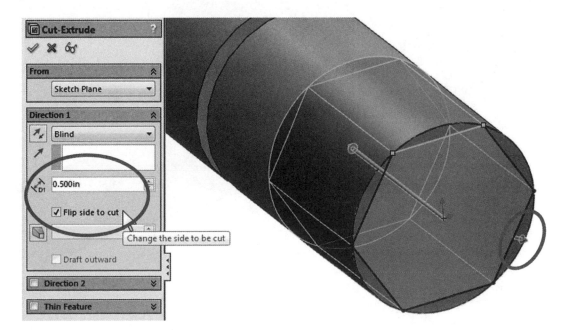

125. - Now we are ready to make the cut. For this operation we'll use a little used but very powerful option in SolidWorks. Select the "**Extruded Cut**" icon from the Features tab as before, but now activate the checkbox "**Flip side to cut**."

This option will make the cut *outside* of the sketch, not inside. Notice the arrow indicating which side of the sketch will be used to cut. Make the cut 0.5″ deep. Rename the feature *'Hex Cut'*.

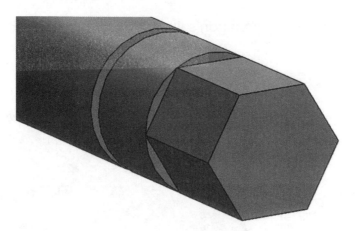

126. - Edit the material for this shaft and select "Chrome Stainless Steel" from the materials library (or the Favorites list if available.)

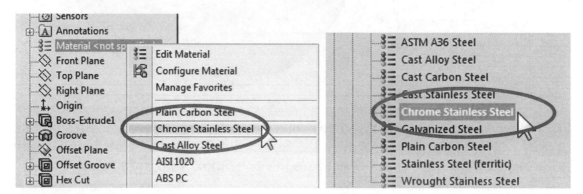

Save the part as *'Offset Shaft'* and close the file.

More about Auxiliary Geometry:

Auxiliary geometry includes **Planes**, **Axes, Coordinate Systems, Points, Mate References and Center of Mass.** Both of these can be created from the "**Reference Geometry**" icon in the Features tab in the CommandManager. Reference geometry can be used for a number of reasons, including locating features and components, as reference, or to use as part of a feature, an axis can be used to define the direction for a circular pattern and planes to add sketch geometry.

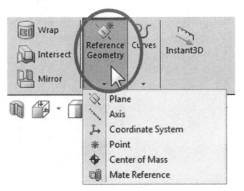

We covered the main options to create **Planes** previously; here are other types of Reference Geometry.

An **Axis** can be made using the following options:

One Line/Edge/Axis – Any linear edge, sketch line, or axis. Every cylindrical and conical face has an axis (Temporary Axis) running through it. To reveal it use the menu "**View, Temporary Axis.**"

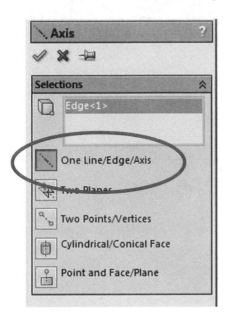

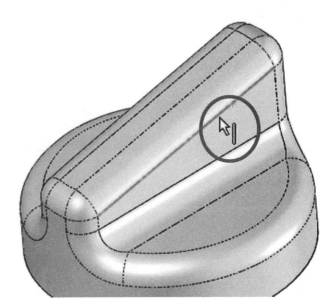

Two Planes – An axis can be created at the intersection of any two planes and/or faces.

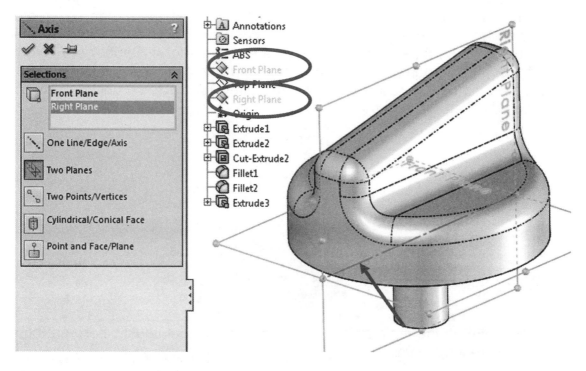

Two points/Vertices – Using any two vertices and/or sketch points/endpoints.

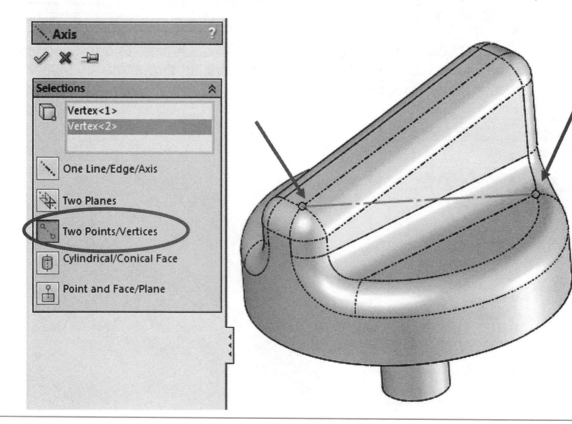

Cylindrical/Conical Face – Selecting any cylindrical or conical face will make an axis using the face's temporary axis.

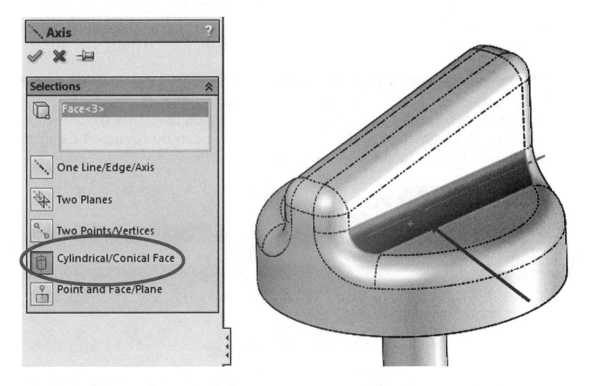

Point and Face/Plane– Selecting a point, sketch point or endpoint, or vertex and a flat face or plane will make an axis running perpendicular to the face/plane that passes through the point/vertex.

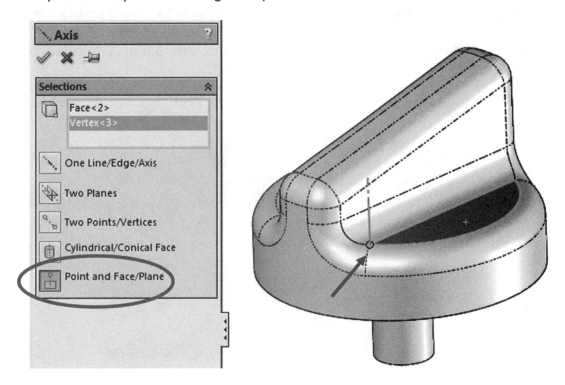

Coordinate Systems can be used for a number of things including to calculate a component's center of mass referenced to a specific location, or when we have to export parts for manufacturing on computer controlled machines using Computer Assisted Manufacturing (CAM). More often than not the origin the designer used for the component is not the best location for the CAM operator to program the machining equipment.

To create a Coordinate System we need to select a vertex or point, and define two axis directions (X, Y or Z) using linear edges, axes or sketch lines; the third direction is defined automatically. Notice that an axis direction can be reversed using the "Reverse direction" icon to the left of each selection box.

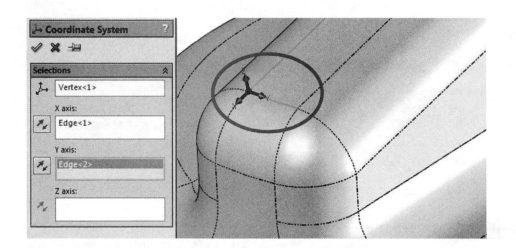

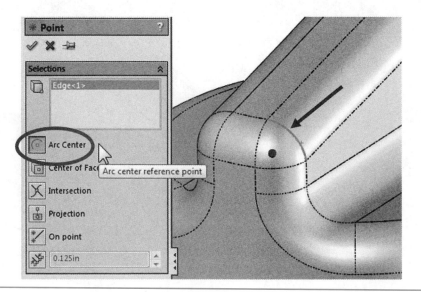

A Point can be added and used as a reference for other features, reference geometry, sketches, etc. Some of the methods to create points are:

Arc Center – Adds a point in the center of a planar arc, either a circular model edge or a sketch arc. Only one reference is needed.

Center of Face – Creates a point at the center of mass of the selected face, either a planar or non-planar face. Only one reference is needed.

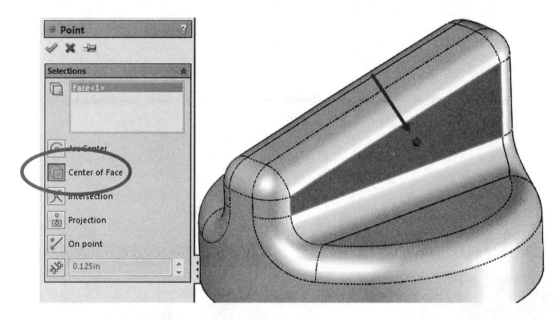

Intersection – Creates a point at the intersection of edges, curves or sketch segments. Two references are needed.

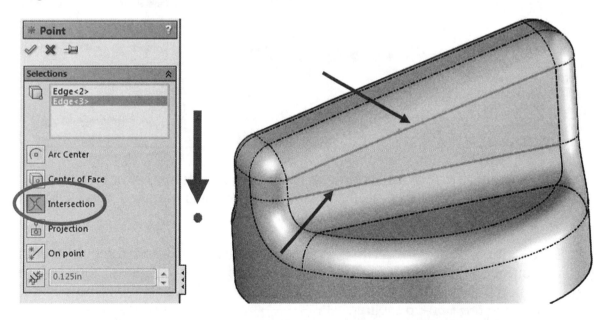

The **Center of Mass** (COM) adds a visual marker at the center of mass of the model, as well as a Center of Mass feature. After adding the COM we can add a **Center of Mass Reference Point** by right mouse clicking in the COM feature and selecting the COM Reference Point that can be used to dimension features from it.

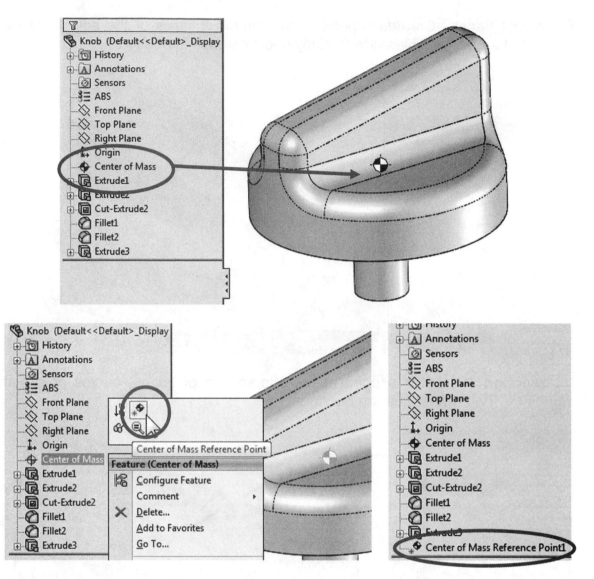

 Important: The "COM Reference Point" is not dynamic, after it is added it will be fixed; what this means is that if the model is modified, the COM *will change*, the COM Reference Point *will not*.

 Remember that we can use sketch geometry from any sketch to create reference geometry (Planes, Axes and Coordinate Systems), but before we can use it, we need to make the sketch visible using the "**Show/Hide**" button in the pop-up toolbar.

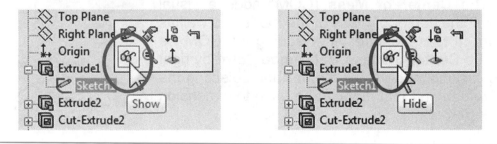

Exercises: Build the following parts using the knowledge acquired in this lesson. Try to use the most efficient method to complete the model.

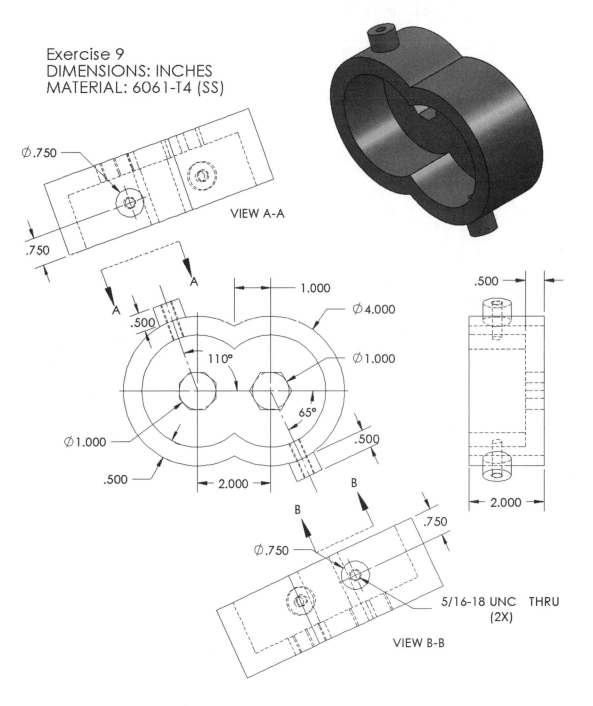

Exercise 9
DIMENSIONS: INCHES
MATERIAL: 6061-T4 (SS)

Ø.750

.750

VIEW A-A

.500

A

A

1.000

Ø4.000

110°

Ø1.000

65°

Ø1.000

.500

.500

2.000

B

B

.500

.500

2.000

.750

Ø.750

5/16-18 UNC   THRU
(2X)

VIEW B-B

HINT: Draw a sketch with centerlines, exit the sketch, and use it as a layout to make the auxiliary planes needed. Hide the layout sketch when finished.

Exercise 10
DIMENSIONS: INCHES
MATERIAL: 2024-O

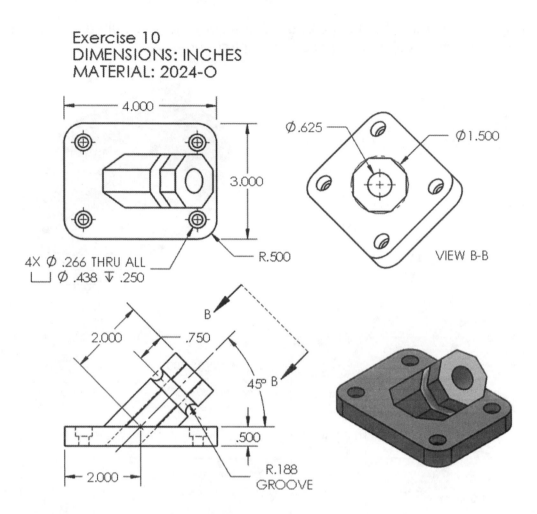

4.000

3.000

R.500

4X Ø .266 THRU ALL
⌴ Ø .438 ▾ .250

Ø.625

Ø1.500

VIEW B-B

B

2.000

.750

45° B

.500

2.000

R.188
GROOVE

Engine Project Parts: Make the following components to build the engine. Save the parts using the name provided. High resolution images are included in the accompanying disc.

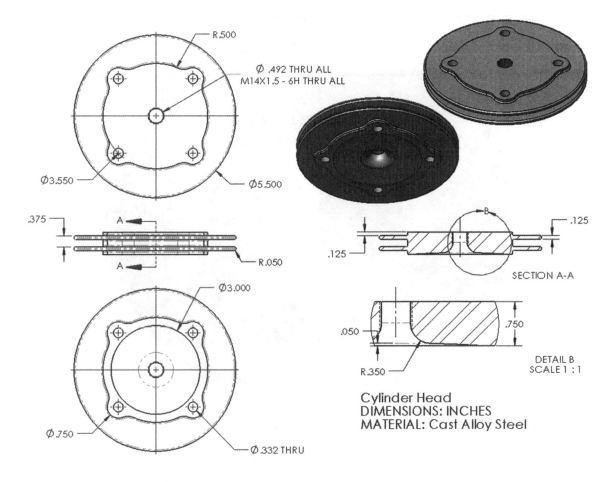

R.500

Ø .492 THRU ALL
M14X1.5 - 6H THRU ALL

Ø3.550

Ø5.500

.375

A

A

R.050

.125

.125

SECTION A-A

Ø3.000

.050

.750

Ø.750

R.350

DETAIL B
SCALE 1 : 1

Ø.332 THRU

Cylinder Head
DIMENSIONS: INCHES
MATERIAL: Cast Alloy Steel

The Worm Gear

Notes:

For the *'Worm Gear'* we will make a simplified version of a gear without teeth. The intent of this book is not to go into gear design, but rather to help the user understand and learn how to use basic SolidWorks functionality. With this part we'll learn a new extrusion (or cut) end condition called "Mid Plane", how to chamfer the edges of a model, a special dimensioning technique to add a diameter dimension to a sketch used for a revolved feature, and how to add a dimension to a circle's perimeter. We'll also practice previously learned commands. For the *'Worm Gear'* we will follow the next sequence of features.

Mid Plane Extrusion	Revolved Cut 1	Revolved Cut 2	Mirror
Chamfer	Fillet	Keyway Cut	

127. - Start by making a new part document and create the following sketch in the "*Front Plane.*"

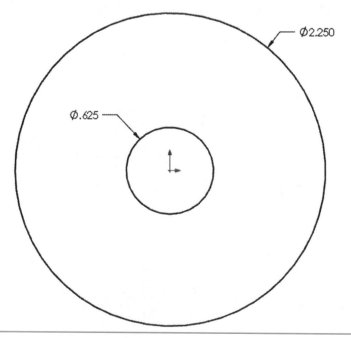

128. - In this case we want the part to be symmetrical about the "*Front Plane*." To achieve this, we'll make an "**Extruded Boss/Base**" using the "**Mid Plane**" end condition; this condition extrudes half of the distance in one direction and half in the second direction. Change the end condition to "**Mid Plane**" and extrude it 1″ (The result will be 0.5″ going to the front and 0.5″ going to the back.) Rename the feature "*Base*."

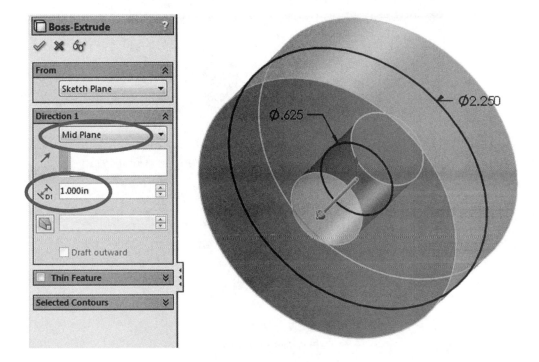

129. - For the second feature we will use a "**Revolved Cut**" to make the slot around the part. Change to a Right view select the "*Right Plane*" from the FeatureManager, and click on the "**Sketch**" icon from the pop-up toolbar as shown. Make the center of the circle coincident to the Midpoint of the cylinder's top edge and <u>don't forget to add the centerline</u>.

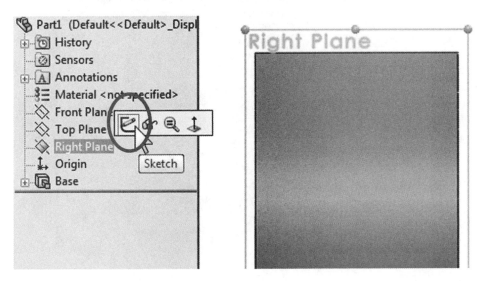

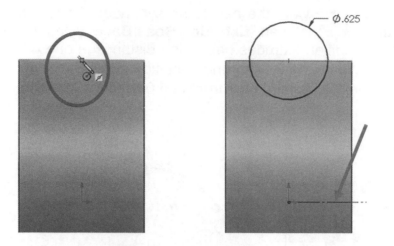

130. - Select the "**Revolved Cut**" command from the Features tab to complete the feature using the default settings. Rename the feature *'Groove'*.

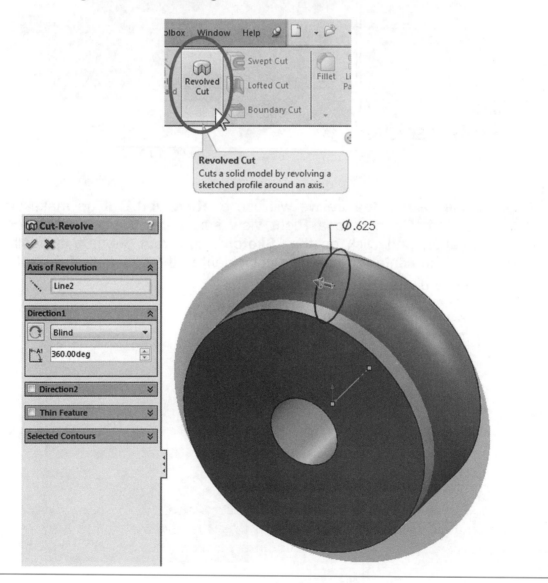

131. - Make a second revolved cut to remove material from one side of the part. Switch to a Right view, and create a new sketch in the "*Right Plane*" as before using the following dimensions. Remember, it is a closed Sketch (four lines; don't forget the vertical line in the right side.) If needed, turn off the Sketch Grid and change to "Wireframe" view mode for clarity.

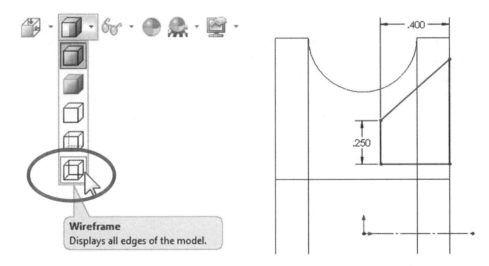

132. - We'll now use a new dimensioning technique to add diameter dimensions for Revolved Features, this way we will have a diameter dimension in the revolved feature when finished. Select the "**Smart Dimension**" tool, and add a dimension <u>from the Centerline</u> (not an endpoint!) to the top endpoint of the sketch. Before locating the dimension, cross the centerline and notice how the dimension value doubles. Locate the dimension, and change it to 2″. Immediately after adding the first dimension the Smart Dimension tool remains in Doubled dimension mode. Select the second horizontal line to add a 1″ dimension from the centerline.

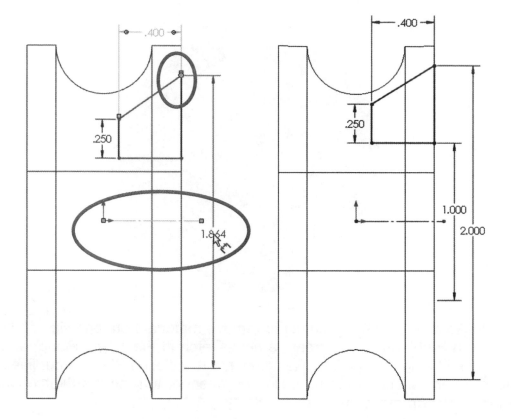

133. - In the next step we will make a "Sketch Mirror" to make the same profile in the other side of the origin. Draw a vertical centerline at the origin as shown and select the "Sketch Mirror" command from the Sketch tab. Select the profile lines in the "Entities to mirror" selection box and the vertical centerline in the "Mirror about:" selection box.

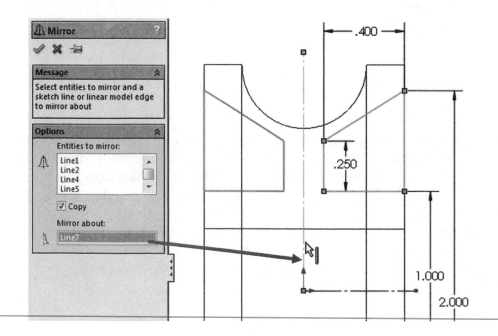

134. - Select the "**Revolved Cut**" command from the Features tab in the CommandManager. In previous operations we only had one centerline and it was automatically selected, in this case we have to select the horizontal centerline to make the revolved cut about it. Notice the doubled diameter dimensions, their purpose is more obvious in this image.

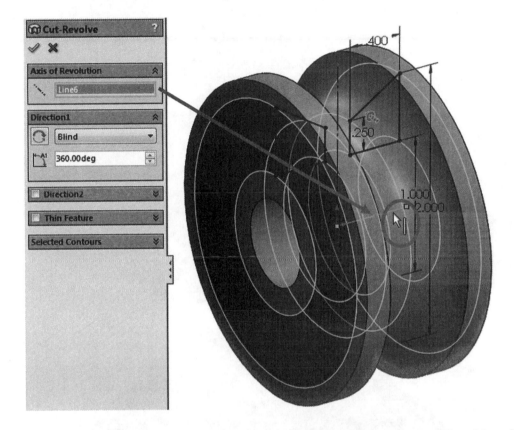

135. - To eliminate the sharp edges on the outside perimeter we'll add a 0.1" x 45° "**Chamfer**." The Chamfer is an applied feature similar to the Fillet, but instead of rounding an edge, it adds a bevel to it. Select it from the drop down menu under "**Fillet**" in the Features tab or in the menu "**Insert, Features, Chamfer**."

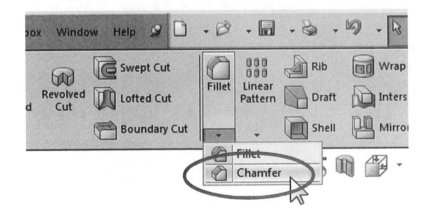

Set the options and values shown for the chamfer and select the two edges indicated. Click OK to finish.

136. - Add a 0.0625″ radius fillet to the four inside edges. Selecting the two inside faces will make selection easier.

137. - For the last step, we'll make the keyway. Switch to a Front view and make a sketch in the "*Front Plane*." Draw a rectangle and add a Midpoint relation between the rectangle's bottom line and the part's Origin.

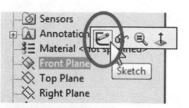

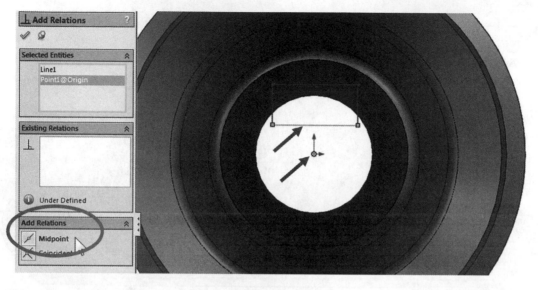

 We could have made the sketch in the front face, but we placed it in the "*Front Plane*" to show additional functionality.

138. - By adding the Midpoint relation, the rectangle will be coincident to, and centered with the origin. Add a 0.188″ width dimension as indicated. If the top horizontal line (blue) is below the center hole's edge, click-and-drag it until it's above the circle as shown. This will allow us to add a dimension to the circular edge in the next step.

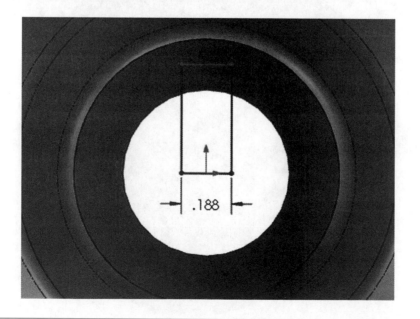

139. - Now we need to add a dimension from <u>the top of the circular edge</u> to the horizontal line. Before adding the dimension, <u>press and hold</u> the "**Shift**" key, by doing this we'll be able to add the dimension from the top of the hole's edge to the top line of the rectangle; Select the circle at the topmost part of the circular edge and the line, click for the location and release the "**Shift**" key; change the dimension's value to 0.094″.

If we don't hold the "**Shift**" key the dimension will be referenced to the circle's center instead.

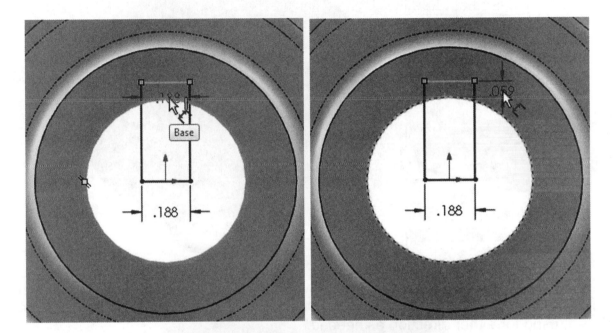

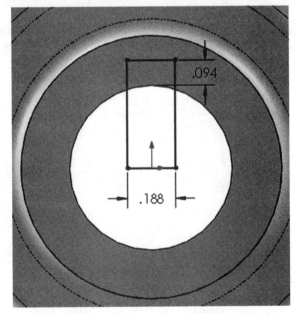

140. - To finish the part we need to make a "**Cut Extrude**." Since the sketch is located in the "*Front Plane*" (in the middle of the part); making a cut "**Through All**" will only go from the center to one side. In this case we need to activate the "Direction 2" checkbox, and set the end condition to "**Through All**" for "Direction 1" and "Direction 2." Being able to select different end conditions for each direction is a very useful and powerful tool.

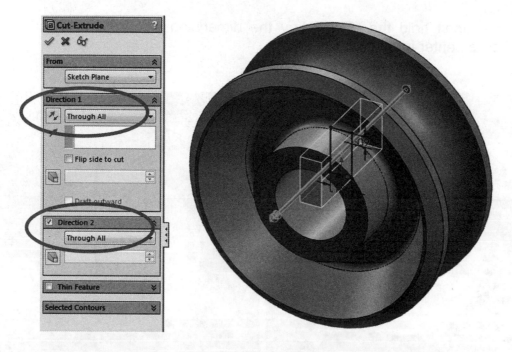

Notice the single and double arrows in the graphics area, indicating which one is "Direction 1," and which "Direction 2." Any "End Condition" can be used for either direction as needed.

Starting in SolidWorks 2014 the end condition "Through All – Both" was added to the Cut Extrude command. When selecting it the "Direction 2" end condition is automatically set to "Through All"

141. - Change the material to "AISI 1020" steel. Save the part as *'Worm Gear'* and close the file.

Exercises: Build the following part using the knowledge acquired in this lesson. Try to use the most efficient method to complete the model.

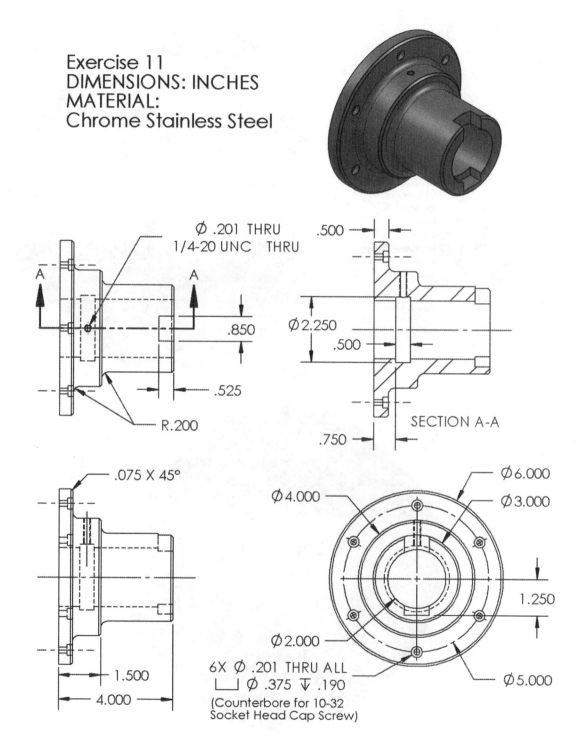

Exercise 11
DIMENSIONS: INCHES
MATERIAL:
Chrome Stainless Steel

Ø .201 THRU
1/4-20 UNC THRU

.500

A   A

.850

.525

R.200

Ø2.250

.500

.750

SECTION A-A

.075 X 45°

Ø4.000

Ø6.000
Ø3.000

Ø2.000

1.250

Ø5.000

1.500

4.000

6X Ø .201 THRU ALL
⌴ Ø .375 ▼ .190
(Counterbore for 10-32
Socket Head Cap Screw)

Engine Project Parts: Make the following components to build the engine. Save the parts using the name provided. High resolution images at mechanicad.com.

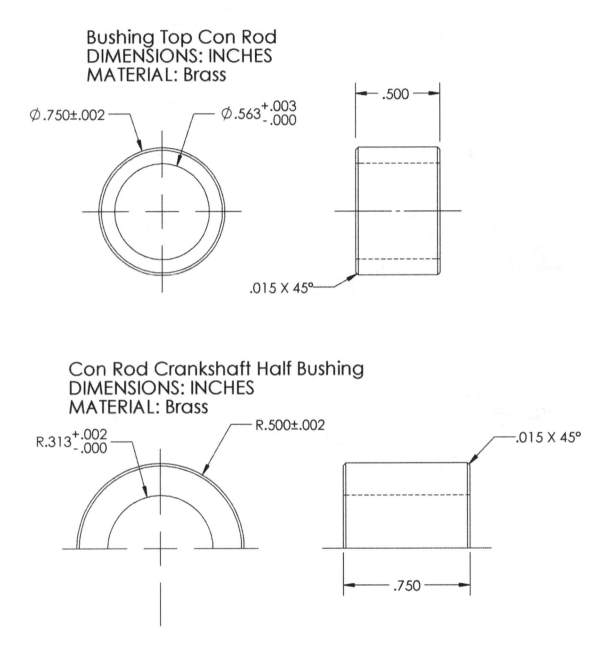

Bushing Top Con Rod
DIMENSIONS: INCHES
MATERIAL: Brass

$\varnothing.750\pm.002$

$\varnothing.563^{+.003}_{-.000}$

.500

.015 X 45°

Con Rod Crankshaft Half Bushing
DIMENSIONS: INCHES
MATERIAL: Brass

$R.313^{+.002}_{-.000}$

R.500±.002

.015 X 45°

.750

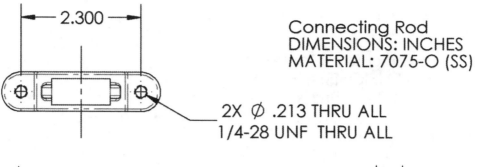

Connecting Rod
DIMENSIONS: INCHES
MATERIAL: 7075-O (SS)

2X ⌀ .213 THRU ALL
1/4-28 UNF THRU ALL

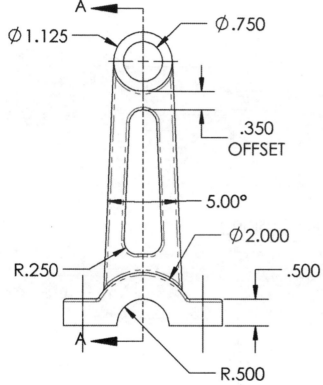

A

⌀1.125

⌀.750

.350
OFFSET

5.00°

⌀2.000

R.250

.500

A

R.500

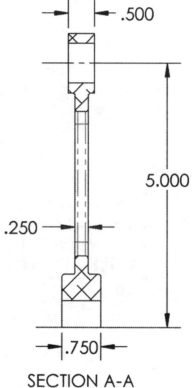

.500

5.000

.250

.750

SECTION A-A

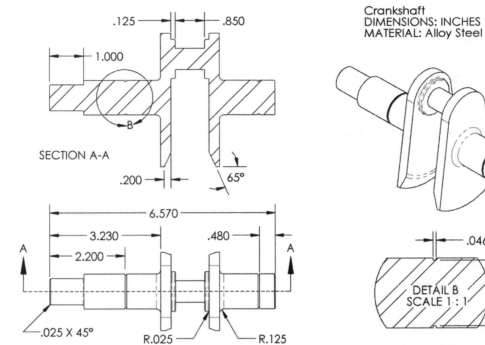

SECTION A-A

.125 .850
1.000
.200 65°

6.570
3.230 .480
2.200
A A
.025 X 45°
R.025 R.125

Crankshaft
DIMENSIONS: INCHES
MATERIAL: Alloy Steel

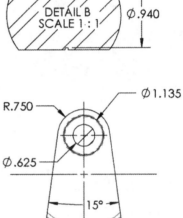

.046
DETAIL B
SCALE 1 : 1 Ø.940

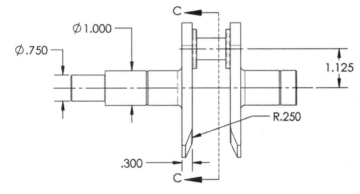

Ø1.000
Ø.750
C
1.125
R.250
.300
C

Ø1.135
R.750
Ø.625
15°
R2.000
SECTION C-C

Pin ConRod-Piston
DIMENSIONS: INCHES
MATERIAL: Alloy Steel

Ø.250 Ø.562

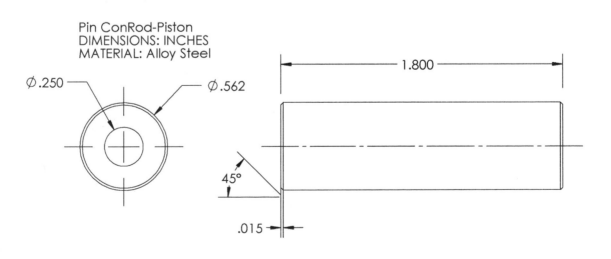

1.800
45°
.015

Notes:

The Worm Gear Shaft

Notes:

For the *'Worm Gear Shaft'* we will review the Revolved Feature previously learned, the sketch Polygon tool, and a Mid Plane cut.

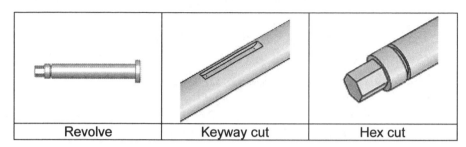

| Revolve | Keyway cut | Hex cut |

142. - In this part we only need to make three features. The first feature will be a revolved extrusion. Make a new part file and insert a sketch in the "*Front Plane*" as shown. It's very important to add the centerline, as we'll need it to add the diameter dimensions as we did in the previous part. Select the "**Revolved Boss**" command to complete the first feature. Rename the feature *'Base'*. Notice the three doubled diameter dimensions using the centerline.

 In a sketch like this is better to add the smaller dimensions before the larger ones. The reason is if the large dimensions are added first, when the geometry updates, the small features may behave unexpectedly.

Add a "Collinear" relation between the two lines indicated before dimensioning.

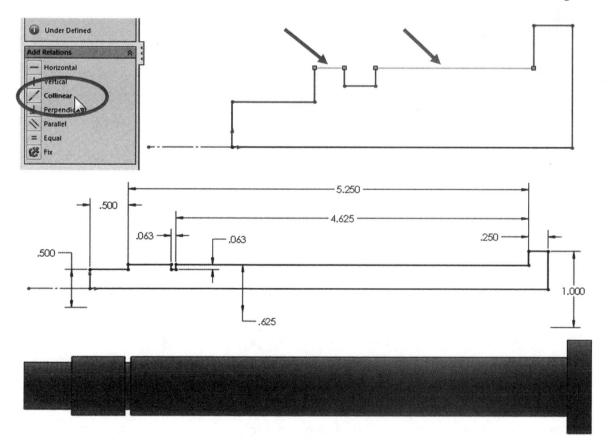

143. - The second feature is the keyway. Select the "*Front Plane*" from the FeatureManager and click in the **"Sketch"** icon from the pop-up toolbar. In this sketch it's OK to leave the top line of the sketch under defined. What we'll do is make a cut using the **"Mid Plane"** end condition. Making the top line beyond the top of the part allows us to "cut air"; this way we are sure we will cut the part. This is a common practice and is OK as long as we make the sketch big enough to accommodate possible future changes. Adding a dimension to ensure the sketch extends past the part is a good idea too. The problem that *may* occur depending on the geometry and the feature being made is that the top line generates a "zero thickness" face error and will not let us continue.

 Remember that we can use Mouse Gestures (right mouse click-and-drag) for the most commonly used commands, or configure it for the tools we use most to help us speed up the design process.

An useful option when drawing lines, is to transition from drawing a line to a tangent arc. To do this we can use the default shortcut key "A" or move the mouse back to the last endpoint. After moving the mouse back, a tangent arc will be started. Depending on the direction that we move out, that's the direction the tangent arc will be created. Select the **"Line"** tool and draw a line, then click in one location, click in the second point to complete the first line, and instead of clicking a third time to add a second line, move back to the second endpoint and move out to add a tangent arc. Press "A" to toggle between arc, and line.

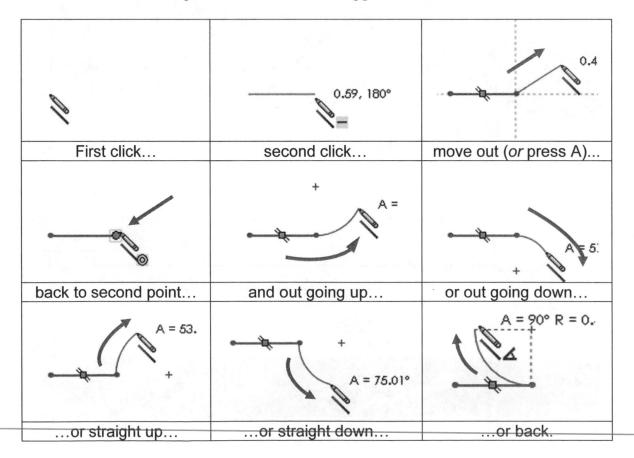

First click…	second click…	move out (*or* press A)…
back to second point…	and out going up…	or out going down…
…or straight up…	…or straight down…	…or back.

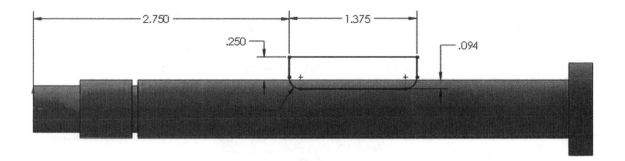

The 0.250" dimension's only purpose is to make sure the sketch cuts through the part by extending the sketch beyond the part. To avoid importing this dimension to the detail drawing later on, right mouse click on the dimension and uncheck the "Mark for Drawing" option.

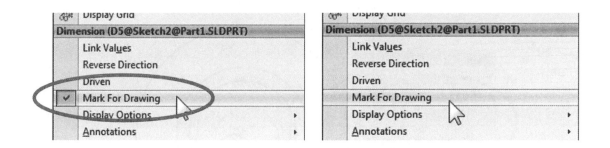

144. - Select the "**Cut Extrude**" command from the Features tab and use the "**Mid Plane**" end condition with a dimension of 0.1875"; this way the keyway will be exactly at the center of the shaft. Notice that the "Direction 2" option box is unavailable when we select the Mid Plane end condition. Rename this feature "*Keyway*."

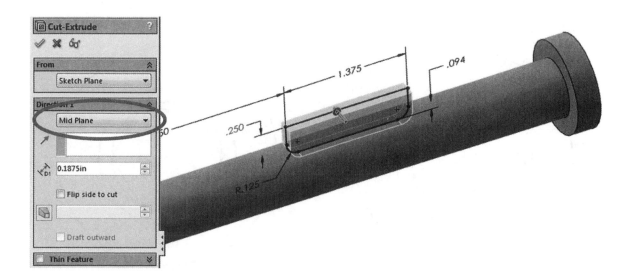

145. - For the last feature we'll make a hexagonal cut just as we did in the '*Offset Shaft'*. Switch to a Left view, select the leftmost face, and create a sketch. Using the "**Polygon**" tool from the Sketch tab draw a Circumscribed hexagon and make the construction circle coincident to the edge at the shaft's end as seen. We changed to Hidden Lines Removed for clarity.

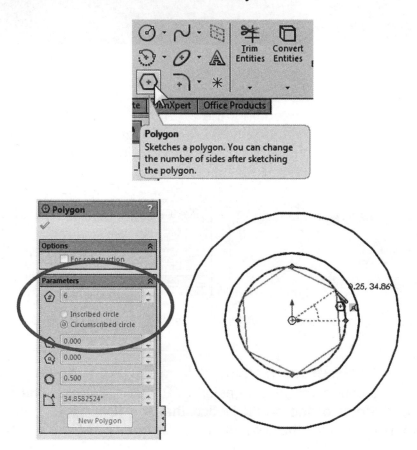

Finally select one line and add a horizontal relation to fully define the sketch.

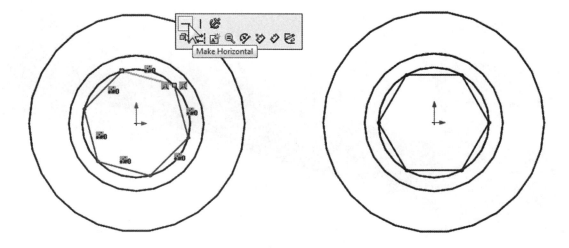

146. - Make a "**Cut Extrude**" using the "Up to Surface" end condition as indicated and activate the option "Flip side to cut" to cut *outside* the hexagon.

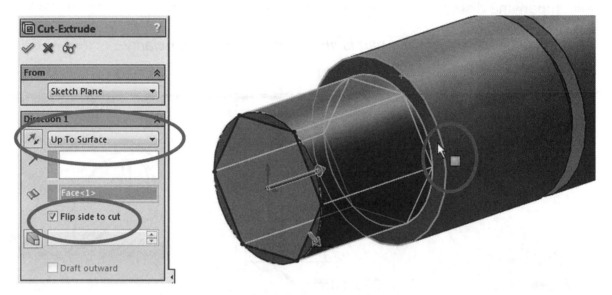

147. - Change the material to "Chrome Stainless Steel." Feel free to add the most commonly used materials using the "**Manage Favorites**" option in the "**Edit Material**" menu.

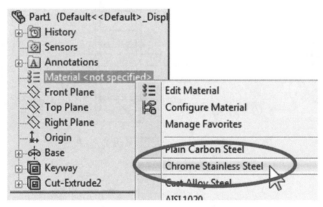

148. - Save the part as *'Worm Gear Shaft'* and close the file.

Engine Project Parts: Make the following components to build the engine. Save the parts using the name provided. High resolution images are included in the accompanying disc.

The following part is shown in three steps for clarity

Sealed Needle Bearing
DIMENSIONS: INCHES
MATERIAL:

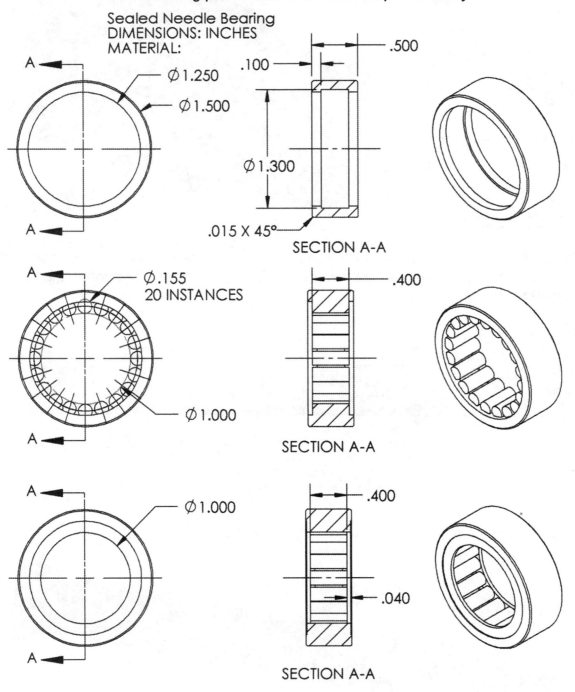

Ø1.250
Ø1.500
.100
.500
Ø1.300
.015 X 45°
SECTION A-A

Ø.155
20 INSTANCES
Ø1.000
.400
SECTION A-A

Ø1.000
.400
.040
SECTION A-A

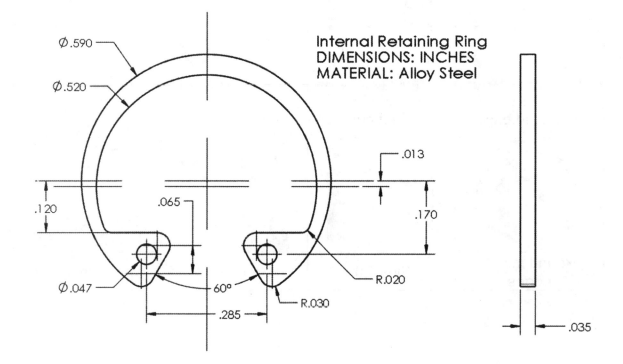

Internal Retaining Ring
DIMENSIONS: INCHES
MATERIAL: Alloy Steel

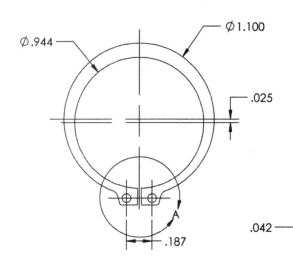

Retaining Ring Crankshaft Bearing
DIMENSIONS: INCHES
MATERIAL: Alloy Steel

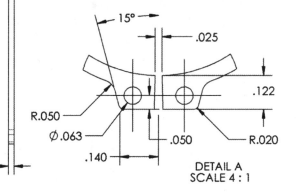

DETAIL A
SCALE 4 : 1

Here is a suggested sequence of features to build the Piston Head for reference.

Revolved base	First cut	First bottom cut	Second bottom cut
Round inside edges	Side Cut	Groove cut	Mirror grove cut

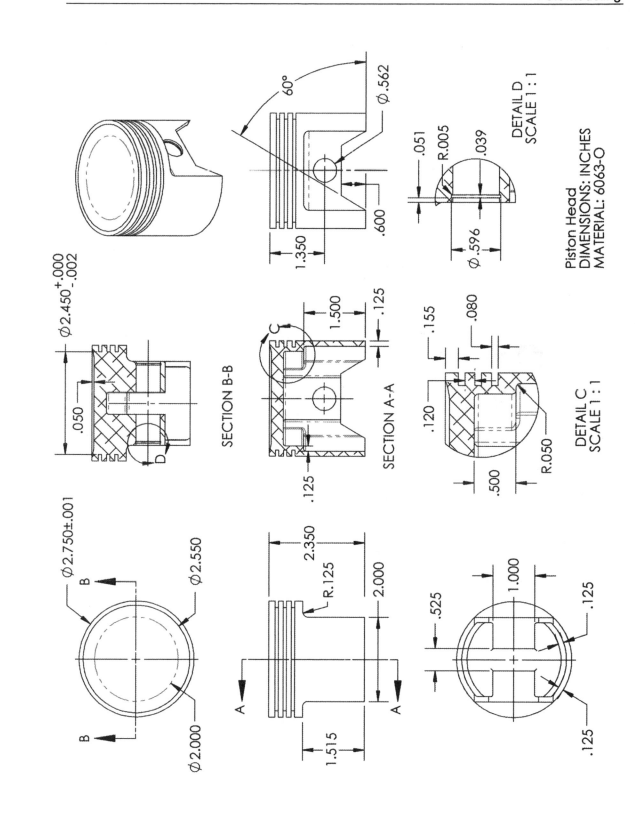

60°

Ø.562

.600

1.350

DETAIL D
SCALE 1 : 1

.051

R.005

.039

Ø.596

Piston Head
DIMENSIONS: INCHES
MATERIAL: 6063-O

Ø2.450 +.000 -.002

.050

SECTION B-B

1.500

.125

.125

SECTION A-A

.155

.080

.120

.500

R.050

DETAIL C
SCALE 1 : 1

Ø2.750±.001

B

Ø2.550

B

Ø2.000

2.350

R.125

2.000

A

A

1.515

.525

1.000

.125

.125

Notes:

Special Features: Sweep, Loft and Wrap

There are times when we need to design components that cannot be easily defined by prismatic shapes. For those features that have 'curvy' shapes we can use **Sweep** and **Loft** features, which let us create almost any shape we can think of. These are the features that allow us to design consumer products, which, more often than not, have to be attractive and appealing, making extensive use of curvature and organic shapes. These products include things like your remote control, a computer mouse, coffee maker, perfume bottles, telephones, etc., and many times the success or failure of these products in the market can be directly attributed to their appearance. They have to look nice, 'feel' right, and of course perform the task that they were intended for. Sweeps and Lofts (also used to create "organic" shapes like those found in nature) are widely used in the automotive and aerospace industry where cosmetics, aerodynamics, and ergonomics are very important in the design.

Sweeps and Lofts have many different options that allow us to create anything from relatively simple to extremely complex shapes. In light of the vast number of variations and possibilities for these features, we'll keep these examples as simple as possible without sacrificing functionality, to give the reader a good idea as to what can be achieved.

Sweeps and Lofts are usually referred to as advanced features, since they usually require more work to complete, and a better understanding of the basic concepts of solid modeling. Having said that, these exercises will assume that commands that we have done more than a couple of times up to this point, like creating a sketch, are already understood and we'll simply direct the reader to create it providing the necessary details. This way we'll be able to focus more on the specifics and options of the new features.

The Wrap feature is a special tool that helps us, as the name implies, to 'wrap' a sketch around a cylindrical surface, this tool helps us create features like cylindrical cams, slots on cylinders or cylindrical surfaces, etc.

These are examples of designs made using advanced modeling techniques.

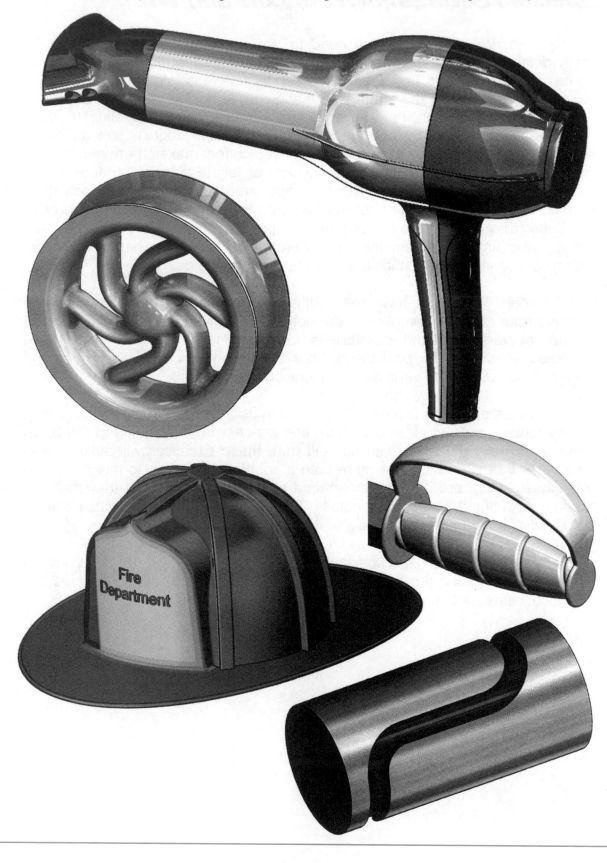

Sweep: Cup and Springs

Notes:

For this exercise we are going to make a simple cup. In this exercise we will learn a new option when creating features called "**Thin Feature**," the Sweep command, a new Fillet option to create a Full Round fillet and a review of auxiliary Planes. The sequence of features to complete the cup is:

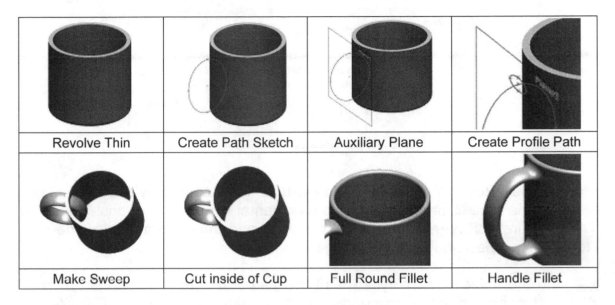

| Revolve Thin | Create Path Sketch | Auxiliary Plane | Create Profile Path |
| Make Sweep | Cut inside of Cup | Full Round Fillet | Handle Fillet |

149. – For the first feature we will create a "**Revolved Feature**" using the "Thin Feature" option. This option makes a feature with a specified thickness based on the sketch that was drawn. Select the "*Front Plane*" and create the following sketch. Notice the sketch is an open profile with two lines, an arc and a centerline. (Remember to make the diameter dimension about the centerline.) a Thin Feature can be made using either an open or closed sketch, but using an open sketch will always make a thin feature.

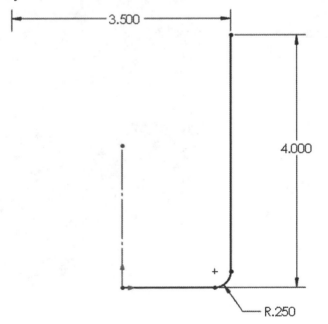

150. - After selecting the "**Revolve Boss/Base**" command we get a warning telling us about the sketch being open. Since we want a thin revolved feature, select "No."

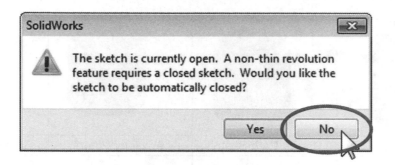

In the "Revolve" options, "**Thin Feature**" is automatically activated. Since we want the dimensions we added to be external model dimensions, select the Thin Feature's "**Reverse Direction**" option to add the material inside the cup. Notice the preview showing the change.

 In the value box we typed 3/16; we can add a fraction and SolidWorks changes it to the corresponding decimal value when we click OK. We can also type simple mathematic expressions including addition, subtraction, multiplication, and division in any value box where we can type a value.

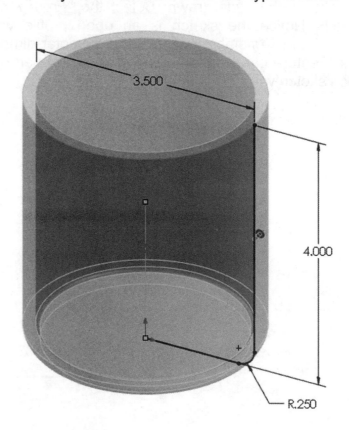

Our part looks like this and *"Revolve-Thin1"* is added to the Feature Manager.

151. - Select the *"Front Plane"* and create the following sketch using an ellipse. Add a "Vertical" geometric relation between the top and bottom points of the ellipse to make them vertical to each other and fully define it. Select the **"Ellipse"** command from the Sketch tab in the CommandManager or from the menu **"Tools, Sketch Entities, Ellipse."** Add the corresponding dimensions to and from the ellipse points at the major and minor axes. To draw an ellipse click to locate the center point, click again to locate one axis and then the other axis.

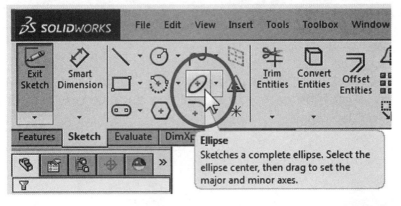

 When looking at a round surface from a front, side or top view we can add a dimension to its silhouette.

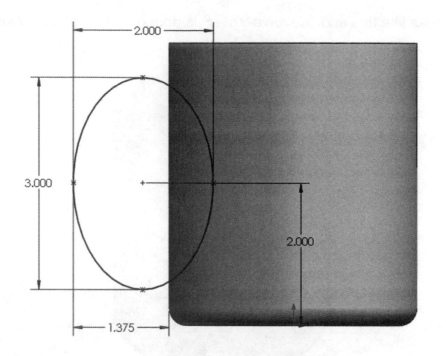

Exit the sketch and rename it *"Path Sketch."* We will not use the sketch for a feature just yet.

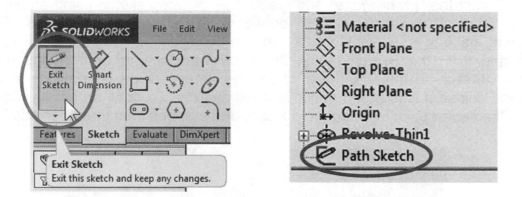

152. - Create an Auxiliary plane parallel to the "*Right Plane*" using the plane as the first reference and the center of the ellipse as a second reference as shown. Click OK to finish the plane.

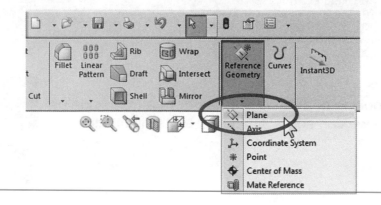

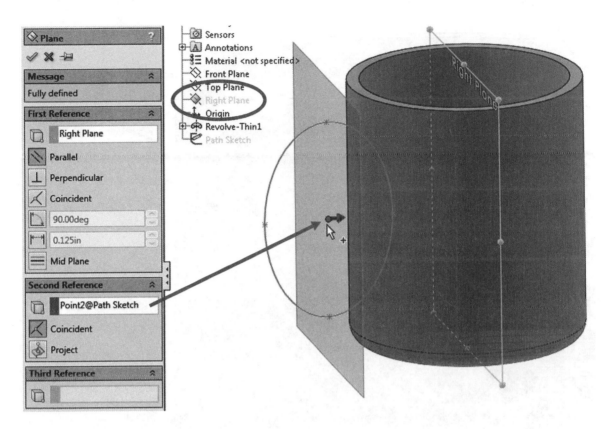

153. - Select the plane just created and draw the next sketch in it. Looking at the plane perpendicular to it helps to visualize the sketch. After adding the sketch press the "Normal To" command (shortcut Ctrl+8.) Pressing it again will show the reverse view. Start the center of the new ellipse at the top point of the previous sketch's ellipse. Add a coincident relation if needed. Remember to add a horizontal relation between the points of the major (or vertical to the minor) axis.

If necessary rotate the part to better visualize and select the top point of the ellipse in the previous sketch. Exit the sketch and rename it *"Profile Sketch."*

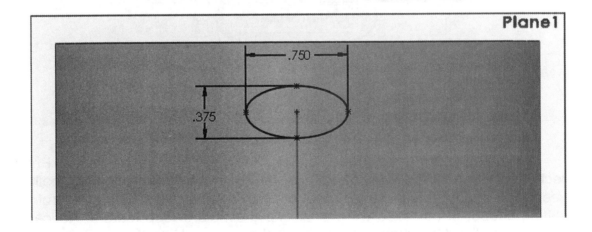

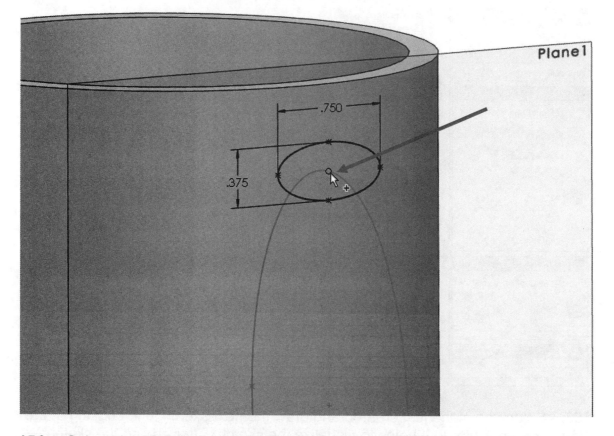

154. - Select the "**Sweep**" icon from the Features tab in the CommandManager or from the menu "**Insert, Boss/Base, Sweep.**" The sweep is a feature that requires a minimum of two sketches: one for the sweep's profile and one for the path (For the path of the sweep instead of a sketch we can also use a model edge or a user defined curve that cross the profile.)

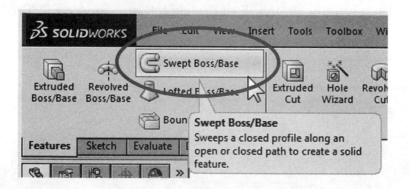

In the "**Sweep**" properties, select the *"Profile Sketch"* in the Profile selection box, and the *"Path Sketch"* in the Path selection box. Optionally, a Sweep can have guide curves and other parameters to better control the resulting shape; in our case we are making a simple sweep feature. Notice the preview and click OK when done to finish the sweep. Hide the auxiliary planes using the "**Hide/Show Items**" toolbar if so desired.

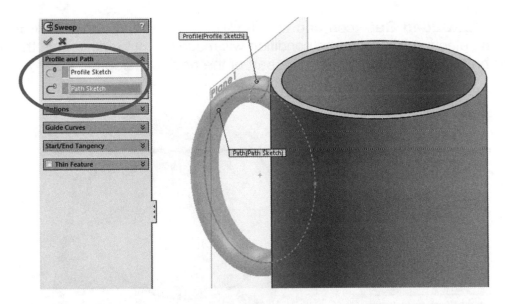

155. - Notice the sweep also goes inside the cup. To fix the cup we'll make a cut. Create a sketch in the flat face at the top of the cup.

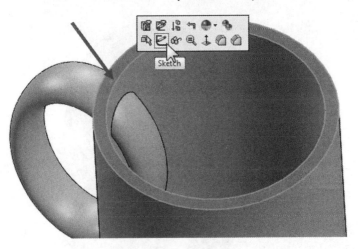

Select the <u>inside</u> edge at the top and use "**Convert Entities**" from the Sketch tab to convert the edge to sketch geometry.

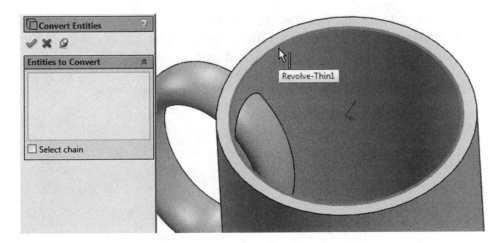

Select the "**Extruded Cut**" icon and use the "Up to next" end condition from the drop down selection list. This end condition will make the cut until it finds the next face (the bottom) effectively cutting the part of the handle inside the cup.

156. - Now we need to round the flat face at the top lip of the cup. To do this we'll add a "**Fillet**" using the "**Full Round Fillet**" option. The full round will essentially remove the flat face at the top, and replace it with a rounded face.

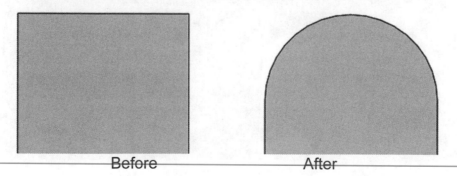

Before   After

We need to select three faces, the middle face will be the one replaced by the fillet. After selecting the Fillet command, select the "Full round fillet" option to reveal the selection boxes. With the first selection box active select the outside face of the cup. Click inside the second selection box and select the top flat face of the cup. Click inside the third selection box and select the inside face of the cup. Note the selected faces are color coded. When done selecting faces click OK to apply the fillet.

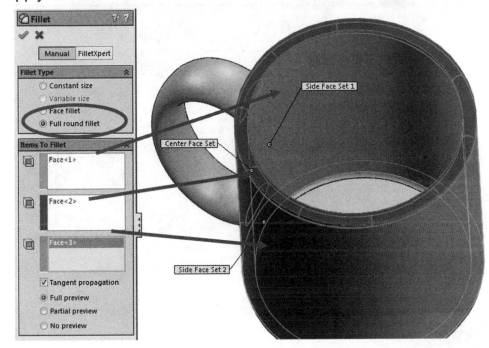

157. - To finish the cup add a fillet to round the edges where the handle meets the cup. Select the fillet command with the "Constant Radius" option, select the handle's surface, and change the radius to 0.25″. Click OK to finish.

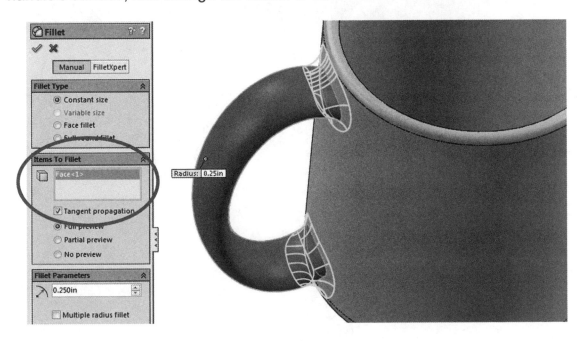

158. - Save the finished part as *'Cup'* and close.

In the next exercise we are going to show how to make a simple and a variable pitch spring. In order to make these springs we'll have to learn how to make a simple and a variable pitch helix to be used as a sweep path. The sequence of features to complete the springs are:

Simple Spring

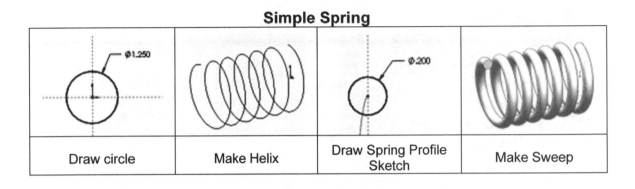

Draw circle	Make Helix	Draw Spring Profile Sketch	Make Sweep

Variable Pitch Spring

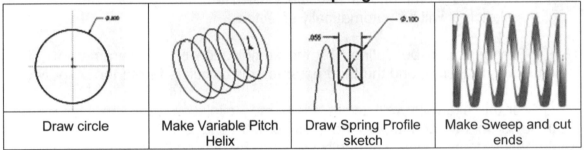

Draw circle	Make Variable Pitch Helix	Draw Spring Profile sketch	Make Sweep and cut ends

Simple Spring

159.- In order to make a helix, first we need to make a sketch with a circle. This circle is going to be the helix's diameter. Select the "*Front Plane*" and make a sketch using the following dimensions. Exit the sketch when done.

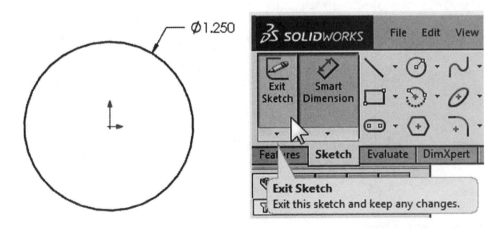

160. - In the Features tab select "**Curves, Helix and Spiral**" from the drop-down icon or the menu "**Insert, Curve, Helix/Spiral**." If asked to select a plane or a sketch, select the sketch we just drew.

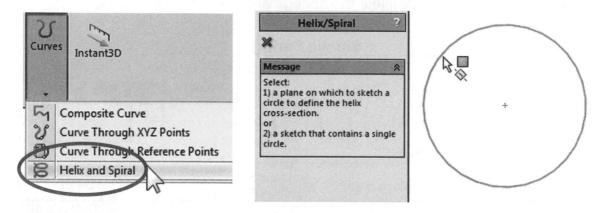

If we don't exit the sketch, we'll only have the "Helix and Spiral" option from the "Curves" command. If we select the "**Helix and Spiral**" before exiting the sketch, it will be automatically selected.

161. - The helix can be defined by the combination of two parameters, Pitch, Revolutions, or Height and the third parameter is calculated from the other two.

For this example we'll select "Pitch and Revolution" from the "Defined By:" drop down menu, and make the pitch 0.325" and 6 Revolutions. The "Start Angle" value defines where the helix will start. By making it 90 degrees it will start at the top, coincident with the "*Front Plane*." If we had made it 0 degrees, it would be coincident to the "*Top Plane*" instead (Feel free to explore the options.) Click OK to finish the helix.

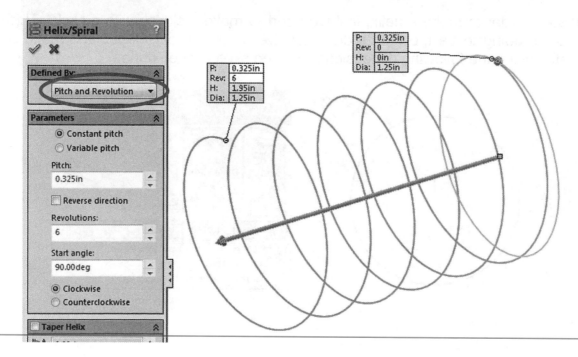

Note the Helix command has options to make it Counterclockwise, Clockwise, Tapered, Variable pitch and reversed (going right or left.)

162. - Once the Helix is done, we need to make the profile sketch for the sweep. Switch to a Right view, and add a new sketch in the "*Right Plane*" as shown. Make the circle close to the Helix...

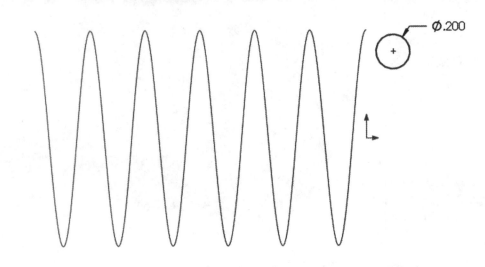

... and add a "**Pierce**" geometric relation between the center of the circle and the helix. This way the path will start at the beginning of the helix. This relation will make the sketch fully defined. Exit the sketch when done.

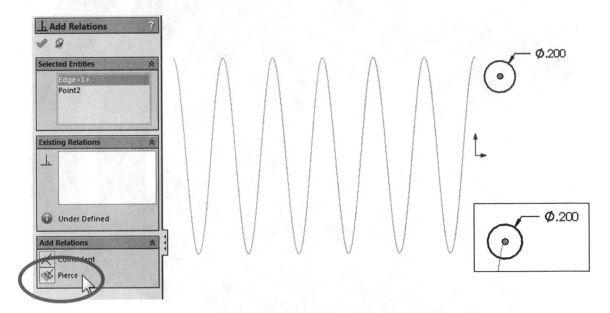

 A pierce relation is done between an element that is oblique or perpendicular to the sketch plane and a point in the sketch. Think of it as a needle piercing through a fabric, the sketch being the fabric and the helix (or curve, model edge or another sketch) the needle.

163. - Select the Sweep command and make the sweep using the last sketch as a profile and the Helix as a Path. Note the Preview and click OK to finish.

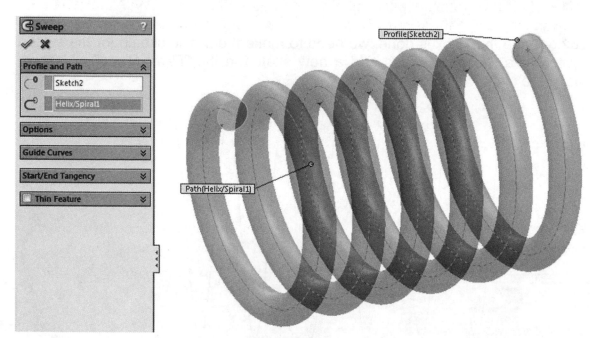

Save as '*Spring*' and close the finished spring.

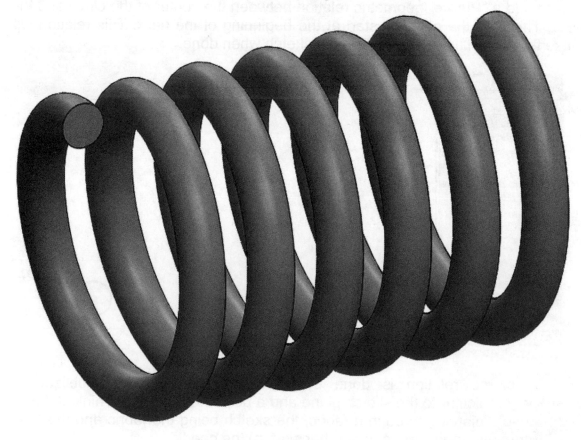

Variable Pitch Spring

164. - For the variable pitch spring we'll start the same way and make the following sketch in the "*Front Plane*." This will be the spring's outside diameter.

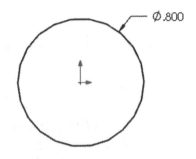

Ø.800

165. - While still editing the sketch, in the Features tab from the **"Curves"** drop down icon select **"Helix and Spiral"**; notice it is the only option available.

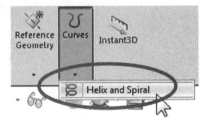

166. - In the **Helix/Spiral** command select "Pitch and Revolution" from the "Defined by:" selection box and "Variable Pitch" in the Parameters box. After selecting it we are presented with a table, fill in the values for the helix using the next table. Click OK when finished to build the helix.

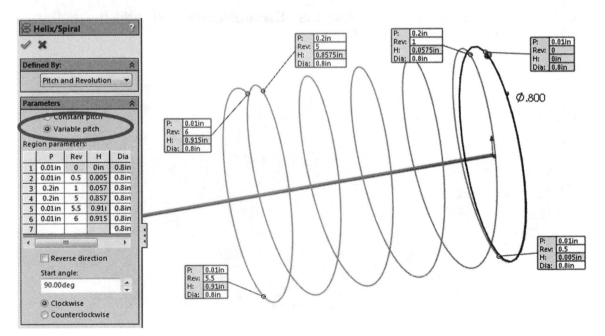

	P	Rev	H	Dia
1	0.01in	0	0in	0.8in
2	0.01in	0.5	0.005	0.8in
3	0.2in	1	0.057	0.8in
4	0.2in	5	0.857	0.8in
5	0.01in	5.5	0.91i	0.8in
6	0.01in	6	0.915	0.8in
7				0.8in

167. - After the helix is complete add a new sketch in the "*Right Plane*." Draw the circle first, then add a center rectangle; trim and dimension as needed.

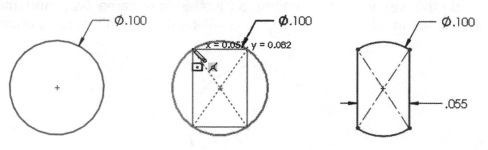

168. - Add a centerline from the center to the top line (make sure it is coincident.) Add a "**Pierce**" geometric relation between the top endpoint of the centerline and the helix to fully define the sketch. Exit the sketch and optionally rename it *'Profile'*.

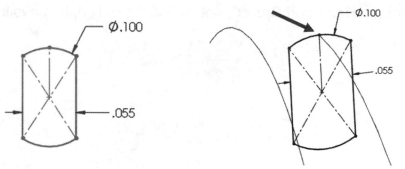

The Pierce relation allows us to fix the profile to the path, and can be added to any part of the sketch. We chose to add it to the top because the original sketch used for the helix is the spring's outside diameter.

169. - Just as we did before, select the **"Sweep"** command, add the path and profile as shown and click OK to finish.

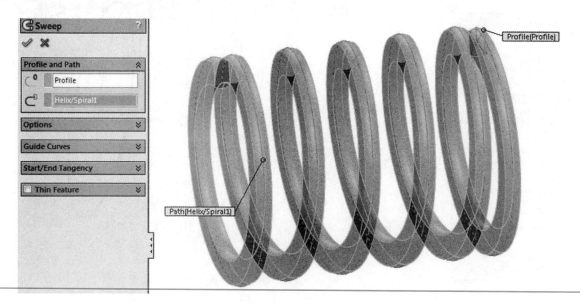

170. – As a finishing touch we'll make a cut to flatten the sides of the spring. Change to a Right view and add a sketch in the "*Right Plane*." Draw a single line starting at the midpoint of the indicated edge and long enough to cross the part.

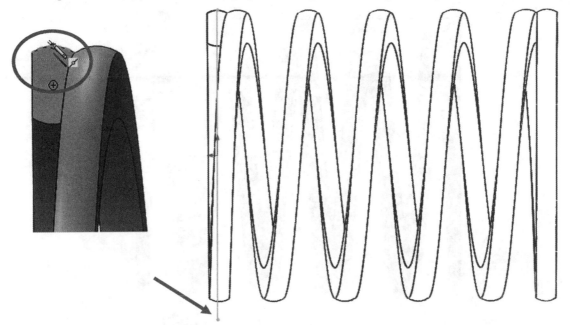

171. - Select the "**Extruded Cut**" command. When we use an open sketch to make a cut, the "Through All" option is automatically selected in both directions. One side of the model is cut using the open sketch. The small arrow located at the center of the line indicates which side of the model will be cut. Use the "Flip side to cut" option if needed to cut the left side. Click OK to complete the cut extrude and repeat it in the right side. Note the cutting plane is shown in the graphics area.

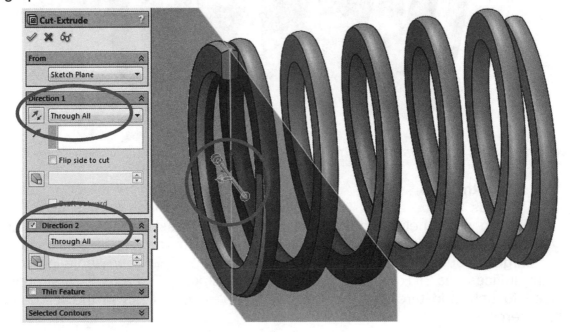

When using an open sketch to cut a model, we can only use a single open profile. If we have multiple open profiles we cannot make the Cut Extrude.

Save the model as *'Variable Pitch Spring'*.

A note about threads

 Threads can be added to a model either by adding a Sweep or a Cut Sweep with a helix. When modeling screws and fasteners in general, it is almost always unnecessary to add a helical thread, as it consumes a large amount of computing resources, and a simple representation of it usually suffices (as a Revolved Boss/Cut or Cosmetic Thread.) It is strongly advised to only add threads when required by the model, as in the following bottle exercise.

For the next exercise we'll build the following bottle using a **sweep feature** with guide curves.

In this model we'll use two sweep features, one for the body and one for the thread. For the body we'll make a sweep with two guide curves, so we need to make four sketches: Path, Guide Curve 1, Guide Curve 2 and Profile, in that order. The reason to make the Profile last is that it has to pierce the Path and both Guide Curves for the sweep to work as expected.

172. - Open a new part, set dimensions to inches, and three decimal places. Make the Path sketch in the "*Front Plane*" and Exit the sketch. Rename *'Path'*.

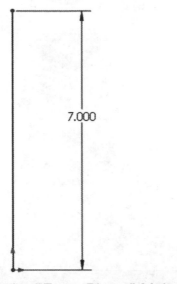

7.000

173. - Add a second sketch in the "*Front Plane*." Make arcs and lines tangent to each other; add centerlines as reference for tangency. All arcs are equal. Exit sketch and rename *'Guide 1'*.

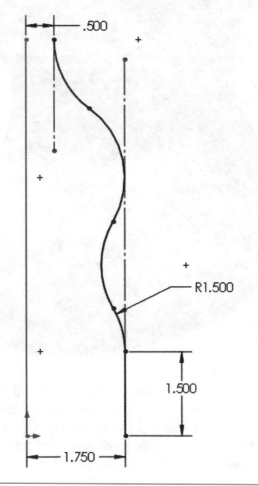

.500

R1.500

1.500

1.750

174. - Add third sketch to "*Right Plane.*" Add geometric relations to previous sketches to maintain design intent. Make the topmost endpoint Horizontal to the topmost endpoint of the '*Path*' sketch. Arcs are equal size and tangent. Make the indicated endpoints horizontal. Only geometric relations and two dimensions are needed to fully define the sketch. Exit the sketch and rename it '*Guide 2*'.

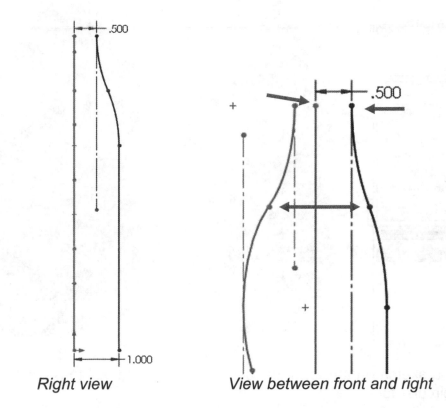

Right view   *View between front and right*

175. - Add a new sketch in the "*Top Plane*", make an ellipse adding Pierce relations between the ellipse's major and minor axes to '*Guide 1*' and '*Guide 2*'. View is in Isometric for clarity. Exit the sketch and rename it '*Profile*'.

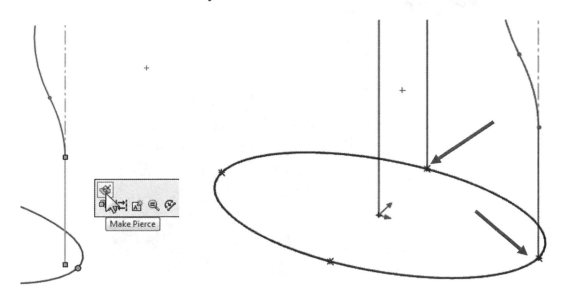

176. - Select the "**Sweep Boss/Base**" icon, add the *'Path'* sketch to the "Path" selection box and the *'Profile'* sketch to the "Profile" selection box. Expand the "Guide Curves" selection box and add both guides to it. Click OK to finish.

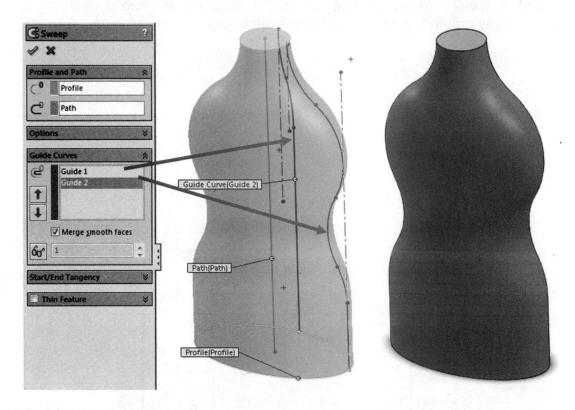

177. - Add a sketch on the top face, use "**Convert Entities**" to project the edge of the top circular face...

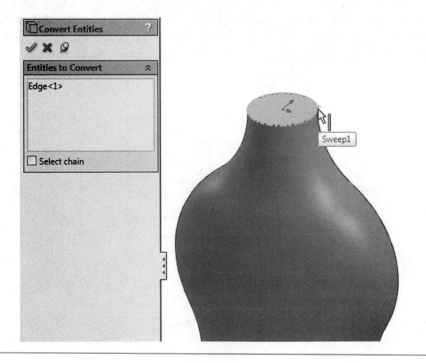

...and extrude it 1".

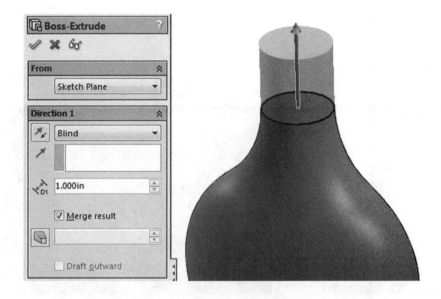

178. - Add a 0.375" fillet at the bottom of the bottle.

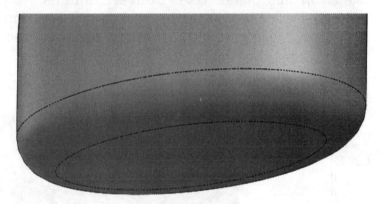

179. - Add a 0.050" shell to the part removing the top face.

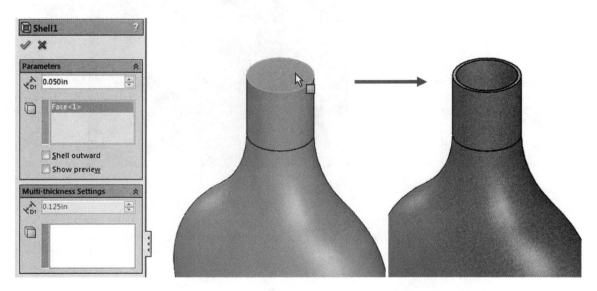

180. - Add a parallel auxiliary plane 0.125" below the topmost face.

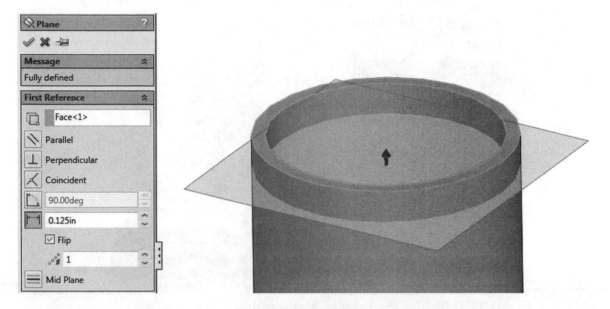

181. - Add a sketch in this plane. Use "**Convert Entities**" to project the top outside edge and make a Helix defined by Pitch and Revolution using 0.2" for pitch and 2.5 revolutions. Make sure the Start Angle is at 0 degrees.

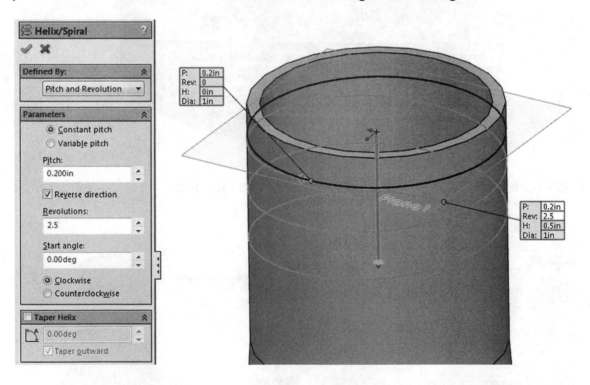

182. – Rotate to a Right View and add the following sketch in the "*Right Plane*" to be the Profile of the thread. Be sure to add a Pierce relation between the profile and the helix at the end of the construction line. Exit the sketch and make a sweep feature using the previous helix and this profile.

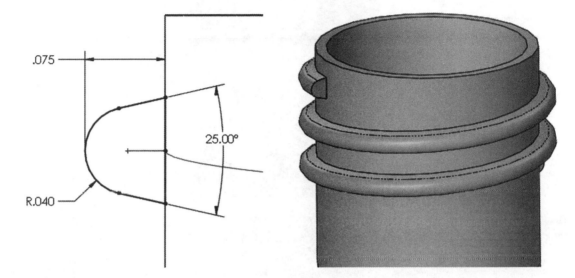

183. - Add a sketch to the flat face at the beginning of the thread, and another at the end of the thread using "**Convert Entities.**" Make a 120 degrees "Revolved Boss" with each sketch using the vertical edge as axis of revolution. The reason to make it 120 degrees is to merge to the body of the bottle.

184. - Add a 0.02" fillet to the thread as a finishing touch. You may need to select multiple edges. Save the part as Bottle and close it.

Engine Project Parts: Make the following components to build the engine. Save the parts using the name provided. High resolution images are included in the accompanying disc.

Intake
DIMENSIONS: INCHES
MATERIAL: Chrome Stainless Steel

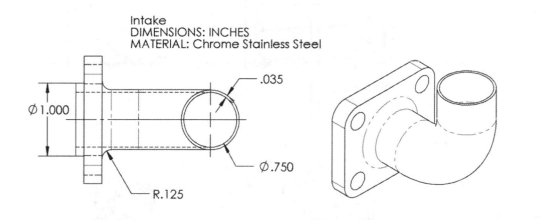

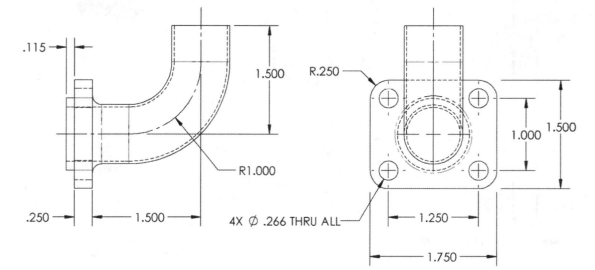

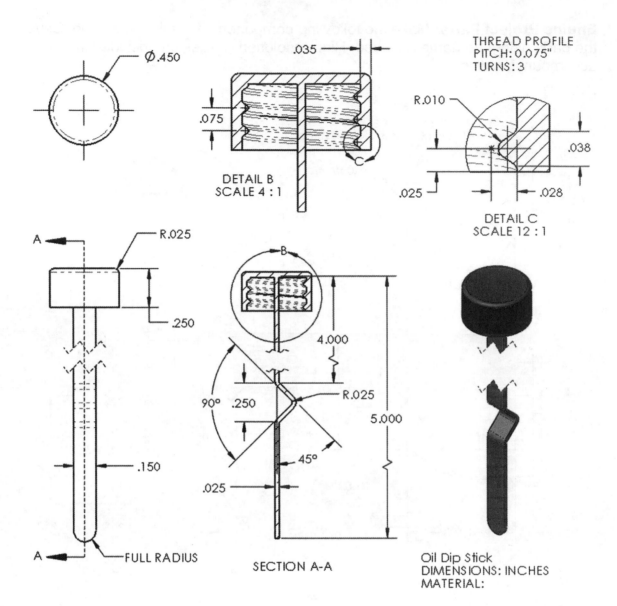

Ø.450

.035

DETAIL B
SCALE 4 : 1

THREAD PROFILE
PITCH: 0.075"
TURNS: 3

R.010

.038

.025

.028

DETAIL C
SCALE 12 : 1

.075

A

R.025

.250

.150

A

FULL RADIUS

B

4.000

R.025

5.000

90° .250

45°

.025

SECTION A-A

Oil Dip Stick
DIMENSIONS: INCHES
MATERIAL:

Loft: Bottle

Notes:

The "**Loft**" feature requires at least two different sketches and/or faces and optionally guide curves to more accurately define the final shape. The **Loft** helps us design complex shapes with more control over the cross section. In this exercise we will make a bottle using a loft with four different sketches.

185. - Make a new part and create three auxiliary planes using the "**Plane**" command. Select the *"Top Plane"* as reference, change the number of planes to 3 and space them 2.5″ as shown. Click OK when done.

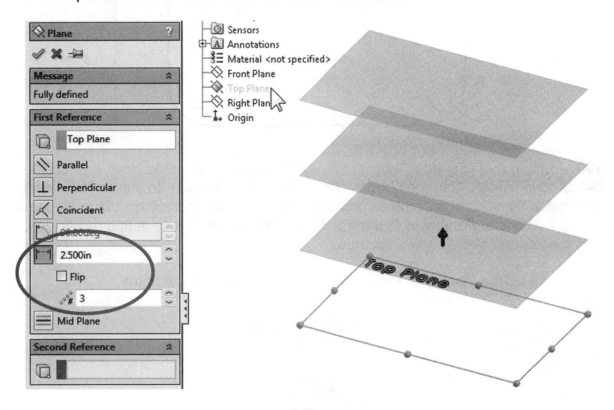

186. - For clarity, select the *"Top Plane"* in the FeatureManager and show it using the "Hide/Show" command from the pop-up toolbar. Turn on Plane visibility if needed in the "Hide/Show Items" command.

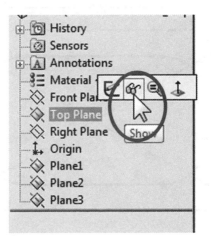

219

187. - Switch to a Top view, select the *"Top Plane"* and draw the following sketch using the "**Center Rectangle**" and "**Sketch Fillet**" tools. Exit the sketch when finished. Plane visibility is turned off for clarity.

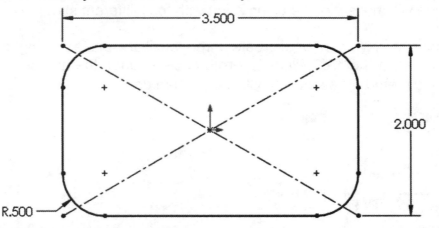

188. - Still in the Top view, select *"Plane1"* from the FeatureManager and create the second sketch. Use the "**Center Rectangle**" tool; be sure to start in the origin and make the rectangle's corner coincident to the previous sketch's diagonal line. Add a 2.5" width dimension and the 0.5" "**Sketch Fillet**" to fully define the sketch. Exit the second sketch when finished.

Turn off the display of Planes for clarity with "Hide/Show Items."

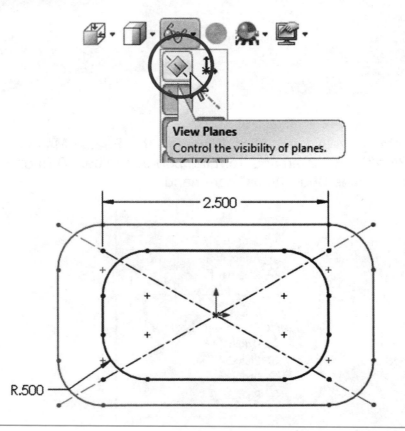

189. - For the third profile, select *"Plane2"* from the FeatureManager and create a new sketch in it. This sketch will be exactly the same as the first one. To help us save time and maintain design intent, we'll use the **"Convert Entities"** tool. In the **"Convert Entities"** selection box, select the entire *"Sketch1"* from the fly-out FeatureManager and click OK to project Sketch1 in the new sketch. Exit the sketch when done.

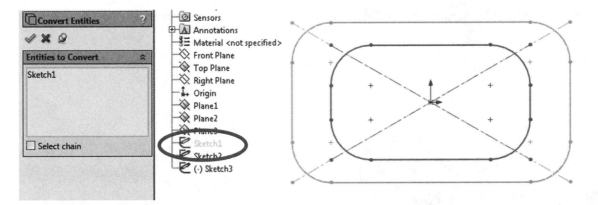

190. - For the last profile select *"Plane3"* from the FeatureManager and create a new sketch. Draw a circle and add a geometric relation to make it "Tangent" to the horizontal line in *"Sketch2"* as indicated. This relation will fully define the sketch. Exit the sketch to finish.

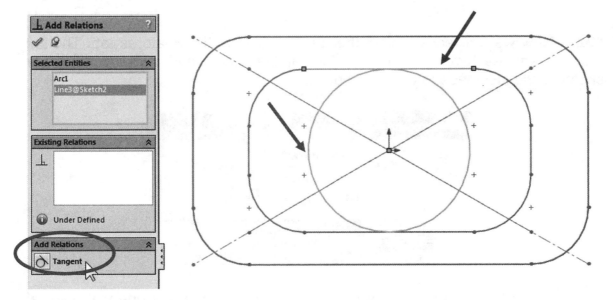

191. - The finished sketches will look like this with the planes visible:

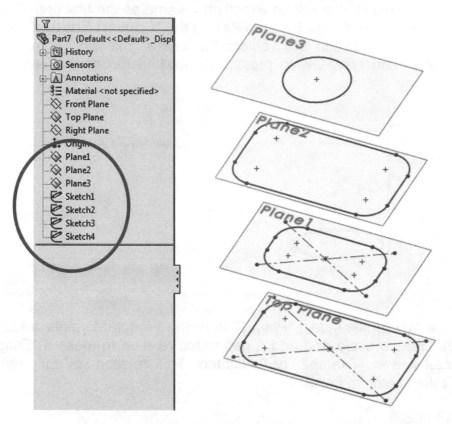

192. - Now we are ready, select the **"Loft"** icon from the Features tab. The loft feature requires two or more sketches and/or faces, and we'll use the four sketches we just made to build the bottle.

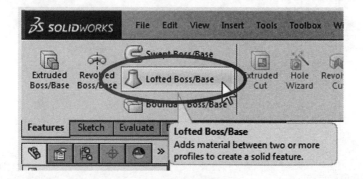

We will select the profiles in order starting with the first one we made at the bottom and finishing with the last one at the top (or from top to bottom, but in order.) It is important to select the sketches thinking that where we select the profile will affect the result. Click in the graphics area near the indicated 'dots', this line indicates the segment of one profile that will be connected to the next profile. If we select points randomly in the profiles, the loft could twist and produce undesirable results. Optionally guide curves can be added to improve control of the resulting shape.

From the "Start/End Conditions" select "Normal to Profile" for both the "Start" and "End" constraint. Notice the difference in the preview after selecting the start and end constraints. Click OK when done.

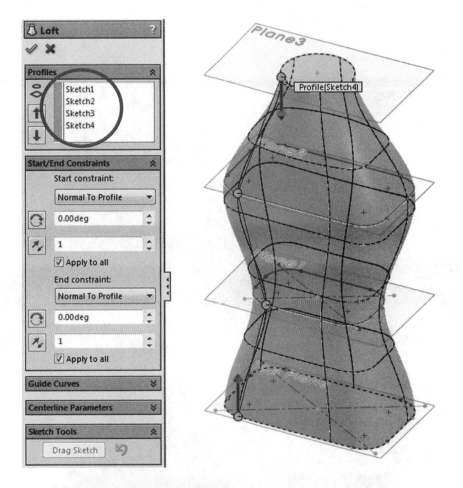

193. - Add a 0.25″ radius fillet in the bottom edge of the part to round it off.

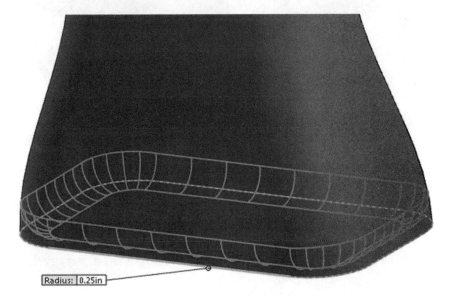

Add a 0.75" extrusion at the top of the bottle and finish using the "**Shell**" command removing the top face making the wall thickness 0.125".

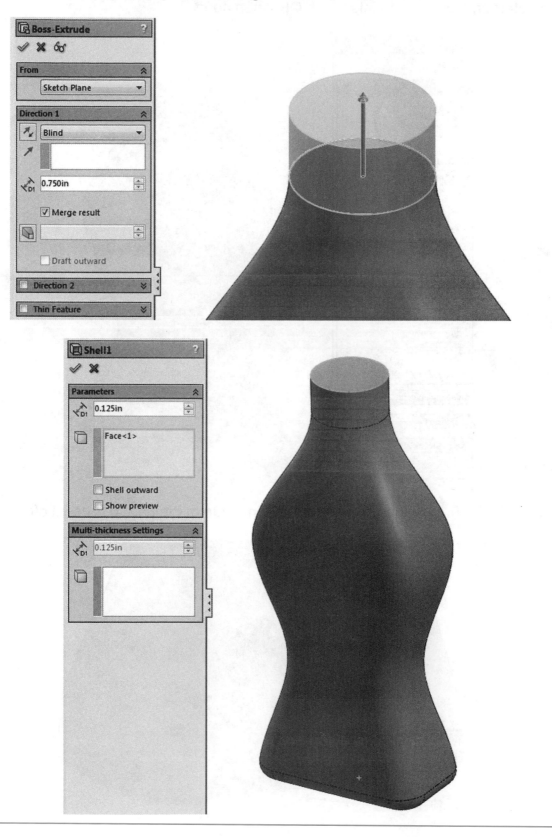

Image shown using Real View

194. - To view the inside of the part, select the **"Section View"** icon from the View toolbar or the menu **"View, Display, Section View."** We can define which plane to cut the model with, the depth of the cut and optionally add a second or third section. If we click OK in the Section View, the model will be displayed as cut, but this is only for display purposes; the part is not actually cut. To turn off the Section View, select its icon or menu command again. This section view can be used along with the **"Measure"** tool to inspect the part.

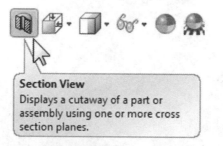

Section View
Displays a cutaway of a part or assembly using one or more cross section planes.

 We can also change the depth of the cut by dragging the arrow in the center of the plane.

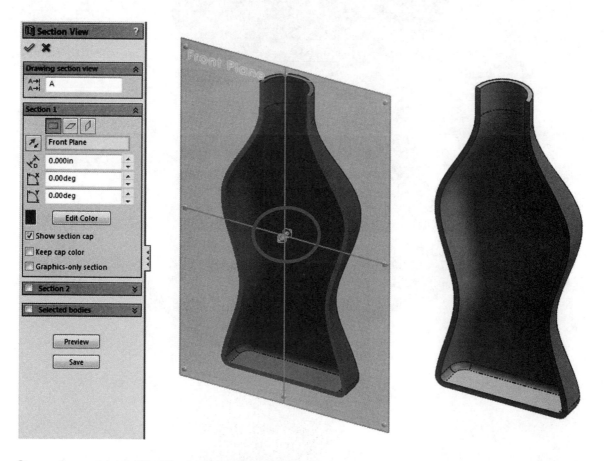

Save the part as '*Bottle Loft*' and close.

Wrap Feature

The wrap feature helps us create cylindrical cams or slots on cylindrical surfaces using a sketch on a plane tangent to the surface we want to make the wrap on.

195. – Make a new part, set units to inches with three decimal places; add this sketch on the *"Front Plane"* and extrude it 3".

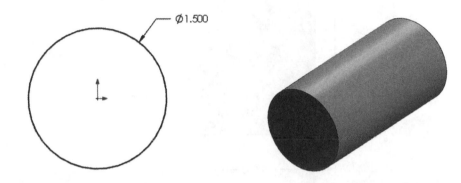

196. – The next step is to make the sketch that will be used for the wrap feature. For the sketch plane we'll make a plane parallel to the *"Top Plane"* tangent to the cylindrical surface. Add a new plane parallel to the *"Top Plane"* 0.75" above and draw the following profile making sure it's symmetrical about the centerline. All arcs are equal radii. The top dimension's value is entered as *1.5 * pi*, since we want the sketch to wrap completely around the cylinder. SolidWorks automatically calculates the resulting value for us.

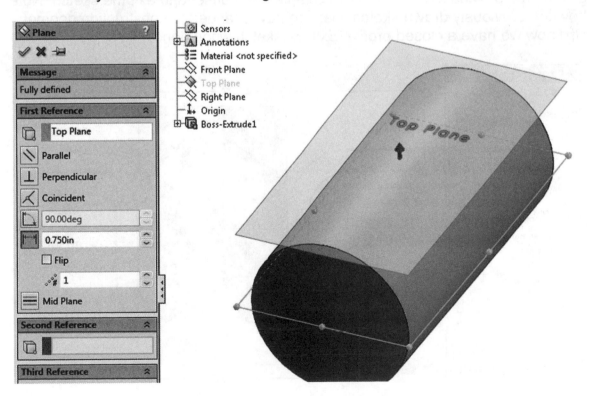

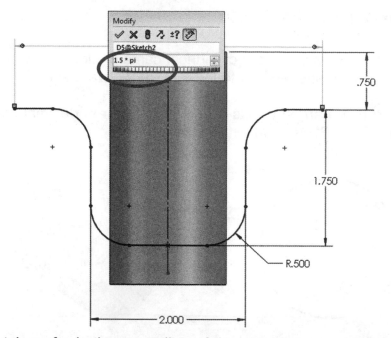

197. -The sketch so far is the centerline of the slot we are going to wrap around the cylinder. Select the **"Offset"** command and turn on the options:

"Select chain" to automatically select the entire centerline picking only one segment, **"Bi-directional"** to make the offset in both directions, **"Make base construction"** to change the selected line (or chain) to construction geometry, and after selecting a segment of the sketch the **"Cap ends"** option is enabled letting us choose to cap the offset with Arcs or Lines. Making the offset 0.25" will give us a 0.5" wide slot. Click OK to complete the offset and exit the sketch. Note how the previously drawn sketch lines are now changed to construction geometry and now we have a closed profile. Exit the sketch when done.

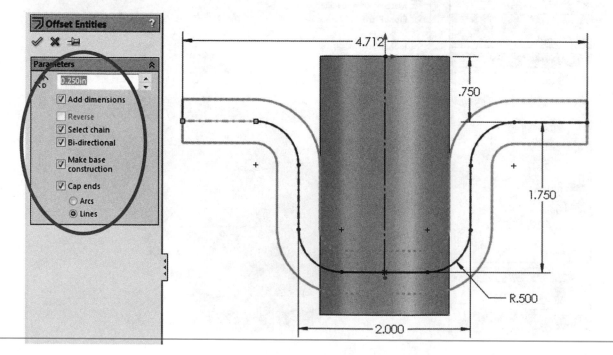

198. – Select the "**Wrap**" feature from the Features tab or the menu "**Insert, Features, Wrap**."

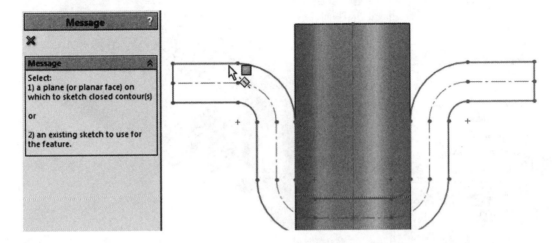

If the sketch is not pre-selected, select the sketch from the graphics area or the fly-out FeatureManager.

199.- In the "Warp" command properties select the "Deboss" option to make a cut in the part (The "Emboss" option will add material and the "Scribe" will split the face.) Select the cylinder's face in the "Face for Wrap Feature" selection box, activate the "Reverse Direction" option* and make the depth 0.1". Click OK to finish.

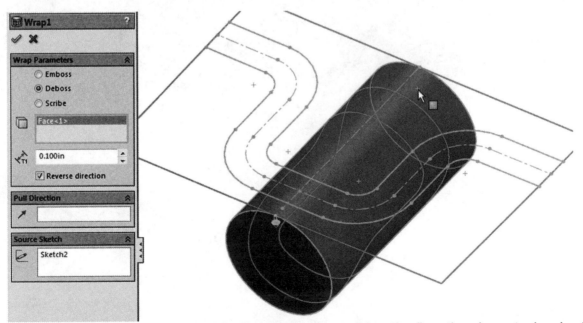

As of the writing of this book, if the "Reverse Direction" option is not checked the wrap feature produces incorrect geometry.

200. – Add a 0.02" fillet to the wrap feature to finish the part and save it as *'Cylindrical Cam'*.

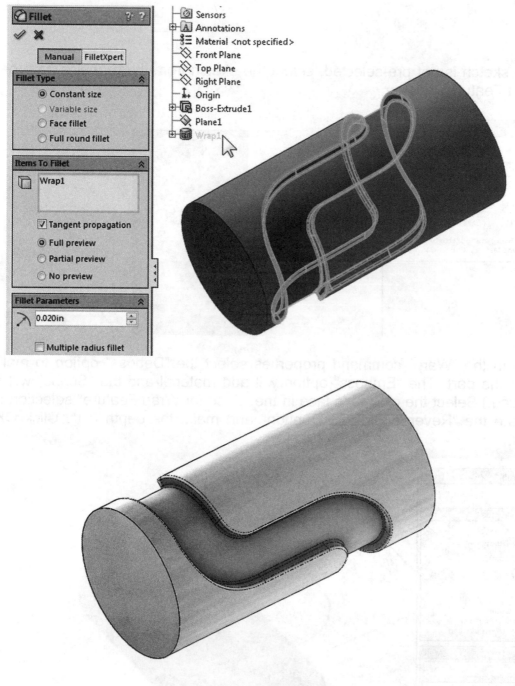

Image made using Real View

Exercises: Build the following parts using the knowledge acquired in this lesson. Try to use the most efficient method to complete the model.

Eccentric Coupler

Notes:

- Both circles are centered horizontally (Right view.)
- Add a guide sketch at the bottom.
- Set the Start and End Conditions for the loft to "Normal to Profile."
- Make as Thin Feature *or* Shell it after making the loft feature.

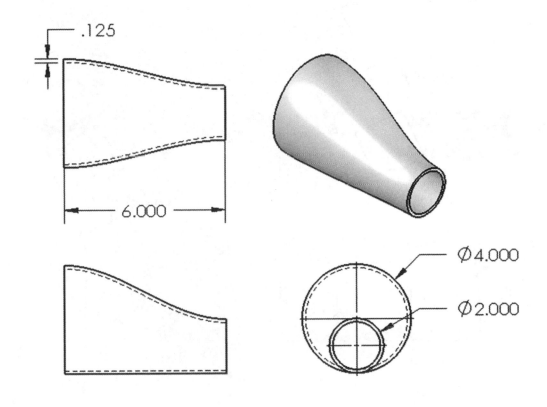

HINTS:

- Draw the 1" circle in the "*Right Plane.*"
- Make an Auxiliary Plane 6" parallel to the "*Right Plane.*"
- Draw a 2" circle in the Auxiliary Plane.
- Draw a sketch in the "*Front Plane*" to make the guide curve.
- Select the guide sketch in the "Guide Curves" selection box.

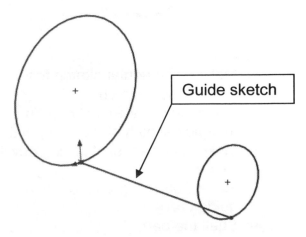

Guide sketch

Bent Coupler

Build the following part using a Loft feature and a shell. The part is 0.15″ thick.

Notes:
- Add a guide sketch along the right side of the part.
- Start and End Conditions "Normal to Profile."
- Make as Thin Feature or Shell after loft.

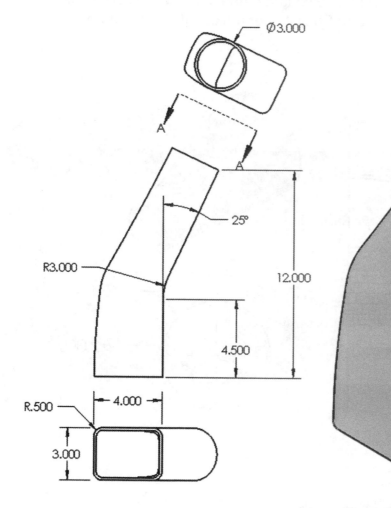

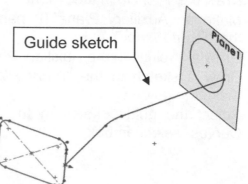

Guide sketch

HINTS:
- Make Rectangular sketch first.
- Make Guide sketch.
- Make Auxiliary Plane perpendicular to Guide sketch at the end point.
- Make circular sketch in Auxiliary Plane.
- Make Loft using Guide sketch as a guide curve.
- Shell the part.

Challenge Exercises: Build the *'Worm Gear'* and *'Offset Shaft'* complete gears using the knowledge learned so far with the information given. High resolution images at www.mechanicad.com.

DISCLOSURE: The gears modeled in this tutorial are not intended for manufacturing, nor is this tutorial meant to be a gear design guide. Its sole purpose is to show the reader how to apply the learned knowledge using a simplified version of the gears.

- **Offset Shaft:** Open the '*Offset Shaft*' and add the following sketch in the "*Front Plane*", Exit the sketch and rename it "*Gear Width*." This will be the length of the full size helix.

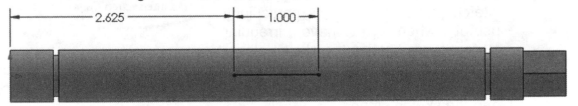

- Build two reference planes parallel to the "*Right Plane*", one at each end of the "*Gear Width*" sketch.

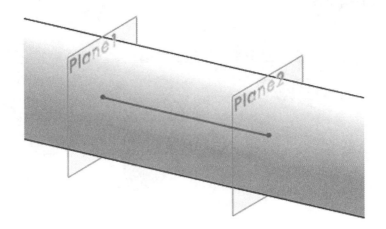

- Add the gear's profile sketch in the "*Front Plane*", at the left side of the "*Gear Width*" sketch. Exit the sketch and rename "*Thread Profile*."

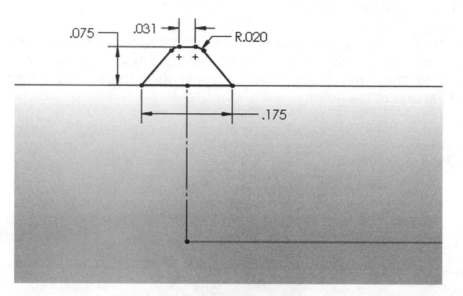

- In the plane located at the left of the "*Gear Width*" sketch add a new sketch; use the "Convert Entities" drop down icon to select **"Intersection Curve"**, this command will create sketch entities at the intersection of the selected surface(s) and the current sketch plane. This tool is particularly useful when we have irregular surfaces intersecting the sketch plane.

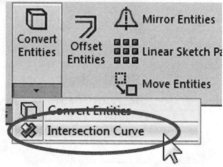

In this case it works the same as "Convert Entities", but for oblique surfaces it's the best option to obtain the intersection of the surface and the sketch plane.

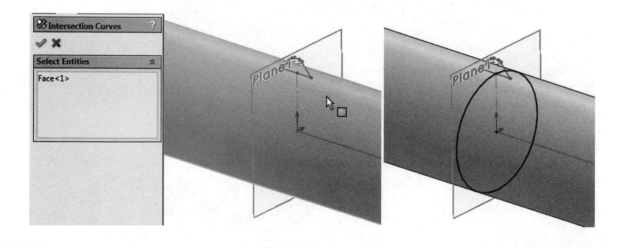

- Make the Helix 1" Height with a 0.25" Pitch

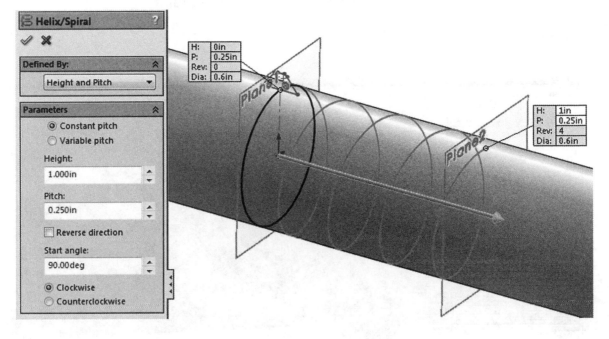

- Make the first sweep using the profile and the first helix.

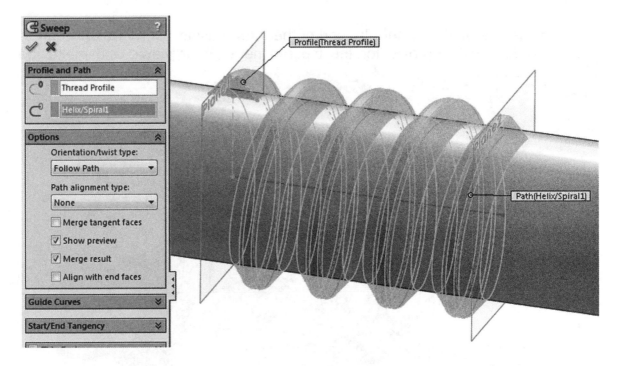

- In the plane at the right of the "*Gear Width*" sketch add a sketch to start a second Helix using "Convert Entities," and make the helix activating the "Taper Helix" option with a 7deg taper.

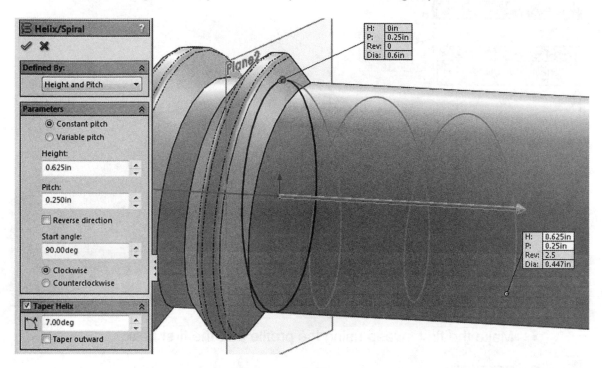

- Add a sketch at the flat end of the thread using **"Convert Entities"** to use as the profile for the tapered helix (Rear view), and make the sweep.

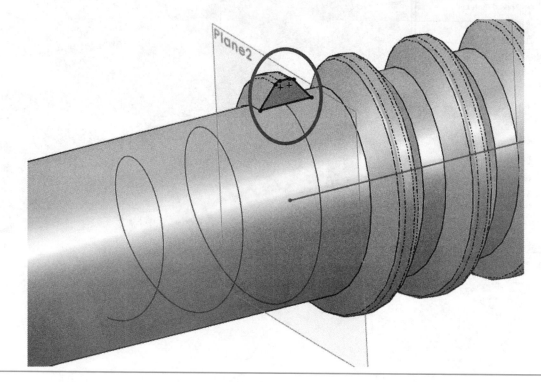

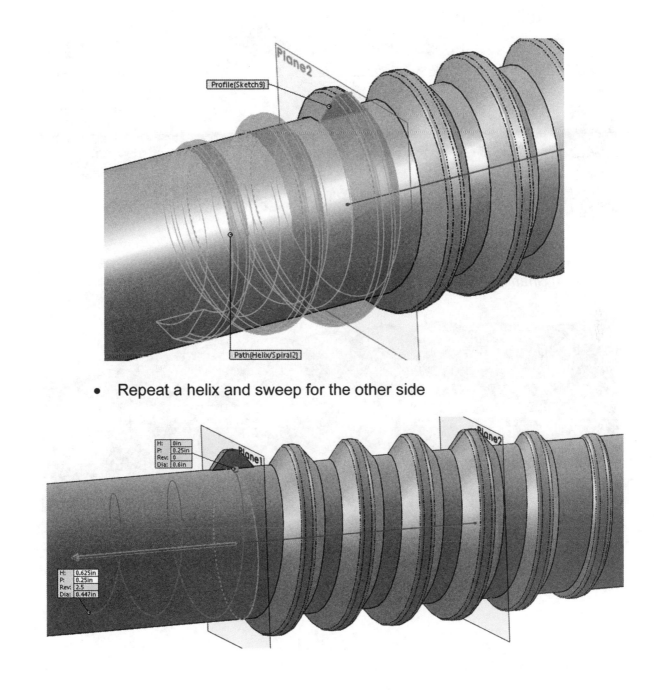

- Repeat a helix and sweep for the other side

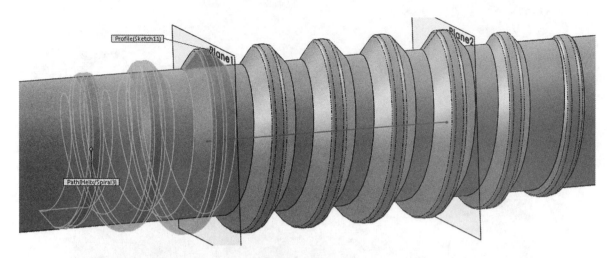

- Add a 0.015" fillet to round the edges of the thread. Save as '*Offset Shaft Gear*' and close.

- **Worm Gear**: Open the '*Worm Gear*' part and change "*Fillet1*" to a 0.031" radius

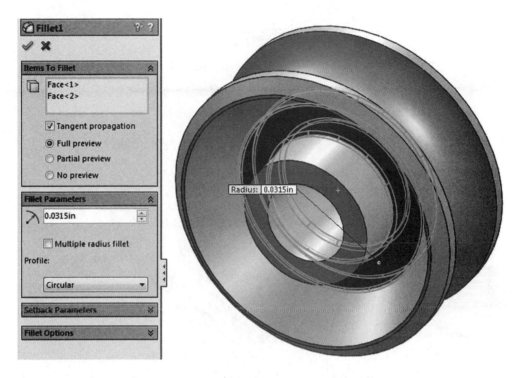

- Modify the following dimensions from the "Cut-Revolved2" feature and rebuild the model to continue.

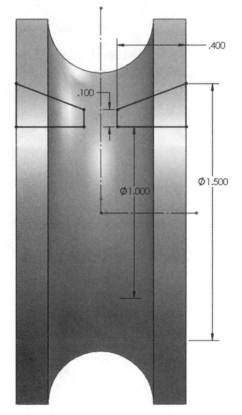

- Add a new parallel plane 0.95" above the *"Top Plane."*

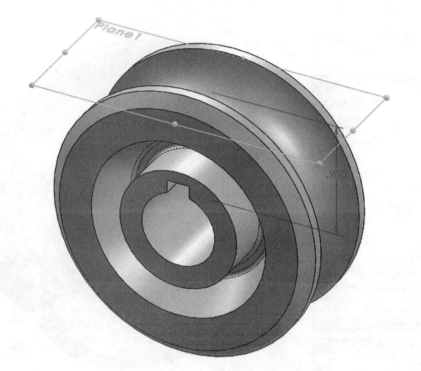

- Add the following sketch in the plane made previously, exit the sketch, and rename it "Path."

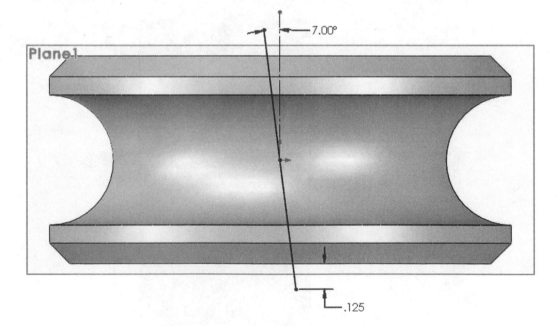

- Add a new auxiliary plane perpendicular to the "*Path*" sketch. Rename it "*Profile Plane*."

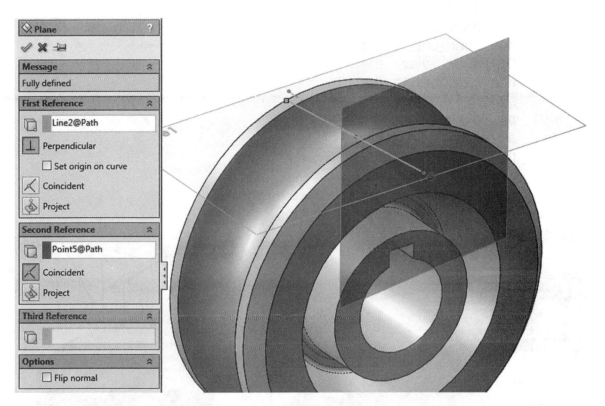

- Add this sketch in the "*Right Plane*" and make a revolved cut. Notice the doubled diameter dimension about the centerline (Auxiliary planes have been turned off for clarity.)

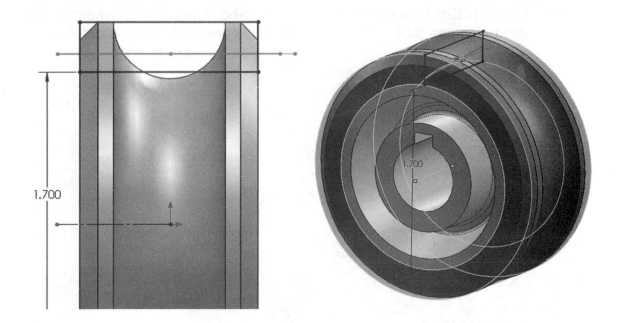

- In the "*Profile Plane*" add the following sketch. This will be the profile to make the gear cut. Press Ctrl+8 to view the plane normal to the screen. Locate the profile sketch adding a pierce relation to the "Path" sketch at the indicated point. Exit the sketch and rename "*Gear Profile*"

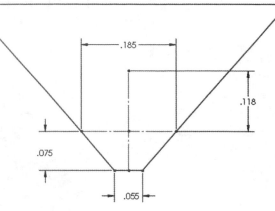

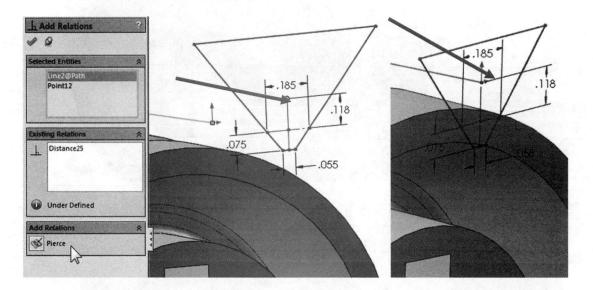

- Make a "**Cut Sweep**" using the "*Path*" and "*Gear Profile*" sketches (In this particular case a "Cut Extrude" would give us the same result.)

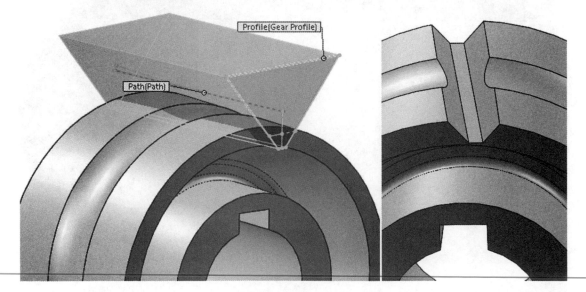

- Add a 0.015" fillet at the bottom of the sweep cut.

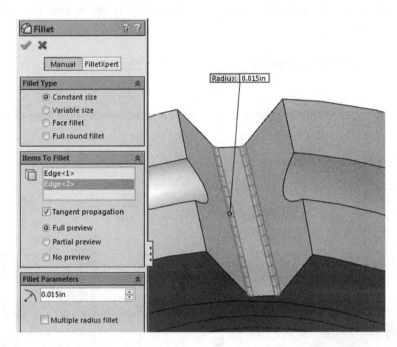

- Make a circular pattern with 22 copies of the Cut-Sweep and the previous fillet. After the pattern is complete add a 0.015" fillet to the "*Cut-Revolve1*" and "*Cut-Revolve3*" features to finish the gear.

Save as '*Worm Gear Complete*' and close.

Engine Project Parts: Make the following components to build the engine. Save the parts using the name provided. High resolution images are included in the accompanying disc.

Hint: Make a revolved boss with the option "Thin Feature."

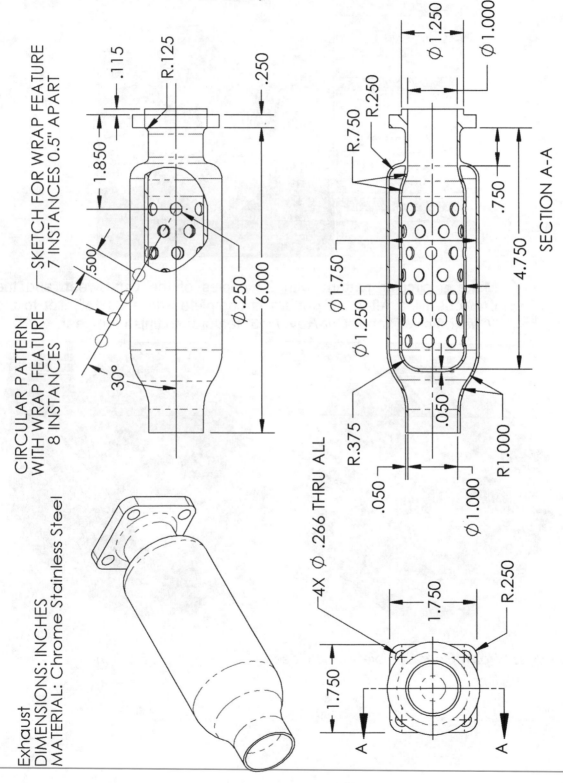

CIRCULAR PATTERN
WITH WRAP FEATURE
8 INSTANCES

SKETCH FOR WRAP FEATURE
7 INSTANCES 0.5" APART

SECTION A-A

Exhaust
DIMENSIONS: INCHES
MATERIAL: Chrome Stainless Steel

Final Parts for the Engine Project: The following components are the last required to complete the engine. Save the parts using the name provided.

Suggested sequence of features for the **Crank case top**

Main body	Corner Fillets	Flange	Bearing mount boss
Mirror bearing mount	Shell part	Top cut	add 0.375" offset plane inside
Add inside bosses. Use Intersecting curve	Add front reinforcement	Add rear reinforcement	Add bearing mount
Add plane for oil dipstick	Add reference sketch for dipstick	Add plane at top of reference sketch	Add dipstick extrusion
Make hole for dipstick	Add sweep cut for threaded cap	Add fillets	Add holes and threads

Crank Case Top (2 Pages)

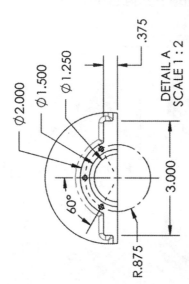

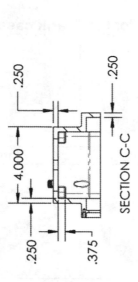

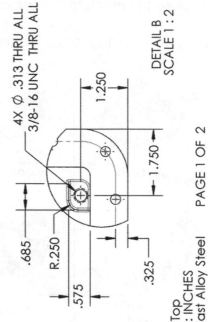

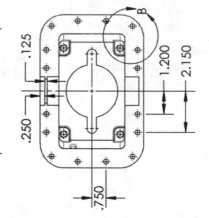

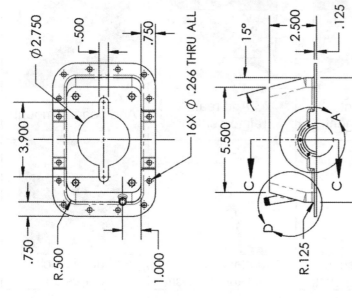

DETAIL A
SCALE 1 : 2

SECTION C-C

DETAIL B
SCALE 1 : 2

Crank Case Top
DIMENSIONS: INCHES
MATERIAL: Cast Alloy Steel   PAGE 1 OF 2

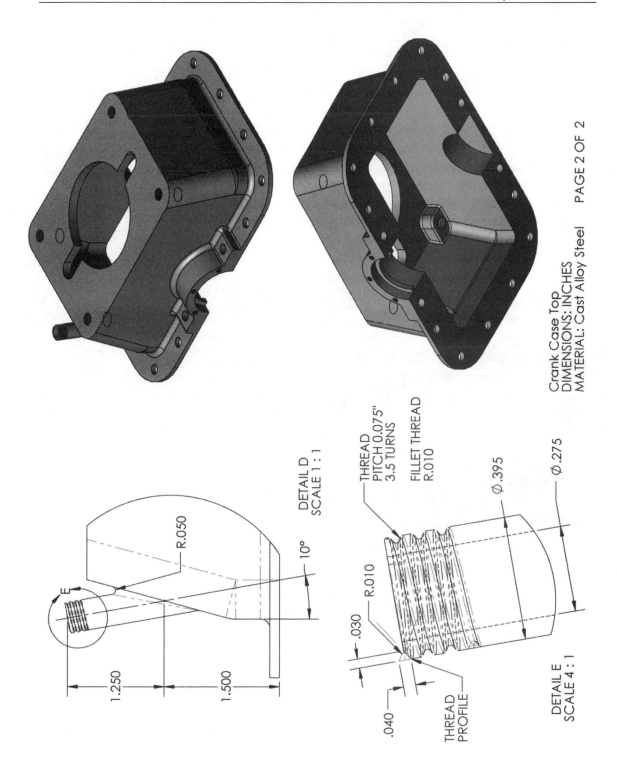

DETAIL D
SCALE 1 : 1

R.050

10°

1.250

1.500

THREAD
PITCH 0.075"
3.5 TURNS

FILLET THREAD
R.010

Ø.395

Ø.275

R.010

.030

.040

THREAD
PROFILE

DETAIL E
SCALE 4 : 1

Crank Case Top
DIMENSIONS: INCHES
MATERIAL: Cast Alloy Steel   PAGE 2 OF 2

Oil Pan

Base extrusion	Fillet corners	Base flange	Bearing mount boss
Shell the part	Reinforcement	Screw mount reinforcements	Fillets
Add bearing mount	Add threads and screws		

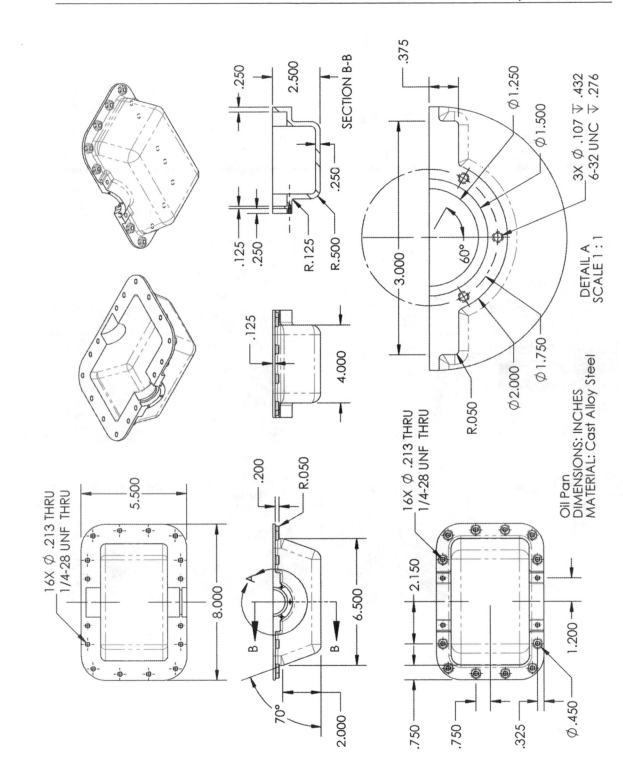

SECTION B-B

DETAIL A
SCALE 1 : 1

3X ⌀ .107 ⫧ .432
6-32 UNC ⫧ .276

⌀ 1.250
⌀ 1.500
⌀ 1.750
⌀ 2.000
R.050

.375
2.500
.250
.250
.125
R.125
R.500
3.000
60°

.125
4.000

16X ⌀ .213 THRU
1/4-28 UNF THRU

5.500
8.000
.200
R.050
6.500
70°
2.000
A
B
B

16X ⌀ .213 THRU
1/4-28 UNF THRU

2.150
1.200
.750
.750
.325
⌀ .450

Oil Pan
DIMENSIONS: INCHES
MATERIAL: Cast Alloy Steel

249

Engine Block

Main body	First fin	Pattern fins	Cuts for Intake/Exhaust
Base extrusion	Intake mount	Exhaust mount	Cylinder Bore
Mounting holes	Screw holes	Exhaust mount hole	Intake mount hole
Head mounting holes	Intake vent hole	Chamfer bottom holes	Round all edges

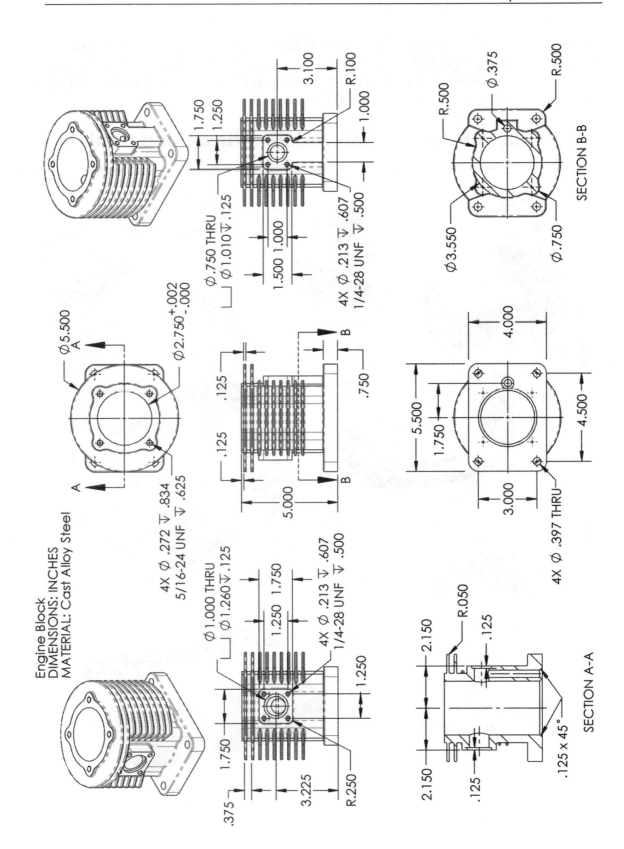

Engine Block
DIMENSIONS: INCHES
MATERIAL: Cast Alloy Steel

SECTION B-B

SECTION A-A

Extra Credit: Visit our web site to download details for the *Gas Grill* project as well as the finished parts for this book, higher resolution images of the exercises and some extra topics not covered in the book. Build these components and after the Assembly lesson make the Gas Grill assembly.

http://www.mechanicad.com/download.html

Detail Drawing

Now that we have completed modeling the components, it's time to make the 2D detail drawings for manufacturing. In SolidWorks, first we make the 3D models and from them we can derive the 2D drawings. By deriving the drawing from the solid model, the 2D drawing is linked and associated to the part. This means that if the part is changed, the drawing will be updated and vice versa. Drawing files in SolidWorks have the extension *.slddrw and each drawing can contain multiple sheets; each corresponding to a different printed page of the same or different 3D models (parts and/or assemblies.)

SolidWorks offers a simple to use environment where we can easily create 2D drawings of parts and assemblies. In this section we'll cover Part drawings only. Assembly drawings will be covered after the assembly section. We will add different model views, annotations, dimensions, sections, and details necessary for a manufacturing department to fabricate the component without missing any details. In this section we will also introduce a new concept called **Configurations**, which allow us to show different versions of the same part, for example, a version for the part as it comes out of the foundry and a version for the machine shop with all the details to machine the finished part.

We can create our 2D drawings using any of the many dimensioning standards available in the industry. In this book we will use the ANSI standard. Once in a drawing, the dimensioning standard can be easily changed to a different one by going to the menu "**Tools, Options**" and selecting the "Document Properties" tab. In the Drafting Standard section we can select the desired detailing standard. It is important to note that after changing a standard, SolidWorks will change the dimension styles, arrow head type, etc. accordingly. For more information on changing units see the Appendix.

The detailing environment of SolidWorks is a true What-You-See-Is-What-You-Get interface. When we make a new drawing, we are asked what size of drawing sheet we want to use unless we are using a template with a predefined sheet size. This size corresponds to the printed sheet size. Do not be too concerned about selecting the right sheet size, as it can be changed to a larger or smaller size at any time if we find that our drawing will not fit the current sheet, and at the time of printing a drawing it can be scaled up or down to fit the available printer size.

Notes:

Drawing One: The Housing

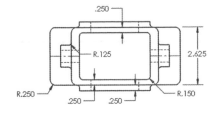

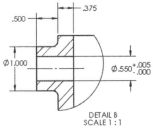

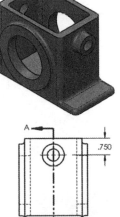

DETAIL B
SCALE 1 : 1

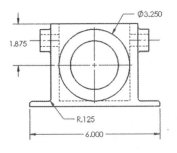

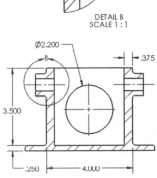

SECTION A-A

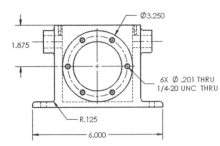

4X Ø .107 ▼ .432
6-32 UNC ▼ .276

DETAIL E
SCALE 1 : 1

DETAIL D
SCALE 1 : 1

Ø.575 +.005 -.000

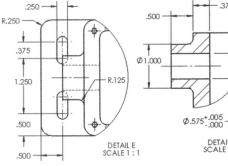

6X Ø .201 THRU
1/4-20 UNC THRU

SECTION C-C

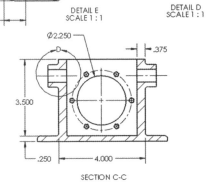

Notes:

In this lesson we'll learn how to make configurations of a part, how to make a multi sheet drawing with the different configurations, add views including sections and details, change a drawing's view display style, move the views within the drawing sheet, import model dimensions and manipulate them. The detail drawing of the *'Housing'* part will follow the next sequence.

Add Configuration	Make new drawing	Insert drawing views	Shaded Isometric
Add Section view	Add Detail view	Import Annotations	Arrange Annotations
Add drawing sheet	Change Configuration	Add new Detail view	Import Missing Annotations

201. - The first thing we need to do is to make a new **Configuration** of the *'Housing'* part. SolidWorks' Configurations allow us to make slightly or considerably different versions of a part without having to make a new part, in order to show or document different states of a component or a different but similar part. In our example, we'll have a configuration of the *'Housing'* as it comes out of the foundry, and another of the finished part for the machine shop including all the details that need to be machined in the cast part. We can configure many different things including dimensions, tolerance, suppressed features, etc.

Open the *'Housing'* part and activate the **"ConfigurationManager"** tab. The Configuration Manager is where we can add, delete and change between the different configurations of a part. We can find it at the top of the FeatureManager; it's the third tab at the top as indicated.

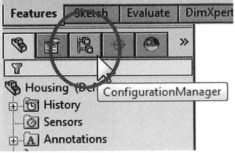

There is always one configuration called *'Default'*. Once the ConfigurationManager is selected, we can add a new configuration by right-mouse-clicking at the top of the ConfigurationManager in the part's name, in this case *'Housing'*, and selecting the "**Add Configuration**…" option. Name the new configuration *"Forge"* and click OK. Adding a comment and/or a description are optional.

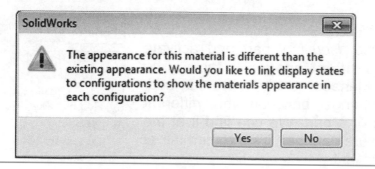

After adding the configuration you may be warned about the material's appearance, and if you'd like to link the display state to show the material's appearance in the configuration. Press "Yes" if asked.

202.- After adding the new configuration, we'll rename the "Default" configuration. Right-mouse-click in it and select "Properties" and change its name to *"Machined*." As before, adding a description is optional. Click OK when finished.

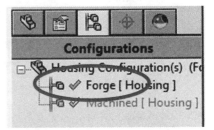

 Configurations can also be renamed using the slow double click method.

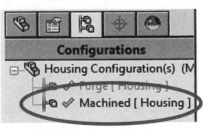

203.- In the ConfigurationManager, the yellow colored configuration with the Green checkmark is the currently active configuration; all others are grayed out. To switch to a different configuration we can double-click an inactive configuration's name or right-mouse-click and select "**Show Configuration**" from the pop-up menu.

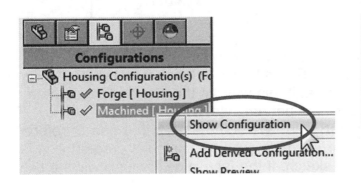

204. - Activate the *"Forge"* configuration (it will have the green checkmark), and change to the FeatureManager tab. Notice that next to the name of the part at the top of the FeatureManager we can see the name of the currently active configuration.

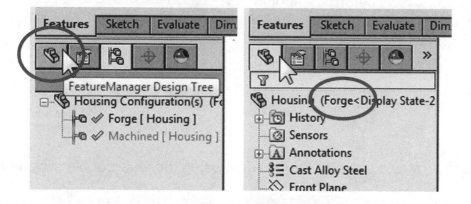

In the *"Forge"* configuration, we'll **"Suppress"** all the features that cannot be made when casting the part, and make the holes smaller to machine them to size later. Essentially, suppressing a feature will tell SolidWorks to *NOT* make it. It will still be listed in the FeatureManager, but will be grayed out. For all practical purposes a suppressed feature doesn't exist in the model, and, since it is not created, the model's mass properties will be affected.

205. - First, select the *'1/4-20 Tapped Hole1'* from the FeatureManager (which cannot be made in a foundry), and from the pop-up toolbar select the **"Suppress"** icon. After suppressing a feature its name will be grayed out. Remember that **we are not deleting it**; it's still there, but it is suppressed.

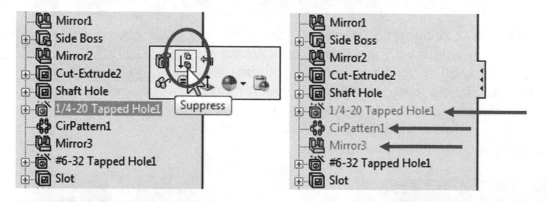

Notice that the two features after the one we suppressed, *"CirPattern1"* and *"Mirror3"* were also suppressed. This is because these features are 'children' of the *"1/4-20 Tapped Hole1."* Look at it this way: if there is no tapped hole, we cannot pattern it, and if there is no pattern, we cannot mirror it either. The "Parent/Child" relations are created when we add features that use or reference existing features in the model. For example, when a sketch is created in a face, the face becomes a parent to the sketch. If the face is deleted, so will the sketch and so on.

Parent/Child relations can be found by right-mouse-clicking on a feature and from the pop-up menu selecting "**Parent/Child**."

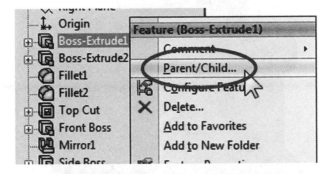

206. - Now suppress the *"#6-32 Tapped Hole1"* and the *"Slot"* features. All the children features of *"Slot"* are suppressed as well.

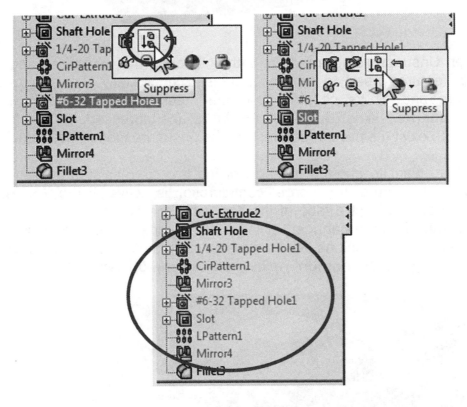

207. -The reverse process to Suppressing a feature is "**Unsuppress**." Select a suppressed feature and click on the "Unsuppress" icon (the icon with the arrow pointing up.) Do not unsuppress any features at this time; we are just explaining how to do it, we'll get to it later.

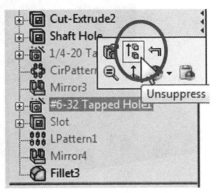

261

Our "*Forge*" configuration now looks like this:

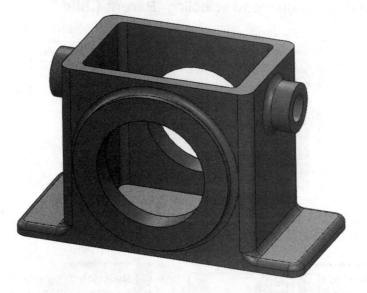

When Unsuppressing a feature with children in the FeatureManager, the child features need to be Unsuppressed individually. To unsuppress a feature and all its children, use the menu "**Edit, Unsuppress with Dependents**." When a feature (child) is unsuppressed, all the features needed for it to exist (its parent features) will be unsuppressed at the same time.

208. - Next we want to change the size of the two circular cuts in the *"Forge"* configuration. Make sure the *"Forge"* configuration is active. If the "**Instant 3D**" command is active, select a face of the first cut in the screen or double click in the feature in the FeatureManager, or in one of its faces in the graphics area to reveal the feature's dimensions. Right-mouse-click in the diameter dimension and select the "**Configure Dimension**" option from the pop-up menu.

In the "**Modify Configurations**" table, change the value of the diameter in the *"Forge"* configuration to 2.200″. The idea is to have a smaller hole made in the forge, and machine it to size later (*Machined* configuration.) Leave the *"Machined"* configuration value as 2.250″ and click "OK" to finish. Notice the change in the hole size. Using this approach we can change a dimension's value for multiple configurations at the same time regardless of the active configuration.

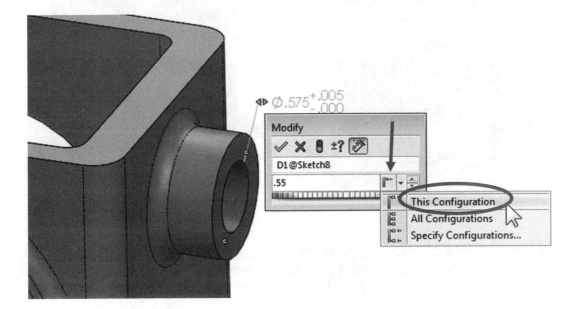

209. - A different way to configure dimensions is by double-clicking a dimension, and when the "Modify" dialog comes up we can select which configurations to modify; after adding configurations, the "Modify" dialog adds a configuration icon at the end of the value. This icon helps us define if we want to change the dimension's value for "This Configuration," "All Configurations" or "Specify Configurations." Keep in mind that this icon will only be visible *IF* we have more than one configuration in the part. Double-click the *"Shaft Hole"* feature to display it's dimensions, double-click the diameter dimension and change the value to 0.55". Make sure we are only changing the value of this configuration by selecting the configuration button and selecting "This Configuration." Click OK to finish. Using "This Configuration" affects only the active configuration.

210. - An easy way to work with configurations is by viewing both the **FeatureManager** and the **ConfigurationManager** at the same time by splitting the FeatureManager pane. Move the mouse pointer to the top of the FeatureManager and look for the "split" feedback icon, then click-and-drag down. We can view Features in the top pane and Configurations in the bottom pane.

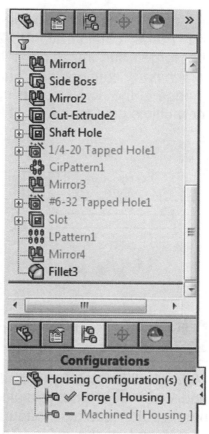

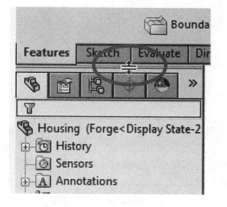

Now that we have made some changes to the *"Forge"* configuration, double click on each configuration to activate it and see what each one of them looks like. Notice the missing features (suppressed) and different sizes of the holes in the *"Forge"* configuration. Save the changes to the *'Housing'* part.

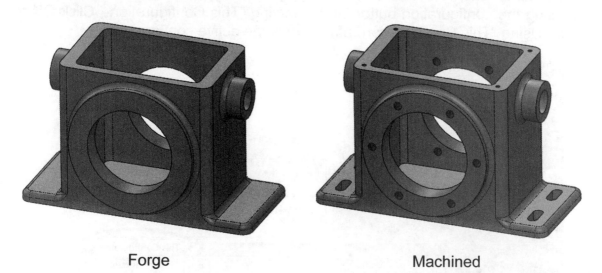

Forge   Machined

We can add as many configurations as needed, but when we have more than 2 or 3 configurations it is easier to manage them with a table. Design Tables are very powerful and will be covered later in the book.

211. - After adding the configurations to the '*Housing*' we'll make the detail drawing. Make sure the *"Forge"* configuration is active and select the menu "**File, Make Drawing from Part**" or from the "**New**" document drop-down command. This way the first drawing will be made using the *"Forge"* configuration. We'll add the *"Machined"* configuration drawing later.

212. - After selecting the drawing template we are asked to select a sheet size to use for this drawing. For Sheet Size select "B-Landscape," and turn off the "**Display Sheet Format**" option.

 The "Sheet Format" is the part of the drawing that contains the title block and related annotations. It will be covered in detail later. We are not including it at this time to focus on basic drawing functionality instead.

213. - After selecting the sheet size, a new drawing is opened and SolidWorks is ready for us to choose the views that we want in the drawing. The "**View Palette**" is automatically displayed; make sure the "Auto-start projected view" option is active, as this option will help us save us time when locating the views in the drawing.

214. -From the "**View Palette**" drag-and-drop the "Front" view onto the sheet.

215. - Locate the "Front" view in the lower left part of the sheet where we have enough room to add the other views. After locating the "Front" view on the sheet, SolidWorks automatically starts the "**Projected View**" command; to add the rest of the views, move the mouse in the direction of the view needed, and click to locate it on the sheet. As a guide, after adding the "Front" view, move the mouse pointer above it and click to locate the "Top" view (you will be able to see a preview), then click above to the right where the Isometric view will be and finally click to the right to locate the "Right" view. When we are done adding views, click "OK" or press the "Esc" key to finish. Your drawing should now look approximately like this:

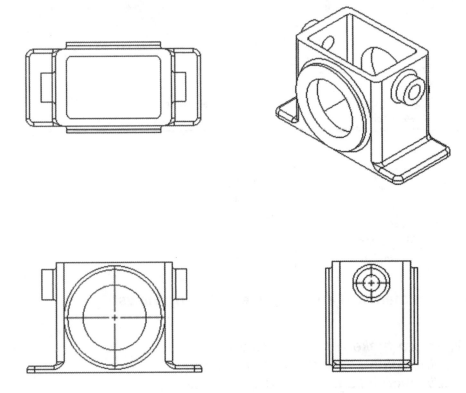

216. - Click to Select the "Front" view in the graphics area and change the Display Style to "**Hidden Lines Visible**" from the view's PropertyManager. This change will update the rest of the views, since they were projected from the "Front" view and by default they use the parent view's display style.

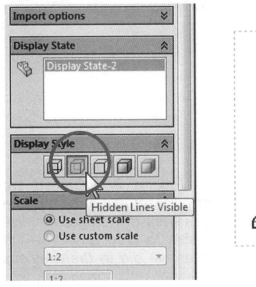

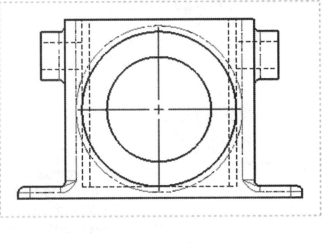

 The option to set the default display style and tangent edge visibility for new views can be changed in the menu "**Tools, Options, System Options**" under "**Display Style**."

System Options - Display Style

| System Options | Document Properties |

General
Drawings
   ├─ Display Style
   └─ Area Hatch/Fill
Colors
Sketch
   └─ Relations/Snaps
Display/Selection
Performance
Assemblies
External References
Default Templates

Display style
- ○ Wireframe
- ○ Hidden lines visible
- ● Hidden lines removed
- ○ Shaded with edges
- ○ Shaded

Tangent edges
- ○ Visible
- ● Use font
  - ☐ Hide ends
- ○ Removed

 ### *Adding standard and projected drawing views*

*When we make a new drawing from a part using the menu "**Make Drawing from Part**," SolidWorks automatically displays the "**View Palette**." However, if we make a new drawing using the "**New Document**" icon, we get a different behavior. To test it, select the "**New Document**" icon and create a Drawing by selecting the "**Drawing**" template using the same settings as before. In this case, we are presented with an empty drawing. (If the "Model View" command is loaded, cancel it.)*

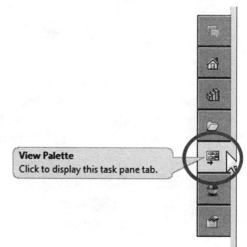

View Palette
Click to display this task pane tab.

To activate the View Palette, click in the View Palette icon from the Task Pane on the right side of the screen to display it.

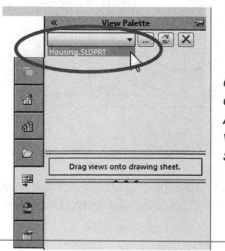

Once the "View Palette" is displayed, we can browse for a part or assembly or select one of the open documents from the drop-down list. At this time we'll be able to drag and drop the views onto the sheet as we did in the previous step.

217. - Now that we have the views in place, we want to show the Isometric view in "**Shaded with Edges**" mode. Click to select the "Isometric" view on the screen, and click the "**Shaded with Edges**" icon either in the "**Display Style**" toolbar or in the PropertyManager as in the previous step. Notice the dotted line around the view; this is an indication that the view is selected. Using this procedure, we can change any drawing view to any display mode as needed.

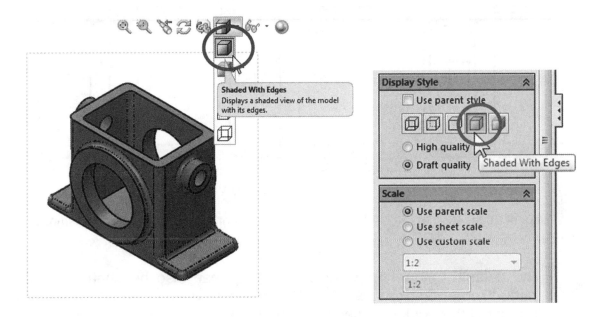

218. - In the drawing views we may or may not want to see the tangent edges of a model. A tangent edge is where a curved face and a flat face have a tangent transition, as in fillets. SolidWorks has three different ways to show them: Visible, With Font, or Removed. Right-mouse-click inside the Front view, and from the pop-up menu select the option "**Tangent Edge, Tangent Edges Removed**." Repeat for the Top and Right views.

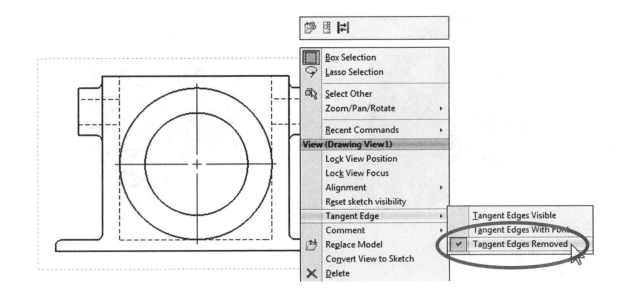

The differences between tangent edge display types are visible in this table. **"Tangent Edges Visible"** shows all model edges with a solid line, **"Tangent Edges with Font"** shows tangent edges with a dashed line, and **"Tangent Edges Removed"** eliminates the tangent edges from the view.

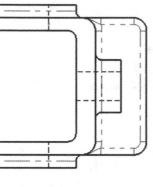

| Tangent Edges Visible | Tangent Edges With Font | Tangent Edges Removed |

The default Tangent Edge display settings can also be changed in the menu **"Tools, Options, System Options, Drawings, Display Style."** For the rest of this book we'll use "Tangent Edges With Font."

219. - The next thing we want to do in the drawing is to move the views to arrange them in the sheet. To move a view, click-and-drag it either from it's border or any model edge in the view.

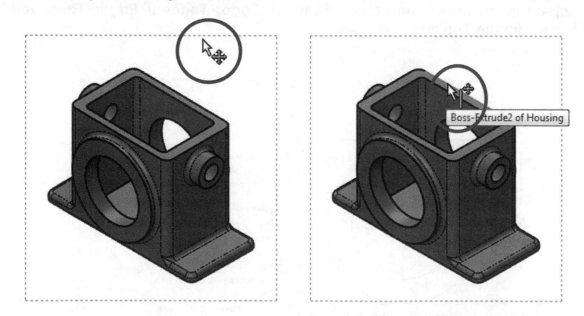

220. - Click-and-drag the drawing views in the drawing sheet and arrange them as shown, with "**Tangent Edges Removed**" for all views, and the Isometric with "**Shaded with Edges**" display. This layout will allow enough space to import the dimensions into the drawing. Make sure the drawing's units are set to inches and three decimal places.

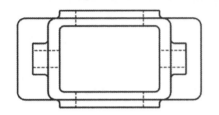

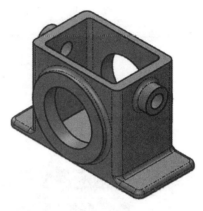

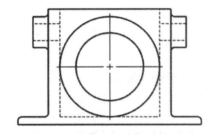

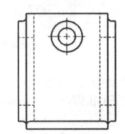

 Notice the toolbars available in the CommandManager were automatically changed to match the detail drawing environment in which we are now. The Features tab was replaced by View Layout and Annotation, with tools and commands for detailing.

221. - To make an easier to read drawing we'll add a section of the Right view. Select the "**Section View**" command from the View Layout tab in the CommandManager.

222. - From the **"Section View"** properties, select "Vertical" from the "Cutting Line" options. In the graphics area move the mouse pointer close to the center of the "Right" view and look for the section line preview. To locate the section line, move the mouse pointer and click when it snaps to the center of the *'Housing'*.

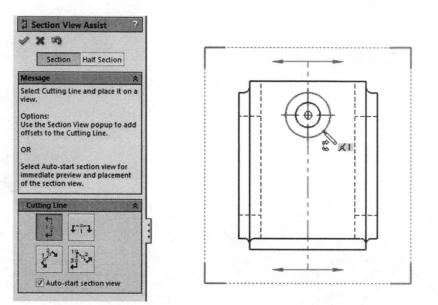

We can zoom in or out in the Drawing using the mouse scroll wheel. SolidWorks will zoom in or out at the location of the mouse pointer.

223. - Immediately after locating the section line in the middle, move the mouse to see a dynamic preview showing the section of the *'Housing'* overlapping the Right view.

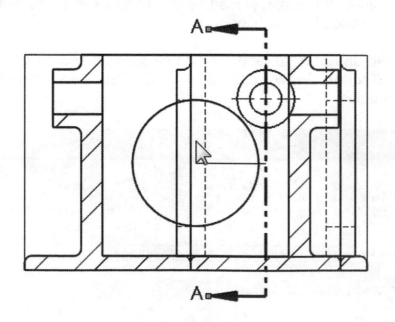

The last thing to do is to locate the section view in the sheet. Move the mouse to the left and click between the Front and Right views to locate it. If needed, after locating the Section view move the other views to arrange and space them.

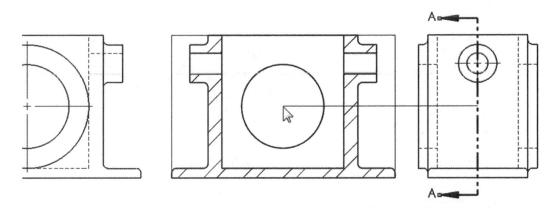

Using the mouse wheel we can manipulate the drawing sheet's view. Use the wheel to zoom in and out and the middle mouse button (Press the wheel down) to move the drawing (Pan). We can do this while positioning the section view or any other view.

Selecting the Section View we can see its Properties, where we can change different options such as the Section Label, reverse the section direction ("Flip Direction"), Display Style, Scale, etc. Change the Section View's display style to "**Hidden Lines Removed**" for clarity if needed. By default, the section will inherit the display style of the view from which it was made.

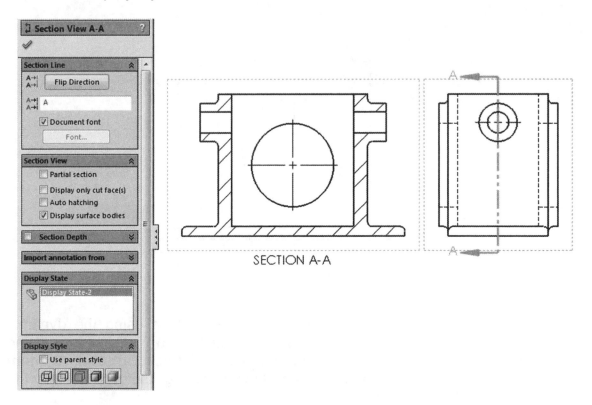

SECTION A-A

224. - The next step is to add a "**Detail View"** to allow us to zoom in an area of the drawing. From the View Layout tab in the CommandManager, select the "**Detail View**" icon. After selecting it we are asked to draw a circle in the area that we want to make a detail of.

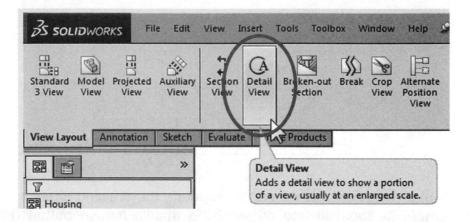

To draw sketch elements without automatically adding geometric relations to other geometry, hold down the "Ctrl" key while drawing. This technique works in the part, assembly, and detailing environments.

225. - Draw a circle in the upper left area of the "Section" view we just made trying not to add automatic relations when drawing the circle by holding the Ctrl key while drawing it, and just like the "Section" view...

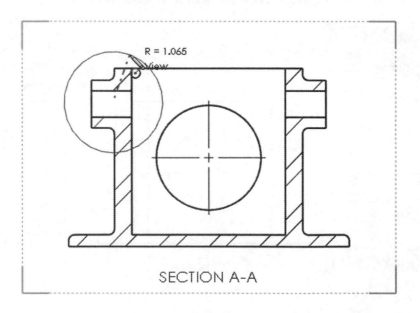

...move the mouse to locate the Detail above the section using the dynamic preview. By default, detail views are two times bigger than the view they came from. This option can be changed in the menu "**Tools, Options, System Options, Drawings**" and change the "**Detail view scaling**" factor to multiply the scale of the view the detail came from.

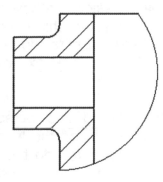

DETAIL B
SCALE 1 : 1

 If the detail is not as big as needed, click-and-drag the detail's circle and/or its center to resize and move the detail area; the Detail view will update dynamically, that is the reason why we don't want to add any geometric relations when drawing the detail's circle, to be able to move it if needed.

 Alternatively we can draw the circle (or any closed contour like an ellipse, a polygon, or a spline) and then select the "**Detail View**" icon and use that profile for the detail view.

226. - Now that we have all the views needed in the drawing, the next step is to import the '*Housing's*' dimensions from the part (the 3D model) into the drawing (the 2D drawing.) If you remember, when we modeled the part we added all the necessary dimensions to define it, and now we can import those dimensions into the detail drawing, effectively reducing the amount of work needed to complete this task.

Select "**Model Items**" from the Annotation tab in the CommandManager or go to the menu "**Insert, Model Items.**"

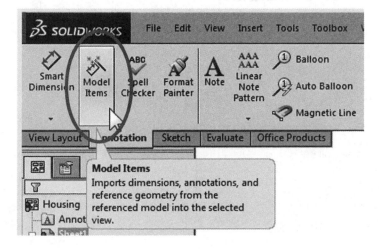

227. - In the "Model Items" options select the type of dimensions and annotations we want to import into the drawing. For this exercise select the options listed below. Remember to select "Source: Entire Model" to import the dimensions of the entire *'Housing'*, and activate the checkbox "**Import items into all views**" to add all dimensions to all views.

"Dimensions Marked for Drawing" is selected by default, optionally we can activate "Hole Wizard Locations" to import the location of holes made using the Hole Wizard command, "Hole Callout" to add the machining annotations to the holes made with the Hole Wizard, and Tolerenced Dimensions to import dimensions with tolerances. 3D model items available for import into a detail drawing include notes, datum, welding annotations, Geometric Tolerances (GD&T), reference geometry (axes, planes, coordinate axes, etc), surfaces, center of mass and others.

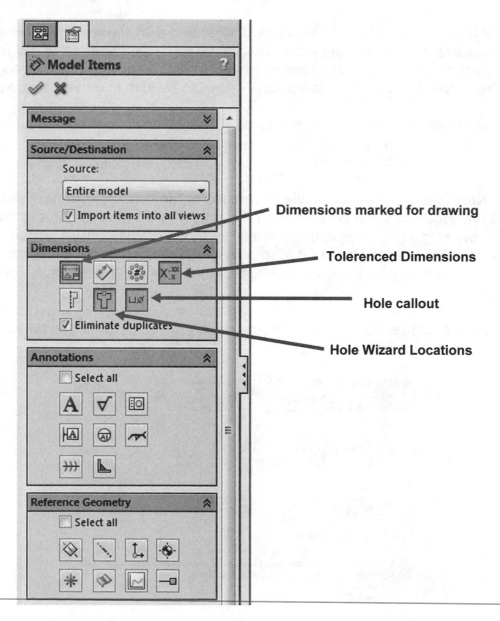

228. - After selecting the model items needed click OK. SolidWorks will import the dimensions and annotations to all views, attempting to arrange them automatically in the view that shows it better. Dimensions are first added to Detail views, then to Section views, and finally main views. The for this order is because Detail Views show more model details, Section Views often show otherwise hidden features, and finally the main views show the major features. While SolidWorks makes a good job at adding dimensions to views, they are not always added to the view that best displays it, and here is where we have to do some work.

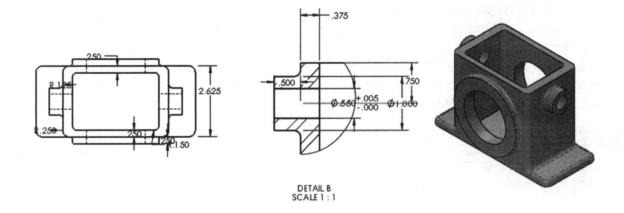

DETAIL B
SCALE 1 : 1

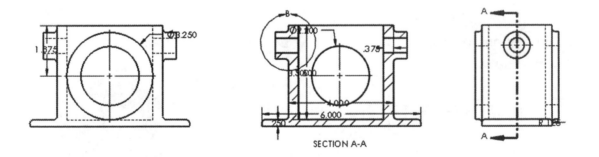

SECTION A-A

 If the drawing's dimensions are not the desired units and decimal places, they can be changed them in the menu **"Tools, Options, Document Properties, Units"** or from the Unit System button in the status bar.

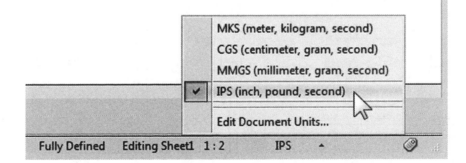

229. - All the dimensions that were added to the part when we made it, including sketch and feature dimensions have now been imported into the drawing. Now we need to arrange them in order to make our drawing easier to read. To arrange annotations in the drawing click-and-drag to locate them as needed.

Some of the dimensions added to a drawing view are incorrectly assigned and we need to move them to a different view. One way to tell which dimensions belong to a view is to move the view. All of the annotations attached to it will move at the same time.

To move a dimension from one view to another, hold down the "**Shift**" key, and while holding it down, drag the dimension to the view where we want it. Remember that the dimension has to be dragged inside the border of the view wanted. Keep in mind that a dimension can only be moved to another view if the dimension can be correctly displayed in it. Arrange the annotations as needed to make the drawing easy to read.

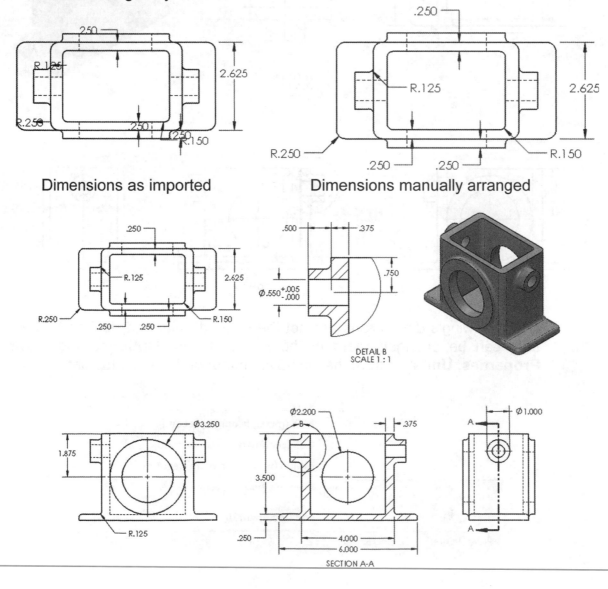

Dimensions as imported

Dimensions manually arranged

230. - If center marks are missing they can be added using the "**Center Mark**" command from the Annotation toolbar by selecting the "**Center Mark**" icon and clicking on the circular edges as needed. Click OK to finish when done.

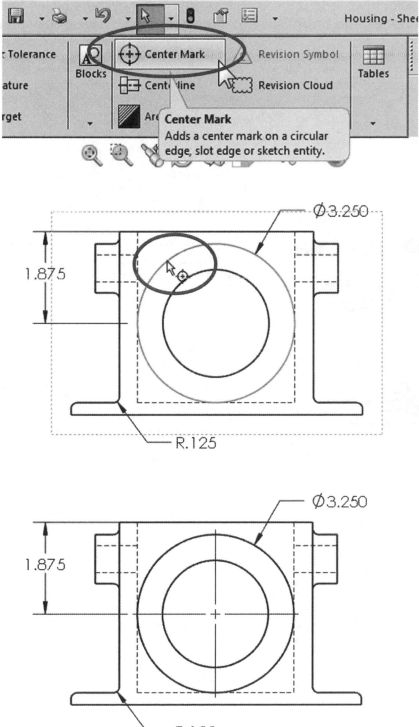

231. - Another annotation that may be missing from our drawing are the centerlines to indicate a cylindrical surface. To add centerlines to our drawing select the "**Centerline**" command from the Annotation tab in the CommandManager, or the menu "**Insert, Annotations, Centerline**." To add a centerline, select two edges or sketch segments, a cylindrical (as is our case) or a conical surface. Add the missing centerlines to all drawing views and click OK to finish.

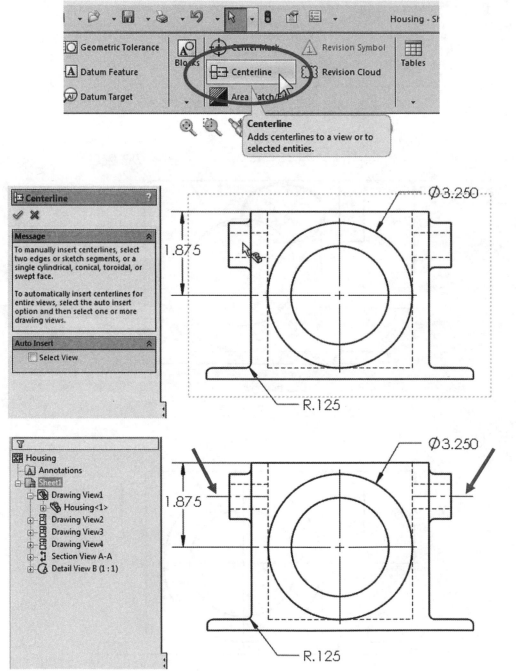

The "Auto Insert" option will add a centerline to every cylindrical face in a view.

232. - When arranging the dimensions in a drawing we may need (or want) to reverse the arrows of a dimension. To do this, select the dimension and click on the dots in the arrow heads to reverse them.

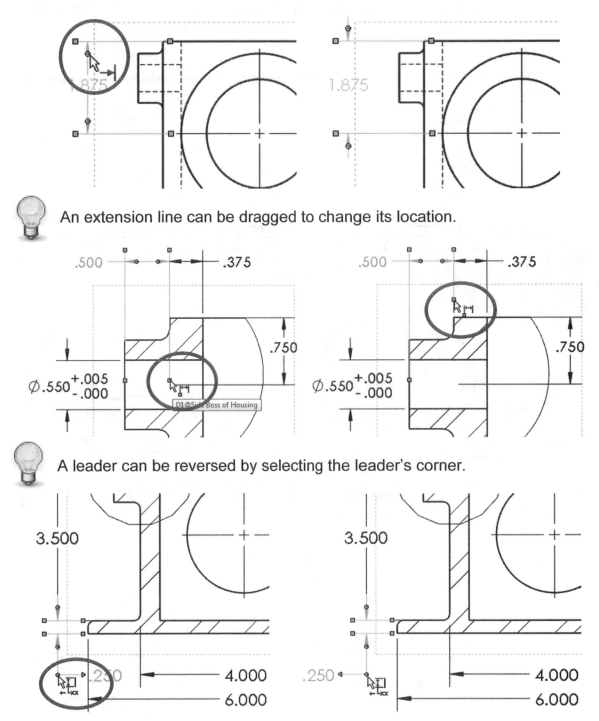

An extension line can be dragged to change its location.

A leader can be reversed by selecting the leader's corner.

To delete a duplicate or unwanted dimension select it and hit the "Delete" key. Note that we are only deleting it from the drawing and not from the 3D model. If the annotations and dimensions are re-imported into a drawing, SolidWorks will only add the missing (deleted) dimensions.

233. - Notice the tolerance for the *"Shaft Hole"* was carried over to the drawing from the 3D model. If we need to add a tolerance, change a dimension's precision or other parameters we can change them in the detail drawing using either the PropertyManager *or* the "**Dimension Palette.**" In the Dimension Palette we can change the precision, tolerance, add notes, parentheses, etc.

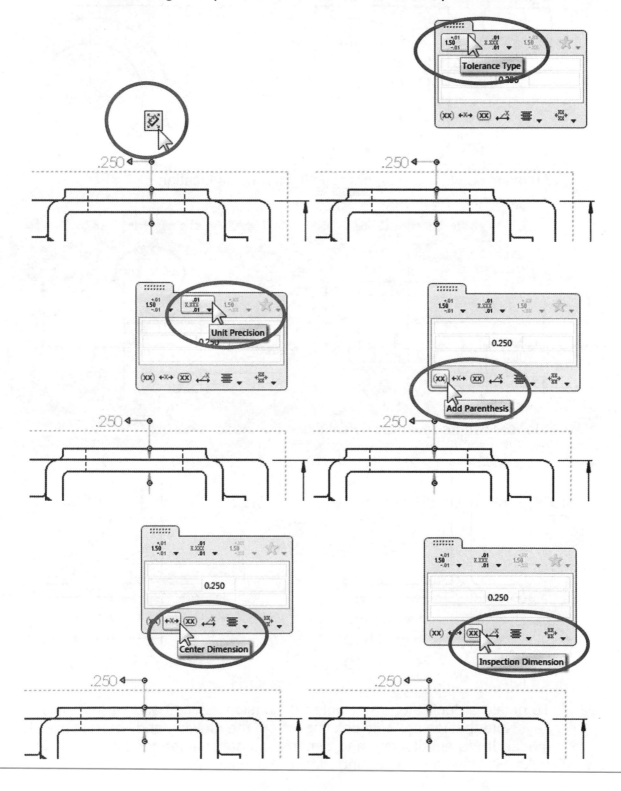

Your finished drawing for the *"Forge"* configuration should look like the next image.

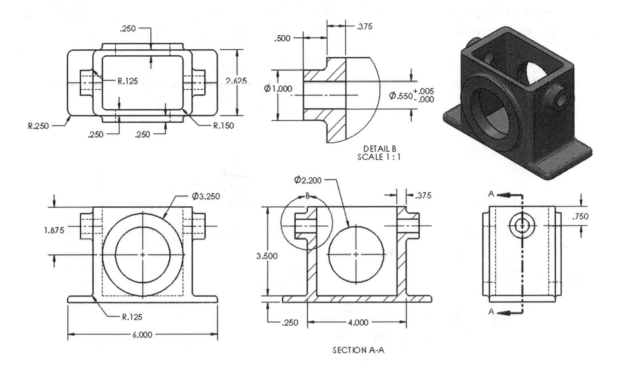

234. - Now that the Forge configuration drawing is finished, we need to add a second sheet to the drawing for the Machined configuration details to complete the '*Housing's* detail drawing. We can add a second sheet and add views and dimensions just as we did in the first sheet. A quicker way is to copy the drawing sheet we just finished, paste it into a new sheet and modify it to add the missing details. In the FeatureManager, right-mouse-click in *"Sheet1"* and select "**Copy**", then repeat and select "**Paste**" *or* select the menu "**Edit, Paste**" (shortcut Ctrl+V.)

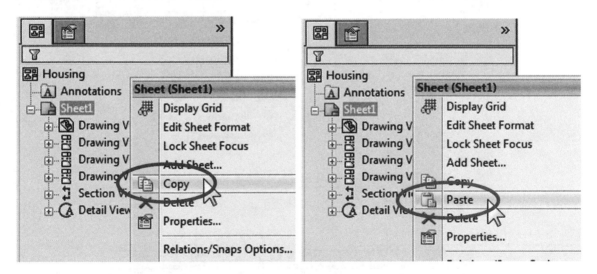

After selecting "**Paste**" from the menu, the "**Insert Paste**" dialog box is presented. Select the "After selected sheet" option to add the new sheet after the first one. When asked about renaming the drawing views, click 'Yes'; this option will rename the section and detail views to use the next available view labels, in our case the new section will become "**C**" and the new detail will be "**D**".

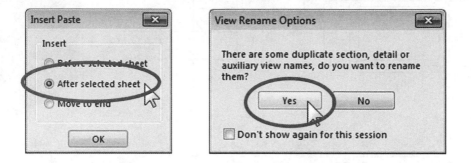

235. - Now we have a second sheet in the same drawing exactly the same as the first one, except for the view labels

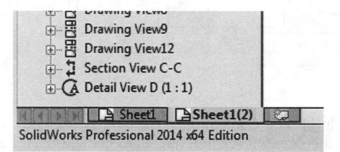

Drawing sheets can be renamed by right-mouse-clicking the sheet's tab or in the FeatureManager and selecting "Properties" or "Rename."
Rename *"Sheet1"* to *"Forge"* and *"Sheet1(2)"* to *"Machined."*

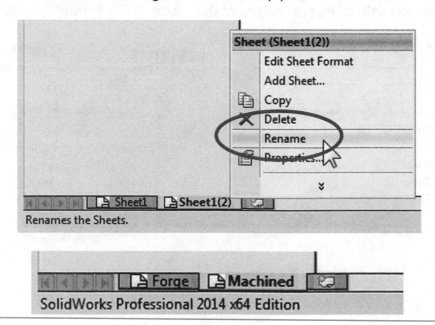

236. - After adding the second sheet we need to tell SolidWorks to show the *"Machined"* configuration in this sheet. If it's not already active, select the "Machined" sheet's tab on the lower left corner of the screen to activate it. Since this is a copy of the *"Forge"* drawing, we'll need to change the configuration displayed to *"Machined."* Select the Front view in the screen; in the drawing's properties select the "Reference Configuration" drop-down menu and select the *"Machined"* configuration. After selecting it the view is automatically updated. The other views will have an option to pick a configuration or link it to their parent view, which in our case is the Front view. The Section and Detail views don't have this option because they are linked to their parent view. As soon as the parent view is updated they are updated too.

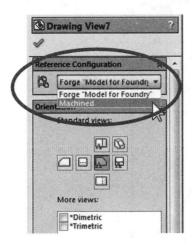

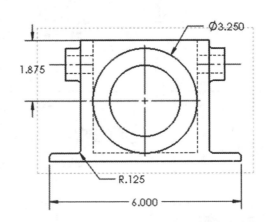

237. - After changing all views to the "*Machined*" configuration repeat the **"Model Items"** command to import the missing dimensions and annotations of this configuration. Be sure to include the "Hole Wizard Locations" and "Hole Callout" buttons. The holes made with the Hole Wizard include annotations with machining information. After the missing dimensions are added arrange them as needed in the different drawing views.

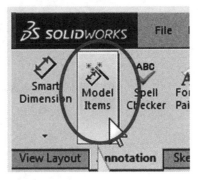

285

238. - Add the missing center marks to the circular array of tapped holes. Select the "**Center Mark**" icon from the Annotation tab, click in one hole's edge, and then click in the Propagate pop-up icon to add Center Marks to all the holes in the array of holes at the same time. SolidWorks recognizes the pattern and adds the corresponding center marks. In the Property Manager we can see the additional options for manually added center marks where we can change the style if needed.

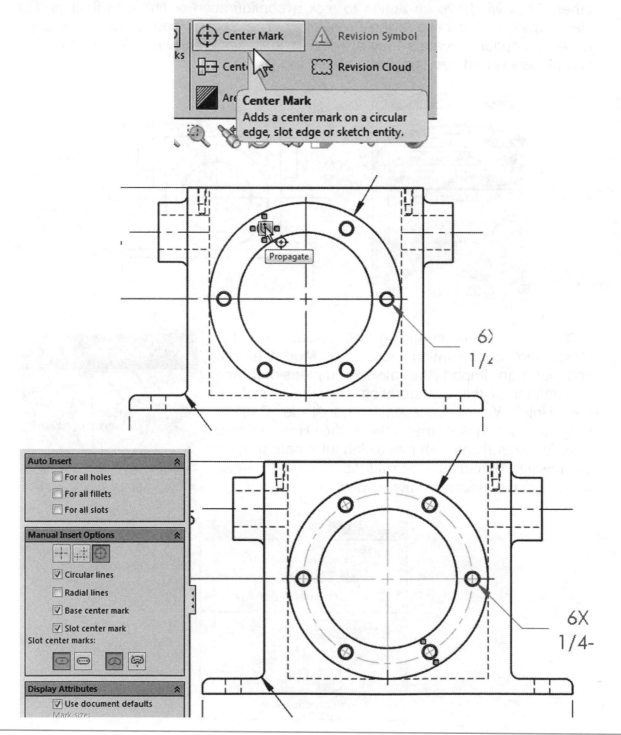

239. - To make the slot dimensions easier to view we'll add a new detail view in the slot area. Add the missing dimensions using the "**Smart Dimension**" tool or move the imported dimensions from the Top view to the new detail view using the "Shift-Drag" method. Remember to add the missing "**Center marks** as well. Next we'll add missing dimensions manually to complete the drawing.

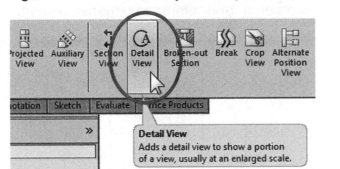

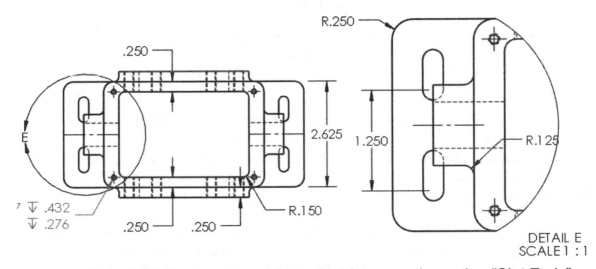

When adding the missing center marks to the slots, use the option "Slot Ends" as we'll need to add dimensions to locate them.

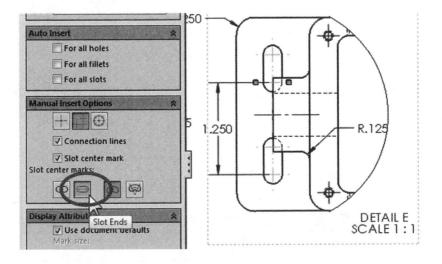

240. - The missing dimensions can be manually added just like we would add dimensions in a sketch. Select the "Smart Dimension" command and add the missing dimensions to locate the slot. These are now reference and not parametric dimensions, the difference is that a parametric dimension can be changed by double clicking in the drawing and the changes will be reflected in the 3D model and vice versa, and reference dimensions cannot be changed.

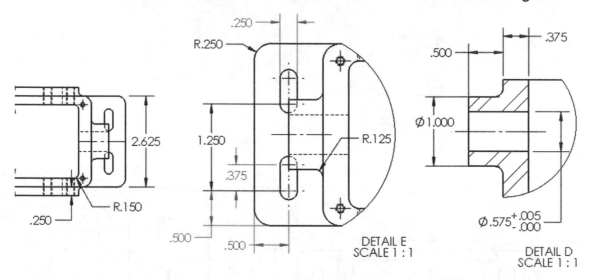

241. - Depending on system and template settings, manually added (reference) dimensions and annotations are grey by default, whereas parametric dimensions and annotations are black. In order to change the color of the reference annotations we need to add a new "Layer," make its color black and then assign the reference annotations to this layer.

If not visible, turn on the "Layer" toolbar. Go to the menu "**View, Toolbars, Layer**" or right-mouse-click in a toolbar and select "Layer." By default it is located in the lower left corner of the screen but can be moved for convenience.

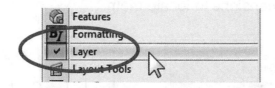

The "**Layer Properties**" command allows us to add, delete, and modify layers as needed.

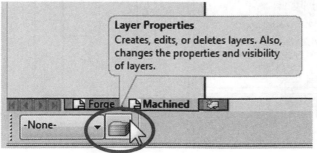

242. - In the "Layers" dialog select the "New" button to create a new layer. After it is created change its name to "Reference." The default color for new layers is black, so we don't need to change it. We'll add the reference annotations to this layer to display them using the layer color. Click OK to finish.

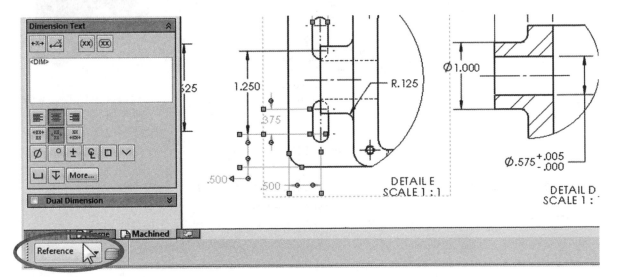

243. - To change annotations or models to a different layer select them in the graphics area and select the new layer from the Layer toolbar. Select all reference annotations (individually or multiple at the same time) and assign them to the new "Reference" layer. Notice their color updating after the change.

244. - Rearrange the views as needed to make room for dimensions and annotations. Delete any duplicate dimensions to make the drawing easier to read. Save the finished drawing as *'Housing'* and close the file. Note the file extension for drawings is *.slddrw.

Forge configuration finished drawing sheet.

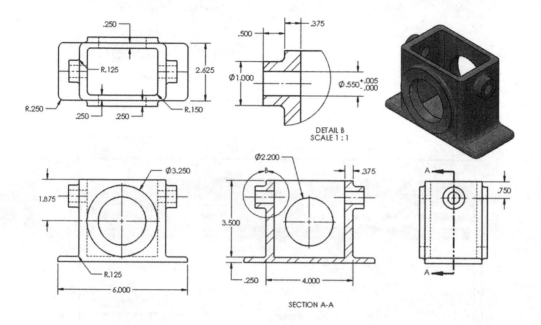

Machined configuration finished drawing sheet.

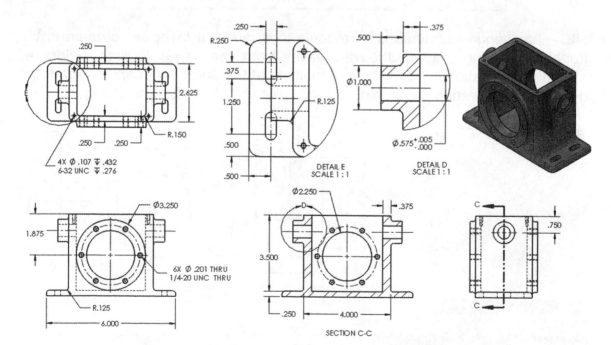

Exercises: Make the detail drawings of the following Engine Project parts that were done in the Part Modeling section to match the drawing previously supplied to make each part. High resolution images are included in the accompanying disc.

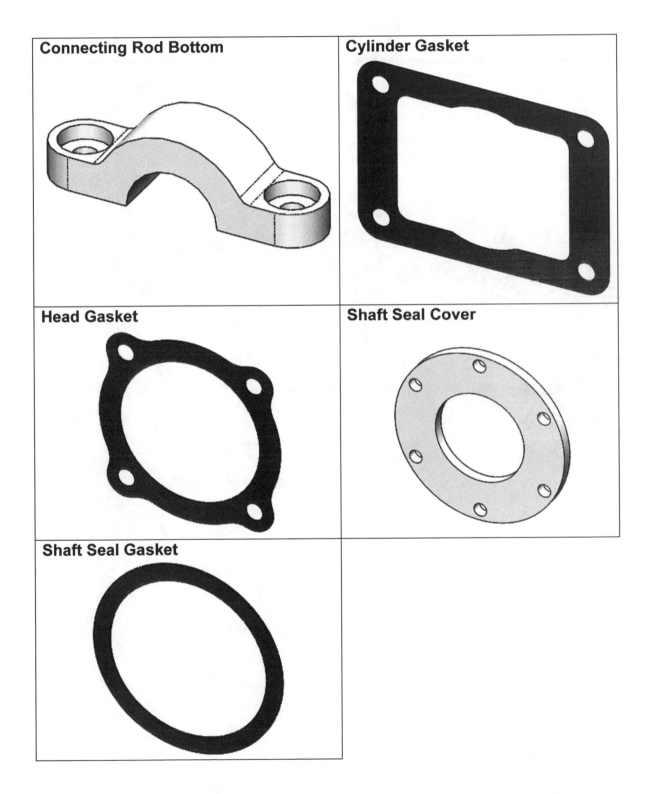

Connecting Rod Bottom	Cylinder Gasket
Head Gasket	Shaft Seal Cover
Shaft Seal Gasket	

Notes:

Drawing Two: The Side Cover

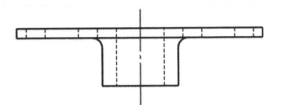

SCALE 1 : 2

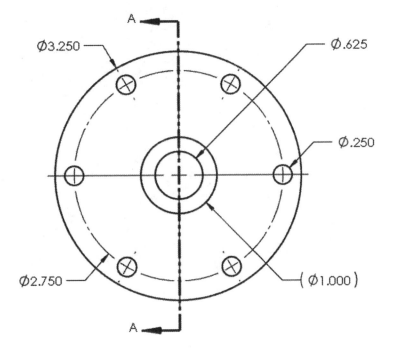

A

Ø3.250

Ø.625

Ø.250

Ø2.750

(Ø1.000)

A

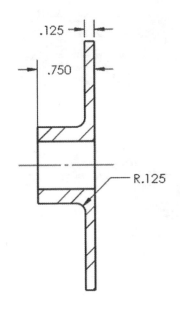

.125

.750

R.125

SECTION A-A

Notes:

In this lesson we'll review material previously covered, including how to add standard views, sections and importing annotations from the model to the drawing. We'll also learn how to add dimensions that are not present or in the desired format, change the sheet's scale and a view's scale.

The drawing of the *'Side Cover'* part will follow the next sequence.

Make new drawing	Insert drawing views	Section View	Import dimensions

| Delete and arrange dimensions | Add Diameter Dimensions | Change Drawing and view scale | |

245. - We will repeat the process that we used with the *'Housing'* including adding a configuration to reinforce the material just covered. Open the *'Side Cover'* part and go to the Configuration Manager tab. Right-mouse-click in the part's name and select "Add Configuration." Enter the name "*Forge*" and click OK to continue.

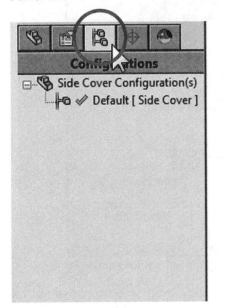
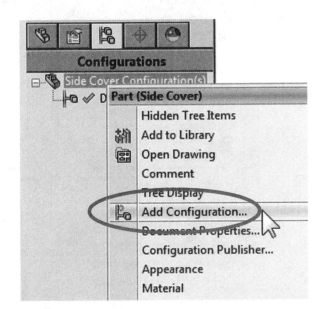

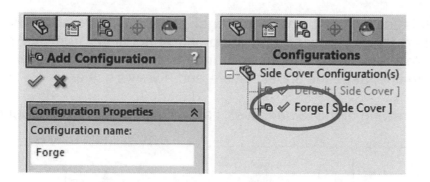

246. - Rename the "*Default*" configuration to "*Machined*" using the slow-double-click method or the configuration properties.

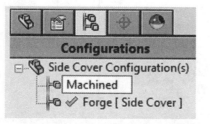

247. - Split the FeatureManager and show the Feature Manager at the top and the Configuration Manager at the bottom. With the "*Forge*" configuration active suppress the "*Cut-Extrude2*" feature, notice that the circular pattern is also suppressed because it's a child feature.

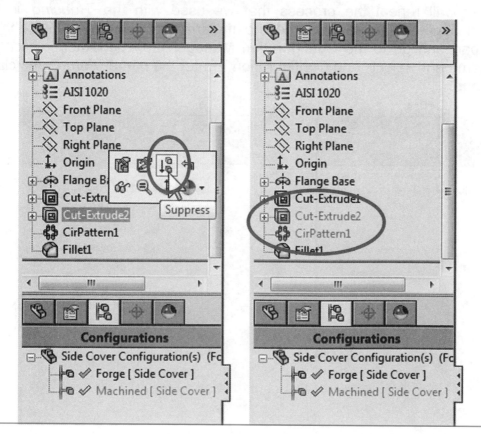

248. - Double click in the center hole to reveal its diameter dimension and then double-click in the diameter. Change its value to 0.6" for the Forge configuration using the "This Configuration" button in the "Modify" value box.

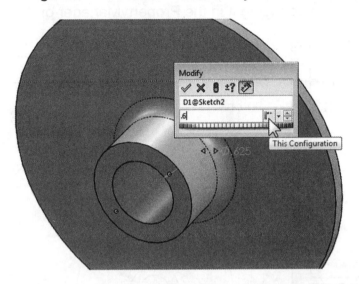

249. - With the "*Forge*" configuration active, select the menu **"File, Make Drawing from Part"** or the icon from the **"New Document"** drop down menu to start the drawing.

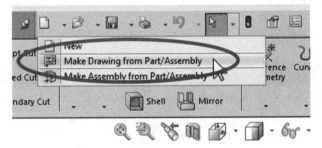

250. - For the '*Side Cover*' part we'll use the "A-Landscape" drawing template without sheet format. After selecting the sheet size add the Front, Top and Isometric views. Drag the Front view from the View Palette and project the Top and Isometric views from it.

251. - From the "**View Palette**" drag and drop the Front view, and project the Top and Isometric views from it. Select the Front view, and if needed, change the Display Style to "**Hidden Lines Visible**" as we did in the previous exercise by selecting the view and changing it in the PropertyManager on the left.

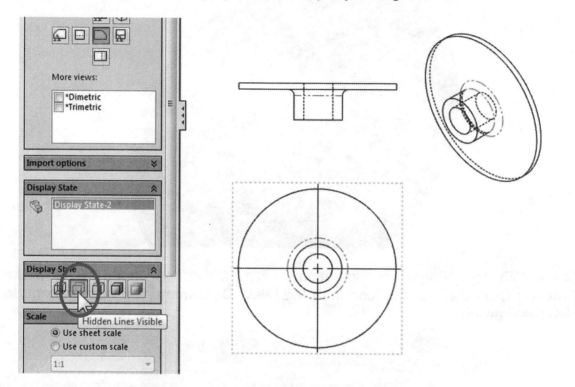

For the Front and Top views change to "**Tangent Edges Removed**," and for the Isometric, choose the "**Hidden Lines Removed**" view mode and "**Tangent Edges Visible**."

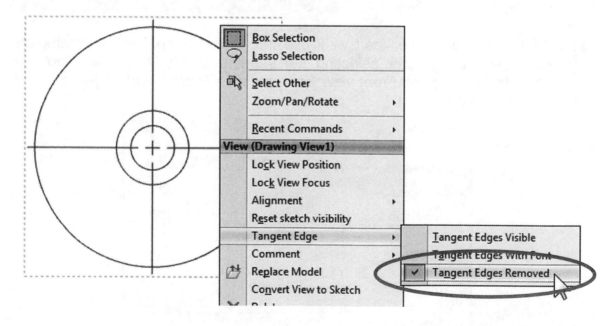

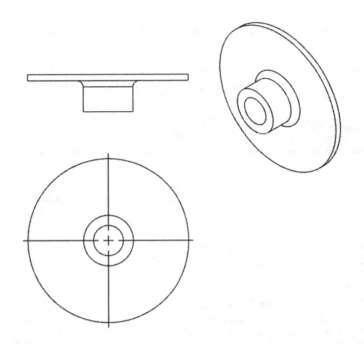

252. - Before adding the dimensions we need to add the centerline to the Top view. Select the "**Centerline**" command from the Annotations tab and click in the cylindrical surface of the Top view to add the centerline. Click OK to finish.

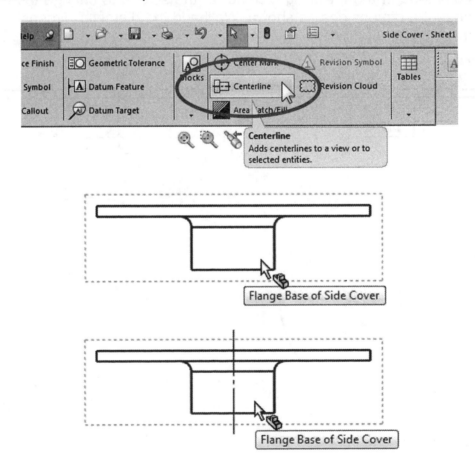

253. - To import the dimensions from the 3D model select **"Model Items"** from the Annotation tab or go to the menu **"Insert, Model Items."** For "Source/Destination" select "Entire Model," activate the checkbox "Import items into all views" and click OK to add the dimensions.

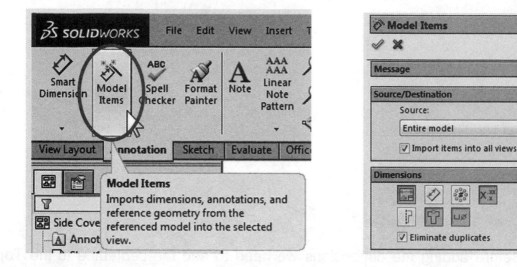

254. - If the document units are not in inches with three decimal places use the "Units" command in the lower right corner of the screen to change them. Delete and arrange the dimensions as shown. We'll add the diameter dimensions in the next step.

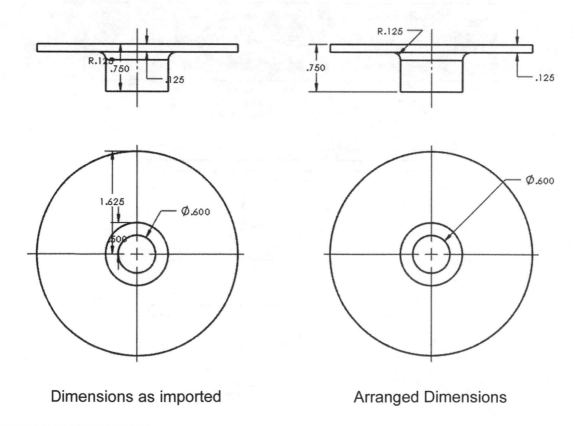

Dimensions as imported   Arranged Dimensions

255. - Select the "**Smart Dimension**" tool and manually add the missing diameter dimensions. Remember we can also select the Smart Dimension command using mouse gestures in the drawing environment.

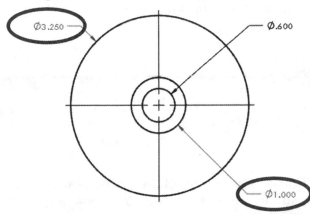

256. - Add a new (black) layer using the "**Layer**" command (feel free to name it appropriately) and change the new reference diameter dimensions to it to show them in black. Arrange the views as shown to finish the "*Forge*" configuration.

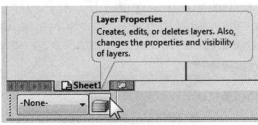

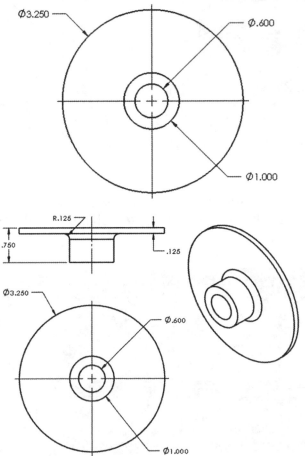

257. - Now we need to add a second sheet to our drawing to add the "*Machined*" configuration drawing. Instead of copying and pasting a complete sheet as we did with the '*Housing*', we'll only copy the Front view. Select the "**Add Sheet**" icon in the lower left corner and rename the sheets "*Forge*" and "*Machined*" respectively to match the configuration.

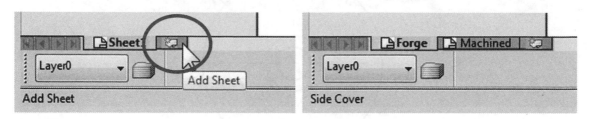

258. - Activate the "*Forge*" sheet, select the Front view and either press **Ctrl-C** or the menu "**Edit, Copy**" to copy the view. Activate the "*Machined*" sheet and press **Ctrl-V** or the menu "**Edit, Paste**" to paste the view. Select the newly added Front view and in the Property Manager select the "Machined" configuration from the "Reference Configuration" drop down list.

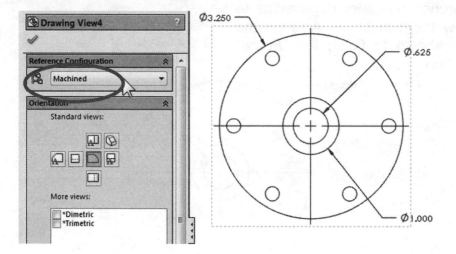

259. - To add the Top and Isometric views we'll use the "**Projected View**" command. Go to the View Layout tab, select the Front view, and click in the "Projected View" icon.

260. – After selecting the Front view the projected view command works like when we add views from the view palette. Move the mouse "up" to add the Top view, then to the top right and add the Isometric view. Click OK to finish. Change the Isometric view to "Hidden Lines Removed" and "Tangent Edge Visible."

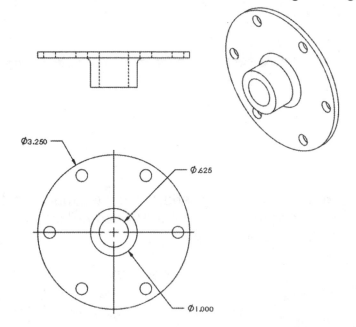

261. – Now we need to add a vertical section using the "**Section View**" command from the View Layout. Select the "Vertical" option, click to locate the section line in the center of the Front view, click OK to add the section line and locate the section view to the right of the Front view.

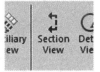

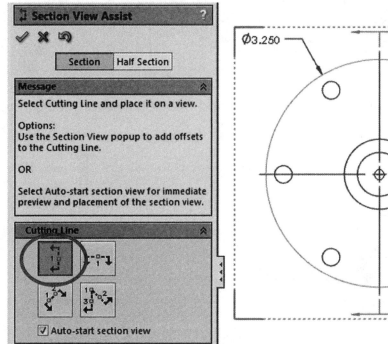

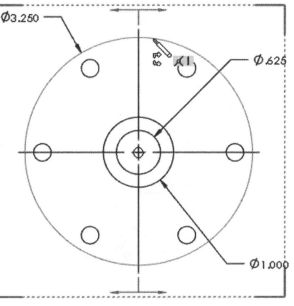

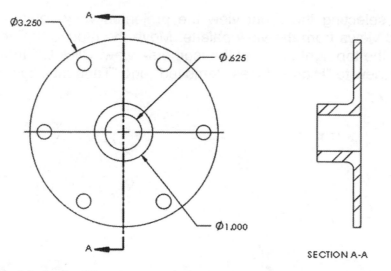

SECTION A-A

262. - Use the "**Center Mark**" tool to add the center marks in the Front view. Select one of the holes, and then click in the "Propagate" icon to add all the holes at the same time. Click OK to finish.

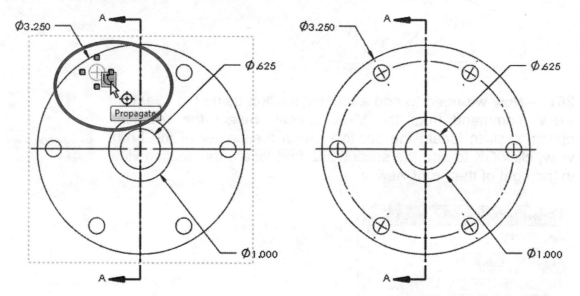

If missing, add the centerlines to the Top and section views using the "**Centerline**" command.

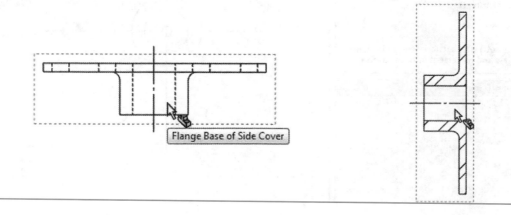

263. - To import the missing dimensions and annotations for the "Machined" configuration drawing select the "**Model Items**" command from the Annotation tab. Use the "Entire Model" and "Import items into all views" options. In the "Dimensions" section include "Hole Wizard Locations," "Hole Callout" and "Tolerenced Dimensions." Click OK to finish and import the dimensions.

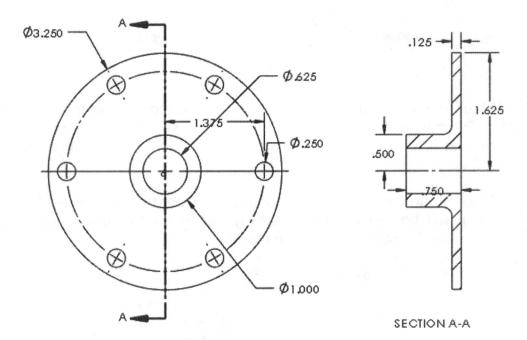

SECTION A-A

264. - Before we add the missing dimensions and annotations select the new layer created early. It will be called "Layer0" unless it was renamed. By selecting a layer, every annotation added will be assigned to this layer. Note that there are two additional options; one is to define annotations based on the drafting standard selected and the other option is to not assign a layer.

265. - After selecting the layer use the **"Smart Dimension"** tool add the missing diameter dimensions and delete the extra dimensions to match the next image. Note that with the new layer selected the new dimensions are added to it and are shown in black.

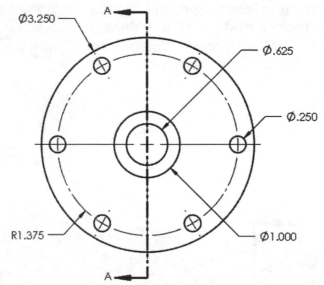

262. - When adding the circle of holes dimension a radius is added instead of a diameter. To change the dimension to show a diameter instead of a radius right-mouse-click in it and from the pop-up menu select "Display Options, Show as Diameter."

 If the "Smart Dimension" command is selected, the "Display As Diameter" option will be displayed immediately, otherwise the option will be listed under the "Display Options" sub-menu.

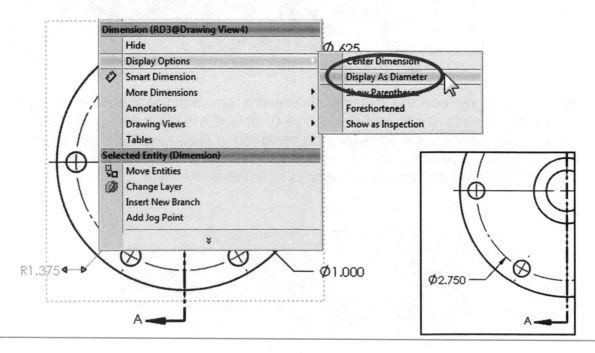

263. - Dimensions manually added to a drawing can be displayed with a parenthesis to indicate it as a **Reference Dimension.** Reference dimensions are used to provide additional information to the drawing, don't have a tolerance and often times their value depends on other dimensions. They should *NOT* to be used for manufacturing or inspection. For this drawing the 1" diameter is not a critical dimension, so we'll mark it as a reference, meaning that its value is not critical to the design. To add a parenthesis, select the dimension and from the Property Manager click in the "Parenthesis" icon.

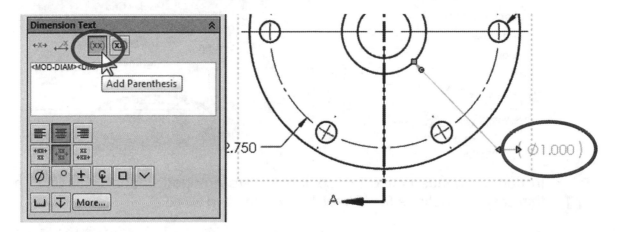

 Parentheses can be added by default to reference (manually added dimensions.) This option is set in the menu "**Tools, Options, Document Properties, Dimensions, Add parentheses by default**." This is an option set by document and is not a system option.

264. - Another way to add or remove parentheses and other annotation options is to use the "**Dimension Palette.**" When we select a dimension the dimension palette appears near it; move the mouse over it to expand the window and modify the dimension's appearance. Here we can change a dimension's parameters including parenthesis, tolerance, precision, etc.

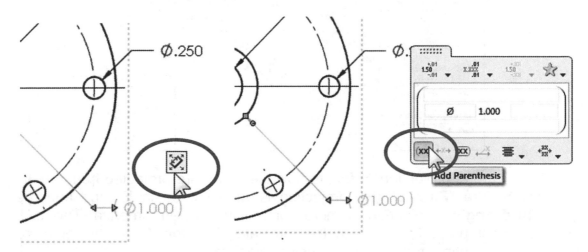

265. - In some instances the drawing sheet is too big or too small for the views. In order to fit them better we can change the sheet's scale. In this case, we need to change the sheet's scale to be 1:1. Make a right-mouse-click *in the sheet* (not a drawing view), or make a right-mouse-click in the sheet's name in the FeatureManager, and from the menu select "Properties."

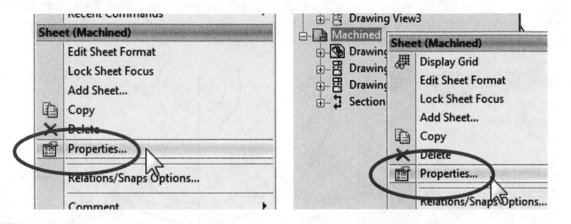

In pop-up menus notice the commands are grouped under a heading; in this case the options for "*Sheet (Machined)*" are listed.

266. - From the options box, make sure we are using a scale of 1:1, "Third angle" projection to match the book images and click OK to finish.

The "Type of projection" refers to how the views are projected from the 3D model. The **"First angle"** projection is widely used in Europe and the **"Third angle"** projection is more commonly used in America. This is a document property saved in the template. See the Appendix for more information in creating, modifying, and using templates.

267. - After arranging the views and dimensions, we notice that the Isometric view is too big to fit in our sheet, so we'll change the isometric view's scale.

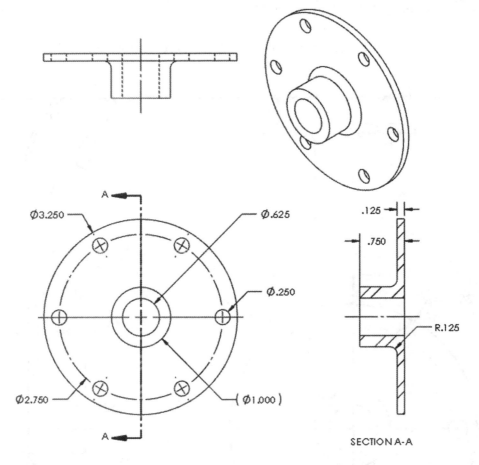

SECTION A-A

Select the Isometric view in the graphics area, and from its PropertyManager, change the view scale to 1:2 from the "Use custom scale" drop down menu in the "Scale" options box.

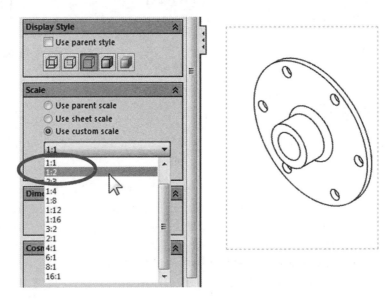

After changing a view's scale to a value different from the sheet's scale a note is added to the view with its value.

SCALE 1 : 2

268. - The drawing is finished. Save it as '*Side Cover*' and close the file.

SCALE 1 : 2

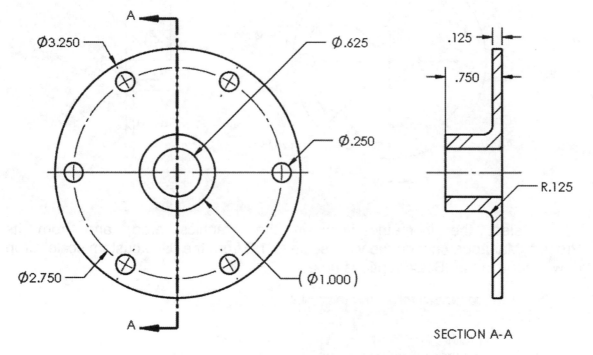

Exercises: Make the detail drawings of the following Engine Project parts that were done in the Part Modeling section to match the drawing previously supplied to make each part.

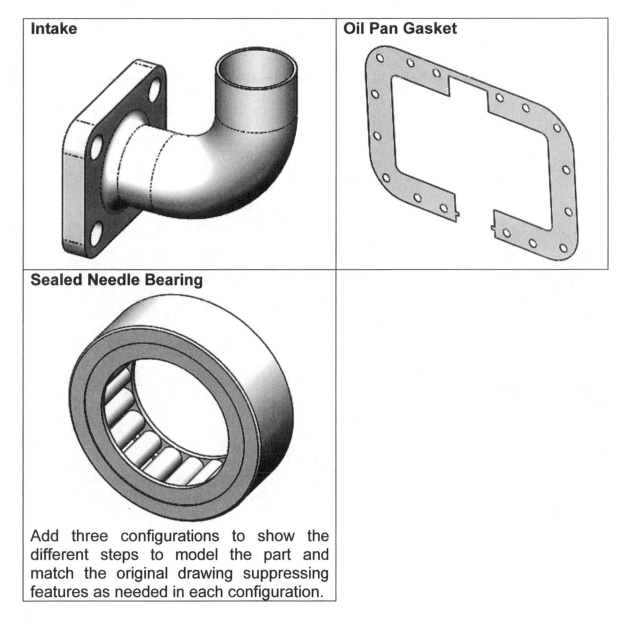

Intake

Oil Pan Gasket

Sealed Needle Bearing

Add three configurations to show the different steps to model the part and match the original drawing suppressing features as needed in each configuration.

Notes:

Drawing Three: The Top Cover

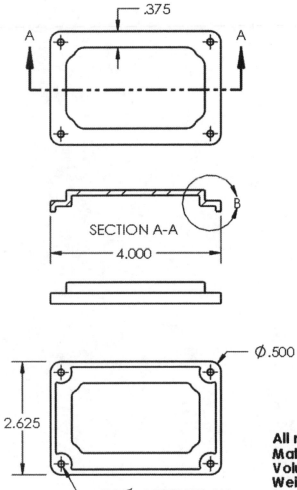

.375

A — A

SECTION A-A

4.000

2.625

Ø.500

4X Ø .150 THRU ALL

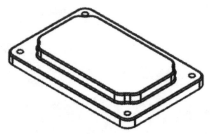

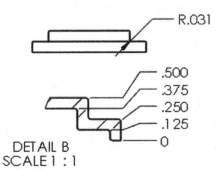

R.031

.500
.375
.250
.125
0

DETAIL B
SCALE 1 : 1

All rounds 0.032" *unless* otherwise specified
Material: Cast Alloy Steel
Volume: 1.82 cu-in
Weight: 0.48 lb
Designer: Alejandro Reyes

Notes:

269. - In this lesson we'll review previously covered material, the section view option "Display only surface", adding Notes, Ordinate dimensions, and adding custom file properties to part and assembly files for use in drawings and bills of materials. The drawing of the *'Top Cover'* will follow the next sequence.

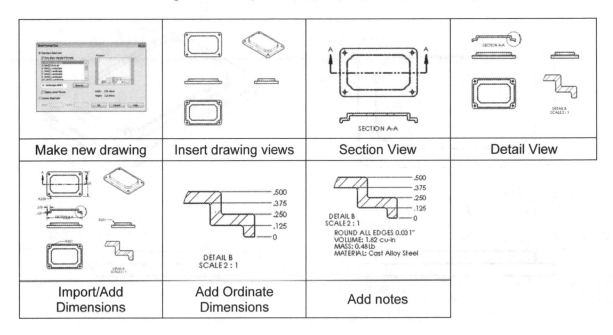

Make new drawing	Insert drawing views	Section View	Detail View
Import/Add Dimensions	Add Ordinate Dimensions	Add notes	

270. - Open the *'Top Cover'* part and select the "**Make Drawing from Part/Assembly**" icon as we've done before. Select the drawing template with an "A-Landscape" sheet size without sheet format.

271. - Click-and-drag the Front view from the "**View Palette**" onto the sheet, and add Top, Bottom, Right and Isometric views by projecting them from the Front view. Change the display style to "Hidden Lines" and "Tangent Edges Removed" for all views except the Isometric, which will have "Tangent Edges Visible."

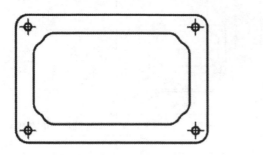
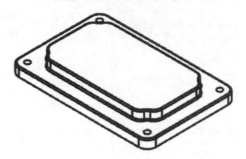

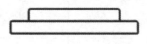

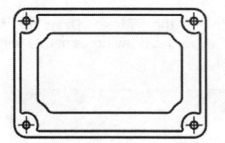

272. - The next step is to make a section through the Top view to get more information about the cross section of the cover. Select the "**Section View**" icon from the View Layout tab, click in the "Horizontal" section icon, and place the section line *approximately* through the middle of the Top view as indicated and locate the new section view just below it.

If the "Auto-start section view" option is checked, the pop-up toolbar is not shown after locating the section line.

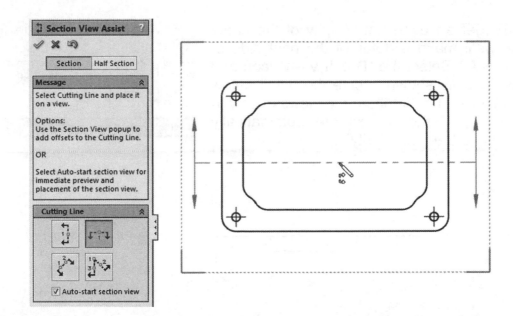

273. - After locating the section view, you may have to activate the "Flip Direction" button to reverse the direction of the section view. Also check the **"Display only cut face(s)"** option to show only the section's surface ignoring the rest of the model behind the section line, the effect of activating this option is as if we had only taken a thin slice of the part at the section line.

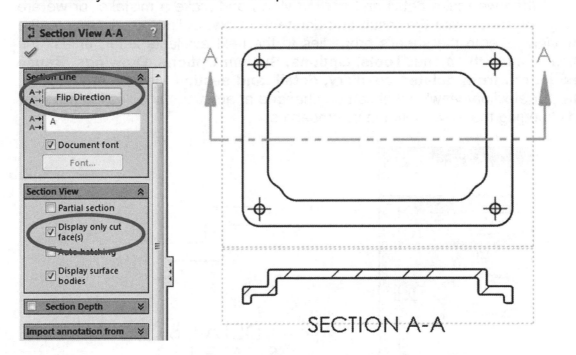

SECTION A-A

 The direction of the section view can also be reversed by a double click in the section line. If the section is reversed this way, the drawing may have to be rebuilt.

274. - To get an even better view of the cross section, we'll make a detail of the right side of "Section A-A." Select the "**Detail View**" icon and draw a circle as shown; locate the detail below the Right view and distribute the views evenly in the sheet. If Center marks are automatically added, delete them for clarity.

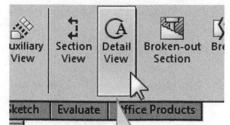

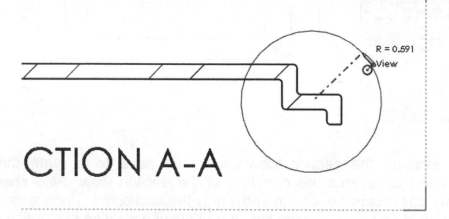

275. - When we make detail and section views and make a mistake, or we are simply not happy with the result and delete the view, SolidWorks increases the *new view label* in the sheet's properties to the next available letter, unless the option is set in the menu "**Tools, Options, System Options, Drawings, Reuse view letters from deleted auxiliary, detail, and section views**." Any section, detail, or auxiliary view's label can be changed at any time by selecting the view and changing the view's letter in its properties.

276. - The next step is to import the model dimensions from the part. Go to the menu "**Insert, Model Items**," remember to select the "Import items into all views" and "Entire Model" options, as well as the "Hole Callout" dimensions.

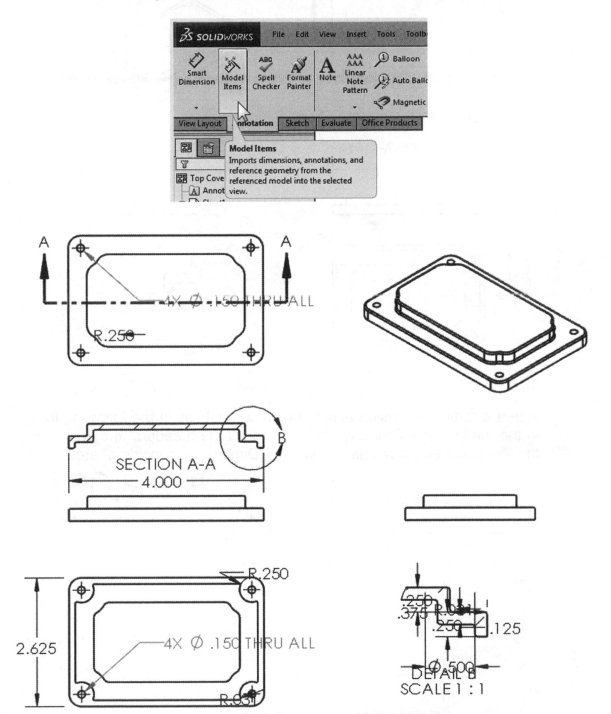

277. - Delete and arrange the dimensions as needed to match the next image.

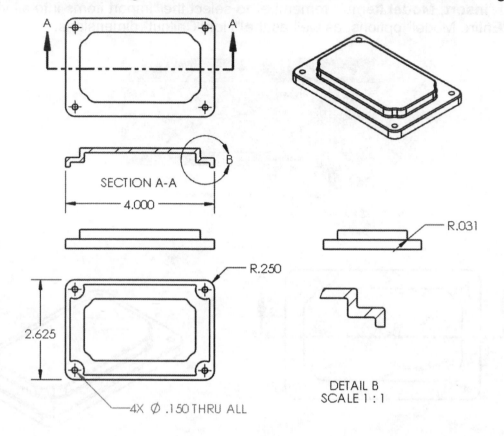

SECTION A-A

4.000

2.625

R.250

R.031

4X Ø .150 THRU ALL

DETAIL B
SCALE 1 : 1

When a radial dimension is not shown correctly as in the following image, in the dimension's Property Manager select the "Leaders" tab and change the Witness/Leader Display options to "Dimension to inside of arc."

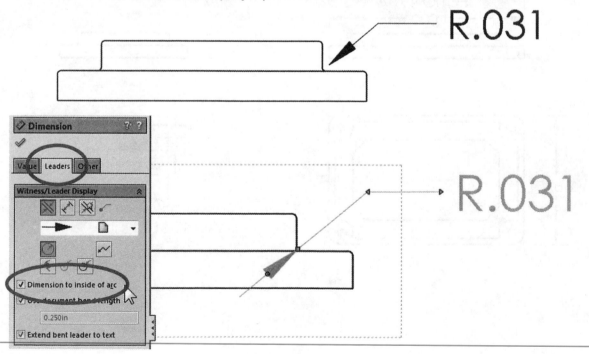

R.031

R.031

278. - If missing, add a dimension to the round edge in the bottom view. When adding a dimension to an arc, SolidWorks automatically defaults to a radial dimension. When selecting a circle we get the diameter dimension.

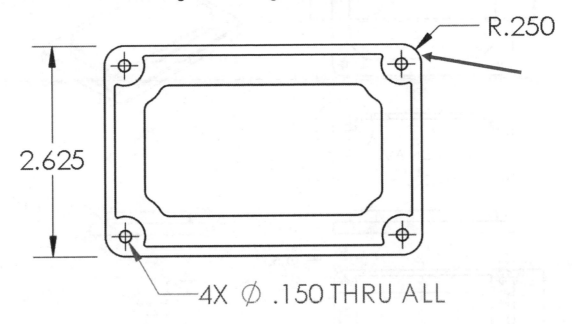

279. - In this example we want to show the dimension as a diameter, not a radius. To change it right-mouse-click in the dimension and from the pop-up toolbar select "**Display options, Display as Diameter**."

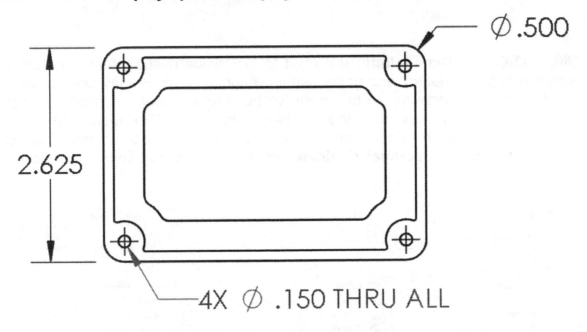

To change the dimension to radial again repeat the previous step and select "**Display as Radius**."

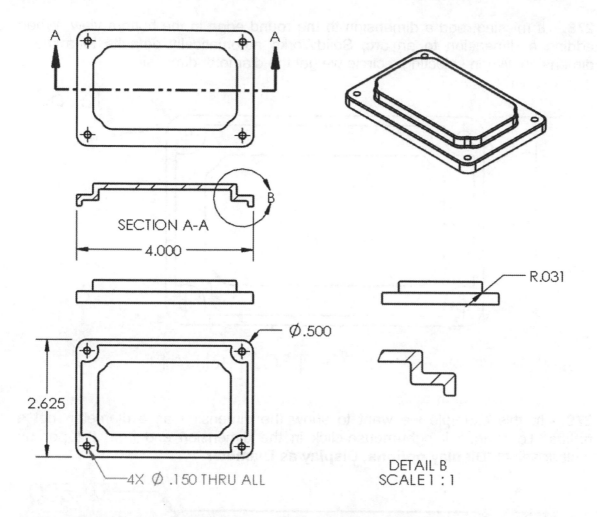

280. - "Ordinate Dimensions" are used to dimension multiple features from a common origin or datum, and under certain circumstances we may need or want to add them to a drawing. In this case we have to add them manually (unless they were added to a sketch and are being imported.) Click anywhere in the graphics area with the right mouse button, and from the pop-up menu select **"More Dimensions, Vertical Ordinate"** or from the "Smart Dimension" icon's drop down menu.

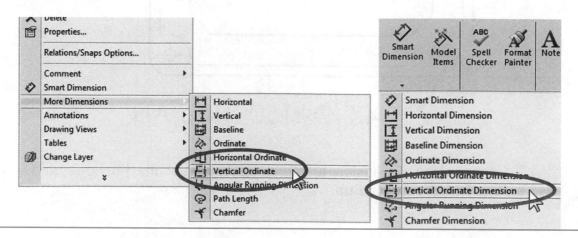

281. - To add ordinate dimensions first click to select the edge that will be the zero reference, then click to locate the "0" dimension and finally click on each horizontal line or vertex to add a dimension to it. The Ordinate Dimensions will be automatically aligned and jogged if needed. In the Detail view, select the lower edge to be the zero reference, click to the right to locate it, and click in the rest of the edges to add the dimensions.

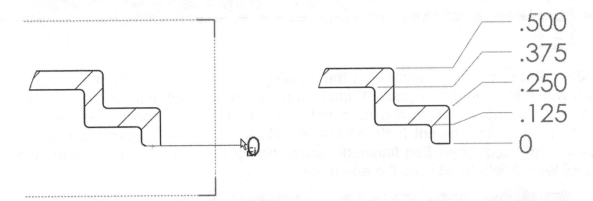

If after adding the ordinate dimensions a dimension is missed, right mouse click in any of the ordinate dimensions, select "**Add to Ordinate**" and click in the edge/vertex that was missed to dimension it.

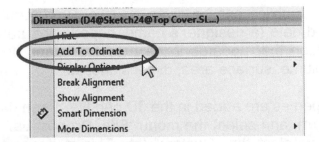

282. - After adding the dimensions we are going to add a note to the drawing. Notes are used in drawings to communicate important information, such as materials, finish, dates, designer, etc. To add a note to our drawing select the "**Note**" command from the Annotation tab or the menu "**Insert, Annotations, Note**"...

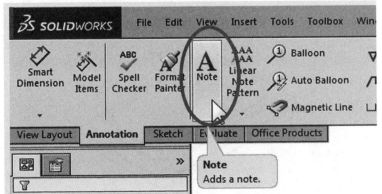

...and click in the drawing to locate the note; the **Formatting toolbar** is automatically displayed next to the note (unless its toolbar is already visible.) The formatting toolbar's functionality is similar to most Windows' applications to change font, color, justification, and style.

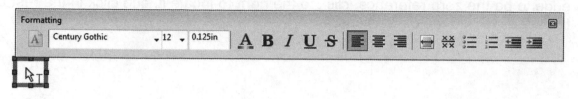

283. - After the note is located in the drawing, we can type and format it just as we would in a word processor. If multiple notes are needed, instead of OK, click in the drawing to locate the next note and repeat the process. Feel free to experiment with different fonts and styles. Click OK in the PropertyManager or press the "Esc" key when finished adding the note. To modify an existing note double-click in it to activate the edit mode.

All rounds 0.032" *unless* otherwise specified

284. - Parts and assemblies can be given specific "**Document Properties**" that contain user defined data (a designer's name, department, part number, etc.) or parametric information that updates if the model changes, like a component's material, weight, volume, surface area, dimensions, etc.

Custom Properties are added in the 3D part file. Open the '*Top Cover*' part file (*Top Cover.sldprt*), and select the menu "**File, Properties**." In the "Summary Information" window select the "Custom" tab. This is document properties are added. In this example we'll add three properties linked to the part's Volume, Weight, and Material, and a user defined property with the designer's name.

 To open a part file directly from the drawing, click in the part in a drawing view and select the "**Open Part**" command from the pop-up menu.

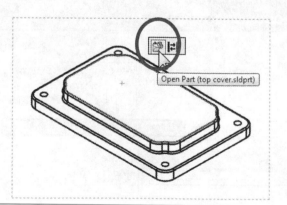

285. - In the "Property Name" column, click in the first cell and select "Material" from the drop down menu; in the "Type" column "Text" is automatically selected; click in the "Value/Text Expression" cell, and from the drop down menu select "Material." SolidWorks fills in the correct expression to make the property's value equal to "Cast Alloy Steel," which is the material we had assigned to this part.

After adding a property a new empty row appears. In the second property name type "*Volume*" and select "Volume" from the value drop-down menu, for the third property name select "Weight" and "Mass" for the value, and for the last property type "*MyName*" in the "Property Name" and fill in your name for the value. If the property values do not update immediately click OK and reopen the properties window to re-calculate them. When finished save the *'Top Cover'* part file.

Property names not listed can be typed in, or if they will be also used in other documents, select "Edit List" to add them to the drop down list of properties used for all components.

286. - After saving the changes go back to the *'Top Cover – Sheet1'* drawing using the "Window" menu. Add a new note and type: "*Material:*" While still editing the note click in the "**Link to Property**" icon from the note's "Text Format" options.

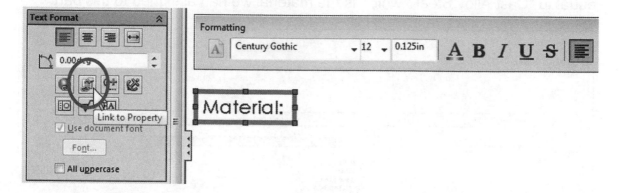

From the "Link to Property" window, select "Model in view specified in sheet properties"; this will tell the note to use the Custom Properties from the part in the drawing. Then select "Material" from the drop down list and click on OK when done to add the property to the note.

Depending on how SolidWorks is configured, you may see in the note "*$PRPSHEET: Material*", this is the code used by SolidWorks to read part properties. If you see this code it will be replaced by the component's property value after we finish the note. Your note should now look like this:

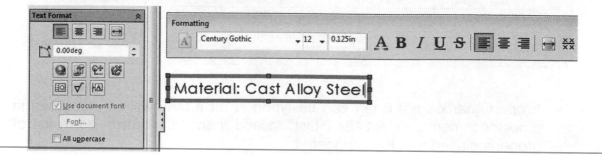

287. -The rest of the parametric notes can be added the same way. Press "Enter" to add a new row in the note; type "*Volume:*" add the link to the "Volume" property; in the next row in the note type "*Weight:*" and add the link to the "Weight" property; finally type "*Designer:*" and link to the "MyName" property.

> A drawback of using parametric notes that return a numeric value is that the units of measure are not listed, and they have to be either manually added to the note or by adding a custom property to the part/assembly with the units. The values are always displayed using the units used in the part. In our example the volume is measured in cubic inches and the weight is in pounds. We can manually add the units to the note. After formatting, the final note will look like this:

All rounds 0.032" *unless* otherwise <u>specified</u>
Material: Cast Alloy Steel
Volume: 1.82 cu-in
Weight: 0.48 lb
Designer: Alejandro Reyes

If a custom property changes in the part, the notes where the property is used in the drawing will be updated to reflect the new value. For example, if the 3D model changes in size its volume and weight will change as a result, and both the volume and mass custom property values will be updated accordingly.

288. - Add a new layer (black) and assign the reference dimensions to it. Save the drawing and close the file.

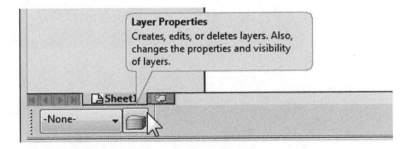

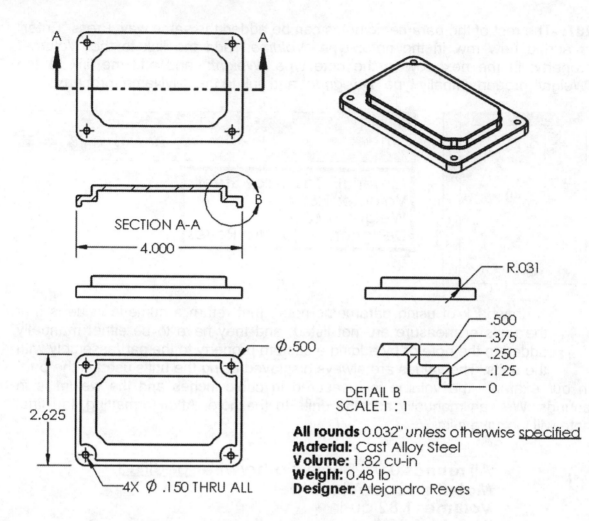

SECTION A-A

4.000

R.031

Ø.500

.500
.375
.250
.125
0

DETAIL B
SCALE 1 : 1

2.625

4X Ø .150 THRU ALL

All rounds 0.032" *unless* otherwise <u>specified</u>
Material: Cast Alloy Steel
Volume: 1.82 cu-in
Weight: 0.48 lb
Designer: Alejandro Reyes

Exercises: Make the detail drawing of the following Engine Project parts that were done in the Part Modeling section to match the drawing previously supplied to make each part. High resolution images are included in the accompanying disc.

Cylinder Head

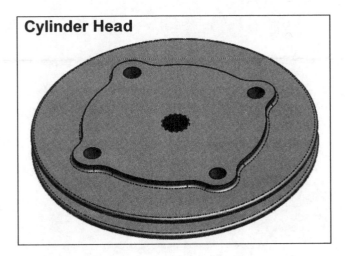

Notes:

Drawing Four: The Offset Shaft

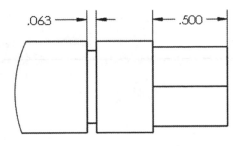

DETAIL A
SCALE 2 : 1

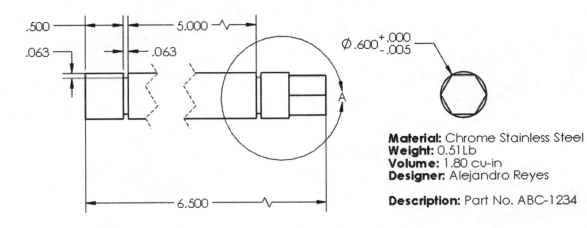

Material: Chrome Stainless Steel
Weight: 0.51 Lb
Volume: 1.80 cu-in
Designer: Alejandro Reyes

Description: Part No. ABC-1234

Notes:

The *'Offset Shaft'* drawing, although a simple drawing, will help us reinforce previously covered commands including standard and detail views, importing dimensions, manipulating and modifying a dimension's appearance, notes and custom file properties, and we'll learn how to add a break to a view. In this exercise we'll make a Front, Right, detail and broken views, import model dimensions, add notes and modify their appearance following the next sequence:

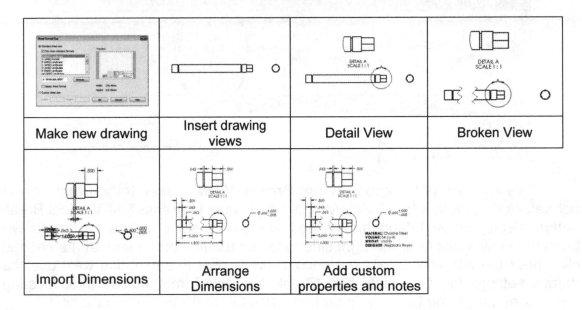

Make new drawing	Insert drawing views	Detail View	Broken View
Import Dimensions	Arrange Dimensions	Add custom properties and notes	

289. - Since we have already done a few drawings, we'll ask you to make a new drawing using the "A-Landscape" sheet size and turn off the sheet format. Add the Front view by dragging it from the View Palette, and project the Right view. Change the display mode to "Hidden Lines Removed" as shown. Right mouse click in the sheet, select "Properties" and change the sheet's scale to 1:1. Add a detail view of the right side of the shaft as shown.

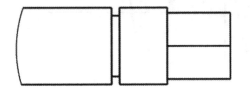

DETAIL A
SCALE 2 : 1

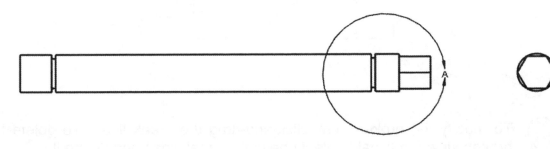

290. - For long slender elements like shafts, it's a common practice to add a **Break** to shorten the view and save space in the drawing. To add a break in the Front view, select the "**Break**" icon from the View Layout tab in the CommandManager or the menu "**Insert, Drawing View, Break**."

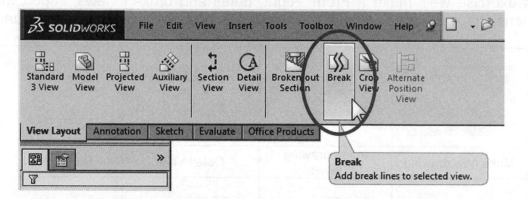

We are then presented with the "**Broken View**" dialog. If the Front view is not selected, click in it to tell SolidWorks which view to break. The Vertical Break option is selected by default, and all we have to do is select where the breaks will be in the view. Click near the right side to locate the first break line, and a second click near the left side to add the second break. For this exercise we'll use the default settings for "Gap size" and "Break line style." Immediately after locating the second break line the view is broken. Click OK to finish the command.

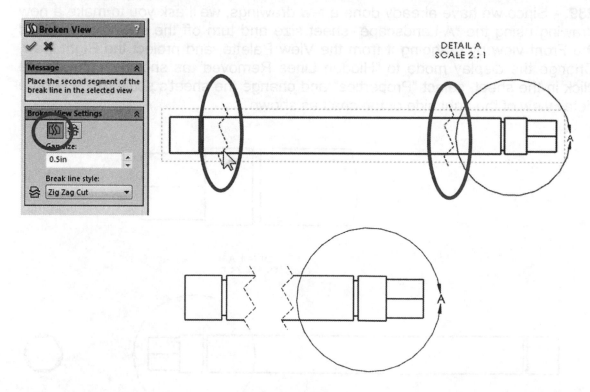

 To modify the broken view click-and-drag the break lines. To delete the broken view (un-break) select one of the break lines and delete it.

291. - You probably know what we are going to do now... Yes, import the dimensions from the 3D model. Go to the menu "**Insert, Model Items**"; remember to select the "Import items into all views" and "Entire Model" options. In this drawing the dimensions are added almost as we need them, we'll just arrange them a little in the next step.

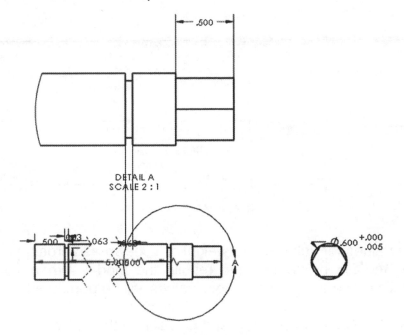

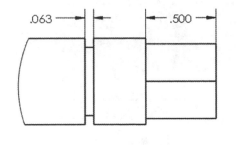

292. - Move the dimensions as shown in the next image; remember to hold down the "Shift" key while moving dimensions from one view to another.

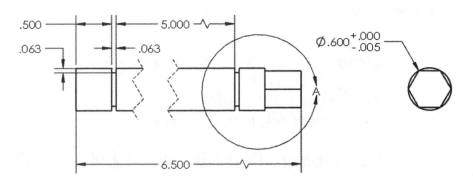

293. - Open the *'Offset Shaft'* part file, and from the menu "**File, Properties**" add the same custom properties as we did in the *'Top Cover'*. Add a new property called "Description" and fill in a description for the shaft. For this example any description will do. We'll use this description in the drawing and the bill of materials later. The "Summary Information" window should look like this when finished:

	Property Name	Type	Value / Text Expression	Evaluated Value
1	Material	Text	"SW-Material@Offset Shaft.SLDPRT"	Chrome Stainless Steel
2	Weight	Text	"SW-Mass@Offset Shaft.SLDPRT"	0.51
3	Volume	Text	"SW-Volume@Offset Shaft.SLDPRT"	1.80
4	MyName	Text	Alejandro Reyes	Alejandro Reyes
5	Description	Text	Part No. ABC-1234	Part No. ABC-1234
6	<Type a new property>			

 If the values for volume and weight are shown as zeroes, you may have to close the file properties and rebuild the model. When you re-open the model's properties window those values will be populated.

294. - Save the *'Offset Shaft'* part and go back to the drawing; add a note using the "**Note**" command from the Annotation tab. The user will have to type "*Material:*" "*Volume:*" "*Weight:*", "*Designer*" and "*Description,*" and link to the corresponding property after each one. Remember to add the units of measure.

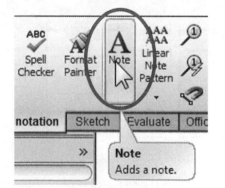

The finished note will be:

Material: Chrome Stainless Steel
Weight: 0.51Lb
Volume: 1.80 cu-in
Designer: Alejandro Reyes

Description: Part No. ABC-1234

295. - Save and close the drawing file.

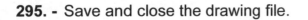

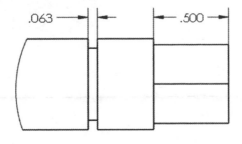

DETAIL A
SCALE 2 : 1

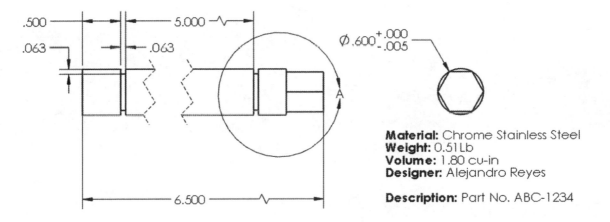

Material: Chrome Stainless Steel
Weight: 0.51Lb
Volume: 1.80 cu-in
Designer: Alejandro Reyes

Description: Part No. ABC-1234

Notes:

•

Drawing Five: The Worm Gear

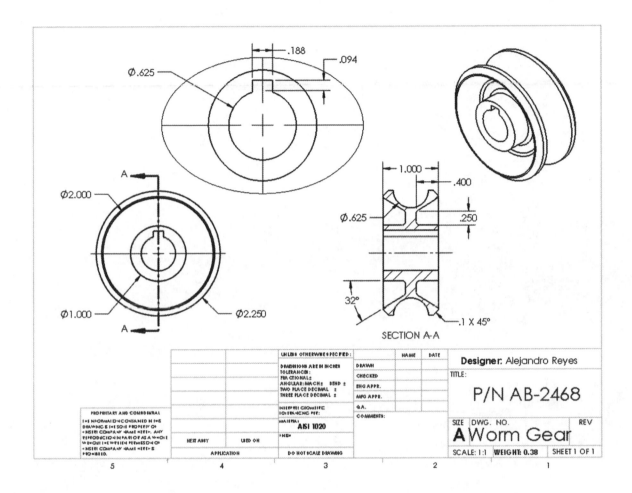

SECTION A-A

UNLESS OTHERWISE SPECIFIED:			NAME	DATE	**Designer:** Alejandro Reyes		
DIMENSIONS ARE IN INCHES	DRAWN				TITLE:		
TOLERANCES: FRACTIONAL± ANGULAR: MACH± BEND ± TWO PLACE DECIMAL ± THREE PLACE DECIMAL ±	CHECKED						
	ENG APPR.				**P/N AB-2468**		
	MFG APPR.						
INTERPRET GEOMETRIC TOLERANCING PER:	Q.A.						
MATERIAL **AISI 1020**	COMMENTS:				SIZE DWG. NO.		REV
FINISH					**A** Worm Gear		
					SCALE: 1:1 WEIGHT: 0.38	SHEET 1 OF 1	

NEXT ASSY | USED ON
APPLICATION | DO NOT SCALE DRAWING

Notes:

In this lesson we'll review previously covered material and a couple of new options, like adding angular dimensions, changing a dimension's precision and adding chamfer dimensions as well as a cropping a view and modifying the Sheet Format. The detail drawing of the *'Worm Gear'* will follow the next sequence.

Add Custom Properties to part	Make new drawing	Insert drawing views	Add view and Crop
Import and arrange Dimensions	Add Angular Dimension	Add chamfer Dimension	Modify Sheet format

296. - As we did in the previous drawing, first we will open the *'Worm Gear'* model and make a drawing, but before we make the drawing, we'll add custom properties to the part. With the *'Worm Gear'* part file open, select the menu "**File, Properties**" and complete it as shown in the next image.

Select the "**Make Drawing from Part/Assembly**" icon. For the 'Worm Gear' use the Drawing Template with an "A-Landscape" sheet size and leave the "Display Sheet Format" option checked in the "Sheet Format/Size" window. We'll learn how to use and edit the sheet format in this exercise.

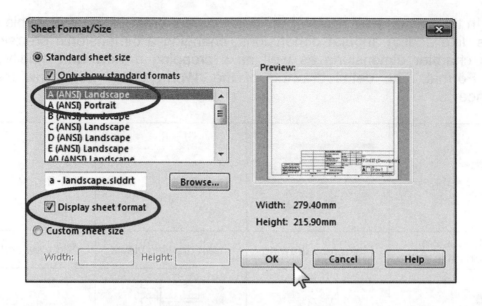

297. - Just as we've done in previous drawings, the first step is to add the main views for the model. Add the Front view from the "View Palette," an Isometric view, and the section view as shown. This is a review of material previously covered. Use "Hidden Line" display mode and "Tangent Edge Removed" for the Front and Section views and "Tangent Edge Visible" for the Isometric.

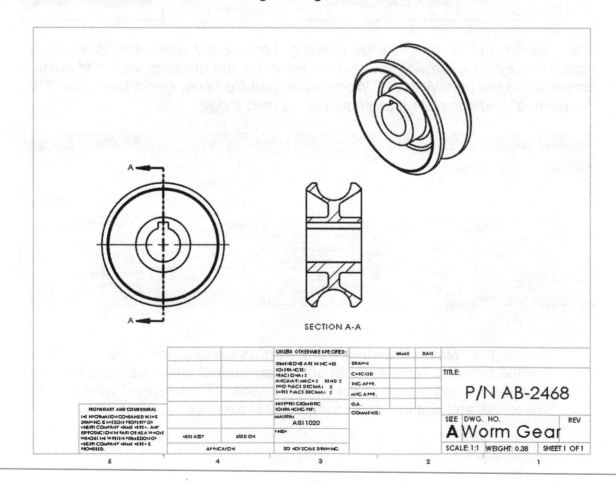

298. - After adding the "Section" view, we need a close-up of the center of the part. We will add a second Front view using the "**Model View**" command from the View Layout tab and then it will be cropped. The reason for not adding a Detail view is that adding another circle may make the Front view confusing.

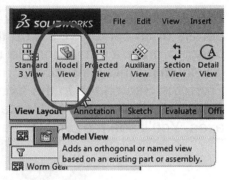

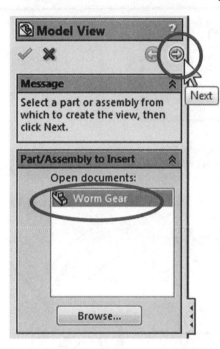

From the "Model View" properties, select the *'Worm Gear'* part from the list of currently open files (or Browse to select it) and click in the "Next" arrow at the top to go to the next step.

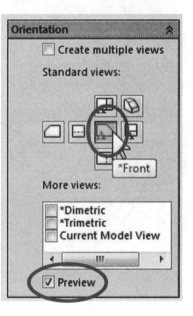

In the next screen select the Front view from the "Standard views," and leave the "Create multiple views" checkbox cleared, as we only need to add one view; to help us visualize turn on the "Preview" checkbox at the bottom.

In this step we can also change the new view's display style to "Hidden Lines Removed" and scale to 2:1 from the view's PropertyManager before we add it to the sheet.

Move the mouse pointer to the graphics area and locate the new Front view in the upper left corner. Click OK when done. Change the new view to "Tangent Edges Removed."

299. - The second Front view is too big, and since we are only interested in the details of its center we'll crop the view. In order to make a "**Crop View**," first we need to draw a closed profile using regular sketch tools. The closed profile can be anything including circles, rectangles, polygons, ellipses, closed splines, etc. From the Sketch tab in the CommandManager select the "**Ellipse**" command. To draw an ellipse, click to locate the center, and then locate the major and minor axes. You'll see the preview as you go. Click OK when finished.

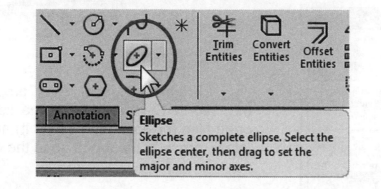

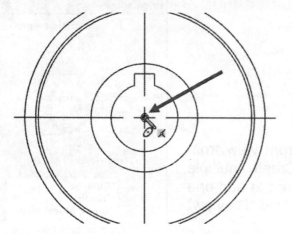
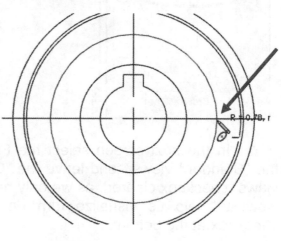

Start the ellipse   Locate major axis

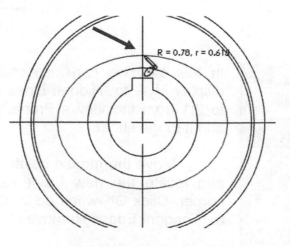

Locate minor axis to finish

344

300. - Select the ellipse we just drew and click in the "**Crop View**" command from the View Layout tab. The view will be automatically cropped to the ellipse.

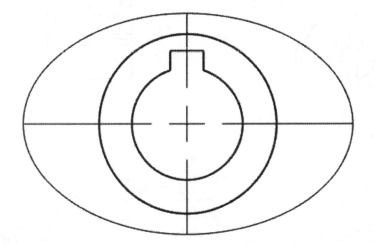

 To change or delete the crop from a view, select the cropped view in the FeatureManager (it will have a scissors icon in it) or in the screen, click with the right mouse button and from the pop-up menu select "**Crop View, Edit Crop**" or "**Remove Crop**."

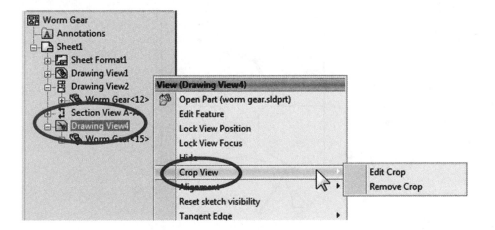

301. - Now import the dimensions from the model using "**Model Items**." Remember to select the options "Import items into all views" and "Entire Model." After importing the dimensions, delete and arrange them (Shift-drag) as needed to match the following image; you may have to change one or more dimensions to display as diameter by right-mouse-clicking in them and select "**Display Options, Display as Diameter**." Add any missing centerlines and center marks.

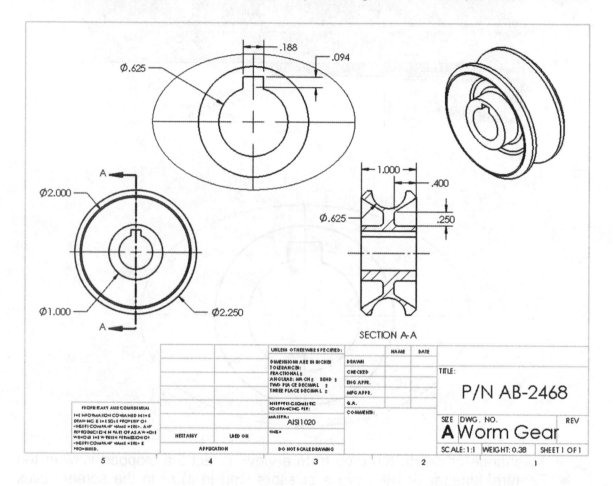

302. - Now we need to add an angular dimension. Using the "**Smart Dimension**" command and select the two edges indicated to add the 32° dimension.

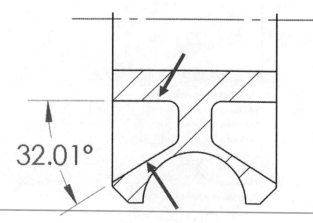

To change the dimension's precision (Significant decimal numbers) select the angular dimension, move the mouse over the "**Dimension Palette**" and change the number of decimal places to "None" from the precision's pull-down menu. Click anywhere outside of the Dimension Palette or hit the "Esc" key to finish.

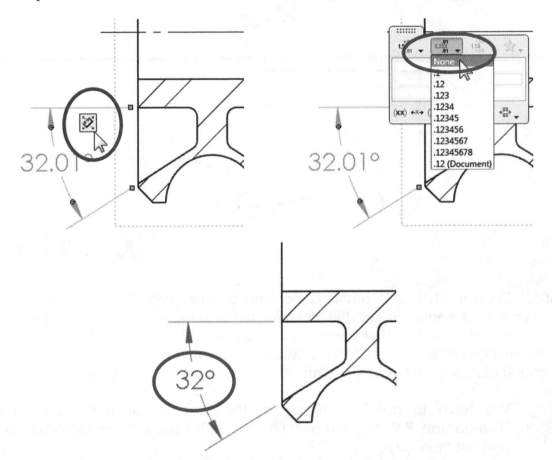

303. - The next thing we need to do is to add a "**Chamfer Dimension**." Click in the graphics area with the right mouse button, and from the pop-up menu select "**More Dimensions, Chamfer**," or the menu "**Tools, Dimensions, Chamfer**" or from the "**Smart Dimension**" drop-down icon.

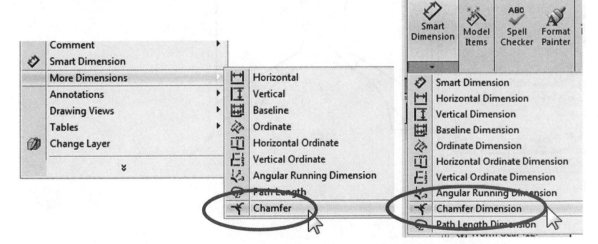

304. - To add a chamfer dimension select the chamfered edge first, then the vertical edge to measure the angle against it, and finally locate the dimension.

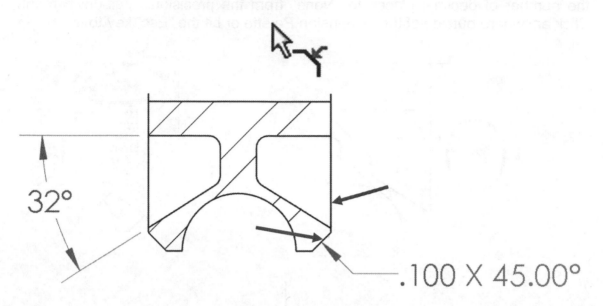

305. - We'll finish the Chamfer Dimension by changing the precision for both distance and angle. Select the chamfer dimension, and from the dimension's properties change the "**Tolerance/Precision**" to ".1" to change the dimension to one decimal place. In the "**2nd Tolerance/Precision**" select "None" to remove the decimal places from the angular value.

 We have to do this change in the PropertyManager, because the "**Dimension Palette**" can only change both values to the same precision, and not individually.

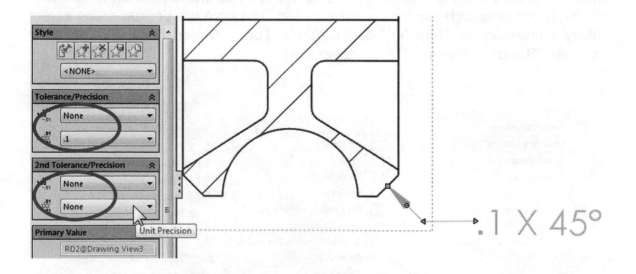

306. - In this drawing we are showing the title block. The title block is the area of the drawing where we can add important drawing information: add our company name, part number, material, etc. In SolidWorks this is called the "**Sheet Format**." One characteristic of the sheet format is that it is "locked," and we cannot change it directly. To change the title block, right-mouse-click in the drawing area *or* in "*Sheet Format1*" in the Feature Manager and from the pop-up menu select "**Edit Sheet Format**."

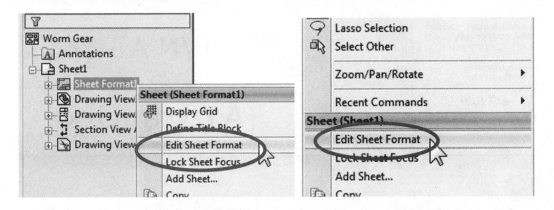

307. - After selecting "**Edit Sheet Format**" we are now editing the title block and are free to change it; all the sketch tools are available to modify it as needed. Notice that the drawing views are automatically hidden when editing the "**Sheet Format**." The default sheet format has a few parametric notes that are linked to component properties like the part's name and material, and other notes are linked to drawing's information like scale and sheet number.

UNLESS OTHERWISE SPECIFIED:		NAME	DATE				
DIMENSIONS ARE IN INCHES	DRAWN						
TOLERANCES:							
FRACTIONAL ±	CHECKED			TITLE:			
ANGULAR: MACH± BEND ±	ENG APPR.						
TWO PLACE DECIMAL ±				P/N AB-2468			
THREE PLACE DECIMAL ±	MFG APPR.						
INTERPRET GEOMETRIC	Q.A.						
TOLERANCING PER:	COMMENTS:						
MATERIAL AISI 1020				SIZE	DWG. NO.		REV
FINISH				**A**	Worm Gear		
DO NOT SCALE DRAWING				SCALE: 1:1	WEIGHT: 0.38	SHEET 1 OF 1	

308. - Edit the notes by double-clicking them to change the font size and style as needed, and add a new note linked to your name. Note that the "Material", "Weight", "Description" (*Title:*) and component name are filled in automatically from the 3D model's properties, and the scale and sheet number are filled in from the 2D drawing's properties. These parametric notes are in the default sheet format. Change the additional notes in the Sheet Format to match the rest of the Sheet Format notes.

Notes, like dimensions and other drawing elements, can be assigned to a different layer to change their color.

UNLESS OTHERWISE SPECIFIED:		NAME	DATE	Designer: Alejandro Reyes			
DIMENSIONS ARE IN INCHES	DRAWN			TITLE:			
TOLERANCES: FRACTIONAL ± ANGULAR: MACH ± BEND ± TWO PLACE DECIMAL ± THREE PLACE DECIMAL ±	CHECKED			P/N AB-2468			
	ENG APPR.						
	MFG APPR.						
INTERPRET GEOMETRIC TOLERANCING PER:	Q.A.						
MATERIAL AISI 1020	COMMENTS:			SIZE A	DWG. NO. Worm Gear		REV
FINISH							
DO NOT SCALE DRAWING				SCALE: 1:1	WEIGHT: 0.38	SHEET 1 OF 1	

3   2   1

After modifying the title block to our liking, exit the sheet format and return to editing the drawing by selecting "**Edit Sheet**" from the right mouse button menu, or clicking in the "**Sheet Format**" confirmation corner.

Zoom/Pan/Rotate ▶
Recent Commands ▶
Sheet (Sheet Format1)
Define Title Block
Edit Sheet
Add Sheet...
Copy
Delete
Properties...
Relations/Snaps Options...

If we modify an empty drawing's Sheet Format and save it as a template, the title block changes will be saved with the template and be available for new drawings based on this template. See the Appendix for more information on creating new templates and changing existing ones.

309. - Change the reference dimensions (grey) to the "Format" layer to change their color to black, save and close the drawing file.

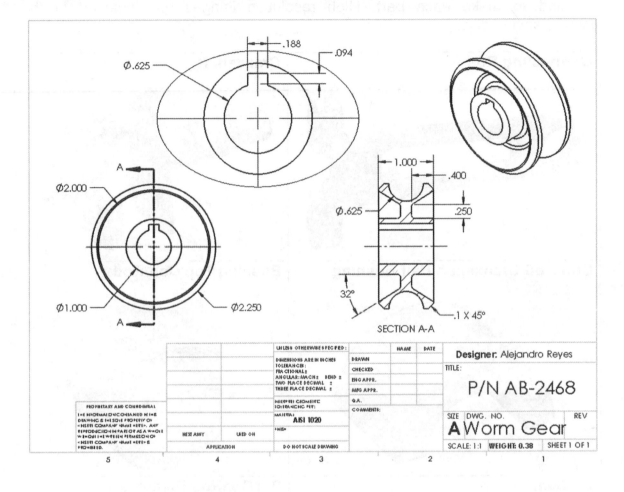

SECTION A-A

UNLESS OTHERWISE SPECIFIED:			NAME	DATE		**Designer:** Alejandro Reyes		
DIMENSIONS ARE IN INCHES		DRAWN						
TOLERANCES:					TITLE:			
FRACTIONAL±		CHECKED						
ANGULAR: MACH± BEND ±		ENG APPR.				**P/N AB-2468**		
TWO PLACE DECIMAL ±								
THREE PLACE DECIMAL ±		MFG APPR.						
INTERPRET GEOMETRIC		Q.A.						
TOLERANCING PER:		COMMENTS:						
MATERIAL					SIZE	DWG. NO.		REV
AISI 1020					**A** Worm Gear			
FINISH								
					SCALE: 1:1	WEIGHT: 0.38	SHEET 1 OF 1	

PROPRIETARY AND CONFIDENTIAL

THE INFORMATION CONTAINED IN THIS DRAWING IS THE SOLE PROPERTY OF <INSERT COMPANY NAME HERE>. ANY REPRODUCTION IN PART OR AS A WHOLE WITHOUT THE WRITTEN PERMISSION OF <INSERT COMPANY NAME HERE> IS PROHIBITED.

NEXT ASSY   USED ON

APPLICATION   DO NOT SCALE DRAWING

5   4   3   2   1

351

Exercises: Make the detail drawing of the following Engine Project parts that were done in the Part Modeling section to match the drawings previously supplied to make each part. High resolution images are included in the accompanying disc.

Connecting Rod	Crankshaft
Con Rod Crankshaft Half Bushing	**Bushing Top Con Rod**
Oil Seal	**Pin ConRod-Piston**

Drawing Six: The Worm Gear Shaft

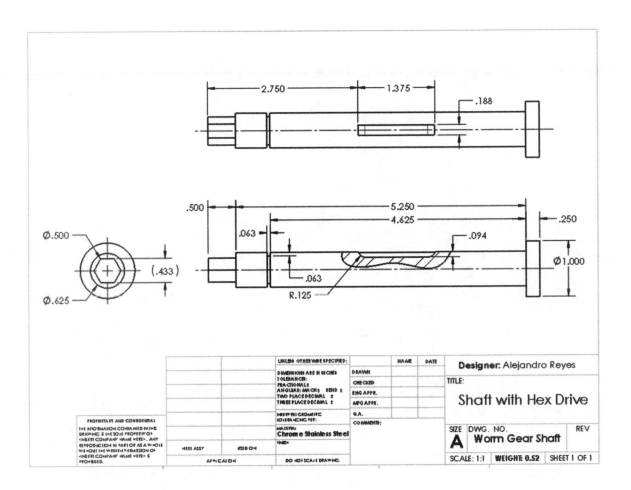

		UNLESS OTHERWISE SPECIFIED:	NAME	DATE	**Designer:** Alejandro Reyes		
		DIMENSIONS ARE IN INCHES TOLERANCES: FRACTIONAL± ANGULAR: MACH± BEND ± TWO PLACE DECIMAL ± THREE PLACE DECIMAL ±	DRAWN		TITLE:		
			CHECKED				
			ENG APPR.		**Shaft with Hex Drive**		
			MFG APPR.				
		INTERPRET GEOMETRIC TOLERANCING PER:	Q.A.				
			COMMENTS:				
		MATERIAL **Chrome Stainless Steel**			SIZE	DWG. NO.	REV
		FINISH			**A** Worm Gear Shaft		
NEXT ASSY	USED ON				SCALE: 1:1	WEIGHT: 0.52	SHEET 1 OF 1
APPLICATION		DO NOT SCALE DRAWING					

Notes:

Just as we did with the *'Offset Shaft'* drawing, we'll reinforce making new drawings, adding views, importing dimensions, moving dimensions from one view to another and changing a diameter's display style. In this exercise we will make Left, Front, and Top views, import and arrange the model dimensions. To complete the drawing we'll learn how to make a new type of view called "**Broken-Out Section**" used to look into the model without having to make a section view.

310. - Open the *'Worm Gear Shaft'* 3D model and add Material, Weight, Description ("*Shaft with hex drive*") and "MyName" custom properties. A quick way to add custom properties to model is by using the "Custom Properties Tab" located at the bottom of the Task Pane. When used for the first time we need to create a new template with the properties we want to add to a model, drawing, or assembly file, but after the template is done adding properties to a file is very quick. Select the "Custom Properties Tab." To create a new template, press the "Create Now…" button to launch the "Property Tab Builder" program.

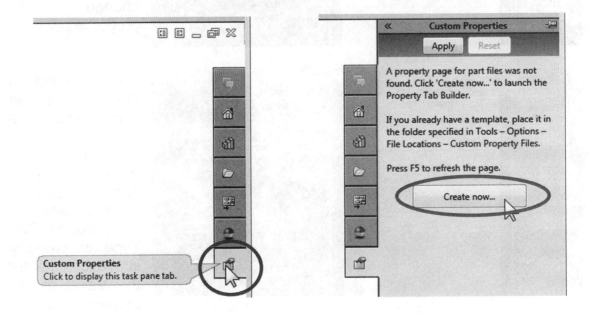

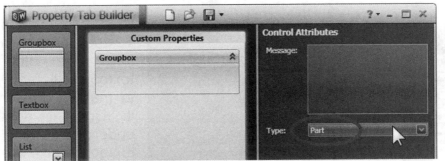

The Property Tab Builder is an easy to use stand alone program to create forms containing the custom properties we want to add to our models using a drag-and-drop interface. In the "Control Attributes" side we can define select if this template is for a part, a drawing, an assembly, or a weldment. In this example we are going to make a Part template.

355

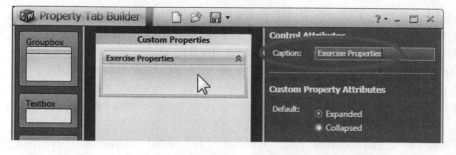

First select the "Groupbox" in the form and change its caption to "Exercise Properties" in the Control Attributes pane.

The next step is to add a "Textbox" to the form by dragging it into the group box and change its properties.

Type "Material" in the Caption to know what the property is. From the Name drop-down list select "Material," this will be the name of the property. The Type of property is Text, and for the Value of the property select "[SW-Material]" from the drop-down list as we did before in the 3D models.

Drag a second Textbox into the form, the other textbox will move to make room for it. Drop it right under the Material textbox at the bottom and fill in the control attributes.

In the "Weight" Attributes type "Weight" in the Caption, select "Weight" from the Name drop-down list and "[SW-Mass]" from the Value drop-down list.

One important detail to keep in mind is that Custom Properties can be configuration specific or not. At the bottom of the Control Attributes pane select the "Show on Custom Tab" option for all properties in this example, otherwise the properties will be added to the "Configuration Specific" tab and to use them later we would have remember to call the configuration properties instead.

Add three more text boxes with the "Volume," "Designer," (MyName property name) and "Description" as shown next.

If the property name is not listed in the "Name" drop-down list, we can type it ourselves, as is the case with Volume.

In the next property use the caption "Designer" to label it, type "MyName" in the custom property Name box, and enter your name in it. This value can be changed later, but for now it will be pre-set to help us save time.

357

For the last property leave the Value field empty, this value will be added when we add the properties to the part files later on.

Other controls that can be added to a Property Tab template include drop-down lists (with typed items, linked to text files, excel spreadsheets, or data bases), numbers, checkboxes and radio buttons for multiple selection items.

Now we need to save this template. Press the "**Save**" command and save it in the default custom property folder. Close the Property Tab Builder and return to SolidWorks.

If the template is saved in a different location, go to the menu "**Tools Options, System Options, File Locations,**" from the drop-down list select "Custom Property Files" and change it to point to the new location.

311. - Back in SolidWorks open the "Custom Properties" tab (If the template is not visible press "F5" to refresh and load the template we just made. The properties added to the template are ready for us to apply to the part. The "Material" property is taken from the assigned part's material, "Weight" and "Volume" are automatically calculated and filled, "Designer" is pre-filled with the value we entered in the template but can be changed if needed, and the only thing we need to do is to add a description, which was intentionally left empty to enter a value for each part. Type a description for the '*Worm Gear Shaft*' and press "Apply" to add the properties to the 3D model and save the file.

312. - Make a new drawing from the '*Worm Gear Shaft*' using the "A-Landscape" drawing template. Add the Front view from the View Palette; click above it to add a Top view, and to the left to add the Left view. Use "Hidden Lines Removed" mode for all 3 views. Change the sheet scale to 1:1. Edit the Sheet Format to add the missing custom property notes and change the formatting to look good.

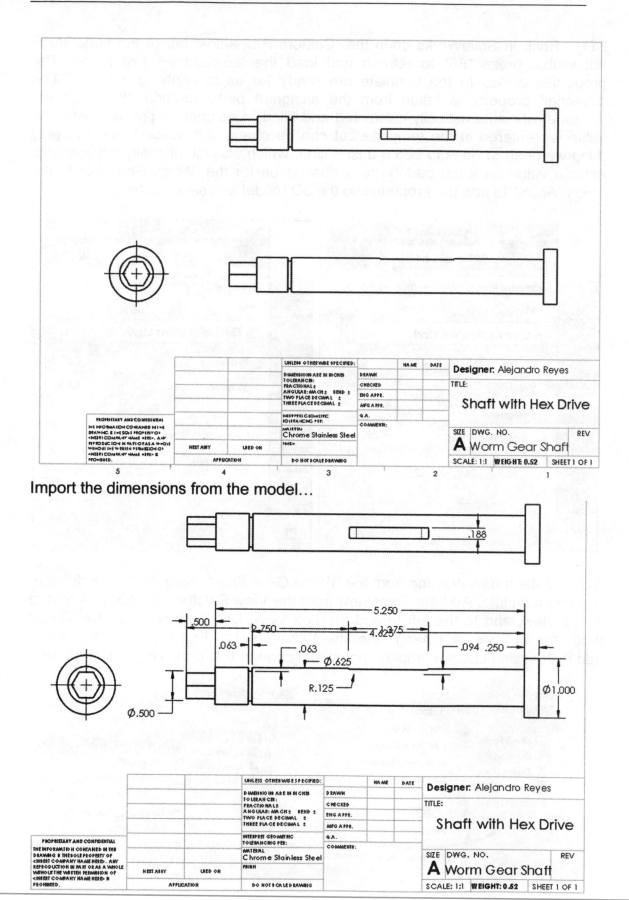

Import the dimensions from the model...

And arrange them.

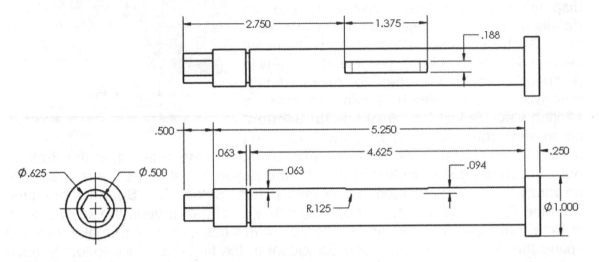

313. - One more thing we need to add to the drawing are the centerlines. SolidWorks allows us to add a centerline to every cylindrical face of the model. To add centerlines to our drawing views, select the "**Centerline**" command from the Annotation Tab, and click in the cylindrical surface that we need to add a centerline to. When finished adding centerlines click OK to finish.

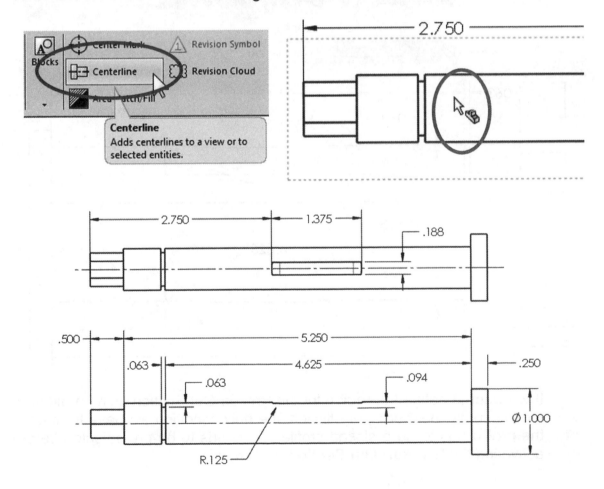

314. - Instead of changing the Front view display to "Hidden Lines Visible" to see the details of the keyway, we will make a "**Broken-Out Section**" view. What the broken out section does is to cut-out a region of the view to a specific depth in order to reveal details otherwise hidden without having to make a section view. Select the "**Broken-Out Section**" command from the "View Layout" tab and

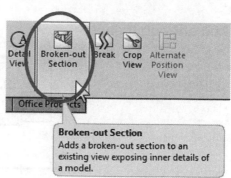

similar to the "Detail" view, where we get a circle tool to define it, in the Broken-out-Section we get a "**Spline**" to define the region to cut. A Spline is a smooth polynomial curve connected by multiple points. Select the "**Spline**" command from the Sketch tab and draw it approximately as shown around the keyway area in the Front view. Splines can be open or, in this case, closed; to make a closed spline the last point will be made coincident to the first one. Click to locate each point of the curve.

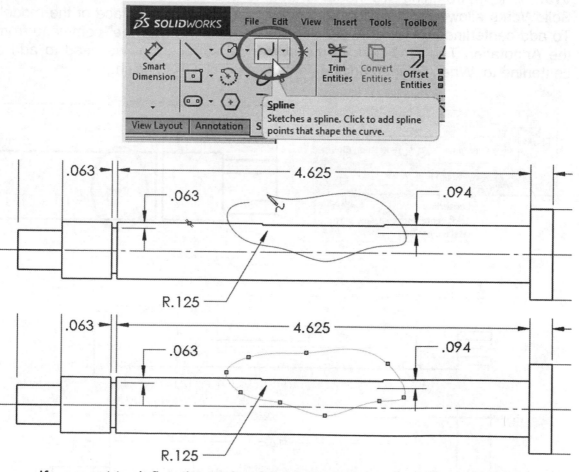

If we want to define the region for the Broken-Out Section using a different tool, such as lines, arcs, or ellipses, the only condition we have to meet is the profile has to be a closed profile and needs to be pre-selected before activating the "**Broken-Out Section**" command.

315. - When the last point of the **Spline** is added, we get the "**Broken-Out Section**" properties, where we are asked to enter a depth to make the cut or select an edge of the model to define the depth. Select the vertical edge indicated in the Top view to define how deep the cut will be. By selecting the vertical edge the section's depth is set to its midpoint, effectively making the cut go to the center of the part. Activating the "Preview" option will allow us to see the resulting section.

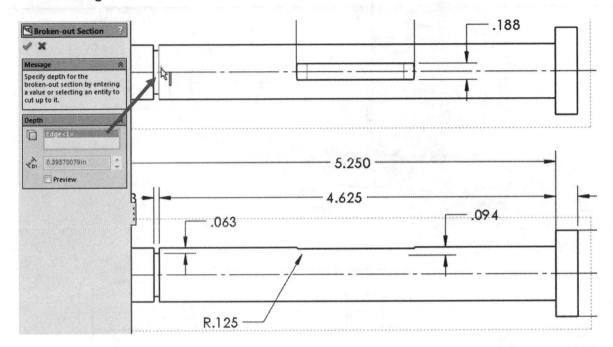

Click OK to finish the Broken-out Section.

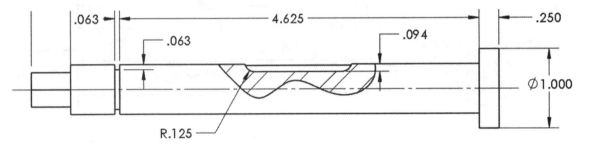

To edit or delete the "**Broken-Out Section**", right-mouse-click <u>inside</u> the section's region and from the "**Broken-Out Section**" menu select "Delete", "Edit Definition" (to change its depth) or "Edit Sketch" to modify the cut-out area.

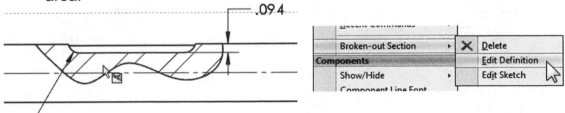

316. - In this drawing, it may be a good idea to manually add a reference dimension for the hexagonal cut. To show the construction circle we can make the sketch for the hexagonal cut visible. Expand the view in the FeatureManager, right-mouse-click in the cut's sketch and select "Show" from the pop-up menu. Save the drawing and close the file.

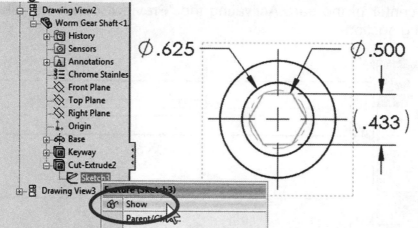

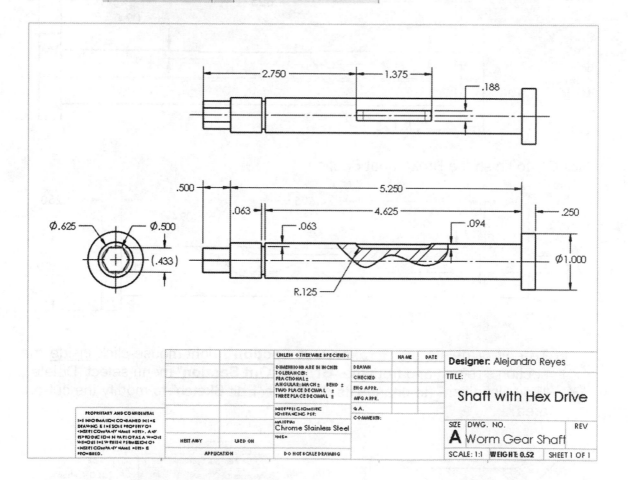

Exercises: Make the detail drawing of the following Engine Project parts that were done in the Part Modeling section to match the drawings previously supplied for each part. These will complete the Engine Project drawings. High resolution images at www.mechanicad.com.

Internal Retaining Ring	**Retaining Ring Crankshaft Bearing**
Exhaust	**Oil Dip Stick**
Engine Block	**Piston Head**
Oil Pan	**Crank Case Top**

Extra Credit: Using the parts made for the gas grill project make the corresponding detail drawings. The finished components can be downloaded from http://www.mechanicad.com/download.html.

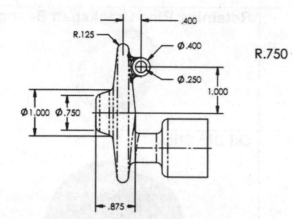

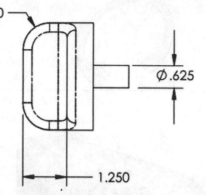

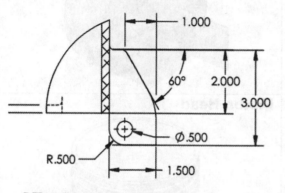

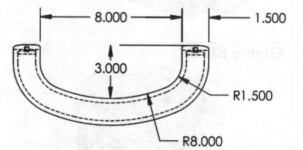

DETAIL B
SCALE 1 : 2

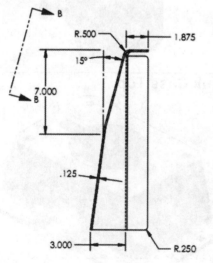

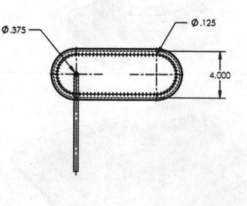

Assembly Modeling

The next step in the design after making the parts and drawings is to get all the parts together into an assembly. The process of designing the parts first and then assembling them is known as "Bottom-Up Design." Think of it as buying a bicycle; when you open the box, you get all the pieces needed ready for assembly. A different approach known as "Top-Down Design" is where the parts are designed while working in the assembly; this is a very powerful tool that allows us to match parts to each other, changing a part if another component is modified. In this book we'll cover the Bottom-Up Design technique, since it is easier to understand and is also the basis for the advanced Top-Down Design, which is covered in the **Beginner's Guide to SolidWorks Level II** book. In general, it's a good idea to design the parts, make the assembly to make sure everything fits and works as expected (Form, Fit and Function), and *then* make the drawings of the parts and assemblies; this way the drawings are done at the end, when you are sure everything works correctly.

So far, we've been working on parts, single components that are the building blocks of an assembly. In an assembly we have multiple components, either parts or other assemblies (in this case called subassemblies.) The way we tell SolidWorks how to relate components (parts and/or subassemblies) together is by using Mates (or relations) between them. Mates in the assembly are similar to the geometric relations in the sketch, but in the assembly we reference faces, planes, edges, axes, vertices and even sketch geometry from the features in the components in order to align them to each other.

In an assembly, the components are added one at a time until we complete the design. In an assembly every component has six degrees of freedom, meaning that they can move and rotate six different ways: three translations along the X, Y and Z axes, and three rotations about the X, Y, and Z axes. By mating components to each other we are essentially restricting how they move in relation to one another based on which degrees of freedom are constrained. This is the basis for assembly motion and simulation.

The first component we add to the assembly has all six degrees of freedom fixed by default. Therefore, it's a good idea to make sure the first component added to the assembly is one that will be a reference for the rest of the components. For example, if we make a bicycle assembly, the first component added to the assembly would be the frame. For the gear box we are designing, the first component added to the assembly will be the *'Housing'* as the rest of the components will be attached to it.

Notes:

The Gear Housing Assembly

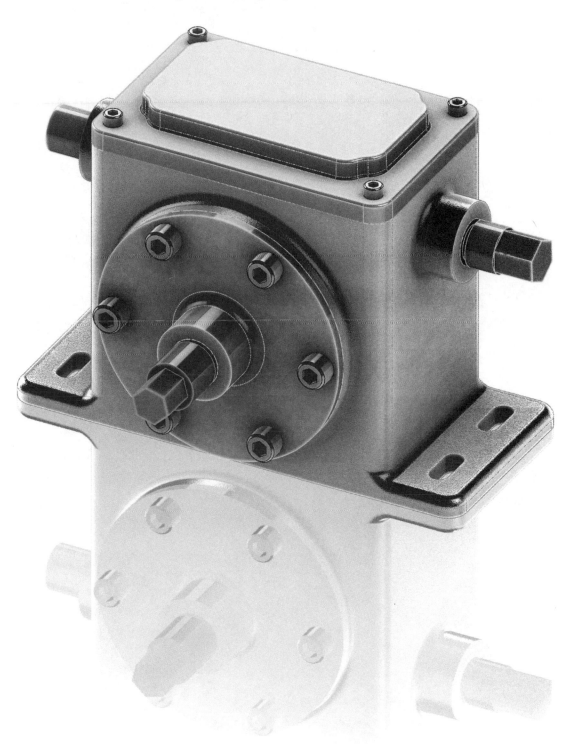

Notes:

In making the *'Gear Housing'* assembly, we will learn about assembly tools and operations, including making new assemblies, adding components, adding Mating relations between them and adding fasteners. We'll cover component design tables, interference detection, assembly exploded views, and how to change a part's dimensions while working in the assembly. The sequence to follow while making the *'Gear Housing'* assembly is the following:

New Assembly	Add the Housing; change configuration	Add and mate the first Side Cover	Add and mate the second Side Cover
Add and mate the Worm Gear Shaft	Change component colors	Add and mate the Worm Gear	Add and mate the Offset Shaft
Add and mate the Top Cover	Add screws	Find interferences and correct them	Make exploded view

317. - The first thing we need to make a new assembly is to select the **"New"** document command, select the Assembly template, and click OK.

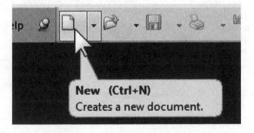

371

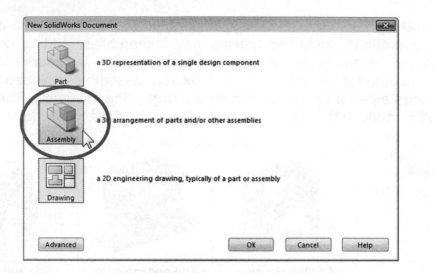

318. - The first thing we see when we make a new assembly is the "**Begin Assembly**" dialog to start adding components. As we discussed previously, the *'Housing'* will be the first component to be added. Click "Browse" to locate the *'Housing'* part file, select it in the "**Open**" dialog box making sure we are using the *"Machined"* configuration in the "Configurations" drop-down menu. If you cannot see the component that you want, make sure you are looking in the correct folder and have the "**Files of Type**" set to *"Part"* in the "Quick Filter." Click "**Open**" when done. If you have the "Graphics Preview" option box checked, you will see a preview of the component being inserted.

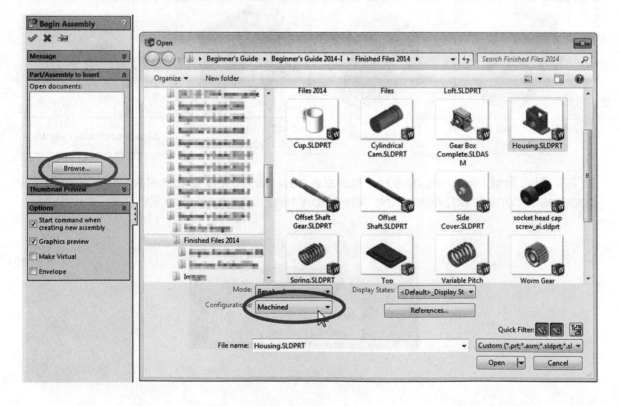

319. - After selecting the *'Housing'* we have to locate it in the assembly; when we move the mouse the part's preview follows it. What we want to do is to locate the *'Housing'* at the assembly origin. If you cannot see the assembly origin (which is hidden in the default assembly template), turn it on by selecting the menu "**View, Origins**" (this can be done while you are inserting a component.) The reason to locate the *'Housing'* at the assembly's origin is to have the *'Housing's* planes and origin aligned with the assembly's planes and origin. To add the *'Housing'* AND align it with the assembly's origin, click the OK button *or* move the mouse pointer to the assembly origin and click on it. (The cursor will have a double origin next to it and you will see the *'Housing'* "snap" in place before clicking.)

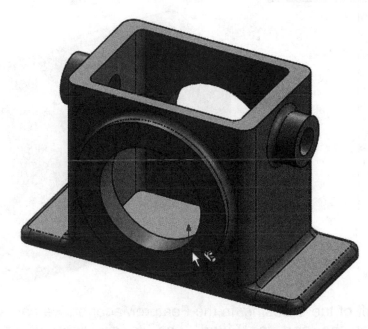

320. - If the *'Housing'* is loaded by mistake showing the *"Forge"* configuration, do not worry, as it can be changed. Select the "*Housing*" part in the FeatureManager and select the "*Machined*" configuration from the pop-up toolbar and accept the change with the green OK checkmark.

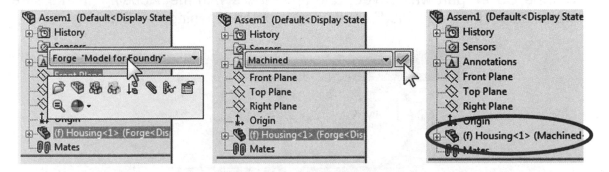

If the component added to the assembly has configurations, the selected configuration is shown next to the part's name in the FeatureManager in parentheses.

321. - Once in the Assembly environment, the toolbars are changed in the CommandManager; now we have an Assembly tab. Also notice at the bottom of the Assembly FeatureManager a special folder called "**Mates**." This is where the relations between components are stored.

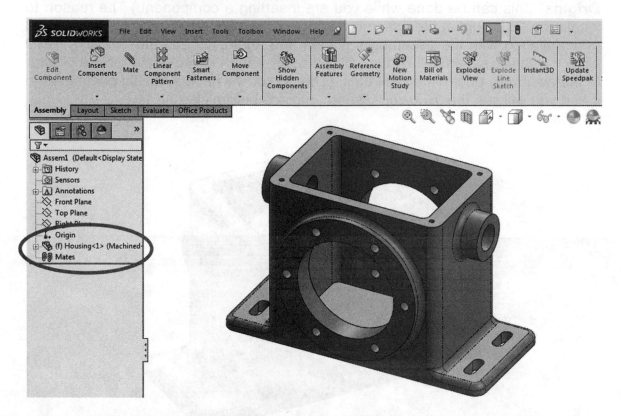

322. - To the left of the *'Housing'* in the FeatureManager, we can see a letter "**f**"; this means that the part is "**Fixed**" and its six degrees of freedom are constrained, therefore it cannot move or rotate about any axis. The first component in the assembly is always automatically fixed and subsequent components are not. To add the second component to our assembly, click in the "**Insert Components**" command in the Assembly tab, browse to the folder where the *'Side Cover'* part was saved, and open it. As with the '*Housing*', make sure we also select the "Machined" configuration before opening the '*Side Cover*'.

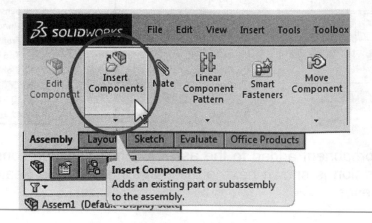

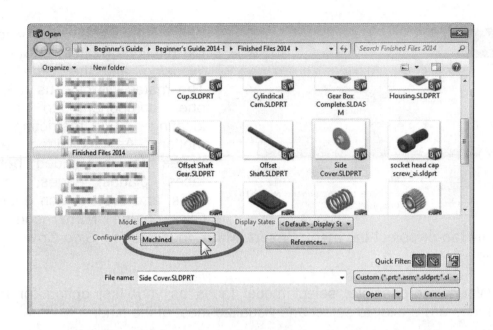

323. - Place the *'Side Cover'* next to the *'Housing'* as seen in the next image. Don't worry about the exact location; we'll locate it accurately next using mates.

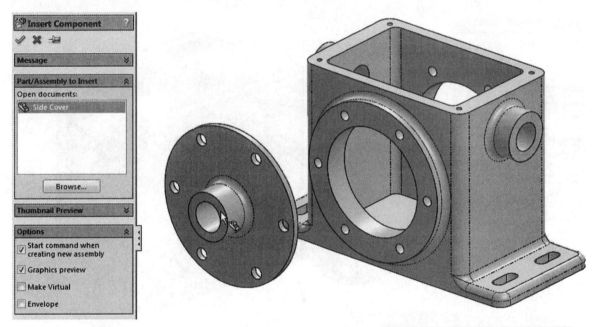

324. - After adding the *'Side Cover'* part, its name in the FeatureManager is preceded by a (-), this means that the part has *at least* one unconstrained degree of freedom. Since this part was just added, all six degrees of freedom are unconstrained and the part is free to move in any direction and rotate about all three axes.

375

325. - Now we are ready to add the relations (Mates) between the *'Housing'* and the *'Side Cover'*. The mates will help us reference one component to another, locating and restricting their motion. As explained earlier, mates can be added between faces, planes, edges, vertices, axes, and even sketch geometry. Click on the **"Mate"** icon in the Assembly tab or select the menu **"Insert, Mate"** to locate the *'Side Cover'* on the *'Housing'*.

Whenever possible, select model faces as your first option for mates, faces are easier to select and visualize most of the time.

326. - For the first mate, select the two <u>cylindrical faces</u> indicated in the next picture.

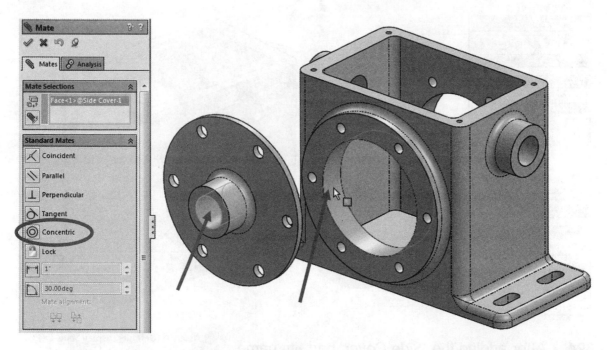

After the second face is selected, SolidWorks recognizes that both faces are cylindrical and automatically "snaps" them with a **Concentric Mate**. (SolidWorks defaults to concentric as it is the most logical option.) The *'Side Cover'* is the part that moves because it is the part with unconstrained degrees of freedom; remember the *'Housing'* was fixed when it was inserted, and therefore, it cannot move. In this case the **Concentric Mate** is pre-selected; click the OK button in the pop-up toolbar to add this mate.

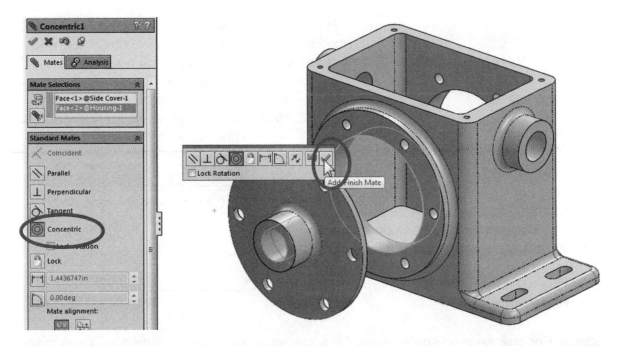

327. - Note the pop-up toolbar shows options to mate the entities. (These options are listed in the PropertyManager, too.) This toolbar helps us to be more productive by minimizing mouse travel. The following table shows the basic mate options available:

Standard Mates	Entities that can be mated
Coincident	Two Faces, Planes, Edges, Vertices, Axes, Sketch points/endpoints, or any combination.
Parallel	Two flat Faces, Planes, linear Edges, Axes, or any combination.
Perpendicular	Two flat Faces, Planes, Edges, Axes, or any combination.
Tangent	Two cylindrical Faces; one flat Face and one cylindrical; a cylindrical Face and one linear Edge.
Concentric / Lock rotation	Two cylindrical Faces, two round Edges, two linear Edges or Axes, one cylindrical Face and one round Edge, one cylindrical Face and one linear Edge.
Lock	This option constrains all degrees of freedom of the component, locking it in place.
1" / Flip dimension	Specify a distance between any two valid entities for Coincident or Parallel mates. "Flip dimension" reverses the direction to one side or the other. Using this mate on two flat Faces or Planes will also make them parallel.

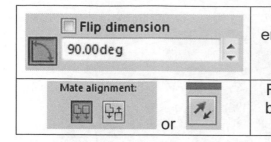	Specify an angle between any two valid entities for Coincident, Parallel, or Concentric mates. "Flip dimension" will reverse the direction of the angular dimension.
Mate alignment: ... or	Reverses the orientation of the components being mated. For two Faces, to look at each other or away.

328. - After adding the first mate, the dialog remains visible; this means that we are ready to add more mates. It will remain active until we click **Cancel** or hit "Esc" on the keyboard. Notice that the mate added is listed under the "**Mates**" box in the PropertyManager. We'll continue adding mates at this time; do not exit the "**Mate**" command.

329. - For the second mate, select the two cylindrical faces indicated (one from the *'Side Cover'*, and one from the *'Housing'*.) SolidWorks defaults again to a **Concentric** mate and rotates the *'Side Cover'* to align the holes; this will prevent the *'Side Cover'* from rotating. Remember we can use the "**Magnifying Glass**" to make selection of small faces easier. Click OK to add the mate. *IF* the *'Side Cover'* is *inside* the *'Housing'*, click-and-drag it with the left mouse button to get it out and allow us to add the remaining mates.

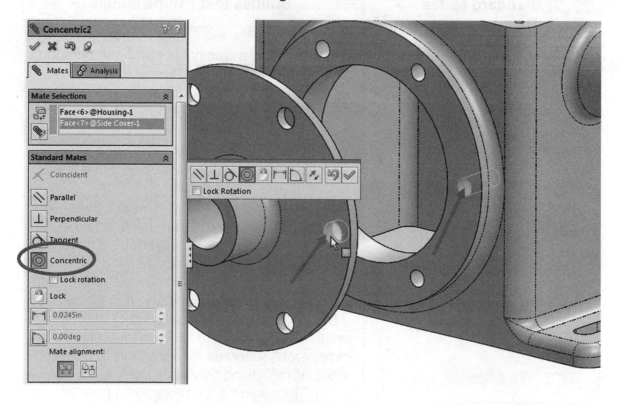

The "Lock Rotation" option in the concentric mate prevents the mated parts from rotating. Checking this option in the first concentric mate would eliminate the need to add the second concentric mate.

In this case the Concentric mate works as expected because both holes are located <u>exactly</u> at the same distance from the center in both parts; in reality, it is generally a better idea to align the two components using Planes and/or Faces, with either a Parallel or Coincident mate, as will be shown in a later in the book.

330. - The last mate will be a **Coincident mate** between the back face of the *'Side Cover'* and the front face of the *'Housing'*; use "**Select Other**" or rotate the view to select the faces if needed (If the *'Side Cover'* is <u>inside</u> the *'Housing'*, click-and-drag to move it out.) After selecting the faces the cover will move until the faces touch; the **Coincident mate** option will be pre-selected. Click OK to add the mate and finish the "Mate" command by either clicking OK, Cancel or pressing the "Esc" key.

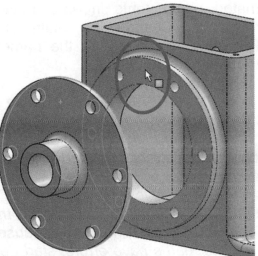

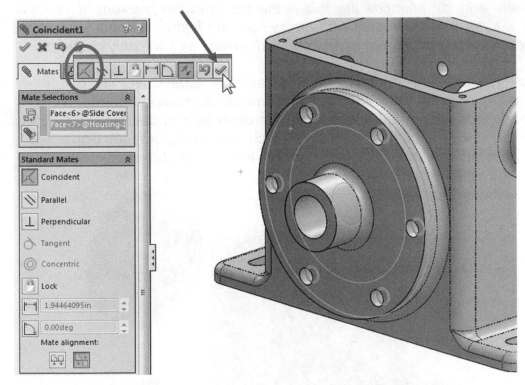

Using the "**Select Other**" tool will allow you us to select hidden component faces without having to rotate the view.

331. - All six degrees of freedom of the *'Side Cover'* have been constrained using mates; this can be seen in the FeatureManager where the *'Side Cover'* is no longer preceded by a (-) sign. Notice that the **"Mates"** folder now includes the two Concentric and one Coincident mate we just added; SolidWorks adds the names of the mated components in each mate for reference. Change the width of the FeatureManager to see the names of the mated components.

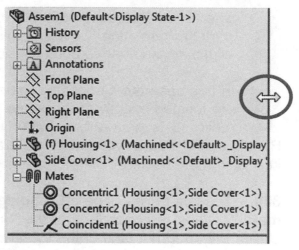

IMPORTANT: *If a (+) sign precedes a part name, you probably also received an error message telling you that the assembly had been **over defined**. If this is the case, it means you added conflicting mates that cannot be solved, or inadvertently selected the wrong faces or edges when adding mates.*

*The easiest way to correct this error is to either hit the **Undo** button or delete the last mate in the "Mates" folder; you will be able to identify the conflicting mate because it will have an error icon next to it. If multiple mates have errors, start deleting the last mate at the bottom (this is the last one added); chances are this is the cause of the problem. If you still have errors, keep deleting mates with errors from the bottom up until you clear all the errors. It's not a good idea to proceed with errors, as it will only get worse.*

332. - We are now ready to add the second *'Side Cover'* to our assembly. Repeat the **"Insert Component"** command to add a second *'Side Cover'* and locate it on the other side of the *'Housing'* as shown. Remember to use the "Machined" configuration. Don't worry too much about the exact location, in the next step we'll move and rotate the part.

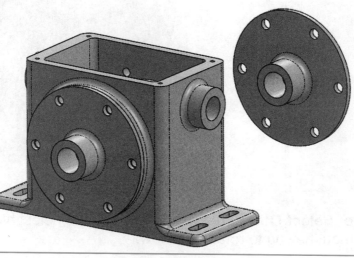

A quick way to add a copy of an assembly component is to hold down the "Ctrl" key and click-and-drag the part to be copied within the assembly.

333. - When the second *'Side Cover'* is inserted, it has a (-) sign next to it in the FeatureManager; remember, this means that it has <u>at least</u> one unconstrained Degree of Freedom (DOF). Since this part was just inserted in the assembly, all six DOF are unconstrained, and the component can be moved and rotated. To **"Move"** a component click-and-drag it with the <u>left mouse button</u>. To **"Rotate"** it, click-and-drag it with the <u>right mouse button</u>. "Move" and "Rotate" the second *'Side Cover'* as needed to align it *approximately* as shown. Remember, we'll add mates to locate it precisely. Turn off the "Origins" (menu **"View, Origins"**) and rotate the view as we did with parts to look at the assembly from the back.

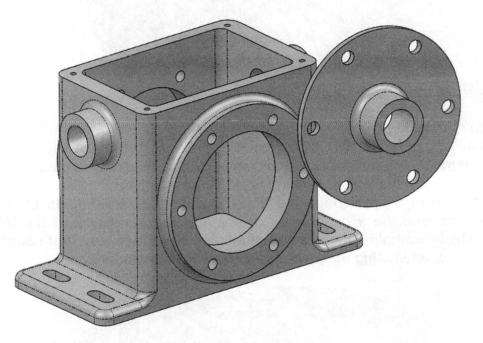

334. - Now we need to mate the second cover as we did to the first *'Side Cover'*. Select the **"Mate"** command from the Assembly tab and add a **Concentric** mate selecting the faces indicated. Rotate the view (not the part) to get a better view of the faces to select. To take advantage of the shortcut menus, instead of the mate command select one of the faces to be mated, and from the pop-up toolbar select the **"Mate"** command, once the command is opened this face will be pre-selected.

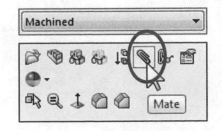

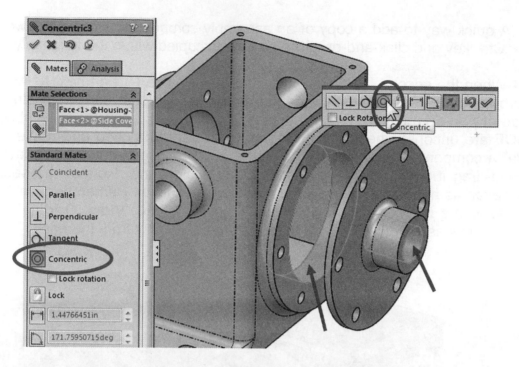

Before adding the second concentric mate click-and-drag the cover. Notice that it can rotate about its center and also move along the axis; under-constrained components are the basis for SolidWorks to simulate motion.

335. - Now add a new concentric mate to align the screw holes between the *'Side Cover'* and the *'Housing'*. Since the part is symmetrical, it doesn't really matter which two holes are selected. If the cover had a feature that needed to be aligned, then orientating the part correctly would be important.

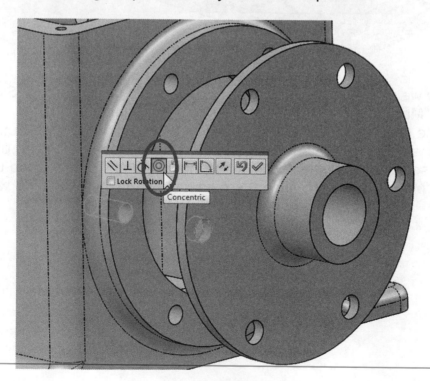

336. - Finally add a Coincident mate between the flat face of the *'Housing'* and the second *'Side Cover'* as we did with the first cover. Use "**Select Other**" to select the hidden face, or rotate the part. Click OK to continue.

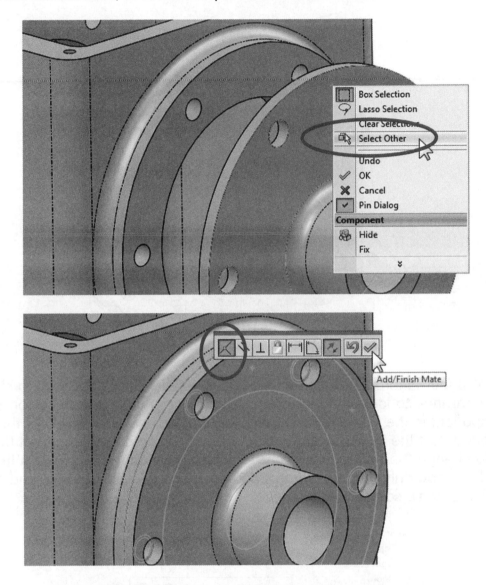

337. - It is very important to notice that these mates could have been added in any order; we chose this order to make it easier for the reader to see the effect of each mate on each part. Whichever order you select, you will end up with both *'Side Cover'* parts fully defined (no free DOF) and six mates in the "Mates" folder as listed next.

338. - Now that we have correctly mated both *'Side Covers'*, add the *'Worm Gear Shaft'* using the same procedure as before and locate it somewhere above the *'Housing'*.

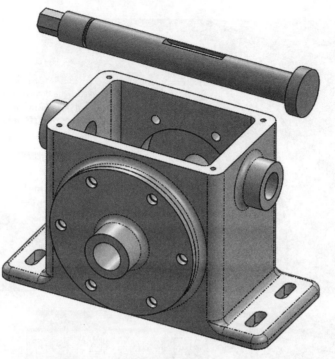

339. - With four different components in the assembly, it's a good idea to change their appearance to identify them easily. To change a component's color, select the component in the FeatureManager or the graphics screen, and from the pop-up toolbar select the "**Appearance**" icon. From the drop-down list, select the first option to change the part's color at the assembly level only. This means that the color will change only in the assembly and not in the part file. The second option changes the part's color at the part level.

We can change a part's appearance in the assembly, or in the part file. Picture it like this: We can paint the part *before* we assemble it, or we paint it *after* we assemble it. In the first case we assemble a painted part, in the second case the part is painted after it is assembled. For this example, we want to change the color at the assembly level.

340. - We are now ready to change the part's color. Select the desired color from the color swatch selection box to change it. Click OK to finish.

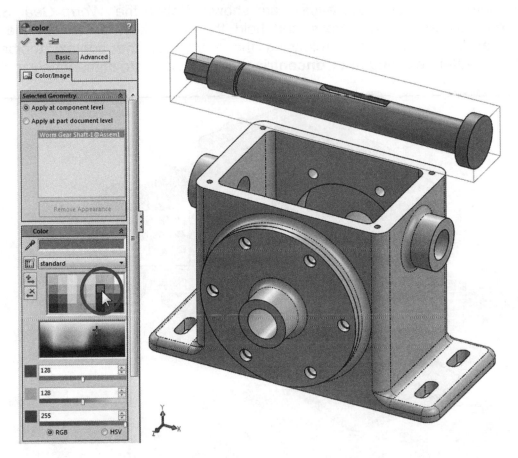

341. - Change the color of both covers to your liking and continue adding mates. (It does look better in color!)

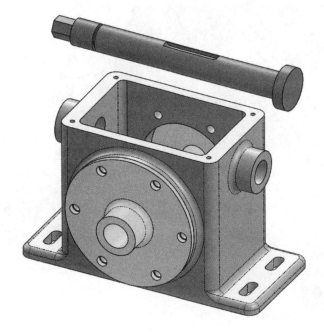

342. - A new way to add mates is by pre-selecting the faces to be mated and selecting the mate to be added from the context toolbar. Only standard mates appropriate for the selected entities are shown. Rotate the *'Worm Gear Shaft'* approximately as shown, press and hold the "Ctrl" key, pre-select the two cylindrical faces, and after releasing the "Ctrl" key the context toolbar is displayed. After selecting the **Concentric** mate the parts are immediately mated.

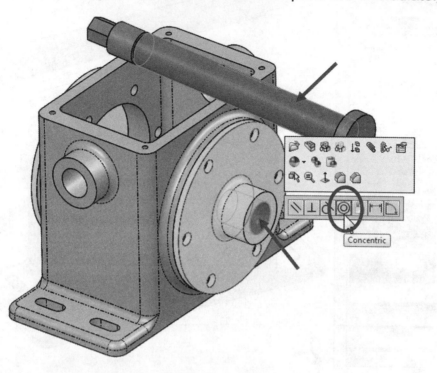

Repeat the same process but now pre-select the flat faces to add a Coincident mate.

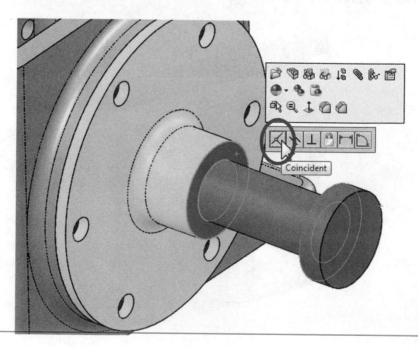

Notice that the *'Worm Gear Shaft'* is not yet fully defined; it still has a (-) sign before its name in the FeatureManager. In this case the only DOF left unconstrained is to rotate about its axis, and that is exactly what we want; the *'Worm Gear Shaft'* is supposed to rotate. If we click-and-drag it, we'll see it rotate. (Look at the keyway while rotating it.)

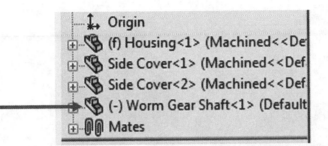

343. - The next component to be added will be the *'Worm Gear'*. Add it with the **"Insert Component"** command as before and place it in the assembly as shown. And now that you know how, change its color too.

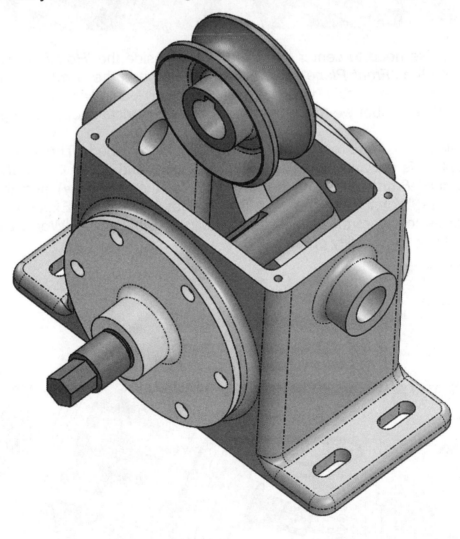

344. - To locate the *'Worm Gear'* in place use either of the two methods presented to add a concentric mate with the *'Worm Gear Shaft'*. Select the cylindrical inside face of the *'Worm Gear'* and the outside face of the *'Worm Gear Shaft'*. Drag the *'Worm Gear'* and see how it moves along the shaft and rotates about it.

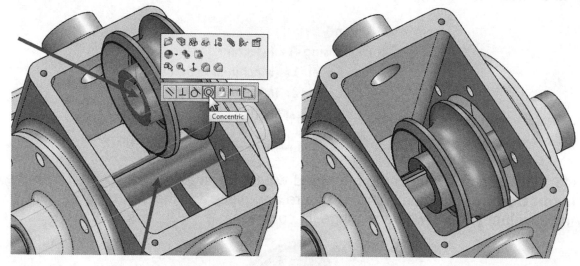

345. - Now we need to center the *'Worm Gear'* inside the *'Housing'*. To do this we can use the *"Front Plane"* of the *'Worm Gear'* and the *"Front Plane"* of the *'Housing'* or the assembly, which are conveniently located in the center of the *'Housing'*. (Remember we made the *'Housing'* symmetrical about the origin? ☺)

Select the **Mate** command if it's not already open (The mate context toolbar option is not available when mating planes) and add a **Coincident** mate selecting the *"Front Plane"* of the *'Housing'* (or the assembly) and the *"Front Plane"* of the *'Worm Gear'* from the fly-out FeatureManager. Expand the parts' feature trees to select the planes. In the following image the 'Worm Gear' was moved outside for visibility purposes.

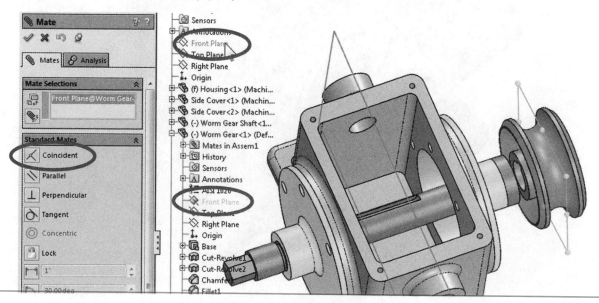

After adding this mate, the *'Worm Gear'* is still under defined, and we want the *'Worm Gear Shaft'* and the *'Worm Gear'* to rotate together. To accomplish this, we'll have to add either a **Coincident** mate using the corresponding planes from the parts, or a **Parallel** mate between the faces of the keyways. We'll add a Parallel mate in this step and let the reader explore the other option.

346. - As luck would have it, the *'Housing'* is obstructing the view to the keyways, and we'll need to hide it in order to add the next mate. Cancel the **"Mate"** command if it's still active. Select the *'Housing'* in the FeatureManger or in the graphics area, and select the **"Hide/Show"** icon from the pop-up toolbar. The part will be hidden, allowing us to see the rest of the components to add the next mate. Keep in mind that the part will be "invisible," not deleted from the assembly. After we are done mating the parts we'll make it visible again.

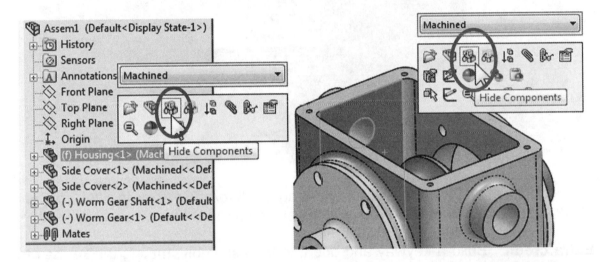

347. - As soon as we hide the part, it disappears from the screen and we can see inside without obstructions. The *'Housing'* icon in the FeatureManager changes to white; this is how we know that the part is hidden.

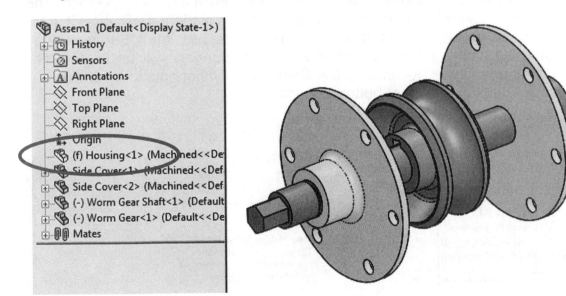

389

348. - Add a new "**Mate**" using the flat faces of the *'Worm Gear Shaft'* and *'Worm Gear'* keyways. In this case, we'll use a **Parallel** mate. The reason for choosing a **Parallel mate** is because it can absorb small dimensional differences that may exist between the parts preventing them from being exactly coincident, and making it parallel gives us the desired result. In general this is a more forgiving option. Click OK to add the mate and close the "Mate" command.

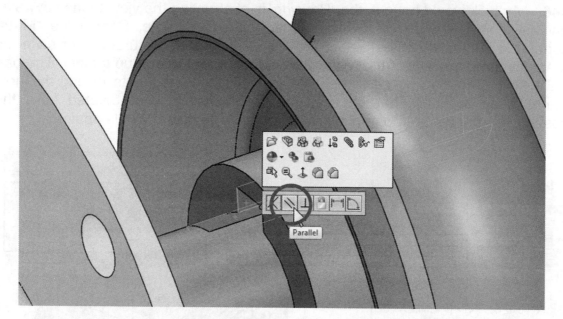

After adding the mate, click-and-drag the *'Worm Gear'* or the *'Worm Gear Shaft'*, see how both of them rotate at the same time, as if they had a keyway.

Extra credit: Build a keyway and add it to the assembly, mating the keyway to the *'Worm Gear Shaft'*, and the *'Worm Gear'* to the keyway.

349. - To show the *'Housing'* select the *'Housing'* in the FeatureManager and select the "**Hide/Show Component**" command from the pop-up toolbar. This command works as a toggle switch. If a component is hidden, it will show it, if the component is visible, it will hide it. Optionally select the "**Show Hidden Components**" command. All currently visible components will be hidden, and hidden components will become visible. Select the components to be shown and click in the "Exit show-hidden" button to finish.

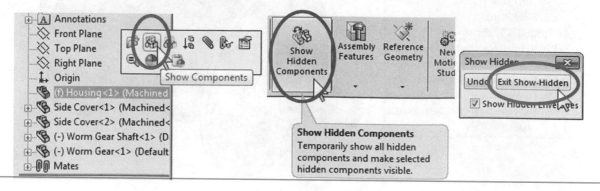

350. - Now add the *'Offset Shaft'* to the assembly using the "**Insert Component**" command and change its color for visibility.

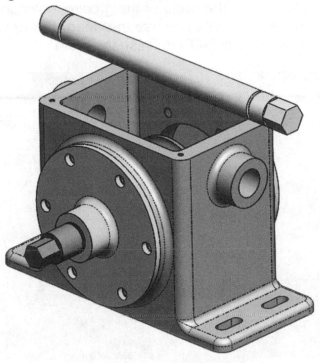

351. - Add mates by selecting one of the model faces to be mated, and from the pop-up toolbar, select the "**Mate**" icon. When the "**Mate**" command is displayed, the model face is pre-selected and we only need to select the other face to add a concentric mate, *or* pre-select both faces and select the "Concentric" mate from the pop-up menu. Do not use the "Lock Rotation" option, we need it to rotate.

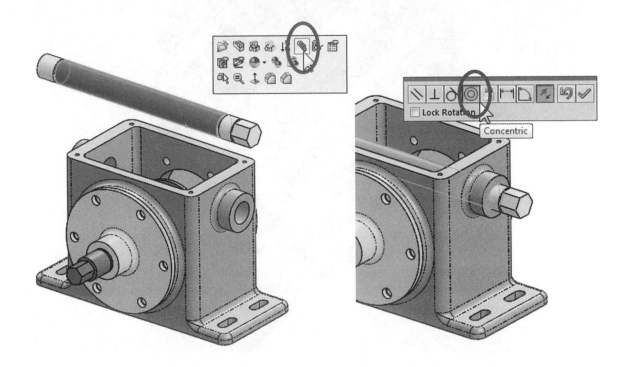

352. - Now we need to add a coincident mate to prevent the shaft from moving along its axis. We'll use the groove in the *'Shaft'* for this mate. In this case, we can use either the flat face or the edge of the groove; selecting the edge may be easier than selecting the face. We can use the **"Magnifying Glass"** tool to zoom in and make our selections. Click OK to finish the mate.

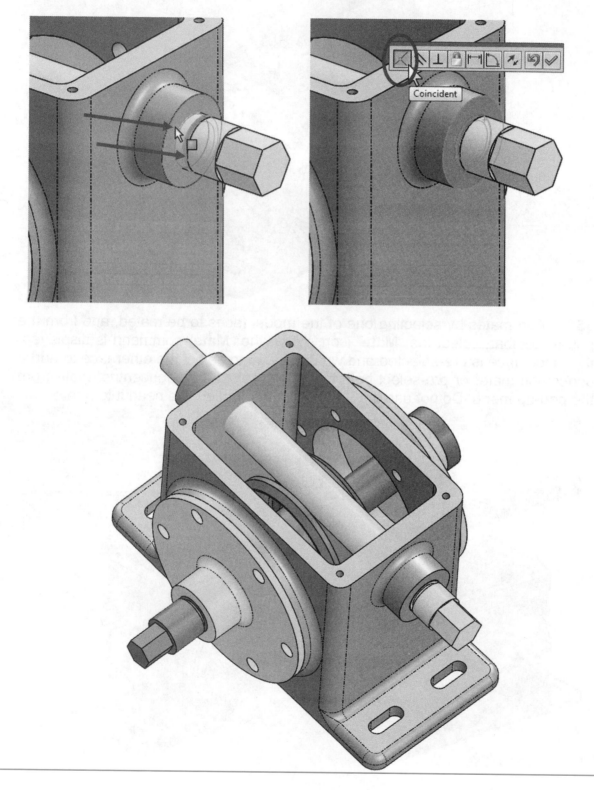

353. - The last component we're adding is the *'Top Cover'*. Add it to the assembly and, if you wish, change its color. Add the first concentric mate to align one of the holes of the cover to the corresponding hole in the *'Housing'*, press and hold the Ctrl key, select both faces indicated, and release the Ctrl key. From the pop-up menu select the concentric mate command. We can select either faces or circular edges for this mate. An interesting detail to know is that a concentric mate removes four DOF from the component: two translations and two rotations when mated to a fixed or fully defined reference.

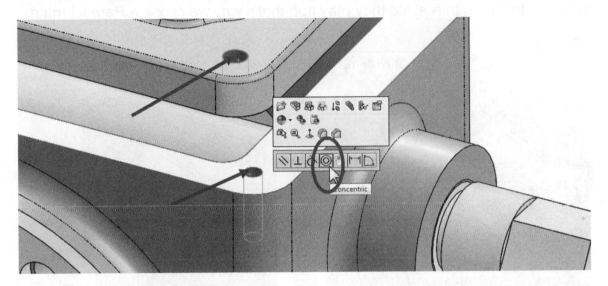

354. - Check the remaining two DOF by dragging the *'Top Cover'* with the left mouse button; it will rotate about the hole we mated and move up and down. By adding a coincident mate between the <u>bottom face</u> of the *'Top Cover'*, and the <u>top face</u> of the *'Housing'* we remove one more DOF.

355. - If we click-and-drag the *'Top Cover'*, it will turn; now we only have one DOF left. To finish constraining the *'Top Cover'* we'll add a **Parallel** mate between the *'Top Cover'* and the *'Housing'*. As we explained earlier, the reason for the Parallel mate is that sometimes components don't match exactly, and if we add a Coincident mate, we may be forcing a condition that cannot be met, over defining the assembly and getting an error message. The Parallel mate can be added between Faces, Planes, and/or Edges. In this particular case, we can use either a Coincident or Parallel mate since the parts were designed to match exactly. However, in real life they may not; that's why we chose a Parallel mate.

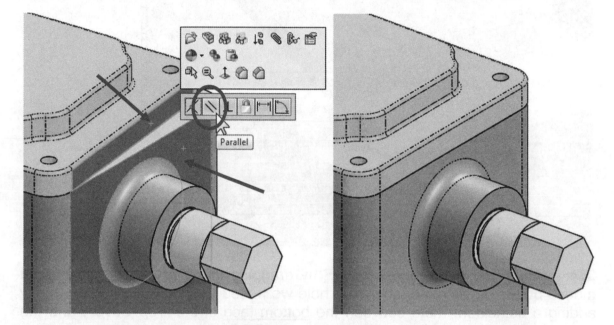

Your assembly should now look like this.

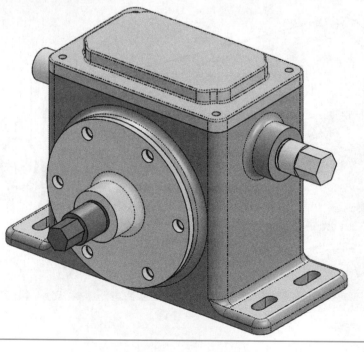

SmartMates

SmartMates are a quick and easy way to add certain mate types between components simply by dragging parts or assemblies onto each other using flat, cylindrical or conical faces, circular or linear edges, vertices, or temporary axes. It works by holding down the "Alt" key while we drag the face, edge or vertex of the component to be mated *onto* the face, edge or vertex of the other component.

We'll re-create the entire assembly up to this point using the SmartMates approach, now that the concept of mates has been explained and we have a better idea of the general process. The next table shows the types of SmartMates available and their corresponding feedback icon when used.

When SmartMates is enabled the icon will change to a clip attached to the face, edge, or vertex being dragged.

Entities to be mated/ Feedback icon	Resulting Mate
2 Flat Faces 	**Coincident Faces**
2 Linear Edges	**Coincident Edges**

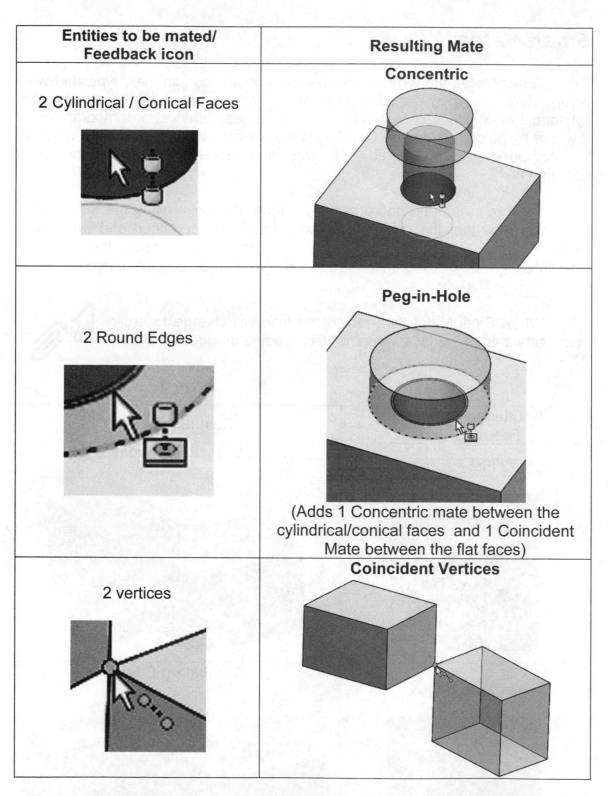

Entities to be mated/ Feedback icon	Resulting Mate
2 Cylindrical / Conical Faces	**Concentric**
2 Round Edges	**Peg-in-Hole** (Adds 1 Concentric mate between the cylindrical/conical faces and 1 Coincident Mate between the flat faces)
2 vertices	**Coincident Vertices**

When using SmartMates to mate two flanged faces, SolidWorks will add a Peg-in-Hole mate and an extra Concentric mate between two holes in the flanged faces to align them.

356. - Let's recreate the entire assembly now using SmartMates. An alternate way to start an assembly is similar to the way we made the detail drawings. Open the *'Housing'* part, and from the "**New**" document icon select "**Make Assembly from Part/Assembly**," or the menu "**File, Make Assembly from Part**." Make sure the selected configuration is "Machined" before making the assembly. Just as we did previously, add the *'Housing'* at the origin. If you cannot see the origin, turn it on in the menu "**View, Origins**."

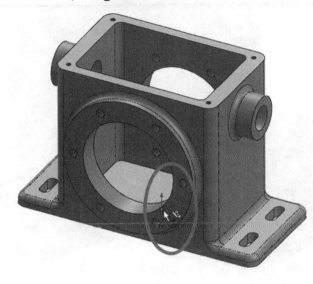

357. - Now, bring in the *'Side Cover'* with the "**Insert Component**" command and put it next to the *'Housing'* with the "Machined" configuration, just as we did before up to this point.

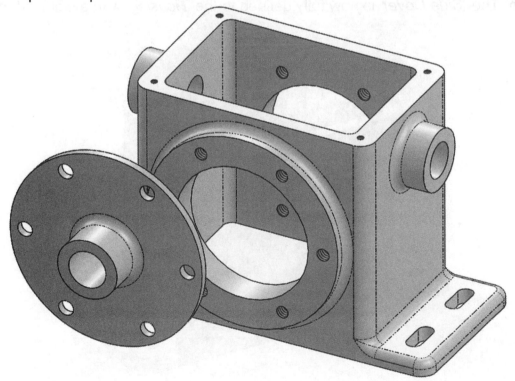

358. - Now we can start using the SmartMates functionality. Press and hold the **"Alt"** key on the keyboard and, while holding it down, left-click-and-drag the *'Side Cover'* from the edge indicated. Notice that as soon as we start moving it, the "Mate" icon appears next to the mouse pointer, and the *'Side Cover'* becomes transparent.

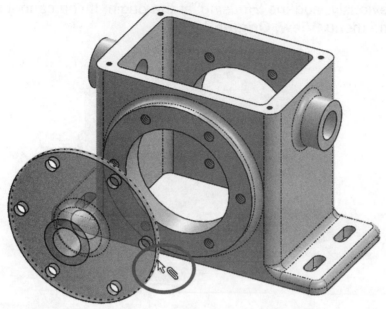

359. - Keep dragging the *'Side Cover'* until we touch the flat face or the round edge in the front face of the *'Housing'*; at this time the *'Side Cover'* will 'snap' into place and will give us the **"Peg-in-Hole"** mate icon. Release the mouse button to finish. The *'Side Cover'* is now fully defined to the *'Housing'* with a single step.

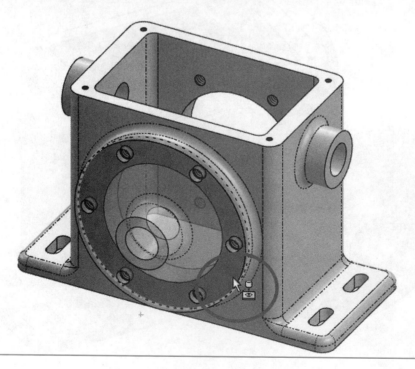

Expanding the "Mates" folder in the FeatureManager, we can see that two concentric mates and one coincident mate have been added. Select the mates to see the faces that were automatically mated in each one.

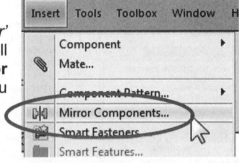

360. - We can mate the second *'Side Cover'* easily with SmartMates, but in this step we'll show how to add it by using the "**Mirror Components**" command. Select the menu "**Insert, Mirror Components**."

361. - Similar to the "**Mirror Feature**" command, we need a plane or flat face to be used as a mirror plane. In this case, we can select the assembly's "*Front Plane*" as the mirror plane (since it is located in the middle of the assembly), and in the "Components to Mirror" selection box, select the *'Side Cover'*. After making your selections, click on the "Next" blue arrow to go to the next step in the "**Mirror Component**" command.

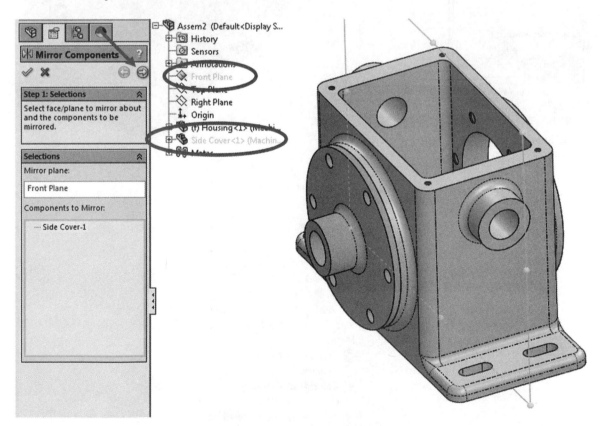

362. - In the second step we get a preview of the mirrored part and we can optionally change its orientation and/or create an "opposite hand" version of it. In this case, the default orientation is correct and we don't need an opposite hand version. Click OK to finish. A new instance of the *'Side Cover'* is added and a *"Mirror Component"* feature is added to the FeatureManager. In case a mirrored component is not correctly oriented, select it and cycle through the different orientations until the desired one is selected.

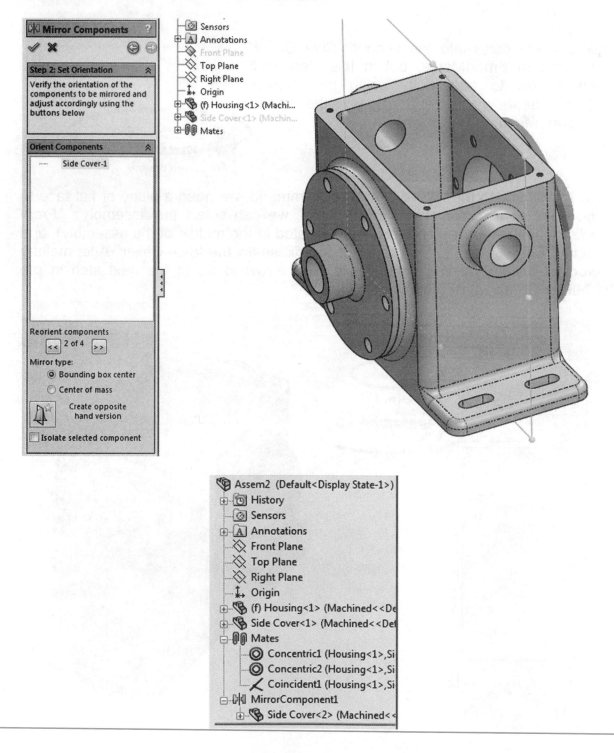

363. - Another way to add parts to an assembly is by dragging them directly from *Windows Explorer*. Open the folder where we have the part files stored and drag-and-drop the *'Worm Gear Shaft'* directly into the assembly window.

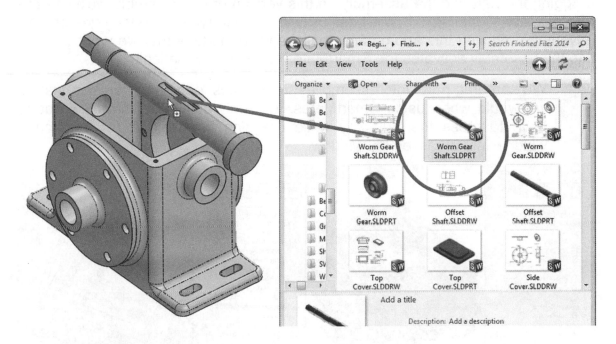

364. - After adding the *'Worm Gear Shaft'* to the assembly, rotate it to a position that will allow us to view both of the edges that we want to mate using the right-mouse-button click-and-drag method. SmartMates has a limitation, in the sense that we need to be able to see both of the mate references for it to work, in this case the edge indicated in the left image and the *'Side Cover'* center hole. Hold down the "Alt" key, then click-and-drag the *Worm Gear Shaft's* edge to the *'Side Cover'* to add a "Peg-in-Hole" SmartMate.

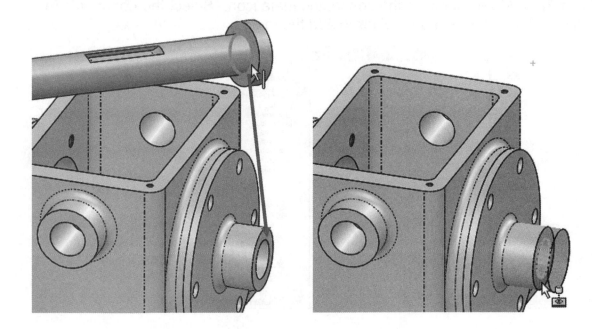

365. - Another way to add a component to an assembly is by opening it in SolidWorks, arranging the part and assembly windows side by side so we can see both windows at the same time (menu "**Window, Tile Vertically**"), and dragging the part *into* the assembly. In this version of the assembly we'll use the '*Worm Gear Complete*'; it will help us with a new type of mate later on. An advantage of using this approach is that dragging the face that we want to mate into the assembly activates the SmartMates function automatically.

We can drag parts into assemblies using faces, edges, or vertices, just as we would when using SmartMates. The only difference is that we don't have to press the "Alt" key while dragging from a part (or assembly) window into an assembly window.

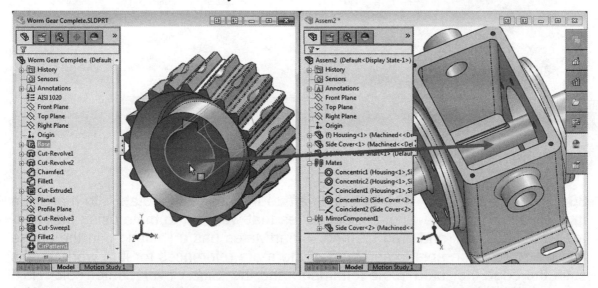

366. - As we drag the *'Worm Gear'* into the assembly window, move the part to the outside face of the *'Worm Gear Shaft'* to add a concentric mate automatically using SmartMates (look for the concentric mate icon.) Select the concentric mate and click OK in the pop-up toolbar to add the mate.

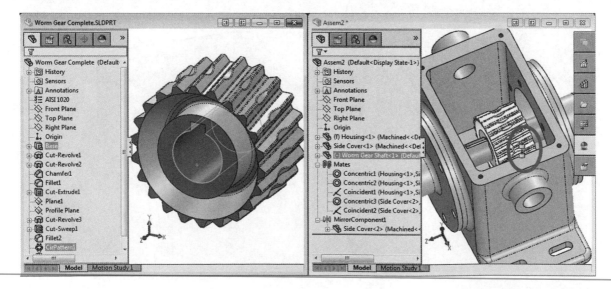

367. - The next step is to center the *'Worm Gear Complete'* inside the *'Housing'*. In the previous assembly we added a mate using the part's and assembly's planes. In this case we'll use a new mate called "**Width**." Maximize the assembly window, select the "**Mate**" command, expand the "**Advanced Mates**" section, and select the "**Width**" mate. In the "Width selections:" select the two inside faces of the *'Housing'*; click in the "Tab selections:" box and select the two outside flat faces of the *'Worm Gear'* (the small round faces.) The *'Worm Gear Complete'* will be automatically centered. The function of the "**Width**" mate centers the "Tab" selections between the "Width" selections. Click OK to finish. After adding the "**Width**" mate don't forget to add the parallel mate between the keyway faces.

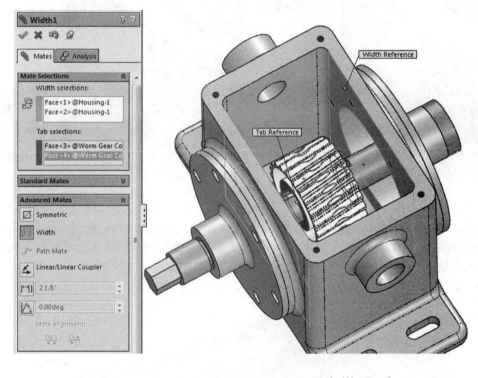

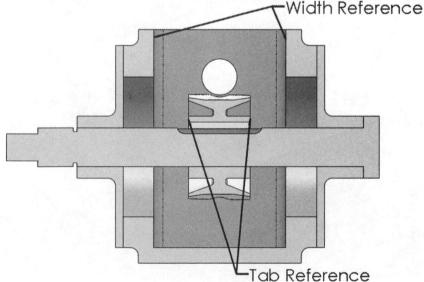

Width Reference

Tab Reference

368. - Add the *'Offset Shaft Gear'* to the assembly and add a "Peg-in-Hole" mate using SmartMates using the indicated edge. **If the part is mated in the wrong orientation**, release the "Alt" key while still holding the left mouse button and press the "Tab" key to reverse the part's orientation. When the correct orientation is displayed release the mouse button.

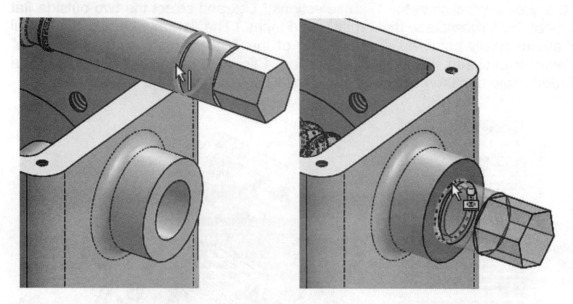

369. - Add the *'Top Cover'* using any of the methods learned so far, and flip it upside down as shown in the next picture using a right mouse button click-and-drag. The reason to flip it is that in order for SmartMates to work, we have to be able to see both entities to be mated, in this case both edges.

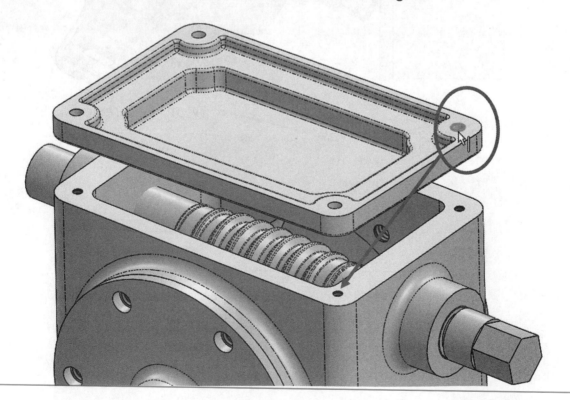

370. - Select the edge indicated, and add a **Peg-in-Hole** SmartMate. Note that the *'Top Cover'* may be upside down in the SmartMate preview. If this is the case, release the "Alt" key, and while still pressing the left mouse button, press the "Tab" key once; notice how the preview changes by flipping the *'Top Cover'* (Pressing the "Tab" key again will flip the mate again.) Make sure you have the correct orientation for the *'Top Cover'* before releasing the left mouse button to add the SmartMate.

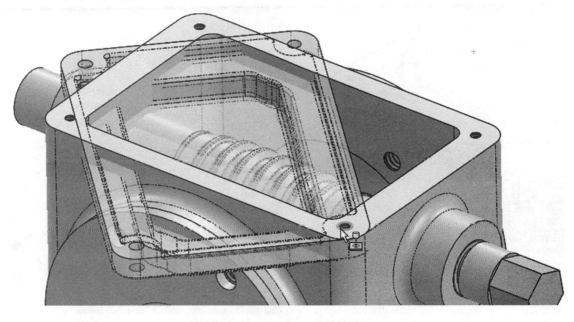

One possible orientation…

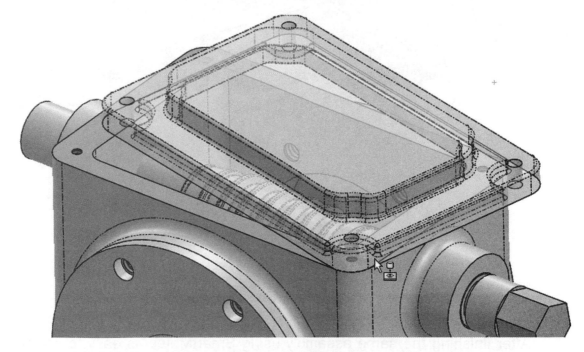

Orientation after pressing the "Tab" key

371. - Now add the final mate to the *'Top Cover'*. Hold down the "Alt" key and drag the edge of the *'Top Cover'* to the face (or the edge) of the *'Housing'* to make them Coincident. Adding this mate will fully define the *'Top Cover'*. Change the color of the parts as before for easier visualization.

NOTE: The rest of the illustrations will be made using the full gear parts, and the reader is free to continue either way.

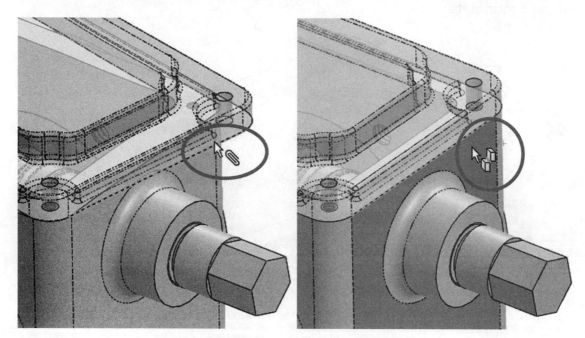

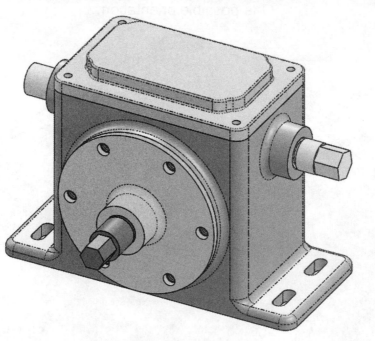

After finishing the same assembly using SmartMates, is easy to see why it's a good idea to learn how to use them, as it speeds up the assembly process making it easier and faster.

Fasteners

The commercial versions of SolidWorks Professional and Premium, as well as the Educational Edition available to schools include a hardware library called "SolidWorks Toolbox" which includes nuts, bolts, screws, pins, washers, bearings, bushings, structural steel, gears, etc. in both metric and imperial unit standards.

372. - The "SolidWorks Toolbox" is an accessory that has to be loaded through the menu "**Tools, Add-ins**." For it to work correctly, we have to load both "SolidWorks Toolbox" and "SolidWorks Toolbox Browser."

With the "SolidWorks Toolbox" we can add hardware to our assemblies by simply dragging and dropping components, and SolidWorks will automatically add the necessary mates saving us time. To make it even more powerful and versatile, we can add our own hardware.

373. - To access "SolidWorks Toolbox" after loading it use the **Design Library**, located in a tab in the Task Pane. If the Task Pane is not visible, go to the menu "**View, Toolbars, Task Pane**" to activate it.

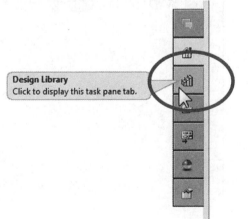

The "SolidWorks Toolbox" <u>was not included in the *Student Design Kit*</u> as of the writing of this book.

Clicking on the "Design Library" icon opens a fly-out pane that reveals the libraries. The "Design Library" contains four main areas:

- **Design Library**, which includes built-in and user defined libraries of annotations, features, and parts that can be dragged and dropped into parts, drawings, and assemblies.
- **Toolbox**, which we just described.
- **3D Content Central**, an internet based library of user uploaded and manufacturer certified components, including nuts, bolts and screws, pneumatics, mold and die components, conveyors, bearings, electronic components, industrial hardware, power transmission, piping, automation components, furniture, human models, etc., all available for drag and drop use. All that is needed to access it is an internet connection and log in.
- **SolidWorks Content** allows the user to download weldments libraries, piping, blocks, structural members, etc.

As we can see, the "Design Library" is a valuable resource for the designer, helping us save time modeling components that are usually purchased or standard, and in the case of the Supplier Certified library, components accurately modeled for use in our designs.

374. - To add screws to our assembly, select the "Design Library" from the Task Pane and click in the (+) sign to the left of the "Toolbox" to expand it.

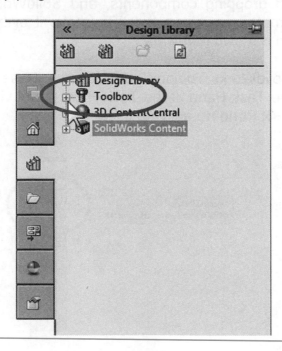

375. - After expanding the "Toolbox" we can see the many options available. Depending on how "Toolbox" is configured, some standards may not be available. In this exercise we'll use "ANSI Inch, Bolts, and Screws" and select "Socket Head Screws."

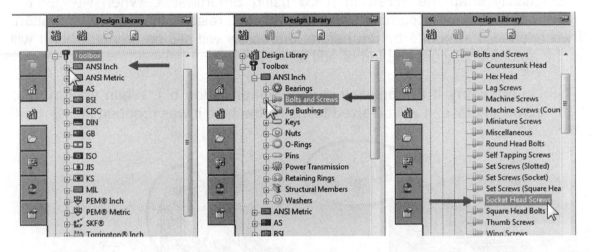

When we select the "Socket Head Screws" folder, we see in the lower half of the Design Library pane the available styles including Button Head, Socket Head, Countersunk, and Shoulder Screws. For our assembly, we'll use "Socket Head Cap Screws (SHCS)."

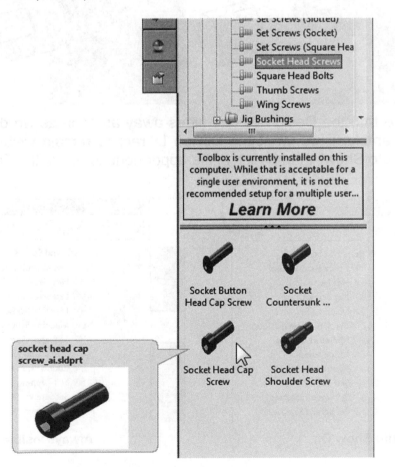

409

376. - First, we want to add the #6-32 screws to the *'Top Cover'*. From the bottom pane of the "Toolbox" <u>click-and-drag</u> the "Socket Head Cap Screw" into one of the holes in the *'Top Cover'*. You will see a transparent preview of the screw, and when we get close to the edge of a hole, SolidWorks will automatically snap the screw in place using SmartMates. When we get the preview of the screw assembled where we want it, release the left mouse button. If we release the mouse button before, the screw will still be created, but it will not be automatically assembled or add any mates.

 Do not worry if the preview in your screen is too big. When we drop the screw in place, it will be sized to match the hole it was dropped in.

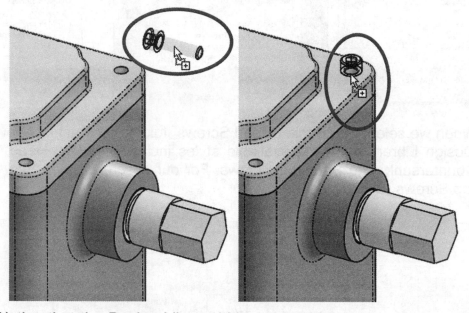

Notice that the Design Library hides away as soon as we drag the screw into the assembly; if we want the Design Library to remain visible we need to press the "Auto Show" thumb tack in the upper right corner of the Task Pane.

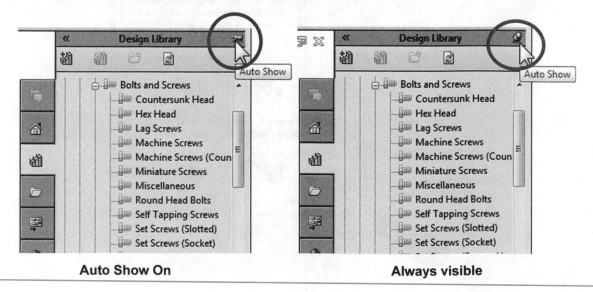

Auto Show On   Always visible

377. - As soon as we drop the screw in the hole, we are presented with a dialog box and a pop-up menu asking us to select the screw parameters, including screw size. In this case, we need a #6-32 screw, 0.5″ long with Hex Drive and Schematic Thread Display. If needed, a part number can be added at the time the fastener is made.

A word on Thread Display options: The "Schematic" thread selected adds a revolved cut to the screw to simulate a thread merely for visual effect. Helical threads can be added as a feature using a sweep as we saw earlier, but it's generally considered a waste of computer resources. If an assembly has tens, hundreds or even thousands of fasteners it would certainly slow down the system noticeably without really adding value to a design in most instances. Helical threads are a resource intensive feature that is best left for times when the helical thread itself is a part of the design and not just for cosmetic reasons. The revolved cut gives a good appearance for most practical purposes and is a simple enough feature that doesn't noticeably affect the assembly's performance.

Toolbox components are stored in a master file that includes the different configurations of each screw type in the Toolbox data folder. If the assembly files are copied to a different computer, the screws used in the assembly will be created there. If the other system does not have SolidWorks Toolbox, the user can use the menu **"File, Pack and go,"** to copy all the files used in the assembly, including the Toolbox components, parts, and drawings.

378. - After selecting OK from the screw size options box, the specified screw is created with the selected parameters and mated in the hole where it was dropped. At this point we can add more screws of the same size to the assembly if needed. In our example, we'll click in the other 3 holes of the *'Top Cover'* to add the rest of the screws. Notice the graphic preview of the screw as we move the mouse, when we get close to a hole the screw snaps adding a Peg-in-Hole SmartMate. Click "Cancel" to finish adding screws.

411

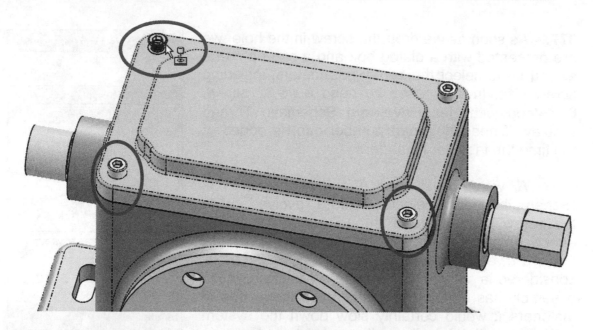

379. - We will now add '¼-20 Socket Head Cap Screws' to the 'Side Covers'. Open the "Design Library" tab and just as the previous step drag and drop the "Socket Head Cap Screw" to one hole of the 'Side Cover', but be careful to "drop" the screw in the correct location. If you look closely, there are two different edges where you can insert the screw: one is in the 'Side Cover', and the other is in the 'Housing'. The screw will be mated to the hole you "drop" the screw in. Use the snap preview to help you find the correct one.

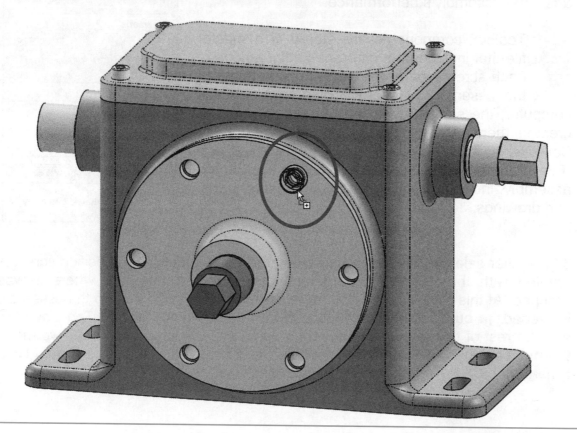

380. - After we drop the screw, the screw properties box is displayed. Select the ¼-20 x 0.5″ long screw with Hex Drive and Schematic thread display. Click OK to build the screw and mate it in the hole where we dropped it and close the "Configure Component" command. In this step we'll be adding a single screw.

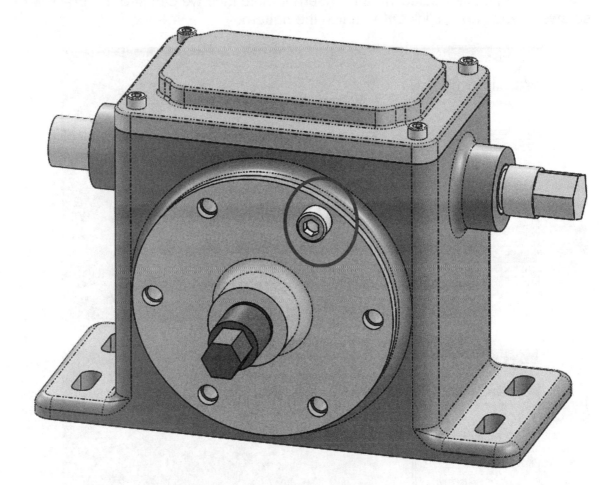

381. - Instead of manually adding the rest of the screws, we'll make a component pattern using the previous screw. Just like with feature patterns in a part, we can add linear or circular patterns of parts, but we also have a special type of pattern that allows us to make a *pattern of parts* to match a *feature pattern* in a part. Think of it this way, we make a pattern of bolts to match the pattern of holes in the *'Side Cover'*, this way, *IF* the pattern of holes changes (more or less holes), the pattern of screws in the assembly changes to match it. From the drop down menu in the **"Linear Component Pattern"** select **"Feature Driven Component Pattern"** or the menu **"Insert, Component Pattern, Feature Driven**."

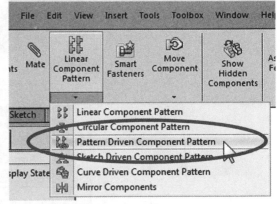

382. - In the "Components to Pattern" selection box select the ¼-20 screw previously made, and in the "Driving Feature" select any of the patterned holes in the '*Side Cover*', except the original hole. When selecting a hole's face, make sure the highlight shows the "*CircPattern1*" name, this way we'll know it's a patterned hole. After selecting the patterned hole face we can see the preview of screws in each hole; click OK to finish the pattern.

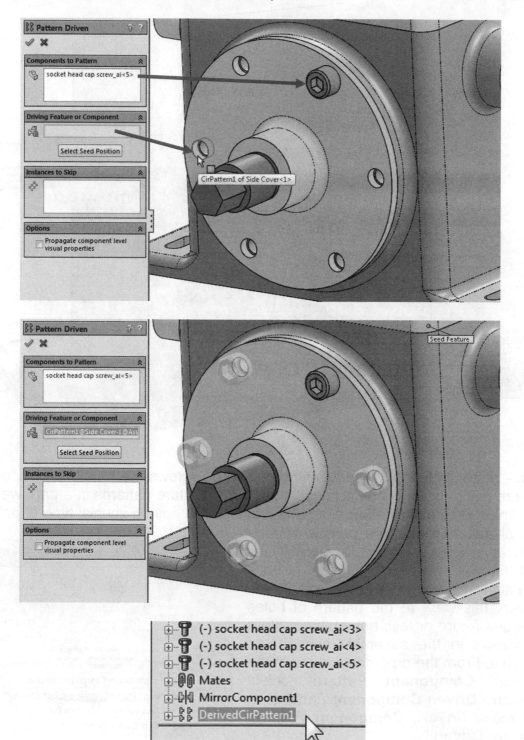

383. - Select the "**Mirror Components**" command either from the menu "**Insert, Mirror Components**" or the drop-down menu in the "Linear Component Pattern" icon.

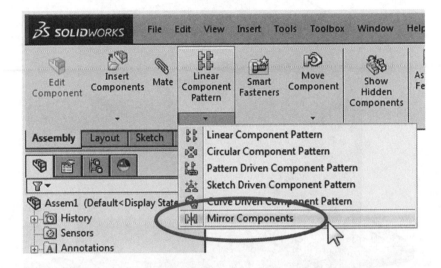

384. – Use the assembly's "*Front Plane*" as the "Mirror Plane" and in the "Components to Mirror:" selection box pick the ¼-20 screw and the "*DerivedCirPattern1*" feature (it will add all the screws in the pattern.) Click in the "Next" arrow to continue to the next step and then OK to finish the mirror.

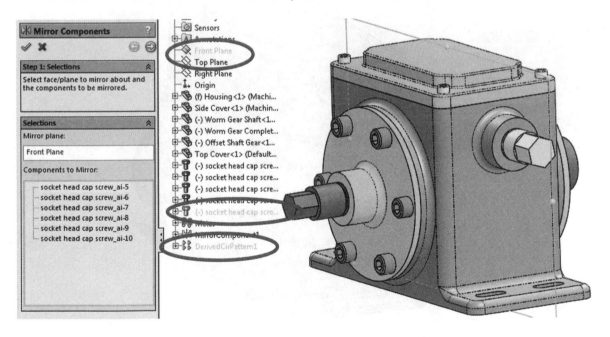

385. – Save the finished assembly as '*Gear Box Complete*'.

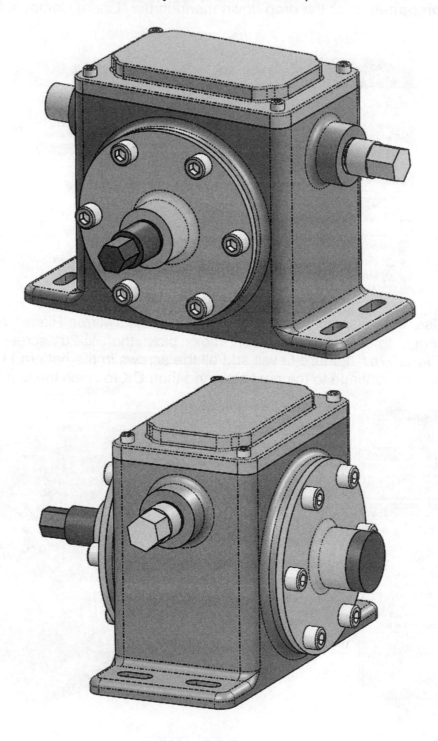

Configurations using Design Tables

Previously we covered how to make configurations of parts by manually suppressing features and changing dimensions. While this approach may be adequate when we have 2 or maybe 3 configurations, it becomes very difficult to keep track of changes when we have 5, 10, 20, or more configurations with multiple configured features and dimensions. This is when controlling configurations with a Design Table is a good idea. A Design Table is an Excel file embedded inside the SolidWorks file that controls dimension values, feature suppression states, configuration names, custom file properties, etc., allowing us to keep track of configurations in a single place.

 To use Design Tables either Excel 2007, 2010 or 2013 is required. Other software's spreadsheets are not supported.

386. - For this example, we'll make a simplified version of a screw with only a handful of sizes. Before we make the design table, we need to have a model to configure. Make a new part and add the following sketch in the *"Front Plane."* Remember to add the centerline for the diameter dimensions.

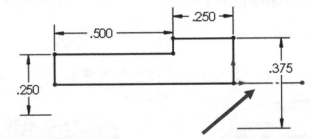

387. - SolidWorks automatically assigns an internal name to all dimensions with the general format *name@feature_name*. We can temporarily see a dimension's name by resting the mouse pointer on top of a dimension, or we can make them always visible (useful when making design tables) using the menu **"View, Dimension Names."**

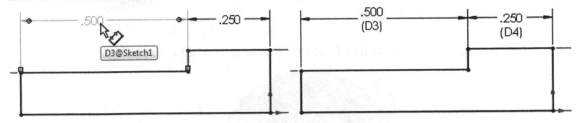

When adding configurations with different dimension sizes, especially with a design table, it is a good idea to give dimensions a name that allows us to easily identify them. To rename a dimension, select it in the screen and type a new name in its properties. When renaming dimensions, do not worry about the part "*@feature_name*"; SolidWorks will add that automatically when we are finished. Turn on the Dimension Names and rename them as shown.

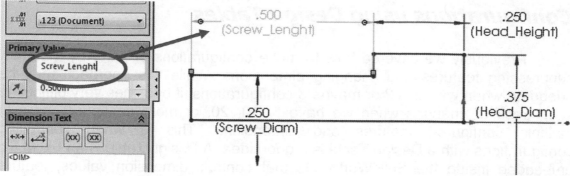

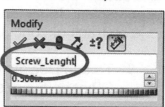

Another way to change a dimension's name is by double-clicking on a dimension as if to change its value, and typing a name in the top box in the "Modify" dialog box.

388 - After completing the sketch make a revolved boss. After we make a feature, the sketch dimensions are hidden as with every feature we've made before. In order to make model dimensions visible while editing the part, right-mouse-click in the "Annotations" folder in the FeatureManager, and activate the option "Show Feature Dimensions."

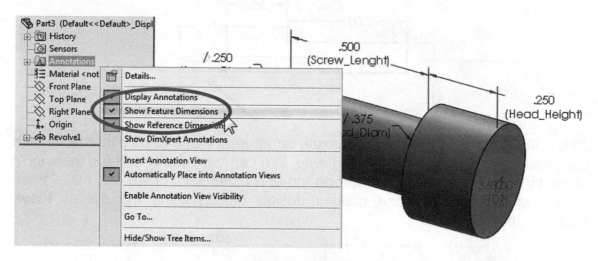

389. - Add a hexagonal cut in the head of the screw; make it 0.125" deep.

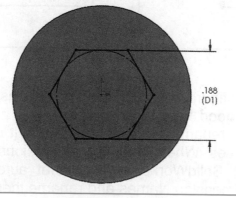

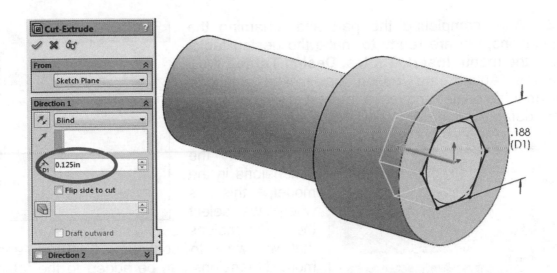

390. - Change the cut dimension's names to "*Hex_Drive*" and "*Hex_Depth*." Note that dimensions added in the sketch are shown in black, and dimensions added by the feature are blue.

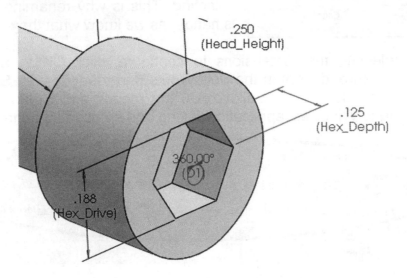

391. - Add a 0.015″ x 45 deg. chamfer to the head and tip of the screw as a finishing touch.

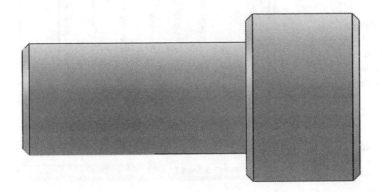

392. - After completing the part and renaming the dimensions, we are ready to make the design table. Go to the menu "**Insert, Tables, Design Table**." We'll use the "Auto-create" option that makes adding a design table easier and leave the rest of the options to their default value. When we click on OK, we are presented with a list of all the dimensions in the model; this is where we select the dimensions that we want to configure. Features and more dimensions can be added to the table later if needed. For this model, select the dimensions indicated. To make multiple selections, hold down the "Ctrl" key while selecting. This is why renaming dimensions is handy, as we know what they are.

393. - After selecting the dimensions to configure, click OK to automatically embed an Excel spreadsheet in the SolidWorks part ready to edit. Since we are using Excel embedded *inside* SolidWorks, the menus and toolbars change to Excel according to Windows' application linking and embedding behavior.

394. -The normal behavior of embedded documents in Windows is to add a thin border around the embedded document. If needed, we can move the Excel file by dragging this border, or resize it from the corners. The borders are very small, be careful not to click outside or you'll exit Excel and go back to SolidWorks.

IMPORTANT: If you accidentally click outside the Excel spreadsheet, this is what will happen: you may be told that that a configuration was created, or not, depending on whether the design table was changed or not. To go back to editing the design table, go to the ConfigurationManager, expand the "Tables" folder, make a right-click in the "Design Table," and select "Edit Table." This will get you back to editing the design table embedded in Excel.

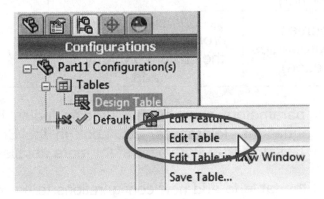

395. - Resize the table and columns if needed. As we always have at least one configuration, "Default" is listed in our Design Table with the corresponding values listed under each parameter. Our Design Table now looks like this:

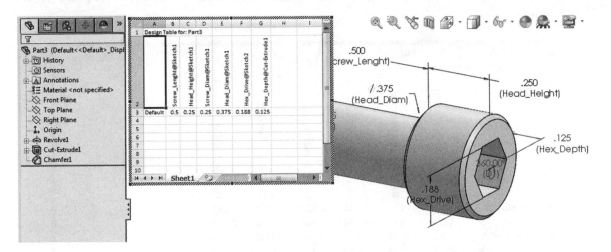

396. - The Design Table holds the information of the parameters that are configured, the configuration names, and values for each parameter in every configuration. The first row holds information about the part. We can type anything we want in this row, as the configuration's data start in the second row.

Configurable parameters are listed in the second row starting at the second column, and configuration names are listed in the first column starting in the third row. Here is a list of the most commonly configured parameters in a part:

Parameter	Format in Design Table	Possible Values
Dimensions (To control dimension value)	*name@feature_name*	Any decimal value
Features (To control if a feature is suppressed or not)	*$STATE@feature_name*	S or *Suppressed* U or *Unsuppressed*
Custom properties (To add custom properties to a configuration)	*$prp@property* *property* is the name of the custom property to add	Any text string

Many other parameters can be configured including hole wizard sizes, description, equations, tolerances, etc. Look in the SolidWorks help for "Summary of Design Table Parameters" for more details.

397. - Now we'll fill the table to add new configurations to the part. Edit the table and fill it out as shown; note that the "Default" configuration was renamed. The configured dimensions were all imported when we created the design table. We don't need to type the dimension names, just the Configuration names, and their values (Cells A3 to G8.) Column "F" was formatted to show dimensions as fractions.

	A	B Screw_Lenght@Sketch1	C Head_Height@Sketch1	D Screw_Diam@Sketch1	E Head_Diam@Sketch1	F Hex_Drive@Sketch2	G Hex_Depth@Cut-Extrude1	H	I	J
1	Design Table for: Part3									
2										
3	6-32x0.5	0.5	0.138	0.138	0.226	7/64	0.064			
4	6-32x0.75	0.75	0.138	0.138	0.226	7/64	0.064			
5	10-32x0.5	0.5	0.19	0.19	0.312	5/32	0.09			
6	10-32x0.75	0.75	0.19	0.19	0.312	5/32	0.09			
7	0.25x.05	0.5	0.25	0.25	0.375	3/16	0.12			
8	0.25x0.75	0.75	0.25	0.25	0.375	3/16	0.12			
9										
10										
11										
12										

Sheet1

398. - After typing the Design Table, click anywhere inside the graphics area of SolidWorks to exit the Design Table (and Excel.) We will be told that the new configurations have been created. Click OK to continue.

SolidWorks

The design table generated the following configurations:

6-32x0.5
6-32x0.75
10-32x0.5
10-32x0.75
0.25x.05
0.25x0.75

OK

399. - Looking at the ConfigurationManager we see the added configurations. Note that configurations created with the Design Table have an Excel icon next to their name. The dimensions configured in the table are now colored magenta (default setting.) Switch between the different configurations to see the screw sizes created with each one.

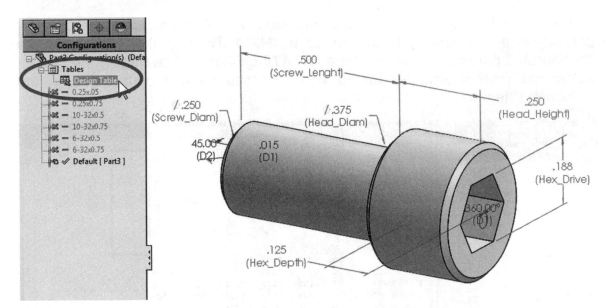

 Delete the *"Default"* configuration since we are not using it. Change to a different configuration first because we cannot delete the currently active configuration.

400. - To configure additional parameters or features we have to edit the Design Table. Right-mouse-click in "Design Table" and select "**Edit Table**." When asked to add Configurations or Parameters, click "Cancel" to continue, as we don't want to add any of those parameters to the Design Table.

401. - When the table is presented, the next available cell for adding a new parameter is pre-selected (in our case "H2".) To add the chamfer as a configurable parameter, we can type *$STATE@Chamfer1* directly in the cell, or select the FeatureManager tab to view the features and double-click in the "*Chamfer1*" feature.

	A	B	C	D	E	F	G	H	I	J
1	Design Table for: Part3									
2		Screw_Lenght@Sketch1	Head_Height@Sketch1	Screw_Diam@Sketch1	Head_Diam@Sketch1	Hex_Drive@Sketch2	Hex_Depth@Cut-Extrude1			
3	6-32x0.5	0.5	0.138	0.138	0.226	7/64	0.064			
4	6-32x0.75	0.75	0.138	0.138	0.226	7/64	0.064			
5	10-32x0.5	0.5	0.19	0.19	0.312	5/32	0.09			
6	10-32x0.75	0.75	0.19	0.19	0.312	5/32	0.09			
7	0.25x.05	0.5	0.25	0.25	0.375	3/16	0.12			
8	0.25x0.75	0.75	0.25	0.25	0.375	3/16	0.12			
9										
10										
11										
12										

Double-click in the "*Chamfer1*" feature will add the correct nomenclature in the table and its current suppression state, in this case *Unsuppressed*. If we leave the value empty, SolidWorks will assume *Unsuppressed*. For short, we can type *S* for *Suppressed* or U for *Unsuppressed*.

402. - Copy the last configuration to the next available row and add "NoChamfer" to the name (SolidWorks does not allow duplicate names for configurations), and suppress "*Chamfer1*" just as an exercise. For short we used **U** and **S** for suppression states. Feel free to format the Design Table to your liking (it's Excel), as long as you don't change the layout.

	A	B Screw_Lenght@Sketch1	C Head_Height@Sketch1	D Screw_Diam@Sketch1	E Head_Diam@Sketch1	F Hex_Drive@Sketch2	G Hex_Depth@Cut-Extrude1	H $STATE@Chamfer1
1	Design Table for: Part3							
3	6-32x0.5	0.5	0.138	0.138	0.226	7/64	0.064	U
4	6-32x0.75	0.75	0.138	0.138	0.226	7/64	0.064	U
5	10-32x0.5	0.5	0.19	0.19	0.312	5/32	0.09	U
6	10-32x0.75	0.75	0.19	0.19	0.312	5/32	0.09	U
7	0.25x.05	0.5	0.25	0.25	0.375	3/16	0.12	U
8	0.25x0.75	0.75	0.25	0.25	0.375	3/16	0.12	U
9	0.25x0.75-NoCahmfer	0.75	0.25	0.25	0.375	3/16	0.12	S

403. - After finishing the changes in the Design Table, click in the graphics area to return to SolidWorks as we did before; as soon as we leave Excel we get a message letting us know that a new configuration was created. Click OK to acknowledge and continue.

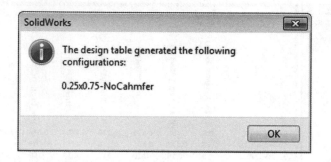

404. - Hide the model dimensions and save the part as "*Screw Design Table*." When adding a configured component to an assembly, remember that it can be configured just like we changed the '*Housing*' from "*Forge"* to "*Machined."* The finished configurations look like this:

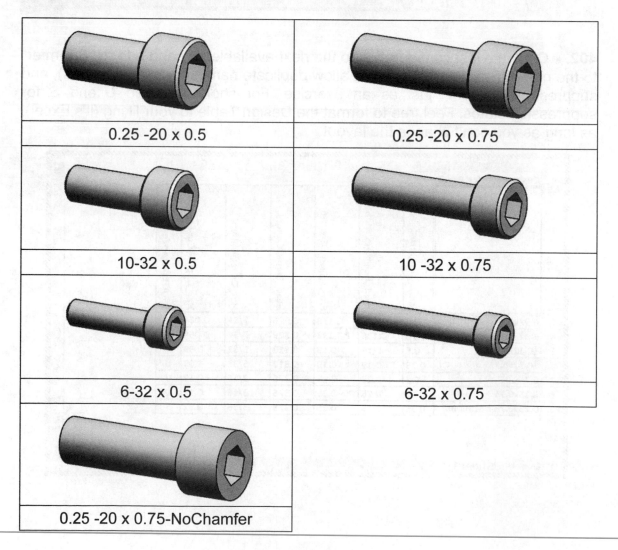

0.25 -20 x 0.5	0.25 -20 x 0.75
10-32 x 0.5	10 -32 x 0.75
6-32 x 0.5	6-32 x 0.75
0.25 -20 x 0.75-NoChamfer	

405. - For the screw we just made to be truly useful we have to add it to our own components library, and give it the ability to auto-assemble using SmartMates, just like the SolidWorks Toolbox components. To do this we need to add a new feature called "**Mate Reference**," this feature will tell a part what type of geometry to look for when we drag-and-drop it into an assembly. Select the menu "**Insert, Reference Geometry, Mate Reference**" or the drop-down menu in the "Reference Geometry" command.

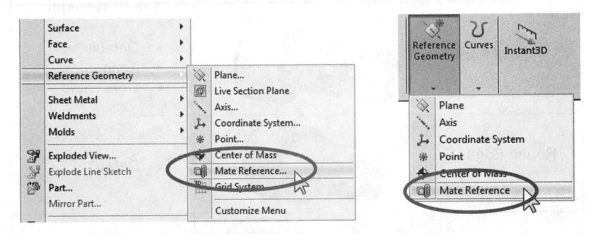

406. - In the "Primary Reference Entity" select the edge indicated. In the "Mate Reference Type" the only option we can use for a circular edge is "Default" and in "Mate Reference Alignment" leave the option to "Any." Click OK to add the reference. By selecting this edge with these options we will get the "Peg-in-Hole" behavior when we drag-and-drop it from the "Design Library" into an assembly. When adding multiple mate references we can rename them for easier reference.

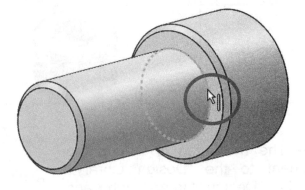

After the Mate Reference is added we can see it in the FeatureManager, where we can edit or delete it if needed. Save the part to continue.

For simple mates we can use a single mate reference, for more complex mates we can use a second or even a third reference. Mate References can be defined using faces, edges, vertices, axes, planes or the origin. The following table shows the type of entity and mate options available. Using "Default" will try to add the default mate type for the entity in the assembly.

Entity		Mate Reference Types available
Cylindrical Face		• Default • Tangent • Concentric
Round Edge		• Default
Flat Face / Plane		• Default • Tangent • Coincident • Parallel
Axis		• Default • Concentric • Coincident • Parallel
Vertex/Origin		• Default • Coincident

407. – The next step is to add the component to the "Design Library." Open the "Design Library" tab, and press the "Keep Visible" push pin as we need the pane to remain visible for the next step.

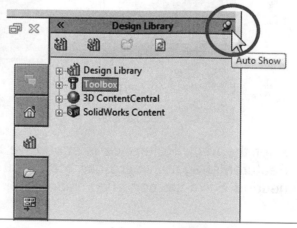

408. – Expand the "Design Library" and select the "parts, hardware" folder. To add the screw to the library we can either select the "Add to Library" icon at the top, or drag-and-drop the screw from the top of the Feature-Manager either into the lower half of the pane or the folder where we want to save it. Both options will show the "**Add to Library**" command.

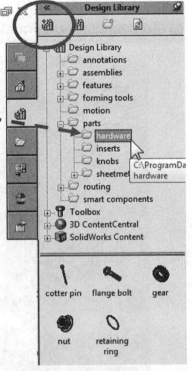

The main difference between the two options is that using the drag-and-drop option pre-selects the part to add to the library, and using the button we have to select the part in the "Items to Add" selection box.

After selecting (or pre-selecting) the screw, select the folder where we want to store the library part and optionally add a description. Leave the "File type" as Part. After pressing OK the screw is added to the hardware folder and is available for use in assemblies. Close the screw file before using it in an assembly, otherwise we'll be asked if we want to use the currently open file.

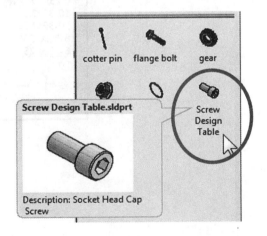

409. - *Alternate to SolidWorks Toolbox:* In case SolidWorks Toolbox is not available, we can use this approach to add the screws to our assembly. Dragging and dropping the screw from the Design Library into an assembly it will have the same assembly behavior as the screw from the Toolbox, the mate reference we added allows it to automatically add the necessary mates after dropping it in. The major difference is that in this case the only screw sizes available will be limited to the configurations made in the part.

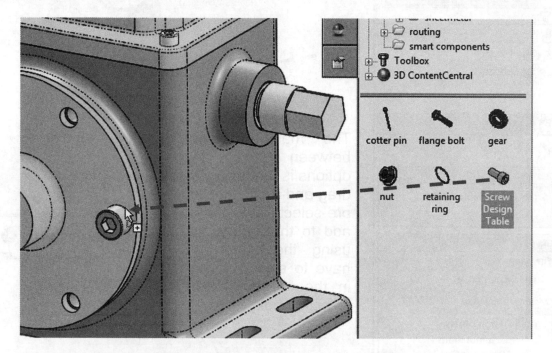

After we drop the screw in the hole it will auto assemble using the mate reference and then we'll be able to select the configuration we want to use.

Interference Detection

410. - Go back to the *'Gear Box Complete'* assembly. One tool that will help us find problems in our assemblies is the "**Interference Detection**" command. We can find it in the "Evaluate" toolbar or in the menu "**Tools, Interference Detection**." We have designed an interference in the assembly to show the user how to use this tool. Select the "**Interference Detection**" command and click on "Calculate." The entire assembly is selected by default.

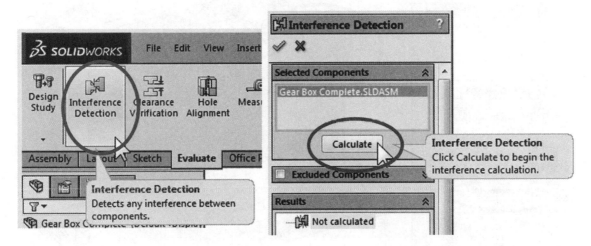

411. - After calculating the interferences, we see multiple interferences listed in the "Results" window. Most of these are fasteners, because the holes they fit in are smaller than the screw threads. Since we are aware of those, we are going to use an option called "Create fasteners folder." When selected the fastener interferences will be grouped together, making it easier to identify problem areas that are not related to a fastener. Turn this option on. The option "Make interfering parts transparent" is on by default, this option will allow us to easily identify the interfering volumes.

NOTE: The fasteners folder option only works with Toolbox generated fasteners.

It's also useful to turn on the "Hidden" option in the "Non-interfering Components" box to temporarily hide all the components that are not related to the selected interference, making the problem areas stand out and easier to find.

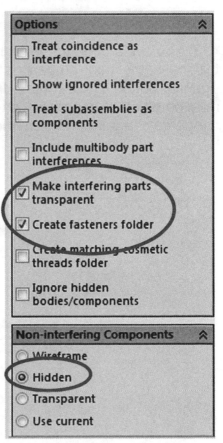

412. – If needed, collapse the "Fasteners" folder and select an interference from the list to see the interfering volumes. Now the designer knows where the problem is, and can take corrective action. In this step ignore the gear-on-gear interferences; we'll work on them later. This is a tool that will help us make better designs, but it will only show us where the problems are, and it's up to the designer to fix them.

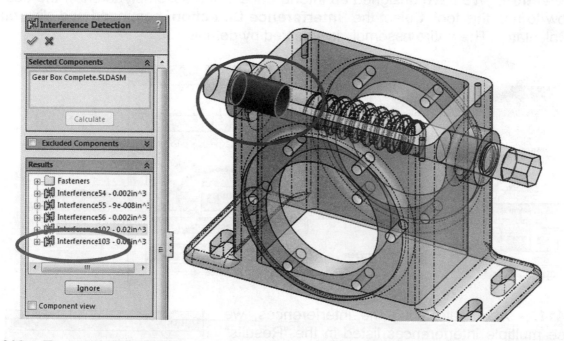

413. –To avoid checking for and displaying interferences we are not interested in, in this case the gear-on-gear, select each of those interferences and click in the "Ignore" button to hide them. In our example we have three instances, your case may be different depending on the position of each gear. Optionally we can rotate the gears to a position where they do not interfere with each other.

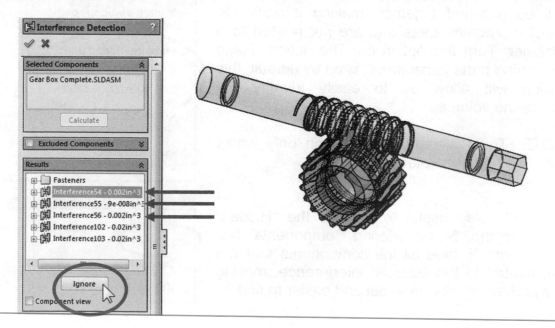

414. - In our case, we know the hole in the '*Housing*' is smaller than the *'Offset Shaft'* diameter, and we need to make the shaft's diameter smaller. To make this change, exit the "**Interference Detection**" command, and double-click on the shaft's cylindrical surface to reveal the feature's dimensions.

415. - Double-click on the diameter dimension and change its value to 0.575″. Click on the "Rebuild" icon as shown, and then OK to complete the "Modify" command. Rebuilding the model will tell SolidWorks to update any models that were changed, like the *'Offset Shaft'* in this case.

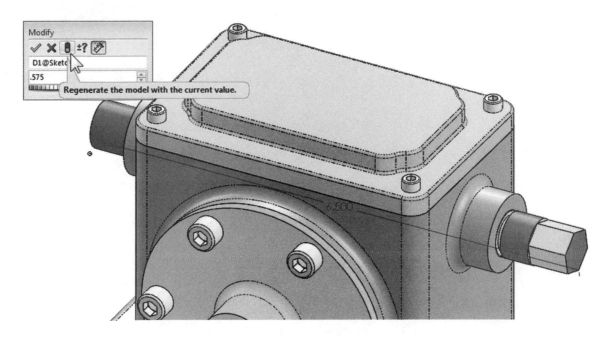

416. - After changing the shaft's diameter run the "**Interference Detection**" command again to confirm that we have resolved the interference between the shaft and the housing, the only interference displayed will be the fasteners. Be aware that the gear-on-gear interferences may have changed when the diameter changed, and we are still ignoring those interferences. Click OK to finish.

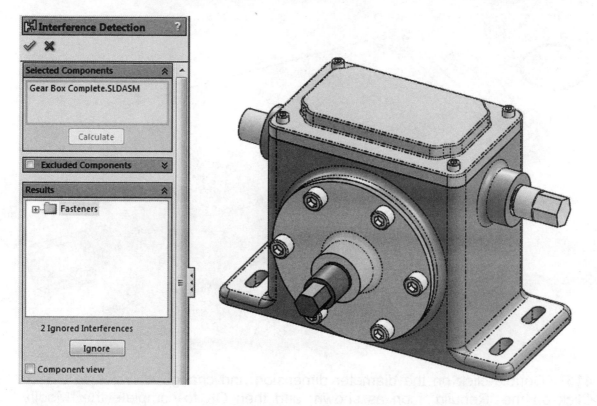

Assembly Configurations

417. - In our book we have two different versions of the *'Offset Shaft'*, with gear and without it. Just as part configurations show different but similar versions of a part, we can add assembly configurations to show, for example, a simplified version of the assembly to be used as a sub-assembly in order to improve assembly performance. Select the ConfigurationManager tab; add two new configurations called *"With Gears"* and *"Simplified."* After adding the new configurations rename the default configuration to *"No Gears."*

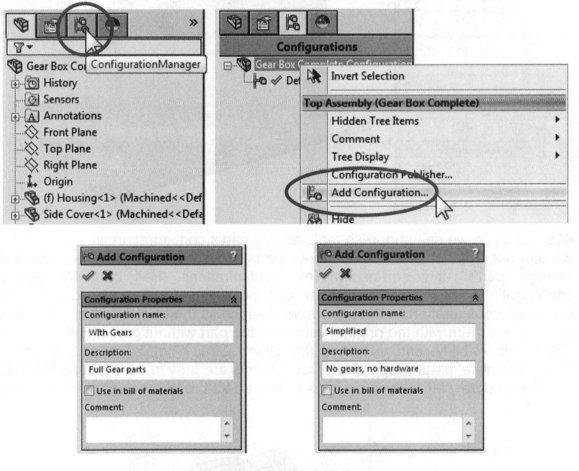

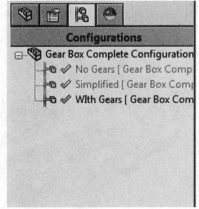

418. - Split the FeatureManager to show parts and configurations, and activate the "*No Gears*" configuration.

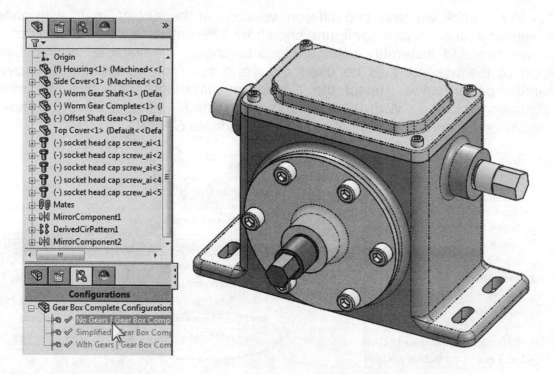

419. - Just as we can suppress features in a part's configuration, in an assembly we can not only suppress components (parts and sub-assemblies,) we can also change part's and sub-assemblies' configurations. For the "*No Gears*" configuration, since the '*Worm Gear*' and the '*Offset Shaft*' parts don't have a simplified configuration without gears, we'll suppress the existing parts with gears and replace them with the original version of the part without gears. Hide the '*Top Cover*' for visibility, and suppress the '*Worm Gear Complete*' and the '*Offset Shaft Complete*' parts. Suppressed components are grey in the FeatureManager, and like suppressed features in a part, they affect the weight and volume of the assembly.

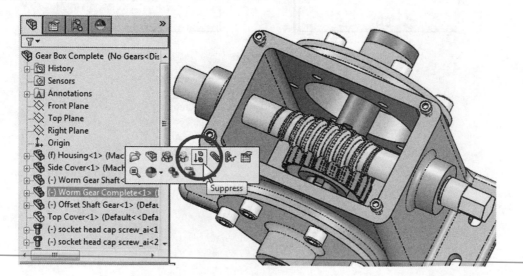

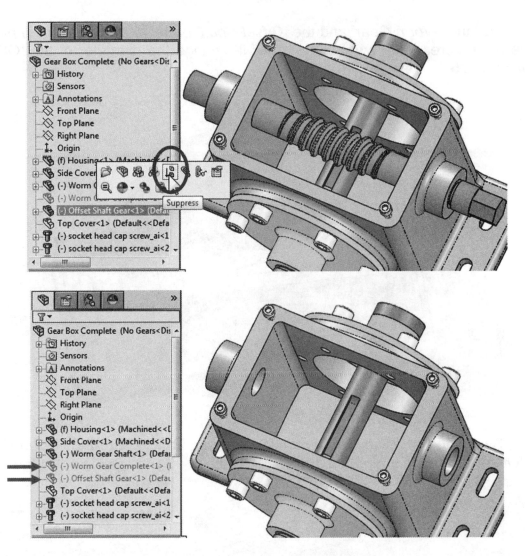

 After suppressing a part in the assembly, the suppressed part mates are also suppressed.

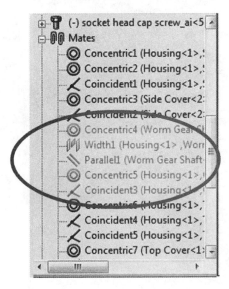

420. – Add the '*Worm Gear*' and the '*Offset Shaft*' parts, and mate them in place as we did before. And now that we know it, change the diameter of the '*Offset Shaft*' to 0.575".

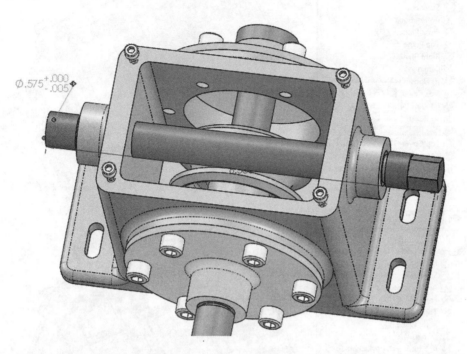

421. – Switch to the "*With Gears*" configuration and make sure the '*Worm Gear*' and '*Offset Shaft*' are suppressed.

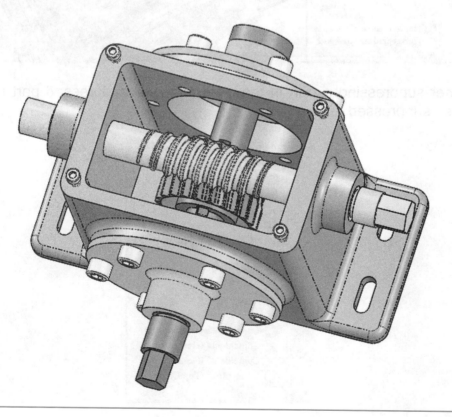

422. – Now switch to the "Simplified" configuration and suppress all fasteners, use the same offset shaft, and worm gear as the *No Gears* configuration. We can select multiple components and suppress/un-suppress at the same time.

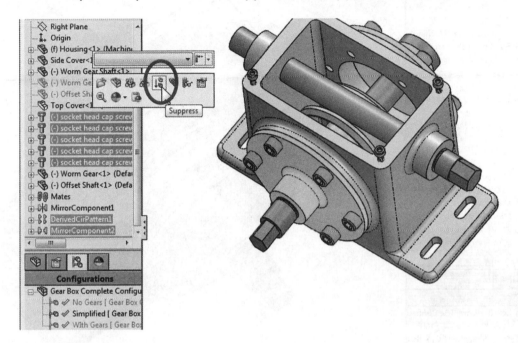

Save the assembly. The finished configurations for the Gear Box are as follow, the '*Top Cover*' has been hidden in all three configurations for visibility:

No Gears

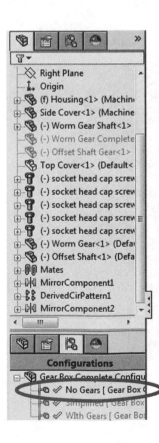

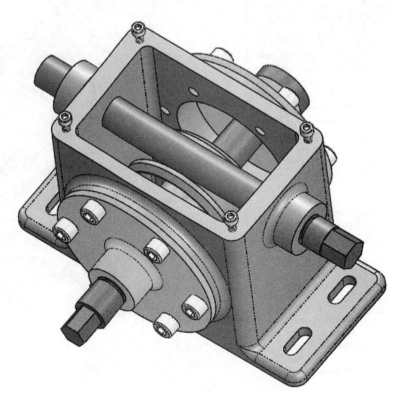

Simplified

With Gears

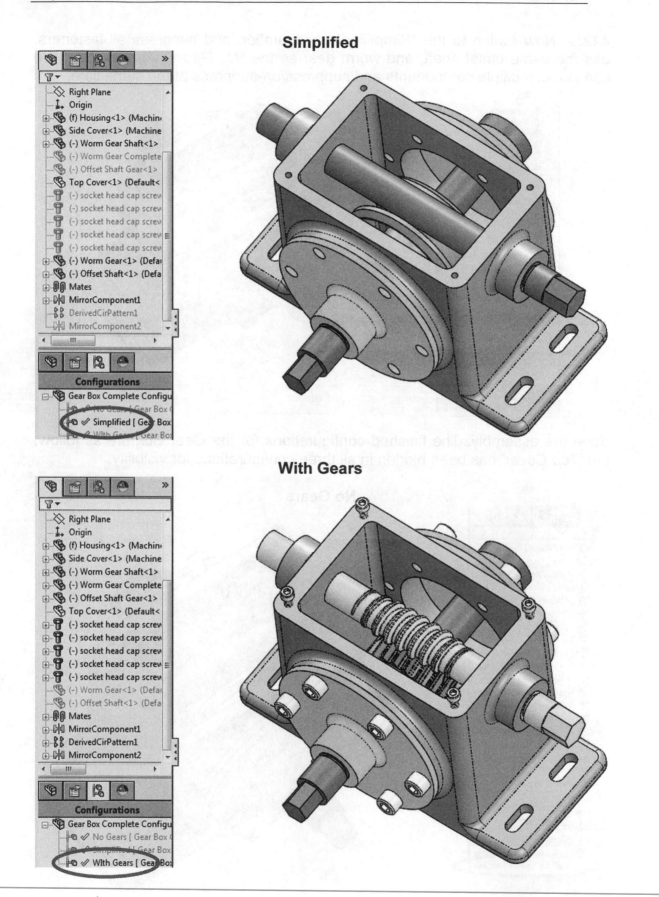

423. – When we change a part's dimension in the assembly, the change is propagated to the part and its drawing. After finishing the assembly and having changed the '*Offset Shaft*' diameter, open it's drawing to verify the drawing is updated. Save and close the drawing file. If asked to save modified files, click on "Save All" to save both the part and the drawing.

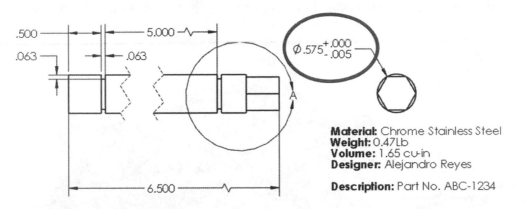

Material: Chrome Stainless Steel
Weight: 0.47Lb
Volume: 1.65 cu-in
Designer: Alejandro Reyes

Description: Part No. ABC-1234

424. – After completing the assembly configurations switch to the "*With Gears*" configuration. With the '*Top Cover*' hidden, we realize that there is another problem with our assembly: The geared shaft cannot be assembled as designed, because it will not fit through the hole in the '*Housing*'. In this case the problem is exaggerated to make it obvious, but most of the time in real life it's not always obvious. To help us find this type of problems we can use a command called **"Collision Detection"** that allows us to move a part through its range of motion and alert us when it hits another component. To allow the shaft to move freely along its axis we need to suppress the coincident mate added in the offset shaft. To locate a part's mates, expand the FeatureManager and go to the **"Offset Shaft Gear, Mates."**

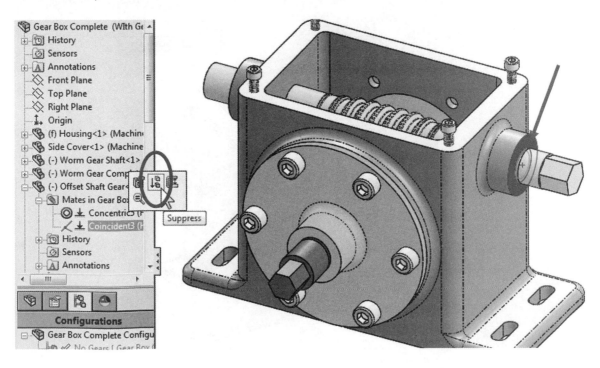

425. – After suppressing the mate we can click and drag the shaft and it will move and rotate about its axis. To simplify the view, hold down the "Ctrl" key and select the shaft and the housing, make a right-mouse-click and select the "**Isolate**" command. Every component that is not selected will be hidden from view temporarily and we'll see a new toolbar that will have an "Exit Isolate" button to return to the previous view state. Isolate temporarily hides all the components we are not interested in.

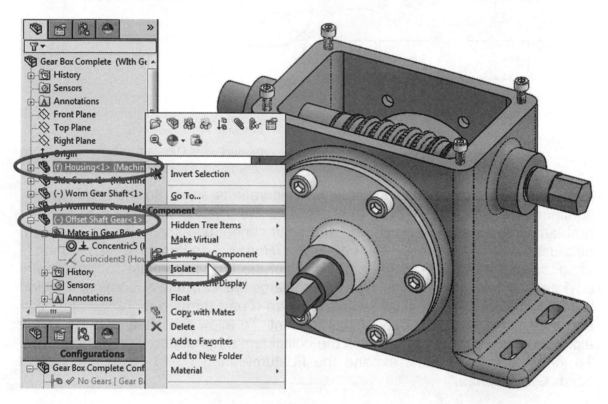

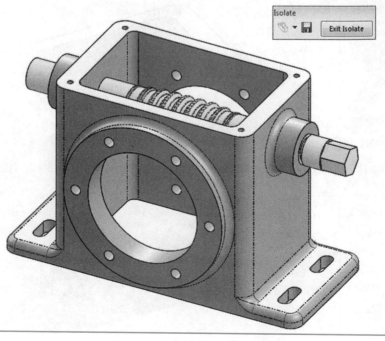

426. – From the Assembly tab select the "**Move Component**" command. In essence it's the same as dragging a component in the graphics area, but this way we have added options including "Collision Detection" and "Physical Dynamics."

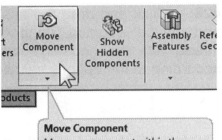
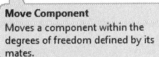

Move Component
Moves a component within the degrees of freedom defined by its mates.

427. – Select the "Collision Detection" and "These Components" options. We'll use this option to calculate collisions only between the housing and the shaft, because the more components are included in the analysis the slower the components will move. Select the '*Housing*' and the '*Offset Shaft Gear*', when finished selecting click on "Resume Drag" to continue the collision detection. Make sure the "Stop at collision", "Highlight faces" and "Sound" options are selected.

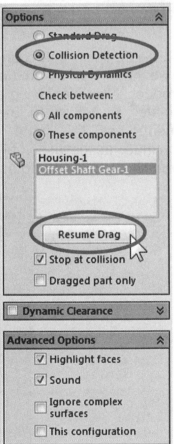

 Using the "All components" option can be used if our assembly has only a few components and we have a fast computer. The maximum number of components depends on geometry complexity, mates, computer speed, etc.

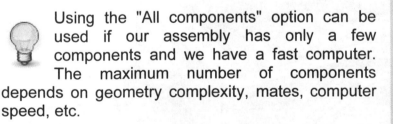 If we start moving the parts with the "Collision Detection" command and there is interference between any two components being analyzed, we'll get a warning letting us know about it and the option "Stop on collision" will be disabled. We will continue to get the sound and highlighted faces. This is another good reason to limit the number of components included in the analysis.

428. – Click and drag the shaft, notice how the movement is slower than usual and maybe sluggish, depending on the computer's speed. When the helical thread hits the housing's wall, it will highlight the colliding faces and stop according to the options selected.

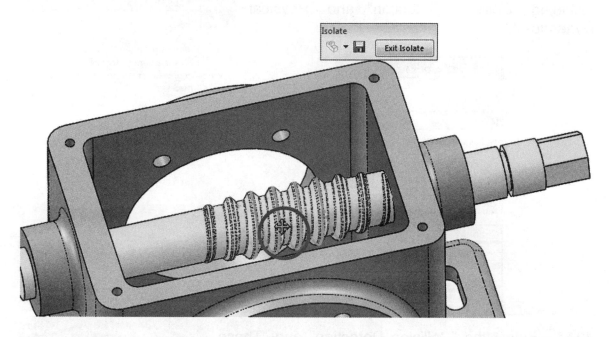

429. – Collision detection and interference detection are tools to help us find out if we have design problems that need to be addressed before fabricating the product. After identifying the interference click in "Exit Isolate" to return to the previous view state and Unsuppress the mate that locates the shaft to continue. In the assembly exercises we'll modify the *'Housing'* to allow us to assemble the shaft.

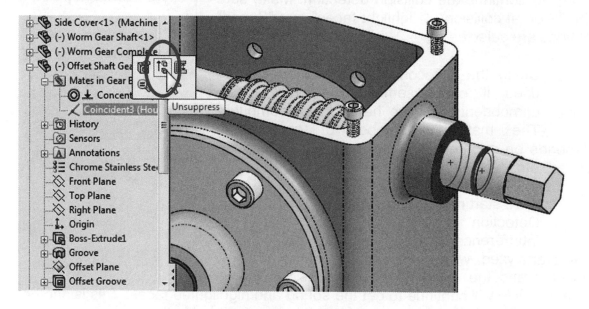

430. – As a final step to finish the assembly we'll add a new type of mate called "Gear." The gear mate allows us to define a rotation ratio between two cylindrical components, and the two components don't need to have any type of alignment to simulate a gear driving another gear. Still in the "With Gear" configuration, select the '*Worm Gear Shaft*', '*Worm Gear Complete*' and '*Offset Shaft Gear*' from the FeatureManager, make a right-mouse-click, and select "Isolate."

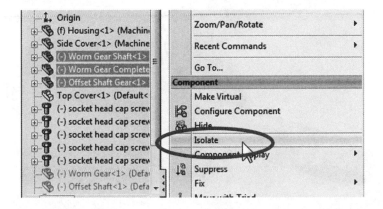

431. – Select the "**Mate**" command, expand the "Mechanical Mates" group, and select the "Gear Mate." Select the indicated faces and enter 1 for the '*Offset Shaft Gear*' diameter and 22 for the '*Worm Gear Complete*' diameter. This is not the actual diameter, but the gear ratio at which one will rotate with respect to the other. If wanted, move the gears to a position where they do not interfere with one another. The "Reverse" option inverts the rotation of the gears if needed. Press OK to add the mate and finish the command.

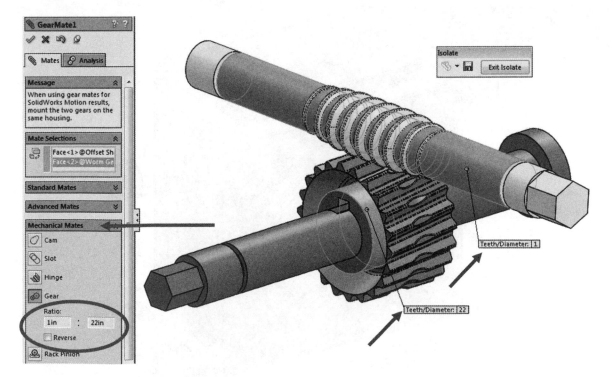

432. – To test the gear mate click and drag with the left mouse button either shaft to see the effect. Dragging the '*Worm Gear Complete*' will cause the '*Offset Shaft Gear*' to turn fast and vice versa.

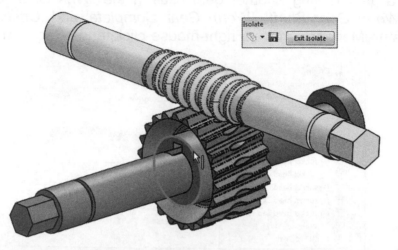

Before adding the "Gear Mate" we can align the gears to a position where there are no interferences between them to make a better looking animation.

433. – Click in the "Exit Isolate" button to return the view to the previous state and show the '*Top Cover*' to finish the assembly. Your assembly '*Gear Box Complete'* is finished and should now look like this.

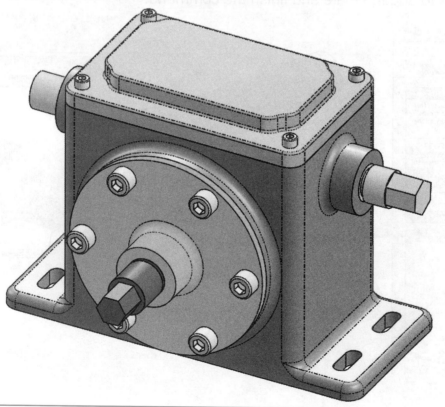

434. – Instead of hiding a component to view inside of it, we can make it transparent. Select the *'Housing'* in the FeatureManager or the graphics area and from the pop-up menu select "**Change Transparency**." Click and drag one of the gears to turn it and see the effect. To make the components opaque again repeat the same process.

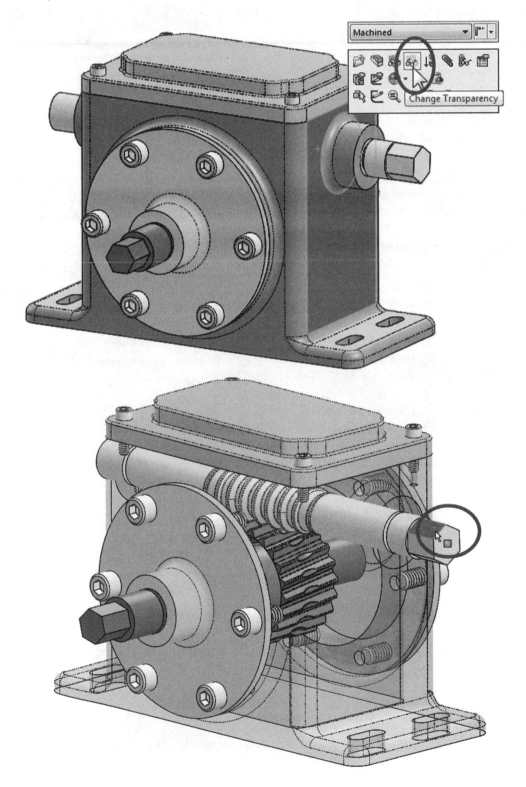

435. – An easy way to manipulate an assembly component's display mode is by using the "Display Pane". The "Display Pane" can be accessed at the top of the FeatureManager, click in the double arrow to expand it. It will be located to the right.

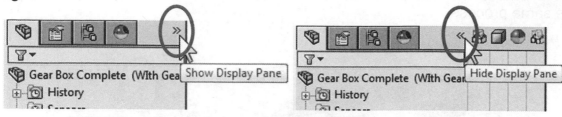

In the "Display Pane" we can:

Click in the first column to Hide/Show a component.

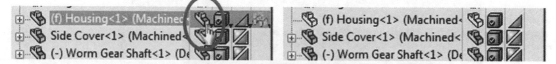

In the second column change a component's display style.

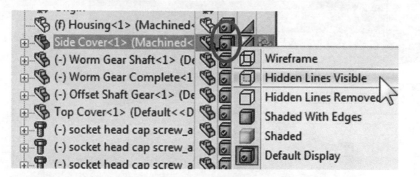

In the third column we can copy/paste, change or remove a component's appearance.

Click in the fourth column to make the component transparent/opaque.

Feel free to explore the different display options for the assembly, more often than not we need to change component's display to be more efficient.

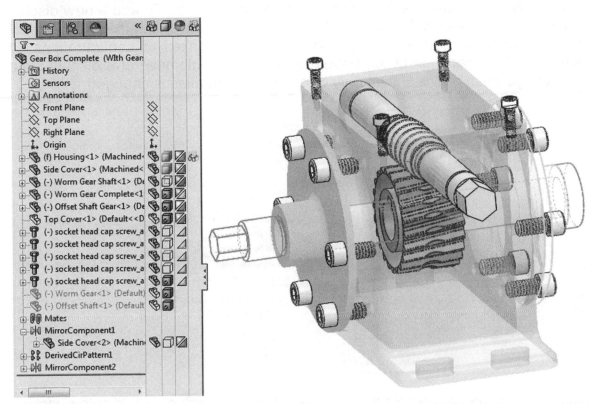

When selecting faces in a transparent component, *IF* there is an opaque component behind the selection, the opaque component is selected, if there are no opaque components, the transparent face is selected. To select the transparent face even if an opaque component is behind it, hold down the "Shift" key while selecting, this is the default setting. To always select the first face even if it's transparent turn off the option in the menu "**Tools, Options, System Options, Display/Selection, Allow selection through transparency.**" Notice the outline of the face to be selected in each case.

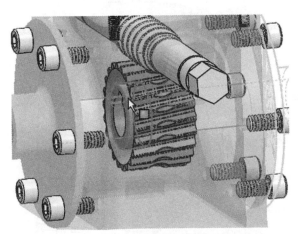

Default selection behavior

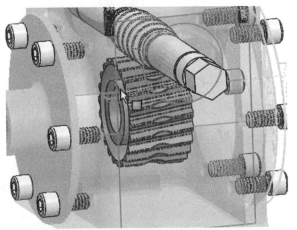

Selection holding "Shift" key

436. – At the bottom of the Configuration Manager, we can see the "Display States" tab. Just like the configurations, a display state stores the hidden state, display style, appearance (color) and transparency setting. To add a new display state, right-mouse-click in the "Display States" pane and select the "Add Display State" command. Display states can be optionally linked to configurations by activating the checkbox at the bottom; this way we only have one display state per configuration and is shown only when the configuration is changed.

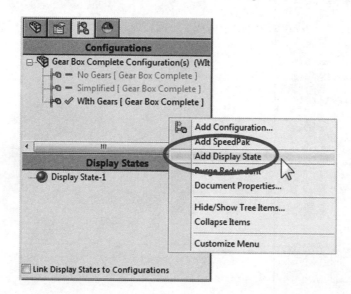

After adding the new display state, change all the components display back to shown (not hidden), no transparency, and default display style. To change between the different display states double click in it to activate it.

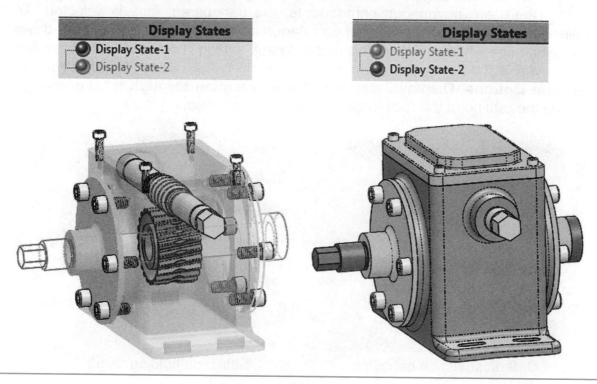

437. – An assembly's weight and mass properties can be calculated the same way as in a part using the "**Mass Properties**" command. The difference is that in the assembly, the weight will be the combined weight of the individual components based on the materials they are made of. This is why it's a good idea to always assign a material to each component. Alternatively, mass properties (weight, center of mass, and moments of inertia) can be overridden if needed by selecting the "**Override Mass Properties...**" button. Keep in mind that each assembly configuration will give us different results because each configuration has different components and some components may be using a different part configuration.

Notes:

Exploded View

438. - The next step in the assembly will be to make an exploded view for documentation. Exploded views are commonly used to show how the components will be assembled together. Activate the "*With Gears*" configuration, and select the "**Exploded View**" icon from the Assembly tab in the Command Manager or from the menu "**Insert, Exploded View**."

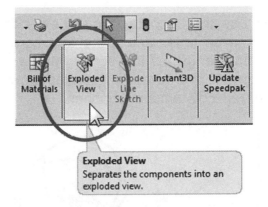

439. - In the Explode PropertyManager we can see the "Settings" selection box is active and ready for us to select the component(s) that will be exploded. For this example, we will leave the option "Auto-space components after drag" off.

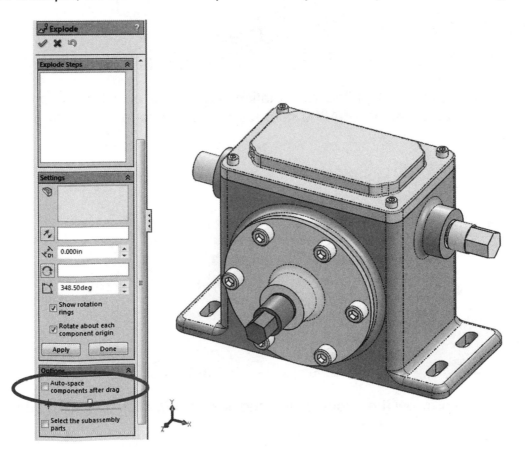

440. - To add the first explode step, select the four screws in the *'Top Cover'* and:

a) Click and drag the tip of the arrow along the axis of the screws upwards as far as you want the screws exploded using the ruler as a guide for the distance,
Or
b) Add specific parameters for the explode step by entering a direction and distance to explode along, and/or an axis to rotate about by entering a rotation angle.

In this step we'll use the second option to explode the top cover screws and rotate them at the same time. Select the four screws in the screen, then select the arrow along the length of the screw for the direction (note that the other arrows are hidden), if the arrow is pointing down check the "Reverse Direction" button, and enter a distance of 3 inches.

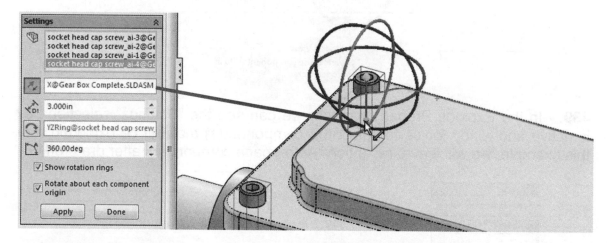

To rotate the screws select the red rotation ring (it will also be the only ring visible) and enter an angle of 1800 degrees in the "Explode Angle" to turn the screws 5 times.

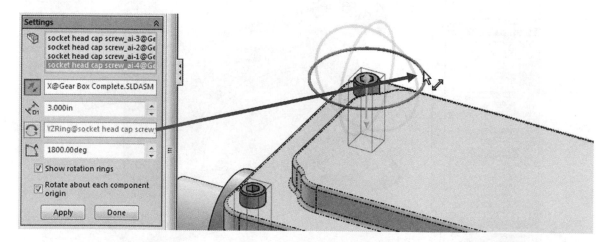

Click "Apply" to preview the explode step and, if satisfied, click "Done" to add this step to continue.

After adding finishing this step, "Explode Step1" is added to the "Explode Steps" list, and the selection box is cleared. Do not click OK yet; we are going to add more explode steps.

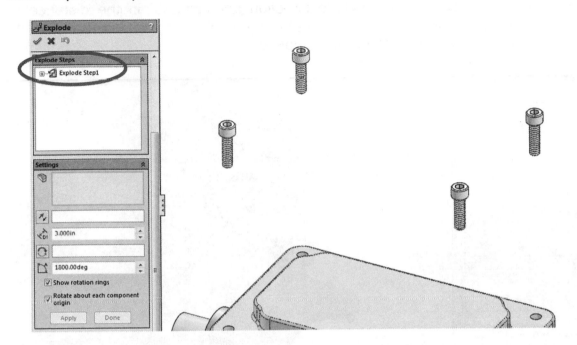

 If we need to modify a step, select it in the "Explode Steps" list and drag the blue manipulator arrow to the new exploded distance.

441. - For the second explode step, select the *'Top Cover'*, and drag the green manipulator arrow up about halfway between the screws and the 'Housing' or add a vertical direction and a distance of 1.5".

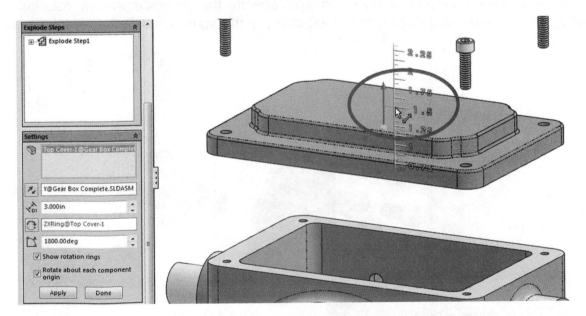

455

442. - For the third step, select the six screws on one *'Side Cover'* and just like the first screws, explode and rotate them in the same step. Select the screws; pick the direction along the screws and the (Red) rotation ring around the direction axis. Reverse the explode direction and enter 5" in the distance to explode box and 1800 degrees (5 turns) in the explode angle. Press "Apply" to preview the step and click "Done" to complete.

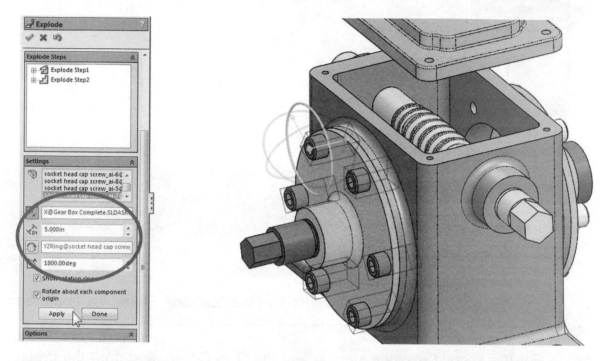

443. - The rest of the explode steps are done the same way. Select the component(s) and either drag the tip of the manipulator arrow along the desired explode direction or pick a direction and specify the distance and/or rotation. Next explode the *'Side Cover'* to the left close to the screws.

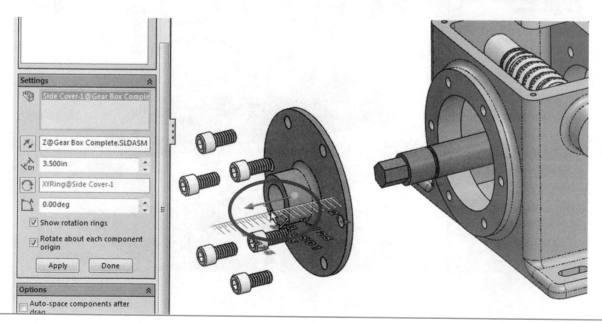

444. - Now explode the *'Worm Gear Shaft'* towards the back about 8".

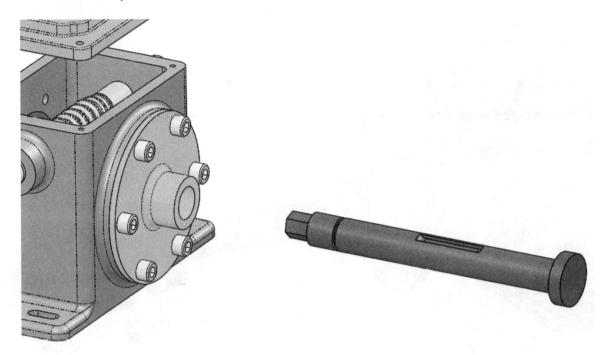

445. - Explode and rotate the last set of screws towards the back approximately 7" and rotate the screws 5 turns (1800 degrees) as we did with the front screws.

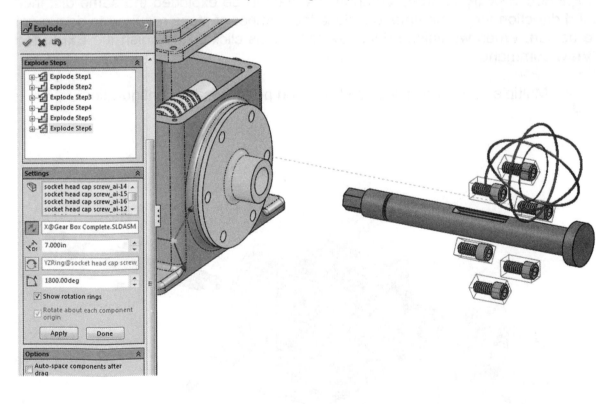

446. - Explode the second side cover towards the back as shown.

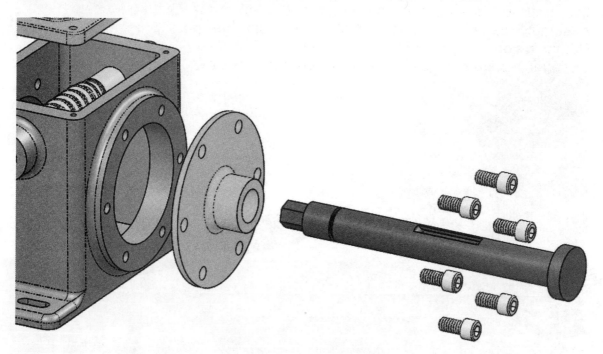

447. - Finally, explode the *'Worm Gear'* and the *'Offset Shaft'* in two different steps to get the exploded view similar to the next image. When making an exploded view try to group components that will be exploded the same distance and direction the same time to reduce the number of steps required to document a design. When we finish adding explode steps click OK to finish the **Exploded View** command.

 Multiple exploded views can be added per assembly configuration.

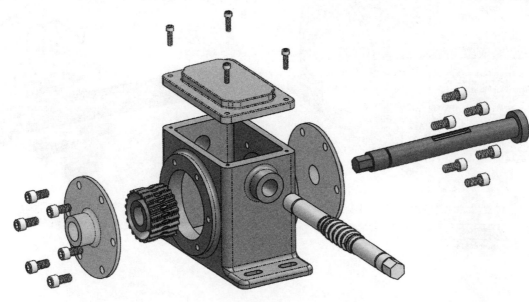

448. - After exploding the assembly, we may need to collapse it. In order to do this, click with the right mouse button at the top of the Feature-Manager in the Assembly name and select "**Collapse**" from the pop-up menu, or in the ConfigurationManager right-mouse-click in "*ExpView1*" and select collapse. Optionally, double click "*ExpView1*" to expand/collapse.

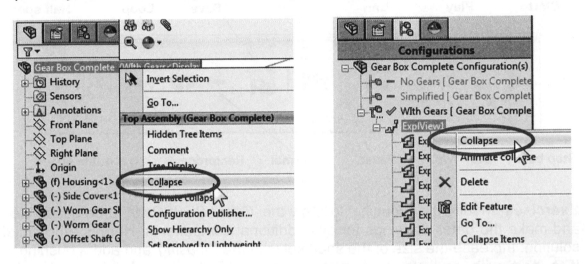

449. - To explode the assembly again, click with the right mouse button at the top of the FeatureManager as we just did, and select "**Explode**," in the ConfigurationManager double click "*ExpView1*" or right-mouse-click in the exploded view and select "Explode." This option will only be available if the assembly has been exploded. In case we need to edit the exploded view steps again, select the "**Exploded View**" icon to bring back the explode PropertyManager.

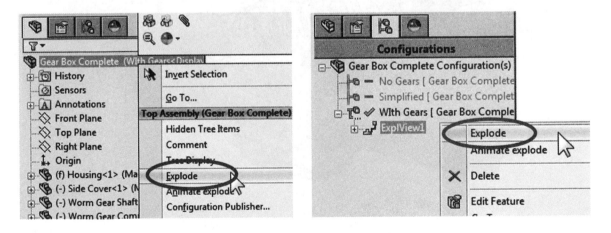

If the assembly has two or more exploded views, exploding the assembly from the FeatureManager will explode the last exploded view used.

450. - From this same menu we can select "**Animate collapse**" if the assembly is exploded, or "**Animate explode**" if the assembly is collapsed. This brings up the Animation Controller to animate the explosion and optionally to save a video with the exploded view animation.

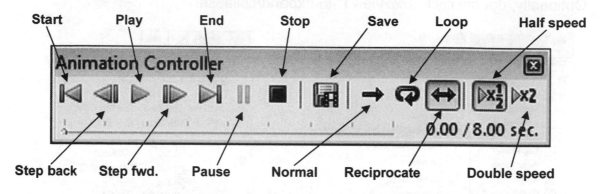

Exercises: Modify the '*Housing*' to allow the '*Offset Shaft Gear*' to be assembled and make the detail drawings for any additional components. Here is a potential solution: Increase the size of the shaft holes in the '*Housing*' and add a bushing. If a part with multiple configurations is modified, remember to make the necessary changes to all configurations affected by the change.

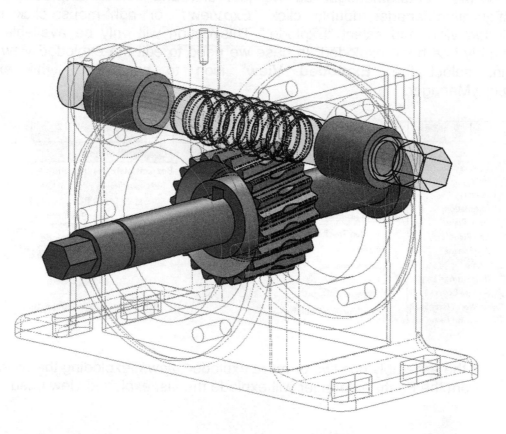

 To create this image the component's display style was changed individually using the "Display Pane."

Engine Project: Assemble the engine using the parts built in the Part modeling exercises, and make an exploded view. First make the following sub-assemblies as indicated (shown in exploded view) before adding them to the final assembly.

Piston Head Sub Assembly

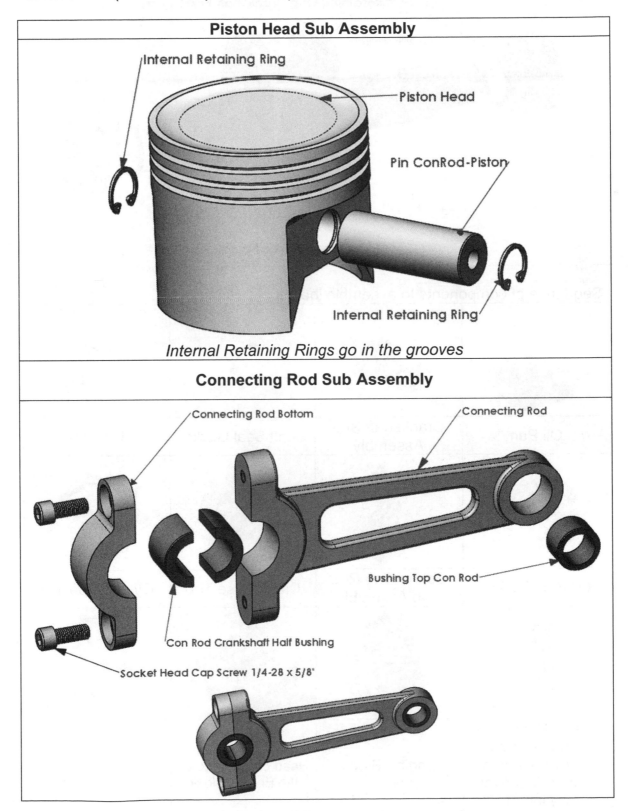

Internal Retaining Ring

Piston Head

Pin ConRod-Piston

Internal Retaining Ring

Internal Retaining Rings go in the grooves

Connecting Rod Sub Assembly

Connecting Rod Bottom

Connecting Rod

Bushing Top Con Rod

Con Rod Crankshaft Half Bushing

Socket Head Cap Screw 1/4-28 x 5/8"

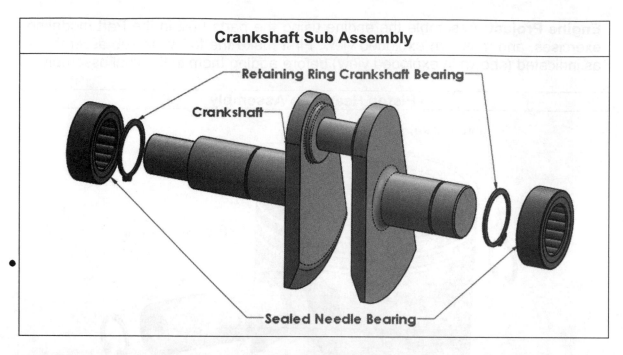

Crankshaft Sub Assembly

- Retaining Ring Crankshaft Bearing
- Crankshaft
- Sealed Needle Bearing

Sequence of components to assemble the engine.

Oil Pan	Crankshaft Sub Assembly	Shaft Seal Gasket	Oil Seal
Oil Pan Gasket	Connecting Rod Sub Assembly	Crank Case Top	Cylinder Gasket
Piston Head Sub Assembly. (Only one Concentric mate to not over define it)	Engine Block	Make the Piston Head **concentric to** the Engine Block	Head Gasket

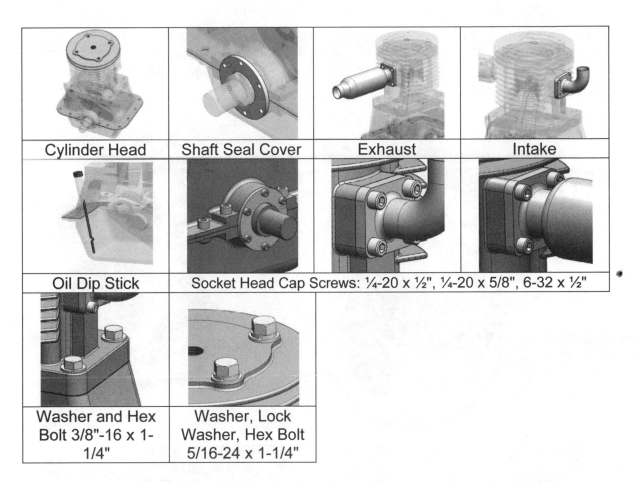

Cylinder Head	Shaft Seal Cover	Exhaust	Intake

Oil Dip Stick	Socket Head Cap Screws: ¼-20 x ½", ¼-20 x 5/8", 6-32 x ½"	

Washer and Hex Bolt 3/8"-16 x 1-1/4"	Washer, Lock Washer, Hex Bolt 5/16-24 x 1-1/4"

As an optional finishing touch before making the exploded view, add a spark plug. You can download one from the 3D Content Central website (Free). You have to sign up and log in to access it. The link to the spark plug we used is:

http://www.3dcontentcentral.com/secure/download-model.aspx?catalogid=171&id=86052

After completing the engine assembly, make a section view as we did in page 226 and move the crankshaft. If the assembly was made correctly the crankshaft will rotate and the piston will move up and down as it should.

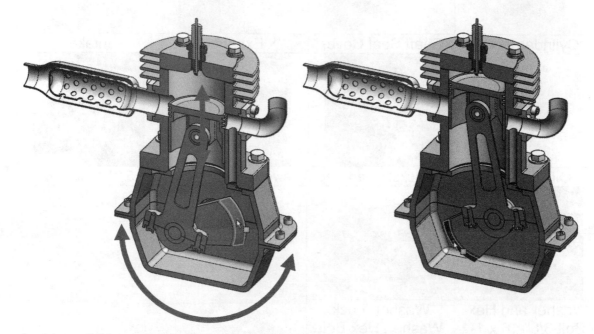

A video of this cross section is available in the accompanying disc.

After adding all the fasteners the FeatureManager will be *very* long. To make it easier to navigate we can group multiple components together using folders. Select all the fasteners in the FeatureManager, right-mouse-click on them, select "**Add to New Folder**" and rename it "*Fasteners*." This way we can hide, suppress, delete, or isolate all of them at the same time. After adding a folder we can drag-and-drop parts to and from it to add/remove items.

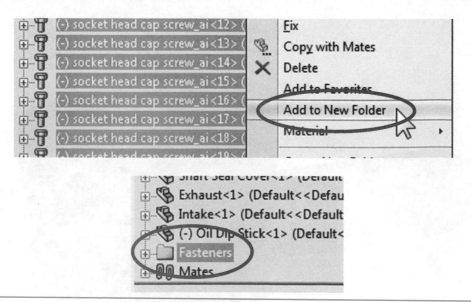

Image created using RealView graphics

For the engine's exploded view we can use the option "Select sub-assembly's parts" to explode sub-assembly components individually, if this option is off the entire sub-assembly will move as a single part.

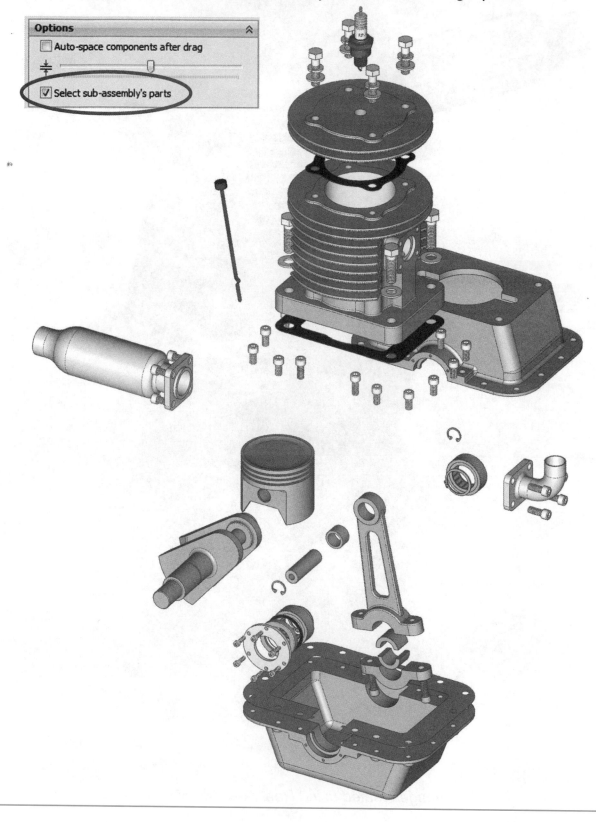

Extra Credit: Make the assembly of the *Gas Grill* using the parts created in the part modeling extra credit project and then add an exploded view for documentation purposes. The grill's cover must be able to open and close. Close the cover using collision detection.

Notes:

Assembly and Design Table Drawings

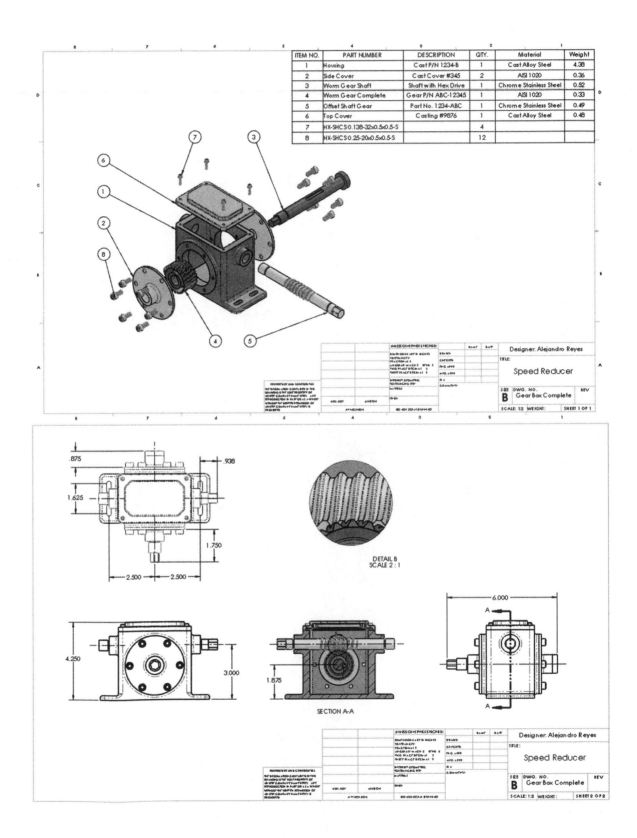

ITEM NO.	PART NUMBER	DESCRIPTION	QTY.	Material	Weight
1	Housing	Cast P/N 1234-B	1	Cast Alloy Steel	4.38
2	Side Cover	Cast Cover #345	2	AISI 1020	0.36
3	Worm Gear Shaft	Shaft with Hex Drive	1	Chrome Stainless Steel	0.52
4	Worm Gear Complete	Gear P/N ABC-12345	1	AISI 1020	0.33
5	Offset Shaft Gear	Part No. 1234-ABC	1	Chrome Stainless Steel	0.49
6	Top Cover	Casting #9876	1	Cast Alloy Steel	0.48
7	HX-SHCS 0.138-32x0.5x0.5-S		4		
8	HX-SHCS 0.25-20x0.5x0.5-S		12		

Designer: Alejandro Reyes

TITLE:

Speed Reducer

DWG. NO. Gear Box Complete

DETAIL B
SCALE 2 : 1

SECTION A-A

Notes:

451. - After finishing an assembly it is usually required to make an assembly drawing with a Bill of Materials for assembly instructions and documentation. In this case, we will make a drawing with an exploded view, Bill of Materials (BOM), and identification balloons. To make the drawing, open the assembly '*Gear Box Complete'* and activate the *"With Gears"* configuration. Select the "**Make drawing from part/assembly**" icon as we did with the parts, and make a new drawing using the "B-Landscape" sheet size, with the "Display sheet format" checkbox activated.

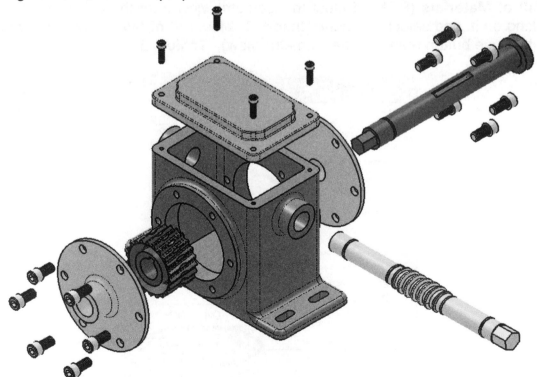

452. - From the "View Palette," drag the "Isometric Exploded" view to the sheet. Change the Display Style to "Shaded with Edges." If the sheet's scale is not 1:2 change it from the sheet properties.

When an assembly has an Exploded View, we can change the view to display Exploded or Collapsed after inserting it in the drawing sheet. Right-mouse-click in the assembly view, select "Properties" from the pop-up menu and turn on/off the option "**Show in Exploded State**." Notice that if we have multiple configurations, exploded views and display states in the assembly, we can also change them in the "Drawing View Properties" window.

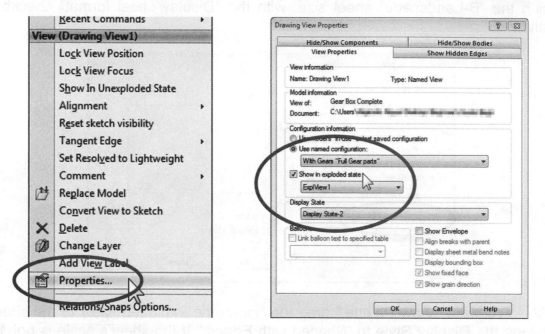

453. - Once we have the exploded isometric view in the drawing, we need to add a **Bill of Materials** (BOM). Select the isometric view from the graphics area by clicking on it, and select the menu "**Insert, Tables, Bill of Materials**", or from the right mouse button menu (in the isometric view), "**Tables, Bill of Materials**."

454. - In this example click OK in the Bill of Materials PropertyManager to accept the default options.

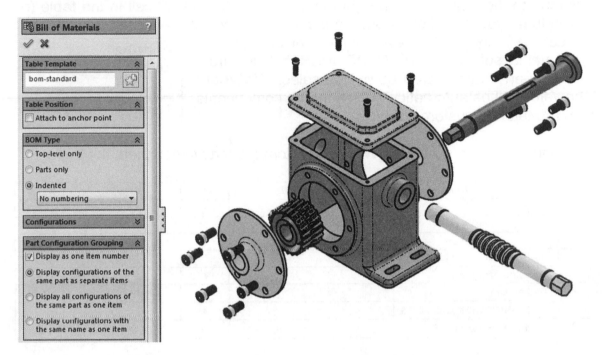

455. - After clicking on OK, we can locate the Bill of Materials in the sheet. Move the mouse and locate the BOM in the top right corner of the drawing. While locating the table, notice the table will snap to the corner. If needed, move the assembly view to make space for the identification balloons that will be added later. The column's width and row's height can be adjusted by dragging the table lines just as in Microsoft Excel. Since we added the "Description" custom property to the *'Worm Gear Shaft'* it is automatically imported into the Bill of Materials. We added a "Description" property to the *'Worm Gear'* and *'Offset Shaft'*, but it was to the simplified version of the parts without gears.

ITEM NO.	PART NUMBER	DESCRIPTION	QTY.
1	Housing		1
2	Side Cover		2
3	Worm Gear Shaft	Shaft with Hex Drive	1
4	Worm Gear Complete		1
5	Offset Shaft Gear		1
6	Top Cover		1
7	HX-SHCS 0.138-32x0.5x0.5-S		4
8	HX-SHCS 0.25-20x0.5x0.5-S		12

456. - It is possible to customize the Bill of Materials by adding more columns with information imported from the components' custom properties. To add columns to the table, make a right-mouse-click in the "QTY" cell in the table (or any column you wish), and from the pop-up menu select "**Insert, Column Right**" (or Left...) to locate the new column. For the "Column type" value select "CUSTOM PROPERTY," and from the "Property name" drop down list, select "**Material**." The value will be automatically filled for the components with a "Material" custom property.

Column type:

CUSTOM PROPERTY ▼

Property name:

Material ▼

Add another column with the "**Weight**" custom property to complete the table.

ITEM NO.	PART NUMBER	DESCRIPTION	QTY.	Material	Weight
1	Housing		1		
2	Side Cover		2		
3	Worm Gear Shaft	Shaft with Hex Drive	1	Chrome Stainless Steel	0.52
4	Worm Gear Complete		1		
5	Offset Shaft Gear		1		
6	Top Cover		1	Cast Alloy Steel	0.48
7	HX-SHCS 0.138-32x0.5x0.5-S		4		
8	HX-SHCS 0.25-20x0.5x0.5-S		12		

457. - Open all the parts with missing information and add the custom properties needed in the table using the "Custom Properties" pane. The material and weight properties are already added, we only need to type a new description for the parts. After adding the properties to a part press "Apply" and save it. After adding the properties to all parts return to the assembly drawing. If the properties are not shown in the table, rebuild the drawing to update the table.

To open a part's file from within the drawing, select the part in the graphics area with the left mouse button and click in the "**Open Part (...)**" icon from the pop-up menu.

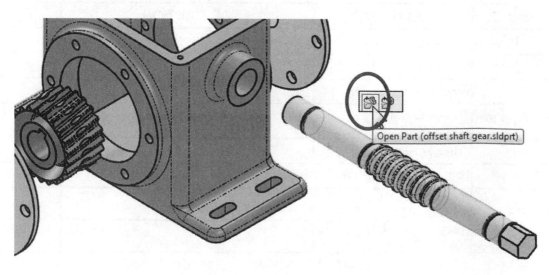

Open Part (offset shaft gear.sldprt)

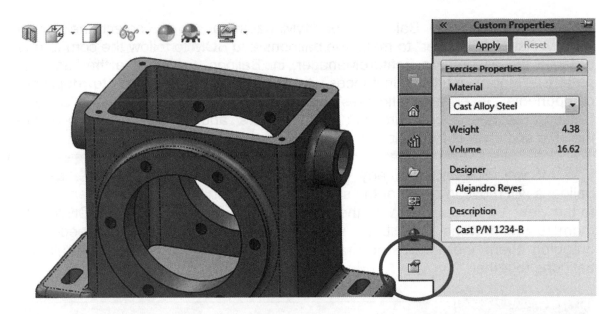

458. - To move the table, click-and-drag it from the upper left corner. Column width and row height can be adjusted as needed, and cells, rows, columns or the entire table can be formatted using the pop-up toolbar, just like Microsoft Excel. When finished, your table should look like this.

ITEM NO.	PART NUMBER	DESCRIPTION	QTY.	Material	Weight
1	Housing	Cast P/N 1234-B	1	Cast Alloy Steel	4.38
2	Side Cover	Cast Cover #345	2	AISI 1020	0.36
3	Worm Gear Shaft	Shaft with Hex Drive	1	Chrome Stainless Steel	0.52
4	Worm Gear Complete	Gear P/N ABC-12345	1	AISI 1020	0.33
5	Offset Shaft Gear	Part No. 1234-ABC	1	Chrome Stainless Steel	0.49
6	Top Cover	Casting #9876	1	Cast Alloy Steel	0.48
7	HX-SHCS 0.138-32x0.5x0.5-S		4		
8	HX-SHCS 0.25-20x0.5x0.5-S		12		

We can add as many custom properties as needed to accurately document our designs and, as we learned, these properties can also be used in the part's detail drawing and the Bill of Materials. Assembly files can also be given custom properties just like individual components.

459. - Now we need to add identification balloons to our assembly drawing to match each item in the assembly view to the item numbers in the Bill of Materials. Make a right-mouse-click in the assembly drawing view, and from the pop-up menu select **"Annotations, AutoBalloon"** or select the assembly view and go to the menu **"Insert, Annotations, AutoBalloon."**

475

460. - When the Auto Balloon PropertyManager is shown, select the option "Follow Assembly Order" to make the balloons and BOM to follow the component order in the assembly's FeatureManager, in "Balloon Layout" use the "Square" pattern, "Ignore multiple instances" to avoid adding balloons to duplicate components, "Insert magnetic lines" to align the balloons to them, in the "Balloon Settings" options select "Circular", "2 Characters" and "Item Number" to define the size and style of the balloons.

If we click-and-drag any of the balloons before we click OK, all the balloons will move in or out at the same time. This can help us locate them closer to the view. When satisfied with the general look of the balloons, click OK to add them to the drawing view. Later we can modify their positions as needed by dragging them individually or dragging the magnetic lines to move all the balloons together.

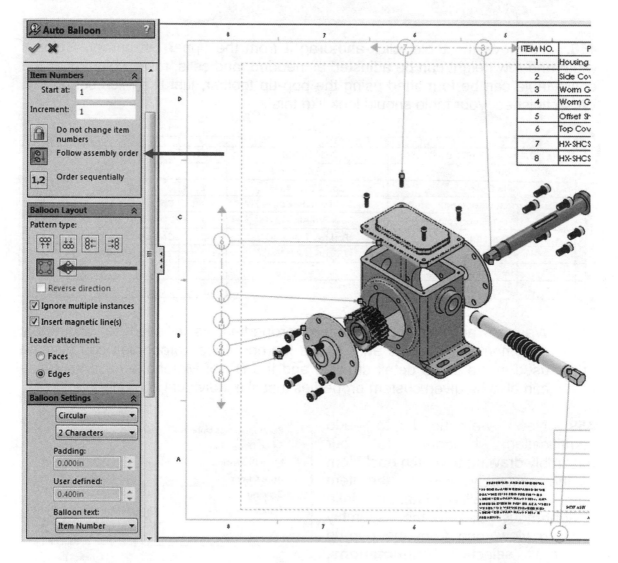

461. - Click-and-drag the balloons individually to arrange them in the drawing. When dragging a balloon it will snap to the magnetic lines, and magnetic lines can also be moved around the drawing. An arrow's tip can also be dragged to a different area of the part for visibility; if the arrow tip is dragged to a different component, the item number will change to reflect the part that the balloon is attached to. Arrange the balloons as needed to improve readability.

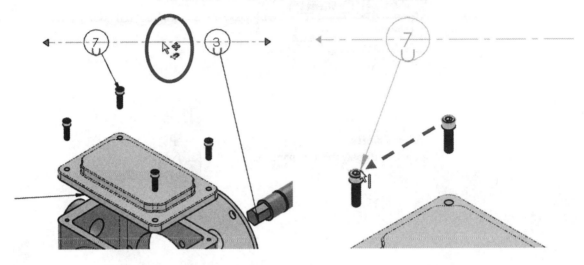

462. - Edit the Sheet Format to add the missing notes in the title block.

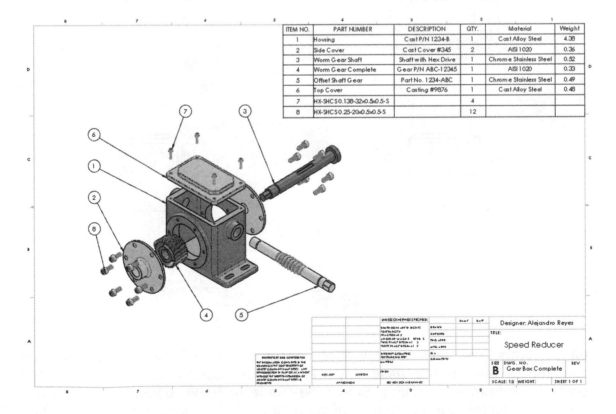

ITEM NO.	PART NUMBER	DESCRIPTION	QTY.	Material	Weight
1	Housing	Cast P/N 1234-B	1	Cast Alloy Steel	4.38
2	Side Cover	Cast Cover #345	2	AISI 1020	0.36
3	Worm Gear Shaft	Shaft with Hex Drive	1	Chrome Stainless Steel	0.52
4	Worm Gear Complete	Gear P/N ABC-12345	1	AISI 1020	0.33
5	Offset Shaft Gear	Part No. 1234-ABC	1	Chrome Stainless Steel	0.49
6	Top Cover	Casting #9876	1	Cast Alloy Steel	0.48
7	HX-SHCS 0.138-32x0.5x0.5-S		4		
8	HX-SHCS 0.25-20x0.5x0.5-S		12		

Designer: Alejandro Reyes

TITLE: Speed Reducer

DWG. NO. Gear Box Complete

SIZE B   REV

SCALE: 1:2   WEIGHT: SHEET 1 OF 1

477

463 . – As we did with the in the part drawings, add a new sheet to the assembly drawing and add a Front, Top and Right views. Click in the "Add Sheet" tab in the lower left corner of the drawing; and from the "View Pallette" drag the assembly's front view, and project the top and right views from it.

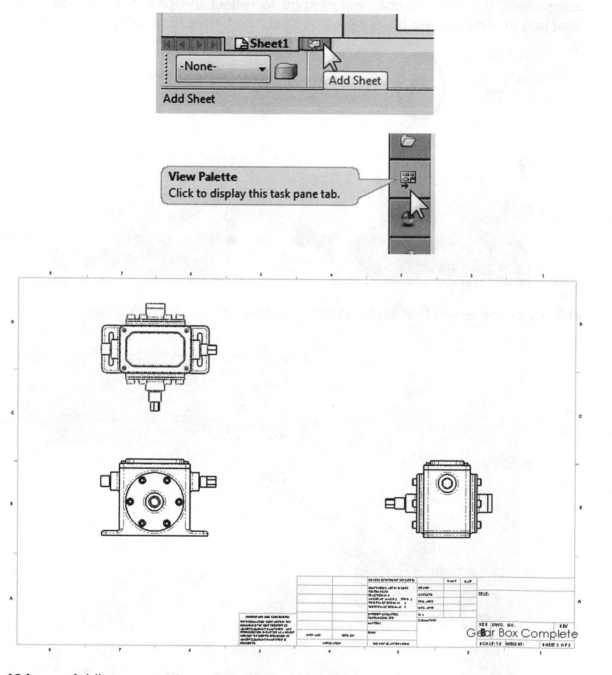

464 . – Adding a section view to an assembly is just like with a part, the exception is that in the assembly we have the option to exclude selected components from the section. Select the "**Section View**" command and add a vertical section through the middle of the right view. After locating the section line a dialog box asks us to select the components that will be exclueded from the section line, in other words, the selected components will not be cut.

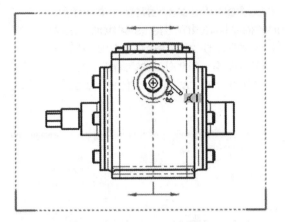

After locating the section line the "Feature Scope" selection box is presented. From the right view click to select the '*Offset Shaft Gear*' click OK to finish and locate the section view. If the section line crosses fasteners we can turn on the "Exclude fasteners" option to exclude all Toolbox components.

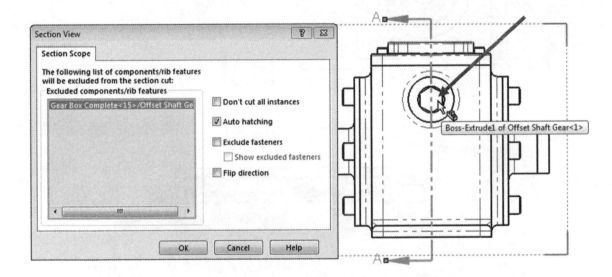

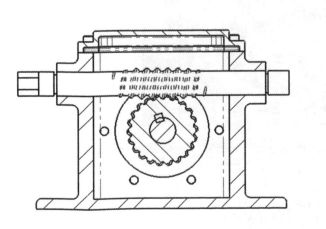

SECTION A-A

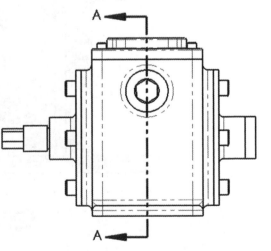

465 . – To exclude additional components from the section line, righ-mouse-click in the section view, select the "Section Scope" tab and select the '*Worm Gear Complete*'. Click OK to continue and change the section view to "Shaded with edges" display style.

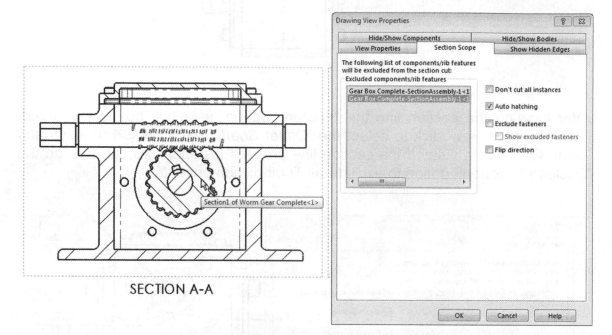

SECTION A-A

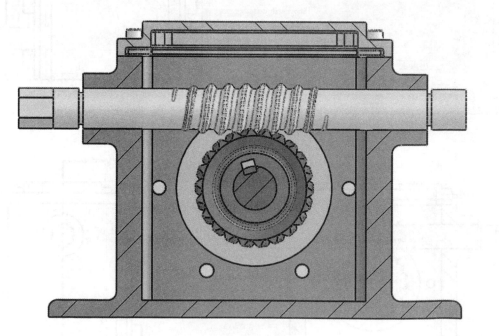

SECTION A-A

466 . – Add a new detail view of the region where both gears mesh and change the detail's scate to 2:1.

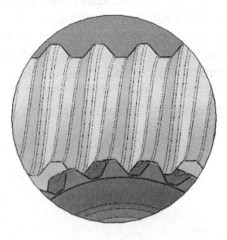

DETAIL B
SCALE 2 : 1

467 . – Since the assembly does not have any dimensions, manually add the overall assembly dimensions to the drawing using the "Smart Dimension" command and move them to the "FORMAT" layer to display them in black.

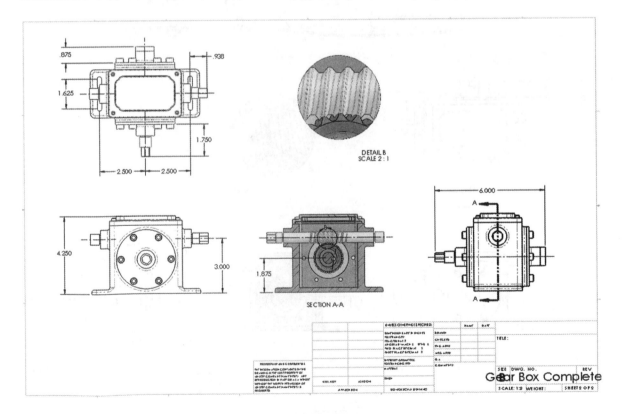

481

468 . – We can modify the sheet format to match the previous sheet, but instead we'll save the sheet format of the first page and apply it to the new sheet. Go back to "Sheet1" and from the menu "**File, Save Sheet Format...**" save it to any location using the name '*Exercises b – landscape*', the extension used for a sheet format is *.slddrt. After saving the sheet format go back to "Sheet2." Right-mouse-click either in the sheet (not a view!), *or* in the FeatureManager in "*Sheet Format2,*" and select "Properties." Browse for the new sheet format and click OK to load it. All notes, modifications, and custom properties added to the sheet format will be added to the new page. Save the drawing and close the file.

469 . – A drawing of a part with a design table is essentially the same as any other drawing, with the only difference that we can add the Design Table to the drawing. Make a new drawing using the '*Screw Design Table*' part, Right-mouse-click in a part's view and select "**Tables, Design Table**" from the pop-up menu. In the drawing we can turn on the dimension names to help identify the dimensions using the menu "**View, Dimension Names**."

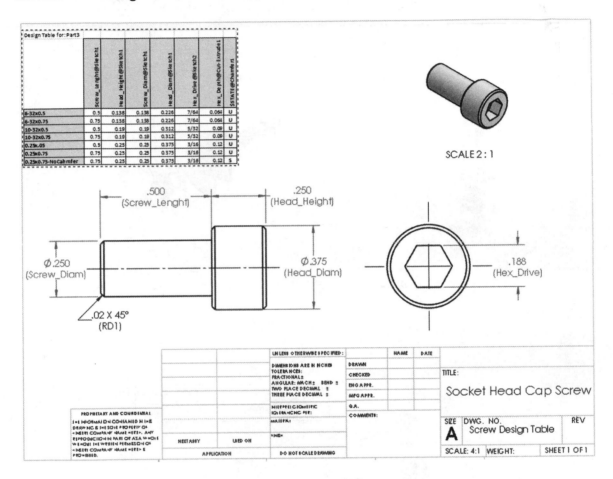

When we add a design table to a drawing, we get a snapshot of the Excel table as it was last edited in the part. To modify the design table we have to go back to the part and edit the design table in the Configuration-Manager.

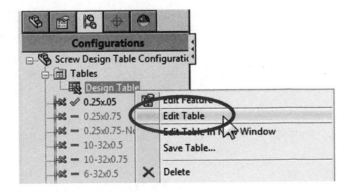

Engine Project: Make an assembly drawing of each sub-assembly and one of the exploded Engine Assembly Use the following images as a guide.

For the "Connecting Rod Sub Assembly" use the "A-Portrait" template, for the "Engine Assembly" drawing use the "C-Landscape" template to better accommodate the large assembly. Feel free to format the BOM to your liking.

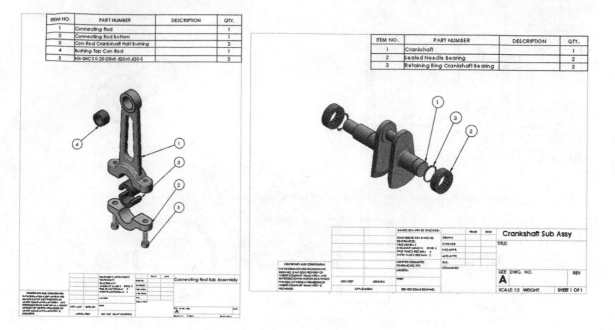

ITEM NO.	PART NUMBER	DESCRIPTION	QTY.
1	Connecting Rod		1
2	Connecting Rod Bottom		1
3	Con Rod Crankshaft Half Bushing		2
4	Bushing Top Con Rod		1
5	HX-SHCS 0.25-28x0.625x0.625-S		2

ITEM NO.	PART NUMBER	DESCRIPTION	QTY.
1	Crankshaft		1
2	Sealed Needle Bearing		2
3	Retaining Ring Crankshaft Bearing		2

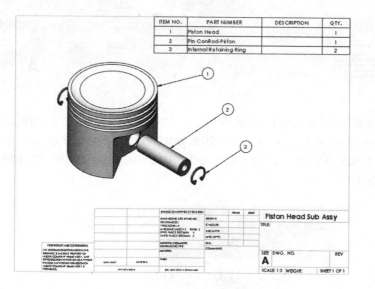

ITEM NO.	PART NUMBER	DESCRIPTION	QTY.
1	Piston Head		1
2	Pin ConRod-Piston		1
3	Internal Retaining Ring		2

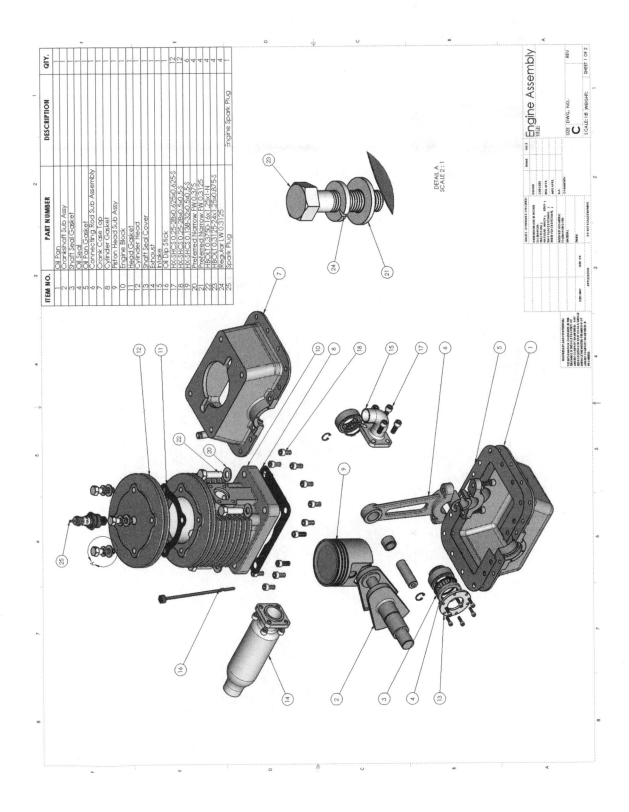

ITEM NO.	PART NUMBER	DESCRIPTION	QTY.
1		Oil Pan	1
2		Crankshaft Sub Assy	1
3		Shaft Seal Gasket	1
4		Oil Seal	1
5		Oil Pan Gasket	1
6		Connecting Rod Sub Assembly	1
7		Crank Case Top	1
8		Cylinder Gasket	1
9		Piston Head Sub Assy	1
10		Engine Block	1
11		Head Gasket	1
12		Cylinder Head	1
13		Shaft Seal Cover	1
14		Exhaust	1
15		Intake	1
16		Oil Dip Stick	1
17	HX-SHCS 0.25-28x0.625x0.625-S		12
18	HX-SHCS 0.25-28x0.5x0.5-S		12
19	HX-SHCS 0.138-32x0.5x0.5-S		6
20	Preferred Narrow FW 0.375		4
21	Preferred Narrow FW 0.3125		4
22	HBOLT 0.3750-16x1.25x1-N		4
23	HBOLT 0.3125-24x1.25x0.875-S		4
24	Regular LW 0.3125		1
25	Spark Plug		1
		Engine Spark Plug	1

DETAIL A
SCALE 2 : 1

Engine Assembly
TITLE:

REV

SIZE C DWG. NO.

SCALE: 1:3 WEIGHT: SHEET 1 OF 2

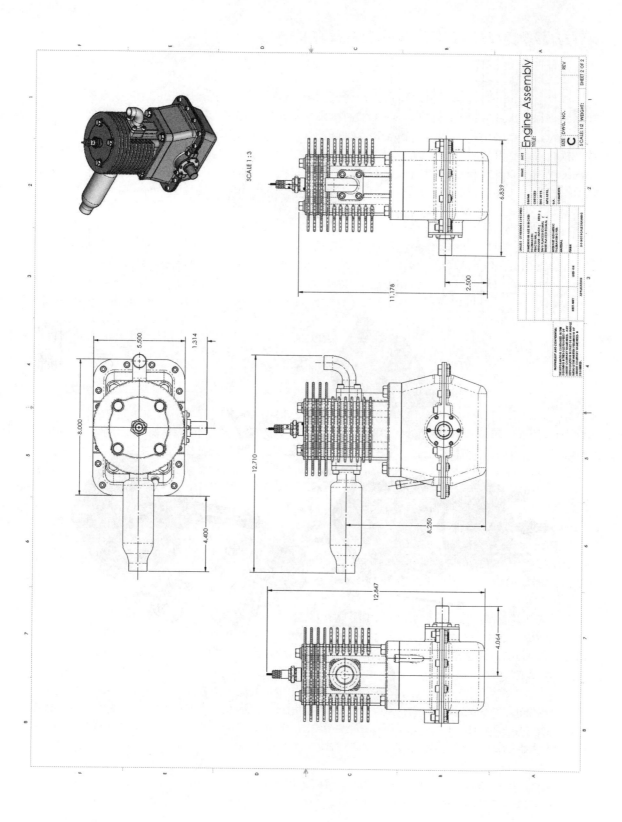

Animation and Rendering

SolidWorks Professional and Educational edition include PhotoView 360, this is the integrated software used to generate photo realistic rendered images of parts and assemblies. Photo realistic images generated before a product or design is finished can be very useful, for example, we can show a potential customer how their product would look, prepare advance marketing campaigns (before the product is made,) promotional videos, etc.

The resulting images can be of such high quality and realism that they can (and often are) confused with pictures taken in a professional photo studio. PhotoView 360 allows us to select component materials, colors, backgrounds, light sources, shadow settings, reflections, and a number of advanced lighting settings; the combination of those and many more parameters takes time to master and a lot of experimenting to see and fully understand their effect in the final result.

To obtain high quality, photo real rendering results, the user will usually have to make multiple iterations, changing and fine-tuning different settings in each pass, especially lighting. In this lesson we'll cover the basic and most commonly used settings to help us understand their effect and how to obtain good rendering results.

Animation is used to show assemblies in motion, to help us see and understand how they work in real life, animate exploded views and collapse them, for example, to explain how to assemble or take apart a product. Also, not only can we animate an assembly, we can change component's transparency, appearance, display settings, hide, and show them, etc. to better illustrate their operation, inner workings or features.

After an animation is completed it can be saved to a file as an *.AVI video or a series of pictures to be used in a third party video editing software. At the time of saving the video we can choose to create the video using the SolidWorks screen (as seen in the graphics area) or a photo realistic animation using PhotoView 360. In the second case, the final result will take considerably longer to generate, as each frame of the animation will be photo realistically rendered, and depending on the rendering settings, the length of the animation, and the size of the image this can take a very long time.

To practice, we'll produce renderings and animations of the parts and assemblies completed so far, including the gear box, the engine, and the grill.

Notes:

PhotoView 360

470 . – To start rendering the first thing we need to do is to load the PhotoView 360 add-in. Go to the menu "Tools, Add-ins…" and select the PhotoView 360. A different way to load the add-in is by going to the Office Products tab in the Command Manager, and select "PhotoView 360." We can also turn on the other add-ins included in SolidWorks, including "SolidWorks Toolbox."

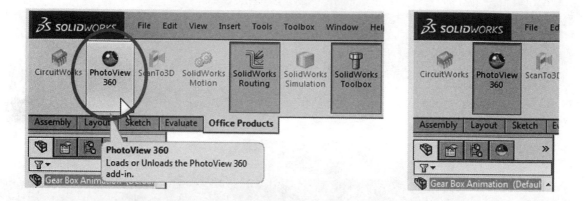

471 . – After loading PhotoView 360 a new "PhotoView 360" menu and "Render Tools" toolbar are added to SolidWorks.

472. – To practice, open the 'Gear Box PhotoView' assembly files included with the book, download it from http://www.SDCpublications.com/ or use the gear box assembly made in the book so far.

473. – The first thing we need to do is to is to activate the "DisplayManager" tab where we can add, edit, and delete a component's appearance, decals, light sources, cameras, and scenes to a model. After activating the tab we can see the different sub-sections for:

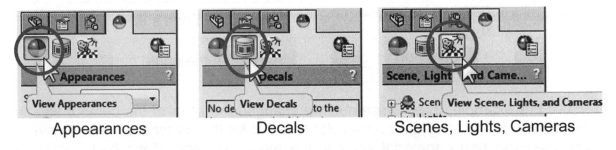

Appearances   Decals   Scenes, Lights, Cameras

After selecting "View Appearances" we can see all the appearances used in the assembly (or part) listed in chronological order (History,) Alphabetical order or by Hierarchy. History lists the appearances in the order they were added and Hierarchy lists the appearances at the level at which they are added.

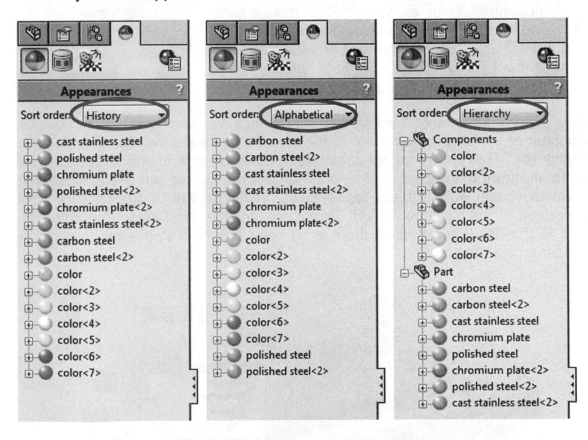

Appearances will be shown depending on the level at which they are added, higher hierarchy appearances will be displayed covering the lower level appearances. The hierarchy for appearance display is:

	Component	Applied to a part or sub-assembly in the assembly.
	Face	Applied to a part's face.
	Feature	Applied to a part's feature
	Body	Applied to a part's body
	Part	Applied to the entire part

For example, in our assembly we changed the color of the components in the assembly covering the part's color (defined by the material.) if we remove it we'll see the part's material color in the assembly, and, if we had applied a different appearance to a face or feature we would see those too, as they are higher in the hierarchy than the part.

In the assembly we can work with appearances at all levels. Right-mouse-click in an appearance and select the option to Add, Edit, Copy, Paste or Remove an appearance to a Component, Face, Feature, Body or Part.

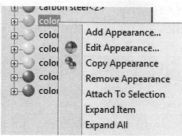

474. – To add, edit or remove an appearance we can work in the Display Manager or in the graphics area. In this step we'll remove the 'Top Cover' color. Select the 'Top Cover' in the graphics area and click in the "Appearances" command from the pop-up menu. In the drop-down list we can see all the levels at which we can work with the appearances. Select the red "X" to delete the color we added at the assembly level. To edit the color instead select the color box next to the assembly level. If there is no color box next to a level, there is no appearance at that level.

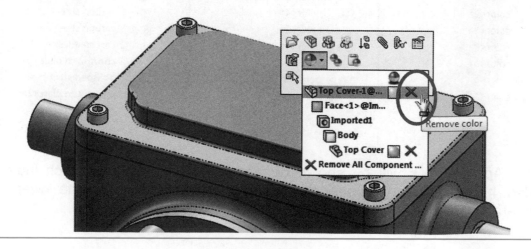

The '*Top Cover*' now looks like this:

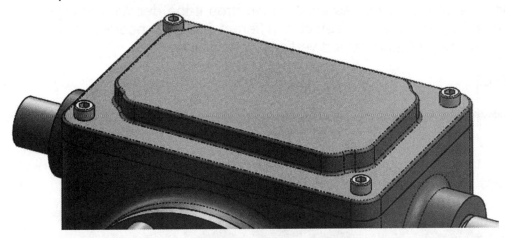

475. – For the next step we are going to add a decal to our assembly. Decals are used to show printed logos, labels, markings, etc. Open the '*Top Cover*', if you are using the disk files for the PhotoView 360 exercise, you may be asked "*Do you want to proceed with feature recognition?*" If this is the case select "No" to continue. After opening the '*Top Cover*' select the Display Manager tab and go to the "View Decals" section. If a part has decals they will be shown in this page. Click in the "Open Decal Library" to show available decals in the library located in the "Appearances, Decals, and Scenes" task pane.

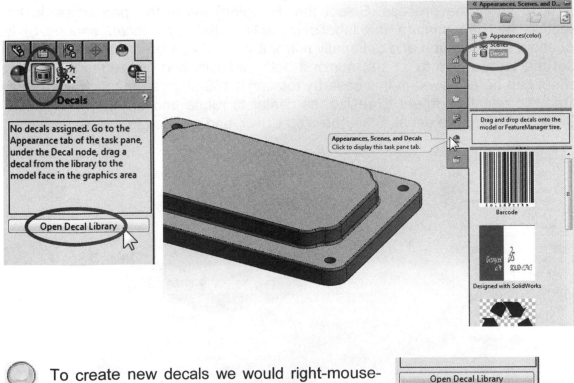

To create new decals we would right-mouse-click in the Display Manager and select "Add Decal."

476. – From the "Decals" library scroll down to the "Recycling" decal and drag it onto the top face of the cover. As soon as we drop it the decal's properties are displayed. In this page we can select a different image if needed. Notice the recycling logo is inverted and flipped vertically in this view.

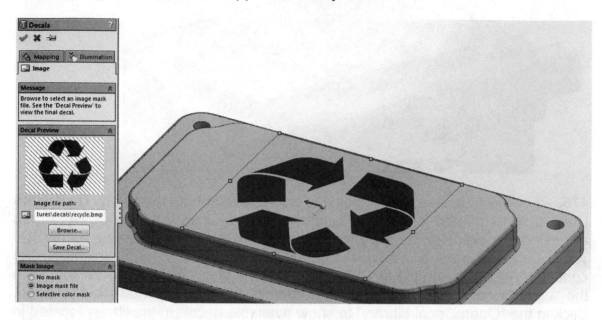

477. – Just as an exercise we are going to reverse the logo in this step. In reality it is not necessary because the part is symmetrical and can be rotated, but we'll do it to show the process. Select the "Mapping" tab in the properties. In this section we can change the label's projection (flat, cylindrical, spherical,) its location, size, rotation and optionally mirror it vertically and/or horizontally.

Set the label's size to 1" and mirror it both vertically and horizontal (The same effect can be achieved in this case by rotating it 180 degrees.) Optionally we can drag the decal's corners to resize, its center to rotate and the edges to locate. Click OK to add the decal. Save the '*Top Cover*' and go back to the assembly.

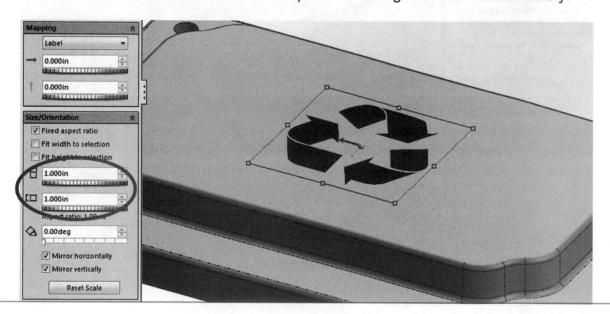

In the assembly we can see the new decal in the "Decals" section.

478. – The next step is to add a scene and lights to our assembly before making the rendering. Select the "Scene, Lights, and Cameras" section.

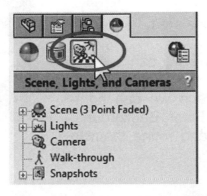

If the hardware supports it, we can activate the RealView graphics in the View toolbar. RealView will show a high quality real time render using the component's materials, appearances, and scenes added. RealView is not required to render an image, but helps when composing images before a final render.

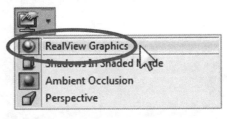

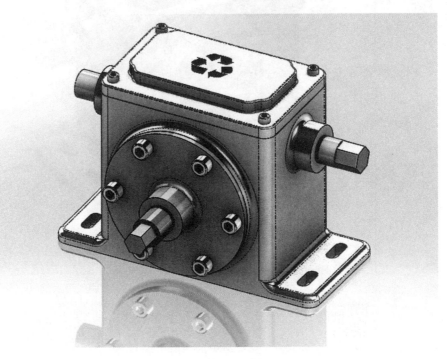

495

479. – To add a scene to our assembly (or a part) open the "Appearances, Decals and Scenes" tab in the Task pane. Scroll down to "Scenes, Studio Scenes" and select the "Reflective Floor Checkered" scene. To apply it to our assembly we can:

- Double click in it
- Right-mouse-click and select "Apply Scene," or
- Drag it to the graphics area.

After adding a scene we can see the new scene parameters in the Display Pane. To further modify the scene we can right-mouse-click in the Scene, Floor, Background, and Environment to edit and refine them to our liking.

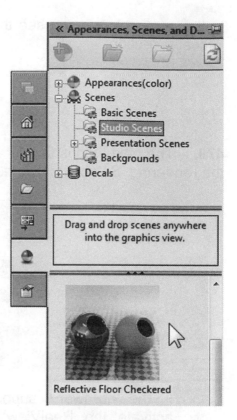

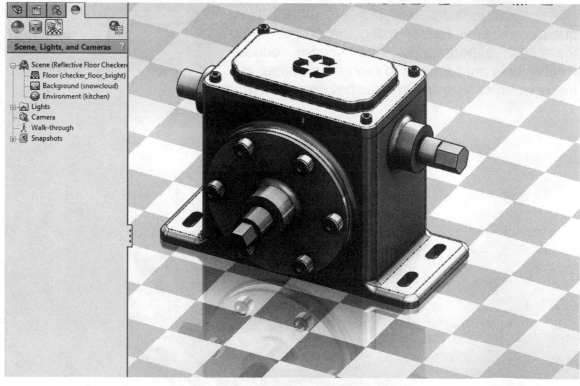

480. – Pre-defined scenes also add lights to match the scene. In the Render Tools tab in the CommandManager turn on the "**Preview Window**" command. A new window will appear showing a preview to help us adjust the settings before rendering the final image. Be aware that computer resources will be used to render the preview image.

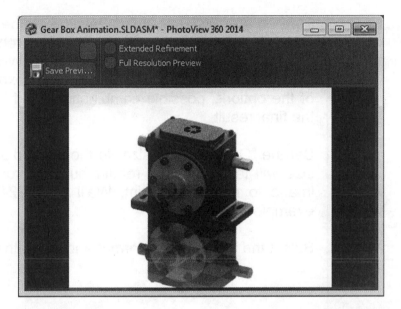

In the preview window we can see that the light is (in this case) too bright. To change the lighting, expand the "Lights" section in the Display Manager. Right-mouse-click in "Scene Illumination" and select "Edit Scene Illumination." This is one of the areas where we have to tweak the settings to obtain the

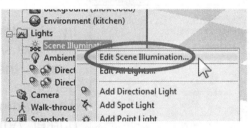

results we want. Change the illumination parameters until the preview shows the desired image and click OK to finish.

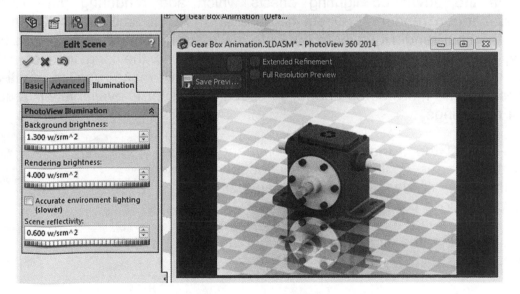

481. – After changing the scene illumination settings select the "**PhotoView 360 Options**" command to set the options for the final render.

Turn on the "Dynamic Help" checkbox to get information on the many options available for a final render, as they are too many to cover in this section. We'll show the most commonly used and let the reader explore the rest of the options, possible combinations and their effect in the final result.

Set the "Output image size" to the desired size. A larger size will take longer to render but will provide a better image to resize and print. We'll use 1024x768 in our example.

Select the image output format and the path to save it.

In "Render Quality" we can change the quality for the preview window and the final render. The higher the quality, the longer the preview and render will take to generate.

The gamma settings will make the scene lighter or darker. Adjust as needed to obtain the desired results.

As a general rule, it's a good idea to set the image size to a small size, turn off the advanced lighting effects which add rendering time (Bloom, contour/cartoon rendering, Direct caustics and Output ambient occlusion) and lower the final render quality to evaluate the resulting image, change positions, lights, colors, environment, etc. before committing to the long time of a high quality final rendering. The rendering engine will make use of multi-core processors, the more cores and faster speed processor is available will result in faster renderings.

482. – Select the "**Final Render**" command from the Render Tools tab. A new window with the final render progress will appear. Each processor's core will render an area at a time, in our case the processor has eight cores, reducing the time needed to get an image.

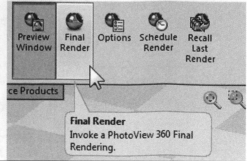

498

After the render is finished select the thumbnail at the bottom and click "Save Image," set the location and save it.

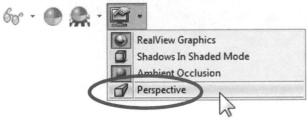

In the next image the part colors were removed from the assembly and gear box was rendered using the appearances assigned by the material selections only.

To add realism to the final renderings activate the "Perspective" view in the View toolbar.

Feel free to explore other options, lighting, and different environments.

Engine Project: Make a render of the engine using the knowledge acquired so far.

 The previous image was made using a "**Cut Extrude**" assembly feature. This is a cut at the assembly level that is not reflected at the part level. Add a sketch in the assembly selecting a face just as we do in a part.

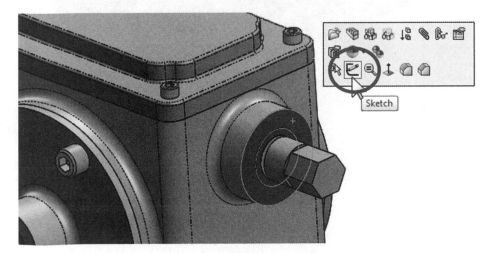

Draw a rectangle or any other profile to make the cut. Make sure it covers the areas of the assembly you want to cut.

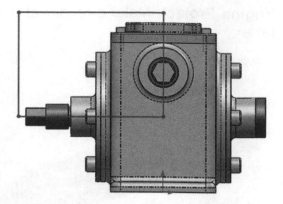

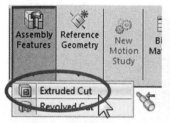

Select **"Extruded Cut"** from the drop down menu under **"Assembly Features"** in the Assembly tab of the CommandManager.

Make the cut using the "Through All" option (only a suggestion.) Under the "Feature Scope" uncheck the "Auto-select" option and select the components that will be cut, this is the same as the assembly section view. Click OK to finish. Add textures to cut faces and render.

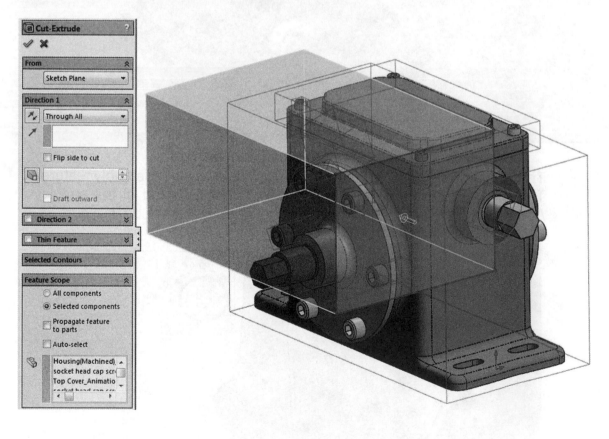

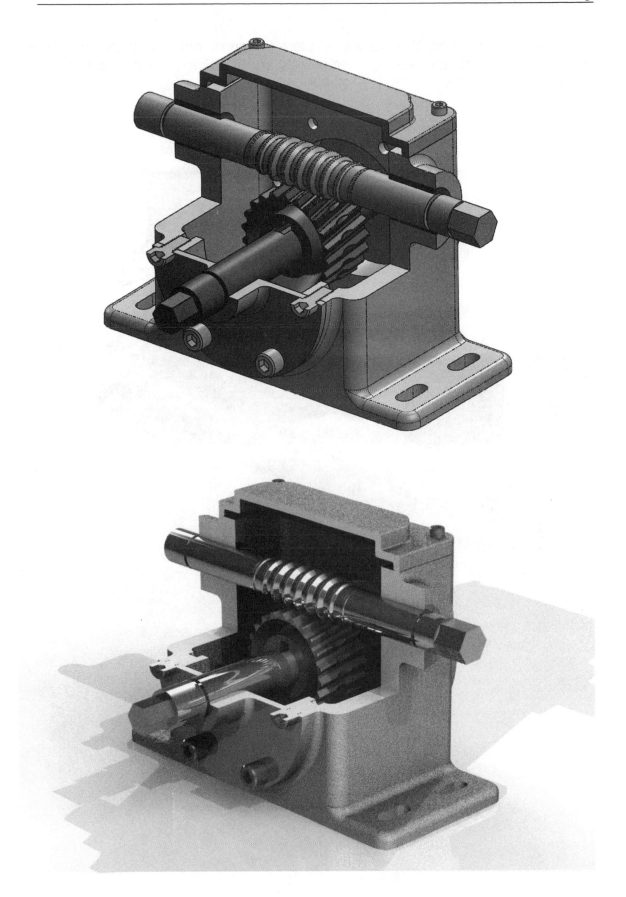

After mastering the basics, explore different options, textures, lighting effects, and the multiple settings available to create photo realistic images of your projects and designs.

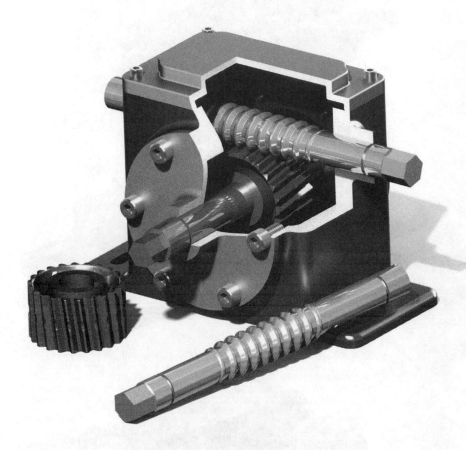

Animation

Notes:

483. – As explained earlier, the animation is where we make a video to show the assembly in motion, functioning as it would in real life, how to assemble (collapse) and disassemble (explode,) etc. Open the '*Gear Box Animation*' assembly from the included disk files, or use the assembly made in the previous lessons. To start an animation, select the "Motion Study 1" tab at the bottom left corner of the window to access the MotionManager.

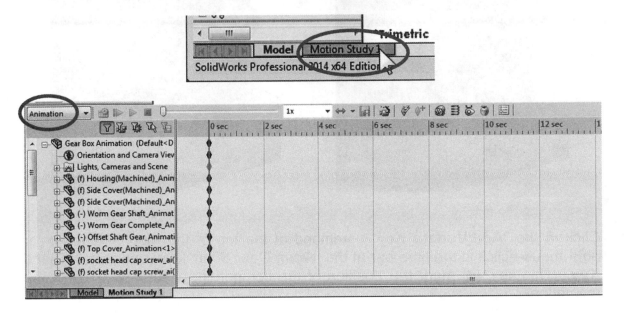

 SolidWorks has two different types of motion studies; the first one is "Animation," where we move components manually or with a motor to a new position using a timeline. The second type is "Basic Motion," the difference is that a basic motion study takes into consideration physics, mass, gravity, etc. and the components are driven by motors, gravity, contact between them, and/or springs. In this lesson we'll cover Animation.

484. – The first type of animation will be made by moving components manually. In the timeline, drag the time bar or click to define the length of the animation at the four seconds mark.

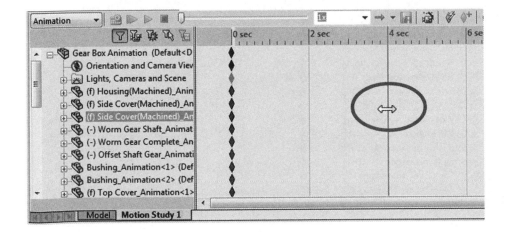

485. – To define the new position of the '*Worm Gear Shaft*' at the four seconds mark, click and drag the shaft approximately ¼ to ½ a turn in the screen. The '*Offset Shaft Gear*' will also rotate because of the gear mate added previously.

 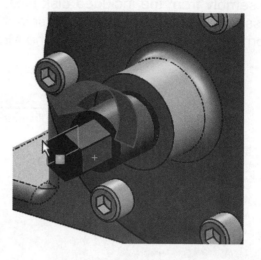

Click in the "**Add/Update Key**" command at the top of the MotionManager, or right-mouse-click in the time bar at the '*Worm Gear Shaft*' level and select "**Place Key**." This key will mark the position of the component at four seconds in the animation.

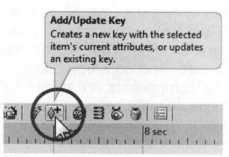

486. – After locating the first key the animation duration bar at the top is extended to four seconds and a green bar is added between 0 seconds and 4 seconds in the '*Worm Gear Shaft*'.

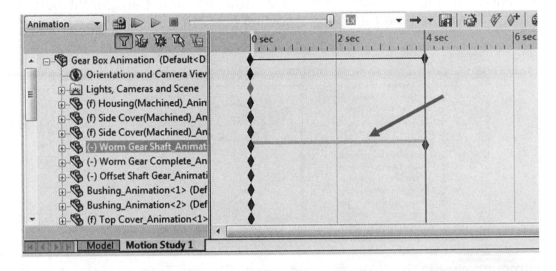

487. – After defining the animation SolidWorks needs to calculate the motion of the components. Click in the "**Calculate**" command. While the animation is calculated the playback may be slower than usual, depending on the number of components and effects being animated. After it is calculated we can press the "**Play**" command to see the video at full speed, since it's only playing the

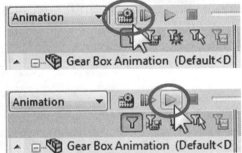

animation and not calculating anything. If we press "**Play**" instead of "**Calculate**" the animation will be played but it will be calculated first. After the calculation is complete a yellow bar is added to the '*Worm Gear Complete*' and the '*Offset Shaft Gear*'. This is to let us know that these components are being driven by the '*Worm Gear Shaft*'.

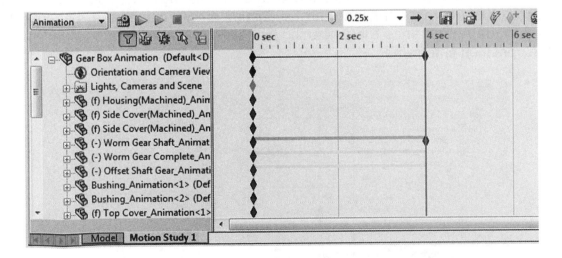

488. – After pressing "Play" the animation runs and we can see the '*Worm Gear Shaft*' turning from the starting point to the end, and the '*Offset Shaft*' following because of the gear mate. During animations we can also change a component's appearance. In this step we'll make the '*Housing*' part transparent during the animation. Move the time bar to the 2 second position.

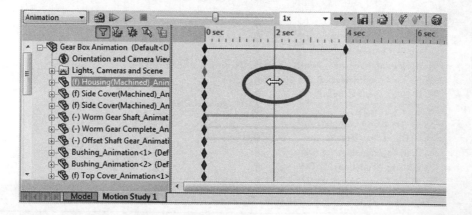

Right-mouse-click in the '*Housing*' and select "Change Transparency. A magenta line will be added from 0 seconds to 2 seconds.

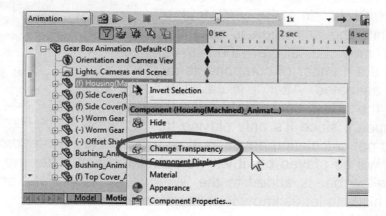

489. – Expand the '*Housing*' in the animation manager to see the different aspects of the component that can be animated. We can see a magenta line added to the Appearance row, meaning that the component has a visual change in the specified timeframe.

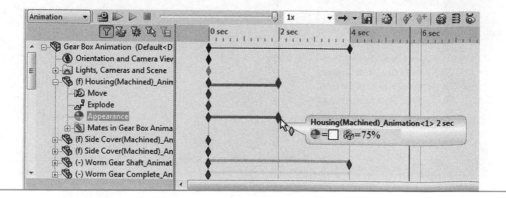

490. – Pressing play will show the '*Housing*' fading starting at 0 seconds and becoming transparent at 2 seconds letting us see the gears moving inside.

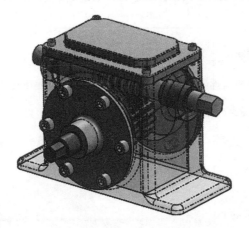

491. – For the next step we'll hide the '*Top Cover*'. Move the timeline to 4 seconds, right-mouse-click in the '*Top Cover*' and select "**Hide.**" A new animation step is added, also in magenta because it's an appearance change, going from 0 to 4 seconds.

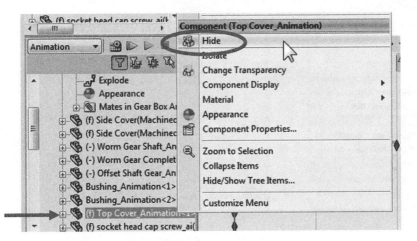

Pressing "Play" will show the animation as before, but now the '*Top Cover*' is fading until hidden at 4 seconds.

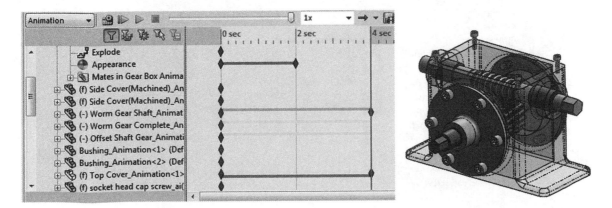

492. – In the timeline we can also make changes to the animation. Just as an example, click in the 'Worm Gear Shaft' marker at 4 seconds and move to 6 seconds. By making this change the shaft will rotate the same as before, but now it will be slower.

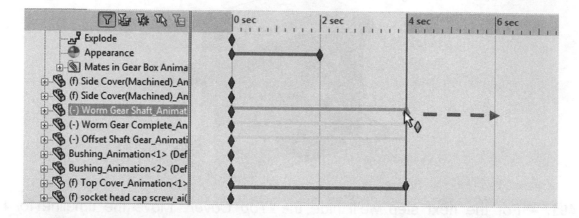

The yellow background at the top of the timeline is now hashed to let us know that we need to re-calculate the animation because changes were made to the movement of components.

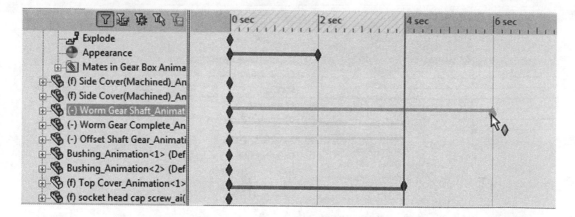

Press "**Calculate**" to continue. After re-calculating the animation the background is solid yellow again.

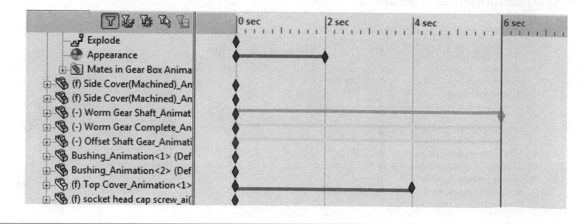

493. – The next step is to change the starting time to hide the 'Top Cover'. Expand the 'Top Cover' in the animation manager to see the animation key points. Click and drag the starting marker to 3 seconds in the timeline.

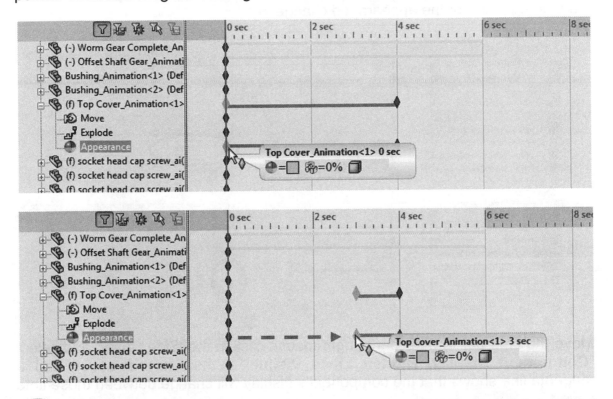

To change a key point to an exact time position right mouse click in it and select "**Edit Key Point Time**" and enter a new time.

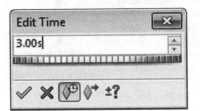

Our animation manager now looks like:

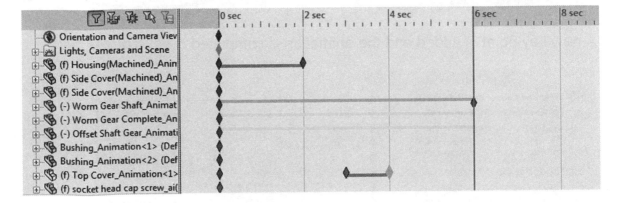

494. – For the last step of this animation we'll change the appearance of the *'Side Cover'* to hidden lines visible mode. Move the time bar to 4 seconds. At the *'Side Cover'* row's level, right-mouse-click and select "**Place Key.**" This will be the starting point for the appearance change.

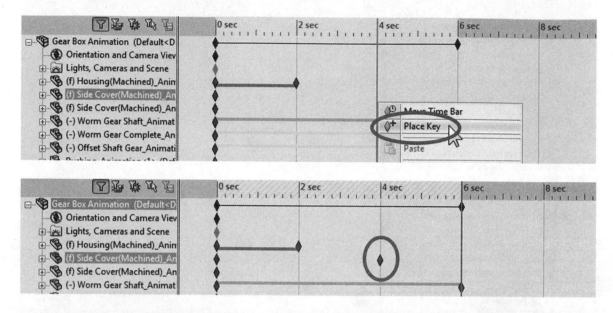

Move the time bar to 6 seconds, right-mouse-click in the 'Side Cover' and select "**Component Display, Hidden Lines Visible.**" A new key is added and a magenta line shows that the component's display will change between those time keys.

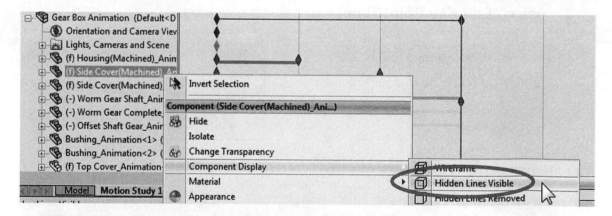

A new key point is added and the animation is completed.

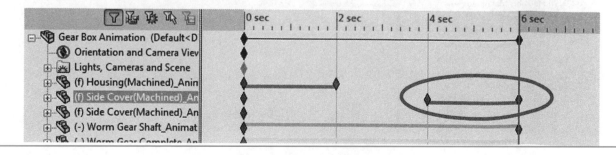

495. – Play the animation to see the result.

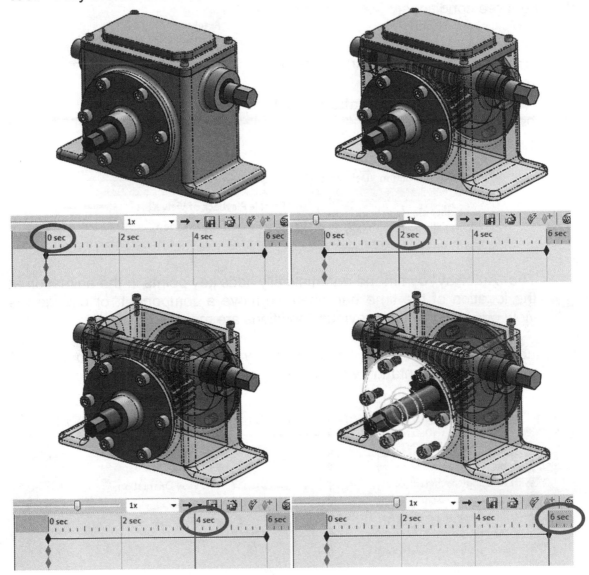

496. – The view is locked automatically when we start a new motion study, and that's why it always goes back to the same orientation when the animation is played, even if we change it. To play the animation regardless of the view orientation right-mouse-click in the "*Orientation and Camera View*" and select "**Disable Playback of View Keys**." After disabling it we can play the animation using any view orientation.

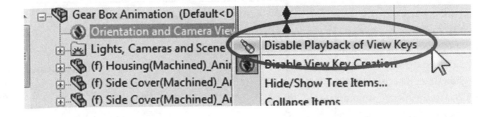

497. – To add view orientation changes to the animation, we have to meet the following three conditions:

- "**AutoKey**" must be ON.
- "**Disable Playback of View Keys**" must be OFF.
- "**Disable View Key Creation**" must be OFF.

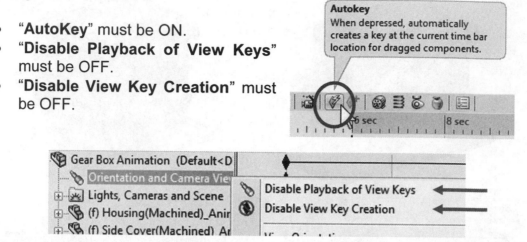

The "AutoKey" command automatically adds key points in the animation at the location of the time bar when we move a component, or change the view orientation if the previous conditions are met.

Move the time bar to 2 seconds and add a key in the "*Orientation and Camera*" row. The icon in the orientation view's row is no longer crossed.

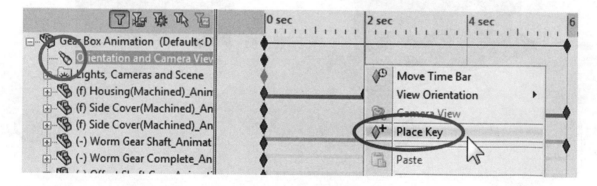

Move the time bar to 4 seconds and change the view's orientation. The new animation step is added to the view orientation automatically. In the resulting animation the view's orientation will change between the 2 seconds key and the 4 seconds key, and remain at that orientation.

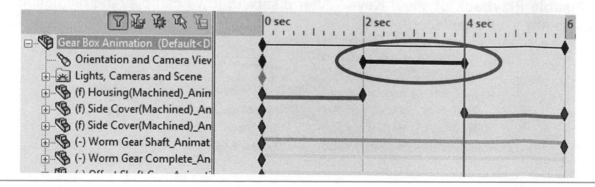

If the "**AutoKey**" command is used for component movement, it's a good idea to turn the "**Disable View Key Creation**" option ON to prevent you from accidentally adding view orientation keys to the animation. Add view orientation animations later to have more control and get the desired results. After finishing the view orientation animations turn the "**Disable View Key Creation**" option back ON.

The Final animation sequence is this. Feel free to explore animating more components to see their effect. We'll see explode and collapse next.

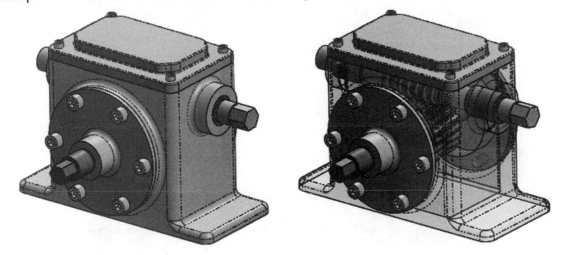

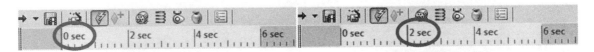

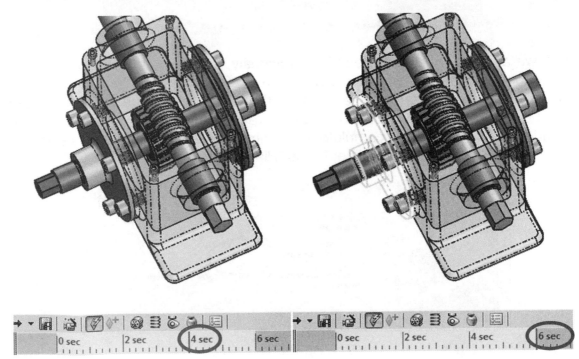

498. – To create a new animation right-mouse-click in the "*Motion Study 1*" tab and select "**Create New Motion study**" from the menu.

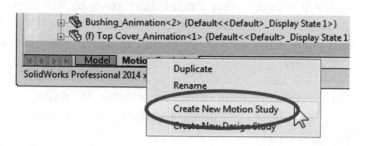

499. – In the new motion study select the "**Animation Wizard**" command, select the "Explode" option and click "Next."

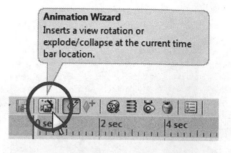

When we animated the exploded view previously, the animation's length is fixed at 8 seconds; if the exploded view has many steps, the steps will run too fast. Using the animation wizard we can change the time to any value we want. In the following dialog enter 16 seconds for the duration and leave the start time at 0 seconds. Click "Finish" to complete the animation. All the explode steps are automatically added to the timeline. Press "Play" to see the result.

500. – Turn the "**Disable Key on View Creation**" option OFF and add orientation view animations to zoom it to the screws when they are exploding out.

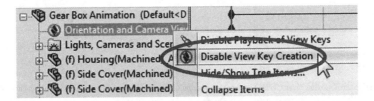

Move the Time Bar to 0.5 seconds and zoom into the '*Top Cover*' to see the screws.

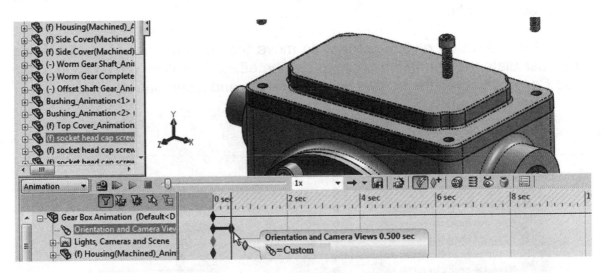

501. – The problem here is that by 0.5 seconds the screws are already half way out of view, and we need to change the time the screws start going out to get a chance to see the screws turning and go out. Scroll down to the top screws in the animation manager and window-select all the top screws' keys in the timeline.

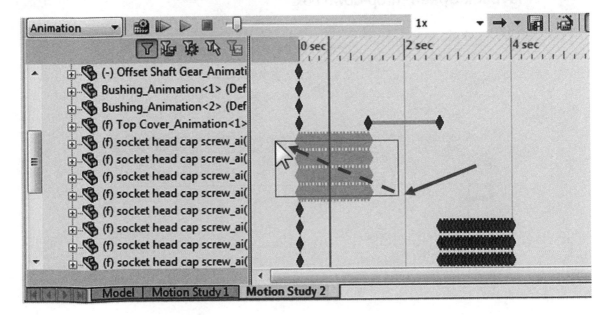

502. – After selecting all the keys right-mouse-click in any one of them and select "**Edit Key Point Time**." By pre-selecting all keys we'll move them all together.

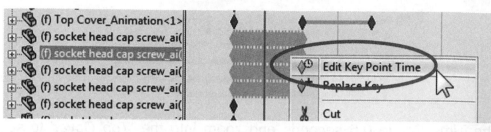

 Individual key points can be dragged in the timeline to make quick time adjustments.

Enter a value of 0.5 seconds to move the screws' keys to start moving later; calculate the animation again to see the effect. The view will zoom in to the '*Top Cover*' and then the screws will start turning and going out.

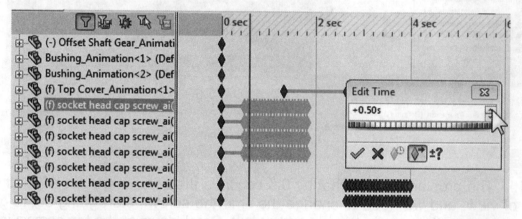

 To change the speed of the animation, select a multiplier from the "**Playback Speed**" drop-down box.

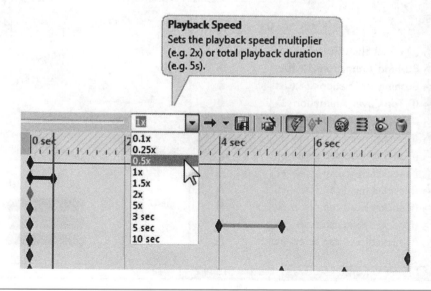

503. – Add similar keys to change the view to zoom into the other components as they explode to finish the animation.

- Add a new key in the timeline where we want to start the view orientation change.
- Move the time bar to the time where we want the view transition to end.
- Zoom and pan into the area of interest.

After setting the view orientation, the new animation step is automatically added between the keys.

Notice that the next timeline does not have a gap between some view orientation steps. This is done by adding a new key, moving the time bar to the new location, and changing the view orientation. The final effect is that the view keeps moving from one orientation to the next without stopping.

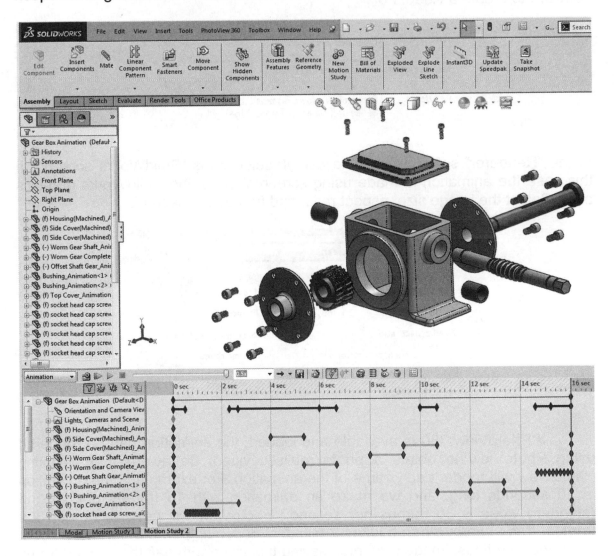

504. – The last step is to save the animation to a file. Select the "**Save Animation**" command.

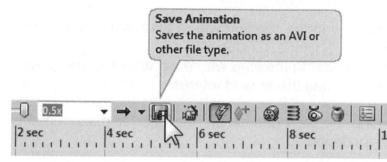

When the "Save As" window comes up, browse to select the location to save the video. In the "Save as type:" we can select to save as a Microsoft AVI file, or a series of images in BMP or TGA format that can be imported into video editing software to create a video. For

In the "Renderer" selection box the default selection is "SolidWorks screen." In this case the animation is made using screen shots of the SolidWorks graphics area. Select the image size, aspect ratio, and frames per second.

If PhotoView 360 is available and loaded, the animation can be rendered using PhotoView to obtain a photo realistic video. Be aware that selecting PhotoView will render each frame of the animation. For example, if the animation is 20 seconds long, and we make an animation with 15 frames per second (standard video is 30 frames per second,) PhotoView will have to render 300 frames. If the average frame takes 2 minutes, depending on the hardware used, PhotoView settings, image size, etc., saving this video with *half* the desired frame rate will take about 10 hours.

Considering the excessive amount of time required to make a photo realistic video, we want to be sure the end result is acceptable, if possible, in the first attempt. To minimize the risk of having to wait a very long time only to find out the resulting animation is not what we expected, here are a few suggestions when saving a video using the PhotoView renderer:

- Make sure the animation runs smoothly, including component movement, component's display, and view orientations.
- In PhotoView adjust all the necessary settings to obtain the desired image quality and write them down.
- Save a video using the SolidWorks screen renderer to make sure the image size is correct and the animation is moving correctly.
- Go back to PhotoView and lower the quality settings to get a fast render for a test.
- Save a new animation using the PhotoView renderer (using the low quality settings), a small (proportional) image size, and low frame rate. This way we'll be able to quickly produce a video to make sure we are getting the desired effect.
- Adjust whatever needs to be adjusted as needed until the result is acceptable using the lower quality settings.
- When the animation is moving correctly using these settings, set the PhotoView settings to the optimal parameters noted before.
- Set the image size and frame rate to the desired values for the final render.
- Wait for the render to complete.

 At the bottom of the PhotoView options there is a section for "Network Rendering." What this option does is to use multiple clients using a shared network directory to split rendering jobs to finish faster.

Exercises:

Generate an animation of the engine assembly using the knowledge acquired in this lesson. This is only a suggestion; it's time to be creative. ☺

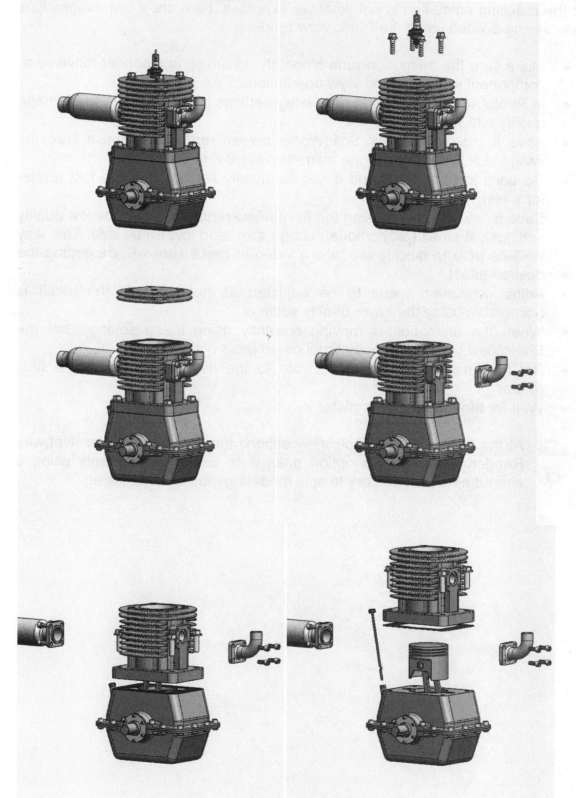

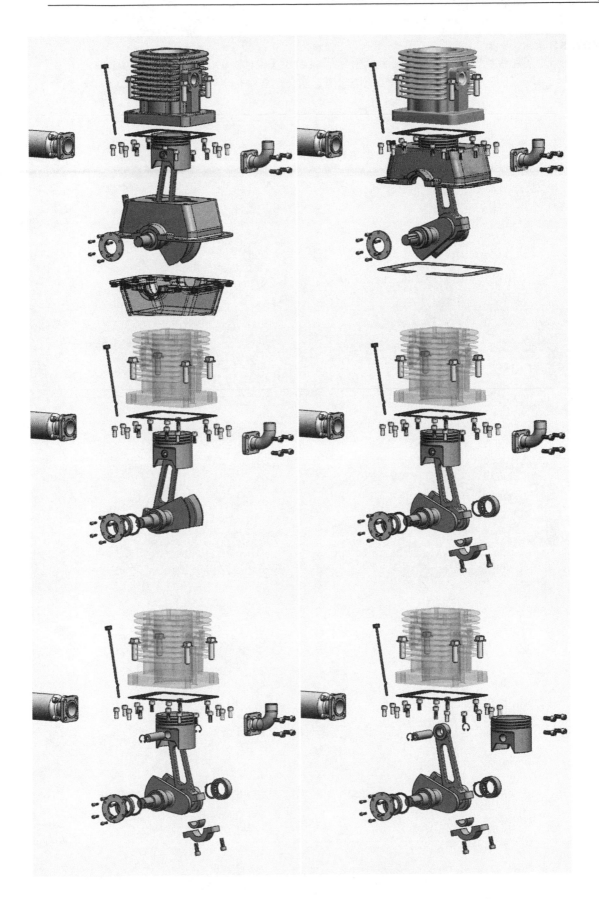

Notes:

Analysis: SimulationXpress

Study name: SimulationXpress Study
Plot type: Static nodal stress Stress
Deformation scale: 15.9445

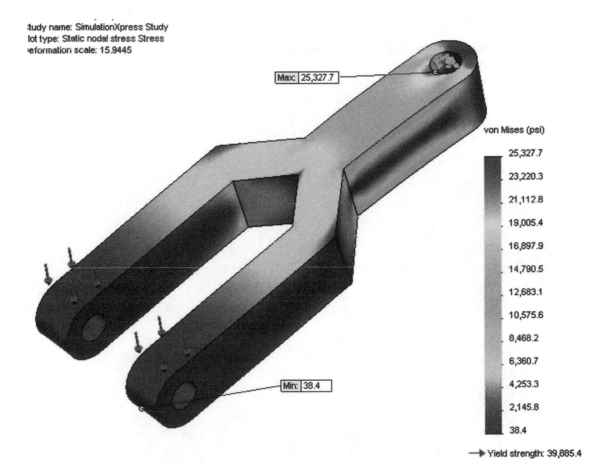

Max: 25,327.7

von Mises (psi)

25,327.7
23,220.3
21,112.8
19,005.4
16,897.9
14,790.5
12,683.1
10,575.6
8,468.2
6,360.7
4,253.3
2,145.8
38.4

Min: 38.4

→ Yield strength: 39,885.4

Notes:

Background: Why Analysis?

Simulation is a very important tool in engineering. Computers and software have come a long way since the early analysis tools first became available, and modern tools have made simulation a lot easier to use, faster, more accurate and more accessible than ever, enabling designers and engineers to check their design, make sure it's safe, understand how it will deform, if it will fail and under what circumstances, or how it will perform in any given environment (temperature, pressure, vibrations, etc.)

The biggest advantage, by far, when analyzing a design is that we will have a safe design, and at the same time, save money by making decisions as to what materials to use, component sizes, features and even appearance early in the design process, when it is still all in "*paper*" (maybe a more appropriate term now would be '*Bites*'☺) and cheaper to modify. As the product development process advances beyond the design stage, making design changes to a product is increasingly more expensive as we approach the manufacturing stage.

Picture it this way: Imagine we design a new cellular phone that looks really nice. We make molds, tooling, order parts, and set up an assembly line. Soon the phones start selling, and a month later, we start getting customer complaints: when a button is pressed hard, the battery cover falls off. Then, *after* we know we have a problem, we run an analysis and find out that *we should have* had a thicker *this or that*, with a *widget* in between the *thingamajig* and the *thingamabob*, and those changes would solve the problem. Now, all we need to do is to change the design, the tooling, the assembly line, marketing, and above all, convince every customer that it is fixed. At this point, our customers' perception of our company and credibility are destroyed. This is usually the most expensive part. It's easy to see why making analysis of our products early in the design process will help us design better products and save money and resources.

With that said, it also has to be noted that the simple fact of making a simulation does not guarantee that our designs will be successful, as there are many factors involved. Reasons for product failure include using the product beyond its designed capacity, abuse, material imperfections, fabrication processes and things and circumstances we could have never thought of. This is where the designer needs to take into account every possible scenario, and of course, simulate it as realistically as possible with the correct analysis tools.

SolidWorks includes a *basic analysis package* called "**SimulationXpress**." As its name implies, it has limited functionality that allows only certain scenarios to be analyzed. In order to understand what these limitations are, first we need to learn a little about how analysis works. A general overview of the inner workings of analysis is as follows:

Analysis, also known as "Finite Element Analysis", is a mathematical method where we divide a component's geometry into hundreds or thousands of small pieces (*elements*), where they are all connected to one or more neighboring elements by the vertices (called *nodes* in analysis.) The elements have simple geometry that can be easily analyzed using stress analysis formulas. Elements are usually tetrahedral or hexahedral for most solid models. There are other types of elements including shell and linear elements. SimulationXpress uses tetrahedral elements.

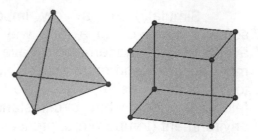

In order for us to make a simulation, we need to know what the component is made of (physical properties of the material), how it is supported (Restraints), and what forces are acting on it (Loads). The next step is to break down the model into small elements; this process is called meshing. The result is called the **mesh**; in SimulationXpress the only input we give, if we choose to, is to define the average element size and SimulationXpress automatically creates the mesh for us.

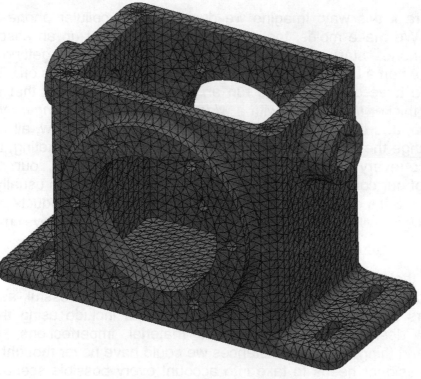

The next step is to define how the component is supported; in other words, which faces, edges or vertices are restrained. Each node has six degrees of freedom, meaning that each node can move along X, Y and Z and rotate about the X, Y, and Z axes. Restraints limit the degrees of freedom (DOF) of the nodes in the face or edge that they are applied to. SimulationXpress limits the user to restraining (Fix) all DOF in faces. In other words, they are completely immovable.

This approach is sufficient for simple analyses, but in order to obtain more accurate solutions, a more realistic simulation must be used that allows selective displacement and rotation of element nodes.

Now that we know how the model is supported, we need to define the Loads (forces) that act upon it. SimulationXpress only allows Forces and Pressures to be applied to model faces. We can define the Loads to be normal to the face they are applied to or perpendicular to a reference plane.

Another limitation of SimulationXpress is it can only make **Linear Static Stress Analysis**. Stress is defined as the internal resistance of a body when it is deformed and is measured in units of Force divided by Area. For example, if we load a bar with a 1 in^2 cross section area with a 1 Lb load, we'll have a stress of 1 Lb/in^2. The stress depends on the forces and the geometry regardless of the material used. The material properties will make a difference as the model will deform more or less.

The "Static" part means the model is immovable; in other words, the restraints will not let the model move when the loads are applied. Loads and restraints are in equilibrium; otherwise the analysis would be "Dynamic."

The "Linear" part implies the deformation of the model is proportional to the forces applied; twice the force, twice the deformation. These deformations are generally small compared to the overall size of the part and occur in the **Elastic** region of the "Stress-Strain" curve of the material used. If we remove the force, the model returns to its original shape like a spring; if we apply a force, the part will deform, twice the force, twice the deformation. If we remove the force, the part returns to its original size.

In general terms, the **Yield Stress** is the point where the stress-strain curve is no longer linear. If a material is stressed beyond the Yield Stress it will be permanently deformed. In this case we will have **Plastic Deformation**. Thinking of the spring before, if we pull the spring too far, it is permanently deformed, meaning it had plastic deformation. Once the yield stress is exceeded, the analysis results of Simulation-Xpress are invalid. In this case we need to change our design, geometry, loads or material so that the maximum stress in the model never exceeds the material's yield stress.

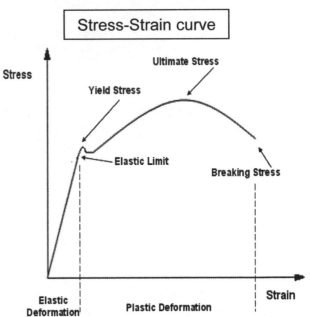

531

Notes:

Analysis of a simple part

505. - To show the SimulationXpress functionality, make the following part to make an analysis. Assign the material "Aluminum 6061-T6." *Tip: Make the part with square ends and round them using a "Full Round Fillet."*

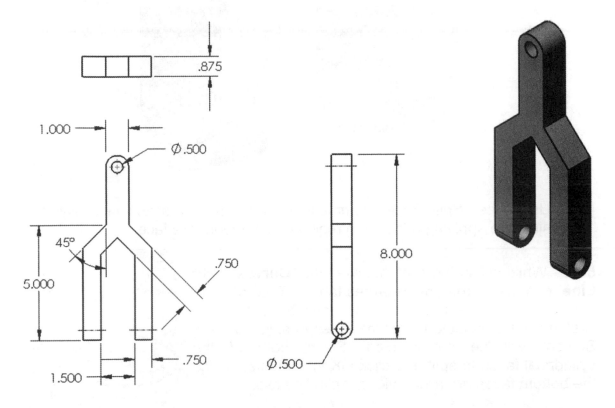

506. - We will add forces in the bottom holes perpendicular to the model and support it from the top hole.

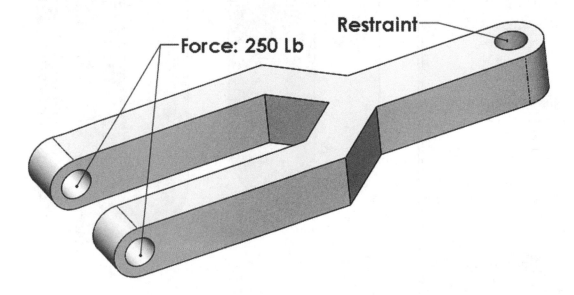

507. - In order to better simulate the force, we need to divide the bottom cylindrical faces in two parts, as the force applied will only be acting in one half of the cylindrical face. To accomplish this, we will use the "**Split Line**" command. The first thing we need to do to split the faces in two is to make a sketch in one side of the model (left or right) as indicated. The sketch is a single line.

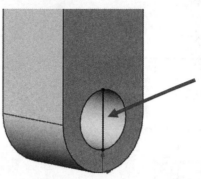

Using the "Split Face" command is a common practice in analysis to simulate applying a load in a region of a component's face.

508. - While still in the sketch, select the "**Curves, Split Line**" command from the Features tab. In "Type of Split" select the "Projection" option; this means that the current sketch will be projected over the faces to split. "Current Sketch" will be pre-selected. Select both of the cylindrical faces to split and click OK to continue. Notice the bottom faces are now divided (split) into two.

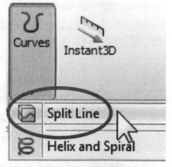

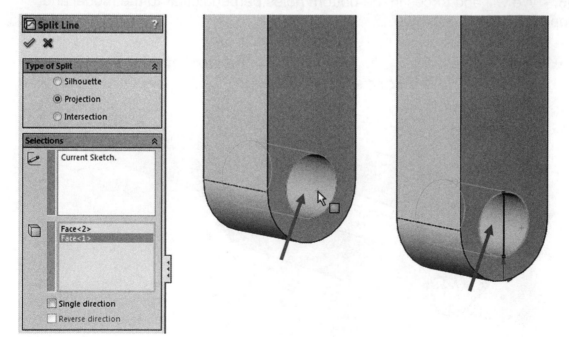

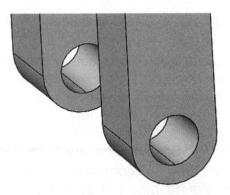

509. - Now that we have prepared our model for analysis, activate the SimulationXpress wizard using the menu "**Tools, SimulationXpress**" or in the Evaluate tab in the CommandManager.

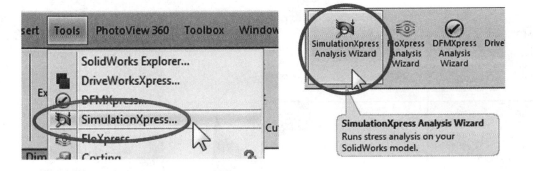

510. - The SimulationXpress wizard is integrated in the Task Pane and is automatically displayed. Select "Options", set units to English, turn the checkbox to display annotations for minimum and maximum in the results plot to ON, and leave the results location to the default 'temp' folder. Click "Next" to continue.

511. - The first step will be to define the "Fixtures," referring to the faces that will be completely rigid (all six degrees of freedom restrained.) We are also given a warning letting us know that the results in the regions close to the fixtures may be unrealistic, and more accurate results can be achieved with *SolidWorks Simulation Professional* by simulating a more realistic restraint condition. Select "Add a Fixture" to define how the part will be supported. We are now presented with the Fixture selection box; select the cylindrical

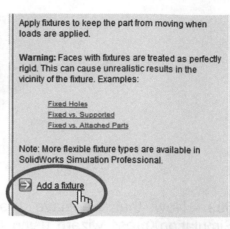

face at the top and click OK to finish. For this example we only need one fixture.

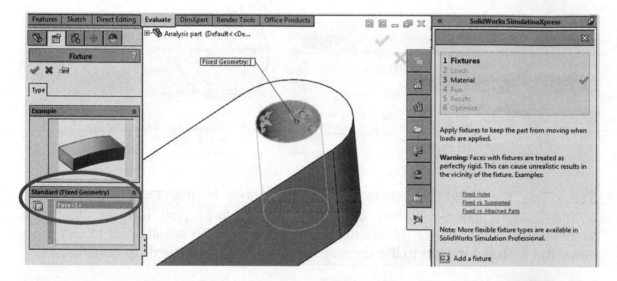

512. - If more Fixtures were needed, select "Add a Fixture" as needed until all the necessary restraints are in place. The SimulationXpress Study now shows the "*Fixed-1*" condition and "Fixtures" shows a green checkmark letting us know this step is complete. Click Next to continue.

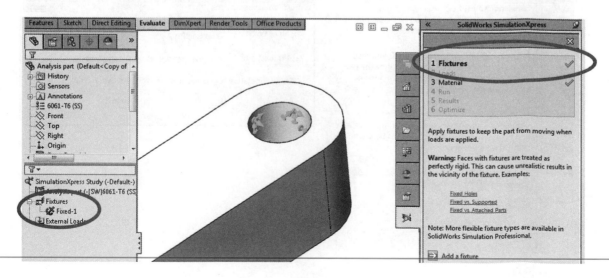

513. - We are now in the "Loads" section of the analysis, and ready to apply the external forces or pressures that will act on the part. The forces that we are adding will be 250 lbf in each face (total of 500 lbf) perpendicular to the part's "*Front Plane*" in each of the two bottom holes.

Select "**Add a Force**" to show the "Force" dialog box. Here we'll select one side of each of the two faces we split earlier; make the force value 250 lbf. To make the forces perpendicular to the part, select the option "Selected Direction" and from the fly-out FeatureManager, select the "*Front Plane*," this way the forces will be perpendicular to it.

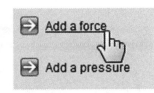

 If we don't give the force a direction, it will be normal to the selected faces, making the force radial to the cylindrical surfaces.

Make sure the option "Per Item" is selected, as we want to apply 250 lbf to each face; if the "Total" option is selected, the 250 lbf force would be equally distributed over the faces selected. In our example the direction of the force doesn't make any difference since our part is symmetrical, but be aware that, if needed, we can change the direction of the force using the "Reverse Direction" checkbox.

Click OK when done and select "Next" from the SimulationXpress wizard at the right to continue. If we need to add more forces or pressures to our analysis click on "Add a Force" or "Add a Pressure" as required.

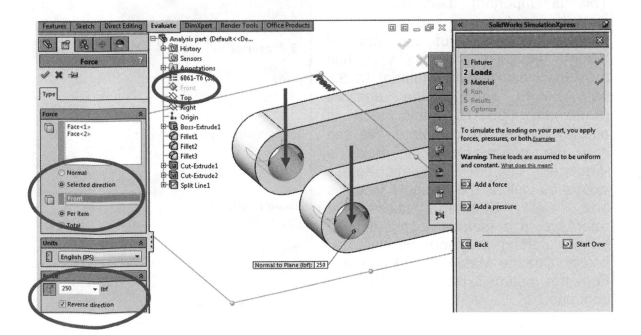

514. - The *"Force-1"* condition is added to the SimulationXpress Study and we can see the preview of the forces applied to the faces and their direction. Now "Loads" shows a green checkmark letting us know this step is complete. If we need to add more forces or pressures to other model faces, or modify this one, we would do it in this step. Click Next to continue.

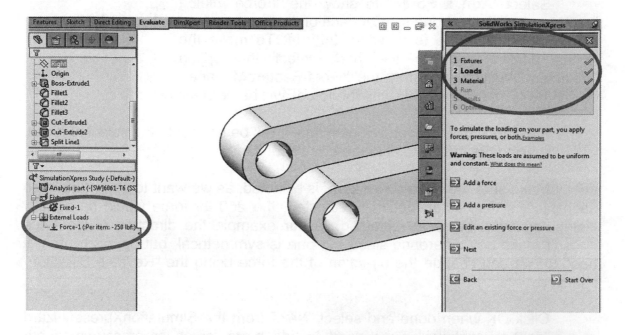

515. - The next step is to define the material that will be used for the part. This is important, because as we explained earlier, we need to know the physical properties of the material being analyzed. Since we had previously assigned a material to the part before starting the analysis (Aluminum 6061-T6), this step is already marked as complete. We can see the green checkbox next to "Material" in the SimulationXpress wizard as well as the Young's Modulus and Yield Strength values for reference. If a material is not defined before starting the analysis, we can select "Change Material" and pick one from the materials list. Click "Next" to continue.

516. - Now that we have given SimulationXpress the minimum information to make an analysis (Fixtures, Forces and Material), we are ready to make the mesh (break the model into smaller 'finite' elements) and run our simulation. At this point we have an option to run the analysis with the default settings for the mesh or change them.

In general, using a smaller mesh size generates more elements that lead to a more accurate solution; however, increasing the number of elements also increases the time and computing resources needed to run the simulation. As a general rule, if our maximum stresses are close to the acceptable limits, try using a slightly smaller mesh element. SimulationXpress allows us to change the mesh density, or the general size of the elements, under "Mesh Parameters." In this example the mesh size will not significantly impact the solver time.

For larger, more complex models there would be a notable difference in computing time. SolidWorks Simulation Professional offers many more options and the ability to analyze entire assemblies; with multiple components, a smaller mesh size will most definitively impact the solution time.

If desired or needed, the mesh parameters can be modified by selecting "Change settings" and then "Change mesh density." In our example we'll use the default mesh settings. Click OK to continue.

539

💡 **ABOUT REDUCING MESH SIZE**: Making the mesh size smaller improves results accuracy up to a certain degree, and it comes a point where reducing the element's size does not significantly improve accuracy in sequential solutions; this is called convergence, and is measured in percentage of change from one solution to the next. For example, if the highest stress value is within a certain percentage of the previous study, we can say that we have reached convergence and call our results valid.

In order to start considering reducing the mesh size and look for convergence, our results MUST be below the yield stress and preferably have no stress concentrations in our analysis. After those conditions have been met, we can start to re-run the analysis reducing the mesh size a little at a time (10% reduction is a good starting point.) Convergence values depend on the accuracy needed and can vary around 2% to 5% or even higher. If these values seem high and/or your design has a low factor of safety you may want to consider analyzing your design with a dedicated analysis package to simulate real world conditions and improve the accuracy of your analysis in order to be safe.

517. - As soon as we click OK in the "Mesh" dialog box, the model is meshed; in other words, breaking the model into many small pieces (*Finite Elements*.) We can tell the model is meshed because the icon in the Analysis Manager is also meshed. At this time our model is ready to run the analysis.

518. - Now that the model is meshed, select "**Run Simulation**" from the SimulationXpress wizard. What happens next, in the simplest terms, is that the solver (the part that actually calculates stresses and displacements) will generate an equation for each element, with an unknown variable at each node. Since adjacent elements share nodes between them this generates a very large matrix of hundreds or thousands of simultaneous equations.

The solver will generate the equations, assemble the matrix, and solve for the unknown variables at every node. The resulting value for each unknown value (one per node) will be the node's displacement or deformation. After a displacement is calculated for each node, the physical properties of the material are used to calculate the stresses in the model at each node.

	1 Fixtures	✓
	2 Loads	✓
	3 Material	✓
	4 Run	
	5 Results	
	6 Optimize	

Your model is ready to solve!

You can solve with the default settings or adjust them to better suit your needs.

→ Change settings

→ Run Simulation

← Back   ↩ Start Over

Since this is a small model it only takes a second to complete the analysis.

SimulationXpress Study

Solving:

Elapsed Time:

☑ Always show solver status when you run analysis

Pause   Cancel   More >>

519. - When the solver is finished with the calculations, we see an animation of the deformed model.

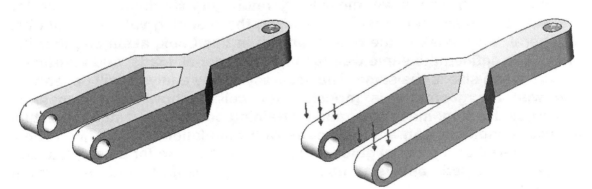

520. - The model deforms as we expected in the direction of the force, so we can proceed to view the results. If the model had not deformed as expected, we would have to go back to modify the fixtures and loads to make the necessary corrections. Select "**Yes, continue**" to view the analysis results.

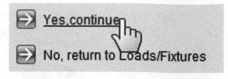

Click in "**Show Von Misses Stress**" to view the resulting stresses calculated using the **von Mises** method, which is the most commonly used criteria for isotropic materials (materials with the same physical properties in all directions, metals are mostly isotropic.) The deformation is exaggerated for visual clarity (in this case 7.5 times.)

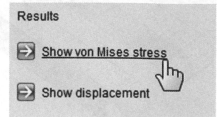

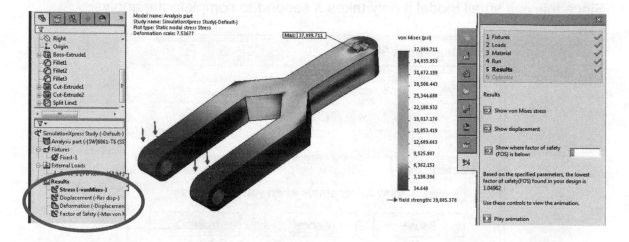

It is important to know that, by the very nature of the Finite Element Analysis process, the results are an *approximation* to the actual physical phenomenon, and solving such a large number of simultaneous equations will most likely return slightly different values for stress and displacement results. However, the resulting values should be, in general, very close to the results shown in this book, assuming that the analysis is defined the same way (geometry, material, loads, and restraints) and the mesh size is the same. The accuracy of any analysis will depend on how well the geometry is modeled, as well as how closely material properties, loading, mesh size, and restraining conditions match the actual physical conditions. An analysis done with SimulationXpress should only be considered as a general guide and never a substitute for a complete and properly modeled analysis using accurate loading and restraining conditions.

521. - In these results, we can see the Maximum Stress in the model is approximately 38,000 psi, very close to the Yield Strength of 39,885 psi. Based on these results, the lowest Factor of Safety in our model is approximately 1.05. The color-coded stress scale will help in finding the stresses in the rest of the model.

The Factor of Safety is calculated by dividing the material's yield strength by the maximum stress in the model. We are interested in finding the lowest value because if any area of the model has a factor of safety below 1, this means the stress is higher than the material's Yield Strength; our model will have permanent deformation and will be therefore considered to have failed.

Results

→ Show von Mises stress

→ Show displacement

→ Show where factor of safety (FOS) is below: `1`

Based on the specified parameters, the lowest factor of safety(FOS) found in your design is 1.04962 ←

Note that we are talking about permanent deformation and not breaking. To yield does not necessarily mean that it will break; it will break if we reach the Breaking Stress. For most practical purposes, a permanent deformation will almost always be considered as a failed design because the part will no longer have the shape it was supposed to have, possibly compromising the integrity, functionality and safety of the product and/or the end user.

The different values for **Factor of Safety** (FOS) mean:

Value	Meaning
> 1 ✓	The stress at this location in the part is less than the yield strength and is therefore safe. Depending on the specific application, we may have to design with a higher FOS to ensure our design is safe and have room for unexpected loads.
= 1 ✗	The stress at this location in the part is exactly the yield strength. This part has started or is about to yield (deform plastically) and will most likely fail if the forces acting on the model are slightly more than the forces used in the analysis.
< 1 ✗	The stress at this location in the part has exceeded the yield strength of the material and the component will fail with the analysis parameters used, either deforming plastically or breaking.

522. - To see how safe our design is, type 2 in the Factor of Safety box, and click "Show where factor of safety (FOS) is below." Areas under the specified factor of safety (*unsafe*) are shown in red, and the areas over the factor of safety (*safe*) are shown blue. Essentially, assuming that our design requires us to have a minimum factor of safety of 2, every area colored in red will fail.

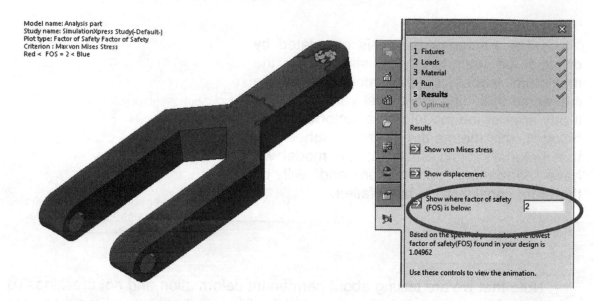

523. - Now activate "**Show Displacement**" to see how much our model deforms using the current conditions. The maximum deformation is 0.1″ at the bottom of the part, as expected since the top is rigidly supported. (The values in the scale are listed using scientific notation.)

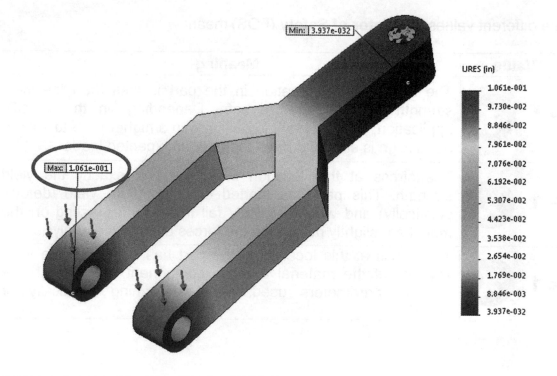

524. - Select "Done viewing results" to move to the next screen where we can generate reports either in Word or eDrawings format. Selecting "Generate report" will generate the files needed for the report and will allow us to fill in additional information before creating it. It will include information as well as screen captures of results and details of the analysis including loads, fixtures, and material properties.

525. - Selecting "Generate eDrawings file" will make an eDrawings file with the analysis results. The main difference from the Microsoft Word report is that, in eDrawings, we can rotate the models, turn the mesh on or off, zoom in or out, and easily share the results with other people.

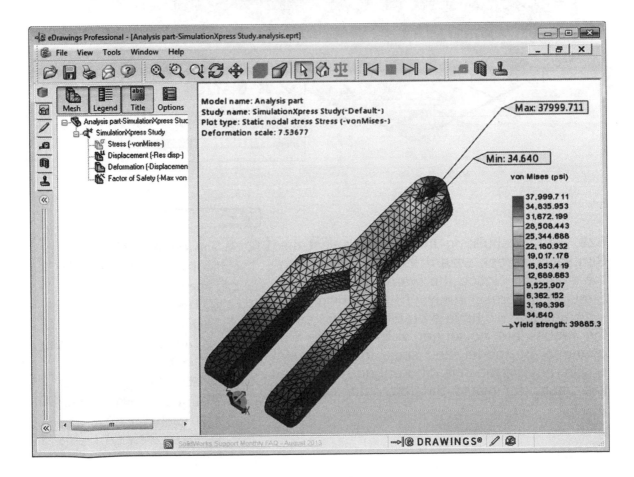

526. - What we are going to do now is to change a dimension in the model and re-run the analysis to see how much the results change. Click to close the SimulationXpress wizard. When asked if we want to save the results select "Yes" from the dialog box.

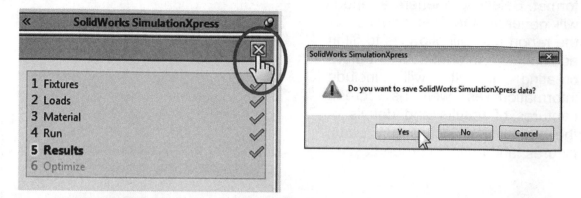

527. – For this example change the 0.875″ thickness dimension to 1.125″ and rebuild the model.

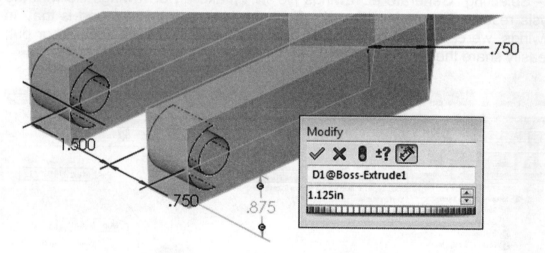

528. - After rebuilding the model, select the SimulationXpress wizard icon to go back to the analysis. Notice the warning icon in the Simulation-Xpress study. This warning icon indicates that we have a problem; in this case the results are no longer valid because we changed the model, and since the geometry is different the mesh is different and therefore the results are invalid, they are outdated.

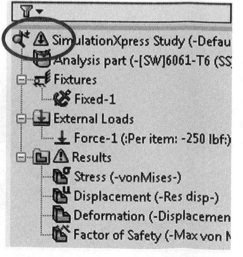

529. - Since we only changed the geometry and no other loading or restraining conditions, to update the results, all we need to do is to make a right-mouse-click at the top of the analysis tree and select "**Run**" from the pop-up menu to update the results. SimulationXpress will automatically re-mesh the model to account for the geometric changes, and run the analysis with the updated geometry.

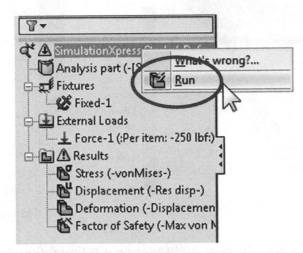

530. - After running the analysis with the updated geometry, we see the updated results. Now we have a maximum von Mises stress of 25,296 psi, giving us a minimum factor of safety of 1.57 and a maximum displacement of 0.05". Depending on the intent of our design, and industry accepted practices, this may, or may not be sufficient to consider our design safe.

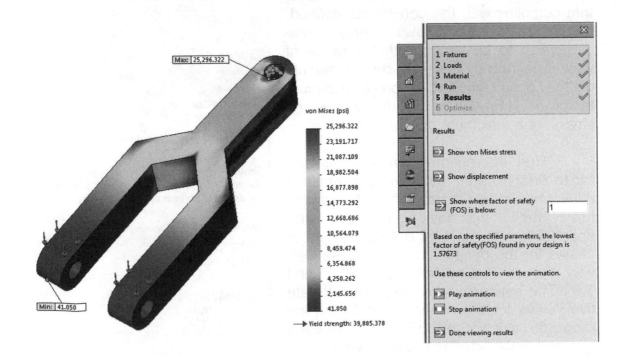

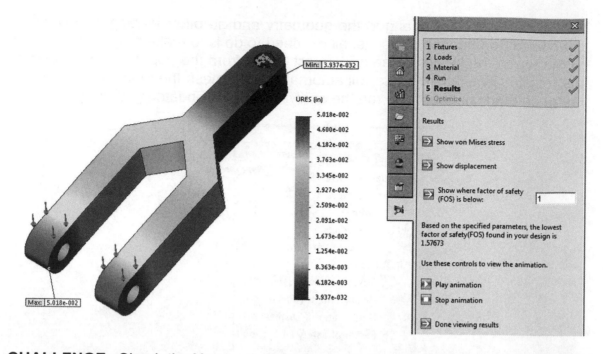

CHALLENGE: SimulationXpress includes an Optimization wizard that can be accessed after reviewing the results and reports; select "Done viewing results" and click on "Next" to continue to the optimization wizard and select "Yes" when asked to optimize your model.

The Optimization wizard helps us find the lightest model (minimum mass) that complies with the constraints defined. SimulationXpress allows only one dimension to be varied within a range of values defined by the user; the constraints of the optimization can be a minimum factor of safety, a maximum von Mises stress, or a maximum displacement.

Run the optimization analysis and try to find a better solution that meets a minimum factor of safety of 1.5 by varying the part's thickness. To run the optimization we have to define a range of values for the dimension, in our case we'll vary the dimension between 0.875" and 1.5". The optimization wizard will calculate five values for the dimension between the range of values, run the analysis for each one and determine the optimum value.

Select the part's thickness dimension in the parameters window.

In the "Variables" section enter a range between 1" and 1.375" for the dimension. In the "Constraints" area, select "Factor of Safety" and make it greater than 1.5. In the "Goals" section select "Mass" and "Minimize" to optimize for the lightest part that meets a factor of safety of *at least* 1.5. Click Run to optimize the model.

After running the optimization, we can see the "Results View" with the initial value and the optimal value. Selecting a column will update the model with those values.

	Initial	Optimal
D1BossExtrude1 (0.027958)	1.125in	1.10071in
Factor of Safety	1.576726	1.504411
Mass	0.50557 kg	0.494564 kg

Note: In order for optimization to work, we need to have a study with a factor of safety higher than what we need, basically *over designed*. If the study has a high factor of safety, we can optimize the model to make the part lighter, and still have a factor of safety that meets our design requirements.

Notes:

A final word on analysis

The analysis world is a very fascinating one that gives us highly sophisticated and powerful tools to predict how machines, products, or designs will perform in any given scenario, and allows us to anticipate the best way to assure their safe operation. However, it is extremely important to make sure the correct assumptions for restraints, loads and external conditions are applied to a model in order to correctly simulate the actual physical phenomena, as the accuracy and reliability of the results are directly tied to them. Talking about results, it's just as important to understand what the results obtained from an analysis mean in order to correctly interpret them and avoid over designing, or putting our designs at risk for failure.

As we explained before, SimulationXpress is a *first-pass-analysis* tool. This means that its purpose is to give us a general idea of how the design will perform within the set of applied conditions. If our design is not *comfortably* safe, and/or we know this is a critical component of the design, it may be better to perform a more complete analysis using the full suite of SolidWorks Simulation software, where we can add more realistic loading, restraining and external conditions. Besides, SimulationXpress is only capable of performing linear static analysis; therefore, if we anticipate that a model will be exposed to temperature, vibrations, large deformations, uses non-linear materials, or other conditions that cannot be correctly modeled with SimulationXpress, those analyses should be done using a version of SolidWorks Simulation (or any other analysis software package) capable of properly modeling those situations.

Analysis and simulation can be a very complex subject depending on the task being analyzed, and depending on the specifics of it, a higher understanding of mechanics of materials, physics, vibrations, heat transfer and many other areas will be likely needed in order to properly setup, analyze and interpret the results. An analysis can be as simple as a linear stress analysis in a small part like our example, or as complex as a space ship re-entering the atmosphere taking into account forces, temperatures, vibrations, pressure, radiation, phase changes, aerodynamics, etc., and based on our analysis and results, astronauts would be returning home safely, or not.

Ultimately, safety is the main reason why we make analysis, and why it has to be done right, with the right set of tools and more importantly, the right knowledge.

Exercise: Make a copy of the *'Crankshaft'* part and rename it *'Crankshaft Analysis'*. Add a split line to divide the face indicated and run an analysis using SimulationXpress using the information given for forces and restraints.

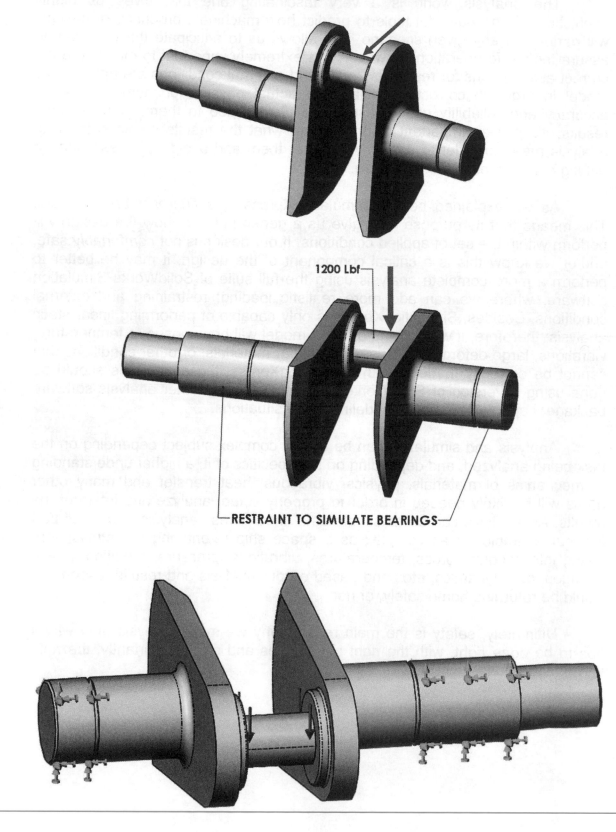

1200 Lbf

RESTRAINT TO SIMULATE BEARINGS

Collaboration: eDrawings

How to collaborate with non-SolidWorks users

Sometimes we need to collaborate with other members of the design team in the same room, same building, or even across the world. With the convenience of e-mail, it's easier than ever to share our designs using eDrawings. We can send our extended design team, customers or suppliers a file by e-mail with all the design information needed for them to review and send back feedback to the designer. A big advantage of eDrawings is that it is available for both Windows and Macintosh computers, and recently for iPad, iPhone, and Android devices.

We can generate eDrawings files from Parts, Assemblies, Drawings, and simulation studies. The only thing we need to do is to press the Publish eDrawings File icon from the "Save" fly-out toolbar, or go to the menu **"File, Publish to eDrawings"** while the document we want to share is active. The eDrawings viewer will be loaded with the same document. After we generate an eDrawings file, it becomes a *read only* file; we cannot modify it, but we can print it, zoom in, or out, section it, etc. For this example, we'll publish an eDrawings file from the '*Gear Box*' assembly drawing. Depending on your installation of eDrawings, your screen will look something like this:

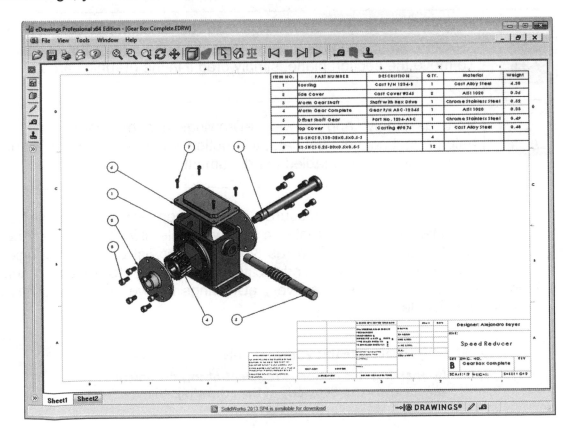

If the eDrawings file is generated using SolidWorks Office Professional or the educational edition, the eDrawings Professional version is loaded. eDrawings Professional includes additional options, including tools to move the components in assemblies, measure, add markups and stamps and, if it's a part or assembly, make section views of the models.

The Previous, Stop, Next and Play buttons will allow you to navigate different views if you have a multiple view drawing, or to go from one view orientation to the next in Parts and Assemblies. Pressing the "Play" icon animates the views, and will change from one to the next. At any time, the animation can be stopped, and the view zoomed in, rotated and panned.

	While in an eDrawings of an assembly, the parts can be moved by dragging them. To return them to their original location, double-click on them or click in the Home icon.
	If the assembly has an exploded view, in the "Explode View" tab we can explode or collapse the assembly and animate as well.
	Part and assembly eDrawings can be sectioned. Select the "Section" icon, and pick a plane to section about from the options. To move the section plane, simply drag it in the graphics area.
	Part, assembly, and drawing eDrawings can be measured. To help protect confidential data, this option is disabled at the time of saving and can be enabled per document.

To activate the "Enable measure" option when saving a published eDrawings file, we have to create an eDrawings file using the menu "**File, Save As...**" and from the "Save as type" selection list pick "eDrawings", press the "Options" button and activate the "Okay to measure this eDrawings file" checkbox. Otherwise every eDrawings file we publish will have the measure tool disabled.

☑ Okay to measure this eDrawings file

By enabling this option, a recipient of this document can measure the geometry in the eDrawings Viewer.

A powerful option in eDrawings Professional is the markup tools to allow anyone to add annotations to a file, and send it back to the generator to make the required modifications.

The markup tools allow us to add:
- Dimensions
- Notes
- Images
- Clouds with text
- Lines
- Rectangles
- Circles
- Arcs and
- Splines, etc.

After creating the eDrawings file, we have to save it. eDrawings allows us to save the files in different ways.

File name:	Gear Box Complete.easm	
Save as type:	eDrawings Files (*.easm)	

eDrawings Files (*.easm)
eDrawings 64-bit Executable Files (*.exe)
eDrawings 32-bit Executable Files (*.exe)
eDrawings 64-bit Zip Files (*.zip)
eDrawings 32-bit Zip Files (*.zip)
eDrawings HTML Files (*.htm)
BMP Files (*.bmp)
TIFF Files (*.tif)
JPEG Files (*.jpg)
PNG Files (*.png)
GIF Files (*.gif)

Hide Folders

Saving as an eDrawings File (*.edrw) will result in a very small file size that can be easily emailed. The only thing the recipient needs to do is to install the free eDrawings viewer in their computer.

Saving as an HTML file (*.html) will create a web page that can be e-mailed. eDrawings will be loaded automatically if it is already installed in the computer; if it is not installed, the web browser will ask to install and run the corresponding plug-in. Optionally, a link to download the eDrawings viewer is listed at the bottom of the web page.

Notes:

Final Comments

By completing the exercises in this book, we learned how to apply many different SolidWorks features and the various options to common design tasks. As we stated at the beginning, this book is meant to be an introduction to SolidWorks, and as the reader was able to see, the breadth of options and possibilities available to the user after completing this book are enough to accomplish many different tasks from part and assembly modeling to detailing in a short time, using the most commonly used commands, including making a stress analysis with the included SimulationXpress software.

We hope this book serves as a stepping stone for the reader to learn more. A curious reader will be able to venture into more advanced features, and take advantage of the similarities and consistency of the user interface to his/her advantage. We tried very hard to make the content as understandable and easy to follow as possible, as well as to get the reader working on SolidWorks almost immediately, maximizing the "hands-on" time.

After completing all parts, drawings, an assembly including the fasteners, exploded view and the assembly drawing complete with a Bill of Materials, the reader is ready to apply the learned concepts in different design projects.

As a follow-up, be sure to continue learning SolidWorks with *Beginner's Guide to SolidWorks 2014 – Level II.* Go further and learn about Sheet Metal, Surfacing, Mold Making and more.

One final tip: If you get lost, or can't find what you are looking for while working in SolidWorks, click with the right mouse button. Chances are, what you are looking for is in that pop-up menu. ☺

Notes:

Appendix

Document templates

One of the main reasons to have multiple templates is to have different settings, especially units. We can have millimeter and inch templates, pre-defined materials for part templates, dimensioning standards, etc. and every time we make a new part based on that template, the new document will have the same settings of the template. A good idea is to have a folder to store our templates, and add it to the list of SolidWorks templates.

Using *Windows Explorer*, make a new folder to store our new templates. For this example we'll make a new folder in the Desktop called *"MySWTemplates*." In SolidWorks, go to the menu "**Tools, Options, System Options, File Locations**." From the drop down menu select "Document Templates."

Click the "Add" button and locate the folder we just made to save the templates. Click OK when done. You will now see the additional template folder listed.

To create a new template, make a new Part, Assembly, or Drawing file, and go to the menu "**Tools, Options, Document Properties**." Everything we change in this tab is saved with the template. The most common options changed in a template are Units, Sketch Grid, Detailing Standards, and Annotation Fonts. Let's review them in the order that they appear in the options.

The first section is "Drafting Standard"; here we can change the dimensioning standard to ANSI, ISO, DIN, JIS, etc.; by changing the standard, all the necessary changes will be made to arrows, dimensions, annotations, etc., according to the selected standard.

The "**Annotations**" and "**Dimensions**" sections contain all the options for annotation and dimension settings including font, size, arrow type, appearance and every configurable option for them. Keep in mind that setting the "Drafting Standard" will modify these sections according to the standard.

In the "Detailing" area we can change what is displayed in parts and assemblies; for drawings we have more options including which annotations are automatically inserted when a new drawing view is created.

In the "Units" section, select the units that we want to use in the template, number of decimal places or fractional values, angular units, length, mass, volume and force, etc. Selecting a unit system will change all the corresponding units to that system, saving us time. Selecting "Custom" will allow us to mix unit systems if so desired.

Document Properties - Units

System Options | Document Properties | Search Options

Drafting Standard
- Annotations
- Dimensions
  - Centerlines/Center Marks
  - DimXpert
- Tables
- Views
  - Virtual Sharps
- Detailing
- Drawing Sheets
- Grid/Snap
- **Units**
- Line Font
- Line Style
- Line Thickness
- Image Quality
- Sheet Metal

Unit system
- ○ MKS (meter, kilogram, second)
- ○ CGS (centimeter, gram, second)
- ○ MMGS (millimeter, gram, second)
- ◉ IPS (inch, pound, second)
- ○ Custom

Type	Unit	Decimals	Fractions	More
Basic Units				
Length	inches	.123		...
Dual Dimension Length	millimeters	.12		...
Angle	degrees	.12		
Mass/Section Properties				
Length	inches	.123		
Mass	pounds			
Per Unit Volume	inches^3			
Motion Units				
Time	second	.12		
Force	pound-force	.12		
Power	watt	.12		
Energy	BTU	.12		

In the "Grid/Snap" section, we can define if we want to have a grid and its settings when we work in a sketch. Most users don't use the grid, but that's precisely why it's called an option. Turn it on if you like it; turn it off if you don't. It may be useful for a new user to help him/her identify when working in a sketch.

Document Properties - Grid/Snap

System Options | Document Properties | Search Options

Drafting Standard
- Annotations
- Dimensions
  - Centerlines/Center Marks
  - DimXpert
- Tables
- Views
  - Virtual Sharps
- Detailing
- Drawing Sheets
- **Grid/Snap**
- Units
- Line Font
- Line Style
- Line Thickness
- Image Quality
- Sheet Metal

Grid
- ☐ Display grid
- ☑ Dash
- ☑ Automatic scaling

Major grid spacing: 1.000in
Minor-lines per major: 4
Snap points per minor: 1

[Go To System Snaps]

Click OK to set the new document properties to the selected options. Another option to save with the template is the material, for this part template select the aluminum alloy 6061-T6. To save the document as a new template, go to the menu "**File, Save As**." From the "Save As Type" drop down box, select "Part Template (*.prtdot)", "Assembly Template (*.asmdot)" or "Drawing Template (*.drwdot)" (depending on the type of document we are working on.) SolidWorks will automatically change to the first folder listed under the "File Locations" list for templates; if needed, browse to the "*MySWTemplates*" folder, give it a name and click "Save." As a suggestion, give the template a name that tells you something about the options set in it, like material, standard, units, etc. or whatever works for you.

After saving the template, when we select the "**New Document**" icon and use the "**Advanced**" option, we'll see a new "Templates" tab with our new templates listed in it.

Drawing templates will include the sheet format and title block with any changes and modifications to it. If editing a drawing, select "Edit Sheet Format" from the right-mouse-click pop-up menu; change the annotations and title block to your needs. When finished modifying it, select "Edit Sheet" from the right mouse button menu and save as a drawing template. When using this template, all notes and annotations will be set.

Index

Notes: